High
Performance
Management

High
Performance
Management

D. D. Warrick
Robert A. Zawacki

UNIVERSITY OF COLORADO AT COLORADO SPRINGS

Library of Congress Cataloging in Publication Data

Warrick, D.D.
    Formerly published as:
    Supervisory management: understanding behavior and managing for results
    (Harper and Row Publishers), 1984.
    1. Supervision of employees. I. Zawacki, Robert A.
II. Title.
HF5549.W346 1984   658.3'02   83-8448
ISBN 0-06-046942-0

From Don to Anna, my wife and most prized friend.

From Bob to the people who challenged my management skills: Martha, Dale, Paul, Carol, Mark, and Laura.

Contents

Part One   The Supervisor's Role

Part Two Supervising Individuals

Part Three   Supervising Groups

Part Four   Supervisory Management Practices

Part Five   Current Issues in Supervision

Preface

The biggest shift in job responsibility often occurs when one becomes a supervisor. Supervisors experience the transition from being primarily doers, whose performance is measured by individual effort and technical skills, to being administrators, whose performance is measured by their ability to achieve results through the multiple efforts of others. This text discusses the challenges that face supervisors in a rapidly changing environment and focuses on sound supervisory practices, how to understand and develop people, and how to achieve high employee productivity.

We have tried to make this a comprehensive and unique book. We have included a wide range of supervisory management subjects from which the reader may select those topics of greatest personal interest. Several factors make the book unique. To help the reader bridge the gap between intellectual learning and internalized learning, and therefore to apply what has been learned, each chapter moves from theory to application to experiential learning. Also, the format of the book provides readers with a logical progression for learning about supervisory management. Chapter 1 presents an overview of the format and the contents of the book, and each of the following chapters is devoted to an aspect of the learning format.

In addition to material traditionally covered in supervisory management texts, we have presented new and fresh material. For example, we have included chapters on building a supervisory philosophy; developing one's personal and supervisory potential; improving group effectiveness; improving formal communications; applying helping skills to supervision; and managing disadvantaged, handicapped, or alcoholic employees, as well as managing labor relations, stress, and one's life and time.

The book has a strong personal development emphasis. We believe that supervisors can best apply what they learn from this book to supervising others when they first learn to apply it to themselves. In addition, we believe that a supervisor's own example has a major influence on employee performance. Our goal in writing this book is to help supervisors develop their own potential so that their positive example will have a multiplier effect on their employees.

ACKNOWLEDGMENTS

We would like to express a special thanks to Anna Warrick, who dedicated a considerable portion of the last two years to typing, editing the manuscript, incorporating numerous revisions, and assuming primary responsibility for writing the teacher's manual. She accomplished all of this while introducing a new member into the Warrick Family (Ryan Matthew Warrick, born December 26, 1981). Jay Schubert also deserves considerable thanks for her painstaking and yet cheerful efforts in proofreading the book and making helpful suggestions as well. Dorothy Cappel, of Harper & Row, earned our respect as a capable and responsible project leader who gently but persistently managed us in completing the book. We would also like to thank Elaine Schantz, who typed some of the early manuscripts. In addition, we would like to acknowledge the following reviewers whose valuable comments helped shape many of our ideas in completing the final manuscript:

Professor Jim Hall
University of Santa Clara

Professor Robert Taylor
University of Wisconsin at Steven
   Point

Mr. Ken Shock
West Valley College

Professor Bill Kindsfather
Tarrant County Junior College

Professor H. D. Ryder
Glouster County College

Professor Bert Weesner
Lansing, Michigan

Professor Ray Mullins
Bowling Green State University

Professor William R. Sherrard
San Diego State University

Professor Charles Beavin
Miami-Dade Community College

Dr. Carl M. Guelzo
Catonsville Community College

Professor James Glover
Essex Community College

Professor John Casey
Herkimer County Community
   College

Professor Sumner White
Massachusetts Bay Community
   College

Professor Richard Herden
University of Louisville

Professor John Zeiger
Bryant College

Professor Charles Manz
University of Minnesota

Professor Robert Richmond
Bucks County Community College

SPECIAL TRIBUTE

ARTHUR H. BOISSELLE, JR.

We want to pay special tribute to Dr. Arthur H. Boisselle, Jr. Dr. Boisselle is a former student of ours who excelled in that role and is now excelling in his role as a professor at Pikes Peak Community College in Colorado Springs. Art has made a valuable contribution to this book by sharing his comments, ideas, experience, and research. He is an energetic resource overflowing with ideas, and we consider ourselves fortunate to have played a small role in his successful career.

D. D. WARRICK
ROBERT A. ZAWACKI

ABOUT THE AUTHORS

D. D. (DON) WARRICK

Dr. Warrick is an associate professor of management and organization behavior at the University of Colorado at Colorado Springs, where he has won six Outstanding Teaching Awards. He has received national recognition as an educator, consultant, and speaker, and in 1982 was named the Outstanding Organization Development Practitioner of the Year by the American Society for Training and Development and was elected chairperson of the Organization Development Division of the Academy of Management. He has also been named to *Who's Who in the West, Personalities in America, Who's Who in Consulting,* and *Certified Consultants International.* He has published over 20 articles and cases, and in addition to this book is the author or coauthor of *Current Developments in Organization Development* (Scott Foresman, 1984), *Managing Organization Development and Change* (SRA, 1984), and *Organization Development: Managing Change in the Public Sector* (IPMA, 1976). In addition, Dr. Warrick is the former editor of the internationally circulated *Academy of Management OD Newsletter.* Dr. Warrick received his bachelor's and master's degrees from the University of Oklahoma and his doctorate from the University of Southern California.

ROBERT A. ZAWACKI

Dr. Zawacki is a professor of management and organization behavior and former associate dean of the College of Business and Administration at the University of

Colorado at Colorado Springs. His teaching and research interests are motivation of people, increasing productivity, job redesign, performance appraisal, and organizational change. In 1979, he received the University of Colorado Chancellor's Award and was elected to *Who's Who in the West.* A keynote speaker at numerous national and state meetings, he has written over 30 articles that have appeared in such journals as *Datamation, Public Personnel Management, Personnel Journal, Supervisory Management, Academy of Management Proceedings, The Personnel Administrator, Management by Objectives Journal,* and *Management Information Systems Quarterly.* Some of the organizations he has consulted with are IBM, GE, GTE, Texaco, Aetna, NCR, ITT, Hewlett-Packard, TRW, Digital Corporation, Hartford Insurance, Arizona State Patrol, New York Department of Labor, U.S. Air Force Academy, Colorado Interstate Gas, and numerous hospitals and banks. In addition to this book, he is the author or coauthor of *Organization Development: Practice, Theory, and Research* (BPI, 1978 and 1983), *The Personnel Management Process: Cases on Human Resources Administration* (Houghton Mifflin, 1982), *Organization Development: Managing Change in the Public Sector* (IPMA, 1976), *Management: Cases in Management and Organizational Behavior* (BPI, 1982), and *Motivating and Managing Computer Personnel* (Wiley, 1981). Bob received his bachelor's and master's degrees from the University of Wyoming and his doctorate from the University of Washington.

High
Performance
Management

PART ONE
The Supervisor's Role

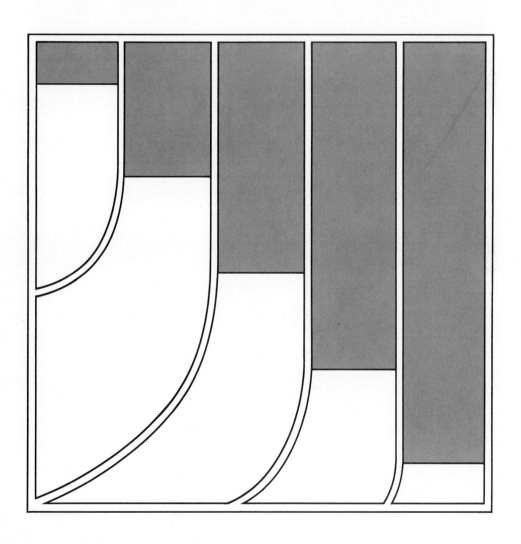

1

An Overview of Supervisory Management

The final decision as to what the future of society shall be depends not upon how near its organization is to perfection, but on the degree of worthiness in its individual members.

Schweitzer

If a man can accept a situation in a place of power with the thought that it's only temporary, he comes out all right. But when he thinks that he is the cause of the power, that can be his ruination.

Truman

The finest combination in the world is power and mercy. The worst combination in the world is weakness and strife.

Churchill

OBJECTIVES

This chapter provides you with the information necessary to:

1. Describe some of the main forces that create pressure on supervisors
2. Describe the major skills used by supervisors

---

3. Identify the components of the supervisor's role
4. Identify some major issues workers are reflecting to management
5. Understand why it is important to develop professional supervisors

OUR CHANGING ENVIRONMENT

It is difficult to describe the total effect created by the relationship of the forces in a dynamic economy, a complex society, and the modern family environment. What is evident is that today's organization, large or small, must cope with these forces and still maintain a competitive position in a free-enterprise environment. Some of the main forces creating these new challenges are

The effects of inflation on economic values
Increased demands of federal, state, and city budgets
Technological explosions in industry
Knowledge explosions in our laboratories and companies
Undertraining of our work force
Underutilization of the disadvantaged
Increased personal and economic freedom
Changing patterns of organizational and interpersonal communication
Increased need by employees to participate in the decision-making process
Increased regulatory requirements and social responsibilities of companies

These forces have created pressures on supervisors and managers to discover skills, innovate techniques, and change strategies to meet the demands of today's modern productive work place. These dynamic and sometimes turbulent situations in which supervisors must perform make it necessary not only that they have an understanding of these forces but also that they have the professional skills to manage human and organizational resources in an increasingly complex and rapidly changing environment.

Evidence of the changing environment in which supervisors must perform their jobs is reported in a Department of Health, Education, and Welfare study on work in America.[1] What the workers want most, as more than 100 studies in the past 20 years show, is to become masters of their immediate environments and to feel that their work, and they themselves, are important. Workers recognize that some of the dirty jobs can be transformed only into merely tolerable jobs. However, the workers reported that the most oppressive features of work were constant supervision and coercion, lack of variety, monotony, meaningless tasks, and isolation. An increasing number of workers want more autonomy in tackling their tasks, greater opportunity for increasing their skills, rewards that are directly connected to the intrinsic aspects of work, and greater participation in the design of work and formulation of their tasks.

[1]David S. Brown, "Rethinking the Supervisory Role," *Supervisory Management,* November, 1977.

Figure 1.1 Skills of supervisors and managers.

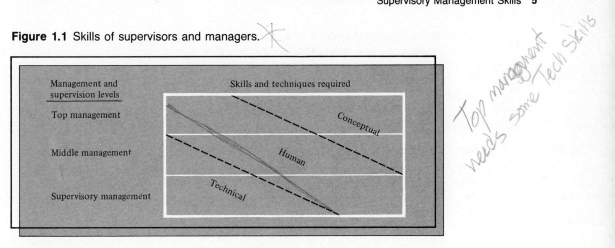

SUPERVISORY MANAGEMENT SKILLS

Anyone to whom people report is in essence a supervisor. While this text is written primarily for supervisors up to first-level management, the skills apply to supervision at any level of the organization.

Major Types of Supervisory Skills

Robert Kahn of the University of Michigan sees the work of supervisors as consisting of technical, human, and conceptual skills (Figure 1.1).

Technical skills are those skills required to accomplish the task. For example, in microelectronics assembly plants, such as those of Honeywell and NCR, the skills required to assemble the microwafer are technical skills learned on the job or in technical courses. At Maytag, the assembly of automatic dishwashers is technical work.

Human skills are the techniques and methods needed to work with and through people. Many people are promoted to supervisory positions on the basis of their technical skills but soon discover that they need human skills. Our own questioning of supervisors suggests that as much as 80 percent of a supervisor's problems are people problems.

Conceptual skills describe one's skills in seeing the "big picture" and being able to plan and organize work. Conceptual skills are required more as one moves up in the organization.

In a study of 311 first-level supervisors in 42 participating companies, the participants identified five major skills needed by supervisors:[2]

Communication skills
Human relations skills
Motivation of subordinates

[2]Arthur H. Boisselle, "Supervisory Training Questionnaire," *Community College Supervisory Training for Business and Industry,* 1979.

Understanding people in groups
Control of the quality of work

The results of this study show a considerable sensitivity by practicing first-level supervisors to the need for improving their skills in working with people.

In another poll of new supervisors, the supervisors stated the following needs in their jobs:

89 percent desired more knowledge of how to work with people.
59 percent needed better communication skills.
40 percent felt deficient in the personnel functions such as records.
39 percent needed better production-planning skills.
27 percent needed better training techniques.[3]

THE SUPERVISORY MANAGEMENT ROLE

A supervisor's role depends on his or her level in the organization and the type of people and tasks involved. However, most supervisors are involved in varying degrees in understanding the management framework, developing a sound supervisory philosophy, supervising individuals, supervising groups, and applying management functions to achieve results (see Figure 1.2).

UNDERSTANDING THE MANAGEMENT FRAMEWORK

Many supervisors are promoted to supervision as a reward for individual performance and have a limited understanding of the management framework in which they will be supervising. This unfortunate dilemma often results in supervisors' making poor or immature decisions and becoming frustrated because of their lack of awareness of the larger picture. A supervisor can acquire an understanding of the management framework by learning to develop a systems view of organizations and by becoming familiar with an organization's objectives, structure, and relationships.

DEVELOPING A SUPERVISORY PHILOSOPHY

Professional supervisors base their supervisory practices on a sound supervisory management philosophy. A supervisory philosophy is developed through an understanding of management theory and evaluating one's assumptions about values important to supervision and about people, groups, and the role of an effective supervisor. Such a philosophy improves supervisory effectiveness and consistency and provides a framework for adding new ideas and discarding ineffective practices.

[3]Quoted by Lester Bittel in *What Every Supervisor Should Know,* 3d ed. (New York: McGraw-Hill, 1974), p. 18.

Figure 1.2 The supervisor's role.

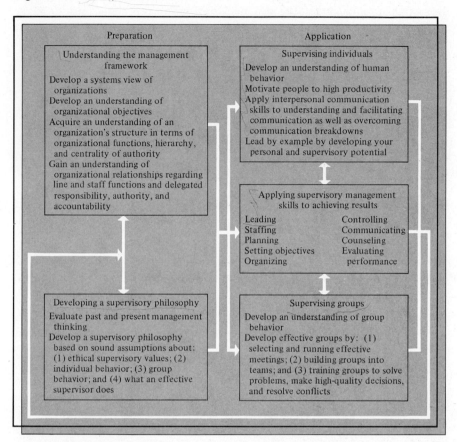

Supervising Individuals

Supervising individuals begins with developing an understanding of human behavior. Next, a supervisor must know how to motivate people. Supervising individuals also requires interpersonal communication skills. Communication skills are used to establish two-way communication with subordinates, one's boss and peers, and others in the organization. They are also used in handling communication breakdowns.

In supervising individuals, one of the most important things that a supervisor can do is to set a constructive example for subordinates. This suggests that a supervisor needs to be willing to develop his or her potential and to continue to grow for the benefit of others as well as the self and the organization.

Supervising Groups

Since supervisors manage people in groups, understanding and managing individuals is only part of a supervisor's job. A supervisor must also understand group behavior and how to develop effective groups. Individuals often respond differently in groups than they would as individuals. The dynamics of a group can either raise or lower individual productivity and morale. Therefore, the wise supervisor stays aware of group dynamics and takes appropriate actions to develop teamwork and group effectiveness.

Applying Supervisory Management Skills

The actual skills used by supervisors and managers are the same. However, the emphasis on various skills and the methods in which they are applied differ. For example, both supervisors and managers plan. Managers, however, place a greater emphasis on planning and focus more on long-range planning, while supervisors are usually more concerned with daily scheduling of work.

The major supervisory management skills are leading, staffing, planning and setting objectives, organizing and controlling, communicating, counseling, and evaluating performance (see Figure 1.3 for definitions).

DEVELOPING PROFESSIONAL SUPERVISORS

The modern organization cannot risk allowing supervisors to develop by chance. If the pressures and demands are real, there must be a concerted, conscious effort made to cultivate successful supervisory practices. There has been extensive research conducted to support these concerns.

The results of a study by Blake Lewis[4] regarding future directions for the supervisory role led to the general conclusion that supervisors believe their job in the future will require the existence of an individual who is more a leader and teacher than the traditional industrial policeman. The future would require that the supervisor concentrate on the "people" side of the organization as opposed to the "thing" side.

Thomas DeLong[5] interviewed 25 middle managers throughout the Midwest to determine two essential facts regarding first-level supervisors:

1. What characteristics they wanted in first-line supervisors.
2. Whether the supervisor who is highly technically oriented is more valuable to the organization than one who can interpret personal skills.

Two of the responses reflect some of the major concerns of those interviewed:

I don't care how intelligent my first-line managers are, the foundation of success is people knowledge.

Automation has changed the nature and scope of the supervisor's job, and he must handle human aspects of the technological change and cope with the most difficult part of the job . . . that which deals with human problems.

[4]Blake D. Lewis, Jr., "The Supervisor in 1975," *Personnel Journal,* September, 1974.
[5]Thomas DeLong, "What Do Middle Managers Really Want from First-Line Supervisors?" *Supervisory Management,* September, 1977.

Figure 1.3 Applying supervisory management skills.

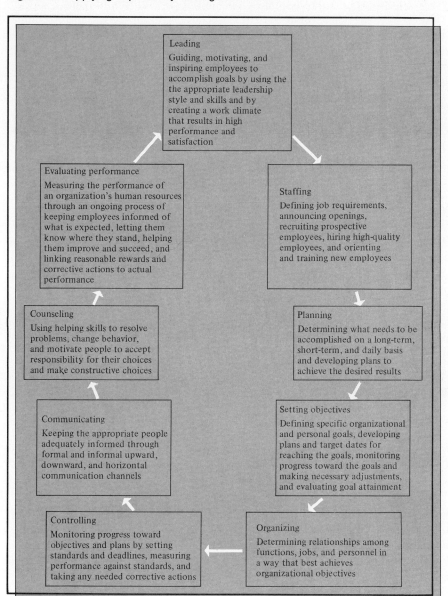

Leading

Guiding, motivating, and inspiring employees to accomplish goals by using the the appropriate leadership style and skills and by creating a work climate that results in high performance and satisfaction

Evaluating performance

Measuring the performance of an organization's human resources through an ongoing process of keeping employees informed of what is expected, letting them know where they stand, helping them improve and succeed, and linking reasonable rewards and corrective actions to actual performance

Staffing

Defining job requirements, announcing openings, recruiting prospective employees, hiring high-quality employees, and orienting and training new employees

Counseling

Using helping skills to resolve problems, change behavior, and motivate people to accept responsibility for their choices and make constructive choices

Planning

Determining what needs to be accomplished on a long-term, short-term, and daily basis and developing plans to achieve the desired results

Communicating

Keeping the appropriate people adequately informed through formal and informal upward, downward, and horizontal communication channels

Setting objectives

Defining specific organizational and personal goals, developing plans and target dates for reaching the goals, monitoring progress toward the goals and making necessary adjustments, and evaluating goal attainment

Controlling

Monitoring progress toward objectives and plans by setting standards and deadlines, measuring performance against standards, and taking any needed corrective actions

Organizing

Determining relationships among functions, jobs, and personnel in a way that best achieves organizational objectives

A report by Baker and Gorman[6] reflects a finding that although a supervisor may have the technical qualifications to assist subordinates in work-related problems, the typical assistance offered frequently fails. This failure is often attributed to inadequate abilities in supervisors for developing rapport and trust with subordinates.

Frank Harwood[7] cites results from 372 executives and supervisors in 160 companies for curricular suggestions on leadership development. They include emphasis on awareness of first-level management problems, communication, skill development, improved human relations knowledge, and the understanding of people to get better results from people.

The supervisory challenge today is to create a productive work group from the collection of single individuals within the organization. The supervisor must understand his or her own definition of performance success and those of each subordinate. The productivity needs of the organization can only be realized if the job goals and the goals of the individual are moved more closely together.

SUMMARY

In this introductory chapter we have discussed the environment in which supervisors must work, the role of a supervisor, and the need for developing professional supervisors. In addition, it is important to understand that: (1) today's supervisor is managing in a turbulent environment, (2) the supervisor is the key link between middle management and the operating worker and plays a major role in the success of organizations, (3) supervision is a professional skill that most people can learn through proper training, and (4) the supervisor must have technical, human, and conceptual skills. Of the three, the human skills are most important.

IMPORTANT TERMS

technical skills   management framework
human skills   supervisory philosophy
conceptual skills

REVIEW QUESTIONS

1. What are some of the main forces in today's busy world that create pressures on supervisors?
2. What does a supervisor do?
3. What is the difference between technical, human, and conceptual skills of supervisors?
4. What is the most significant change that a new supervisor must undergo?

[6]Kent H. Baker and Ronald H. Gorman, "Why Don't They Accept Help from Supervisors?" *Supervisory Management,* March, 1978.
[7]Frank R. Harwood, "Can This Business Profile Help You?" *Journal of Business Education,* 1975.

EXERCISE

1.1 Supervisory Perception

Complete the following statements by applying your feelings about working and interacting either as a supervisor or as a worker under the supervision of others. (Use your answers in a discussion of supervisory perception.)

1. Anybody will work hard if . . .

2. People will think of me as a good supervisor if . . .

3. Nothing is so frustrating on the job as . . .

4. There are times when I . . .

CASE

1.1 The Transition into Supervision

Carol A. Mark has been an electronics technician at Digital Electronics Corporation for the past 10 years. Based on the technical skills she demonstrated at the Massachusetts plant, she was selected for promotion to supervisor of assembly line A at the Colorado Springs division of Digital. On the airplane to Colorado Springs, Carol is going over in her mind what type of challenges the new job will hold and what to tell her subordinates at her first staff meeting.

Questions

1. What do you think her most important concern would be?
2. What advice would you give Carol?
3. What should she strive for as an outcome for her first meeting?
4. Which of the three major supervisory skill areas is important to Carol for this first meeting?

SUGGESTED ADDITIONAL READINGS

"A New Era of Management," *Business Week,* April 25, 1983, pp. 50.

Banathy, Bela H., et al. *The Effects of Learned Leadership/Membership Skills on Work Performance.* San Francisco: Far West Laboratories for Educational Research and Development, 1976.

Calhoun, Richard P., and Jerder, Thomas H. "Determining Supervisory Training Needs." *Management Review* (November, 1975).

Hershey, Gerald L. "Supervisory Development." *Management World* (December, 1974).

Hoeffer, Edward. "The Foreman and Learning to Use New Tools." *Industry Week,* October 7, 1976.

James, Muriel. *The OK Boss.* Reading, MA: Addison-Wesley, 1975.

Welch, Robert C. "The Care and Feeding of Blue-Collar Management." *Training Digest,* May, 1976.

2

The Management Framework

Order is Heaven's First Law.
                    Pope

OBJECTIVES

This chapter provides you with the information necessary to:

1. Know why supervisors need a "big picture" view of the management framework
2. Describe the components of the management framework
3. Know how systems theory can be used to understand organizations
4. Know why organizations need objectives
5. Understand how organizations are structured in terms of functions, hierarchy, and centrality of authority
6. Describe organizational relationships in terms of line and staff functions and the delegation of responsibility, authority, and accountability.

THE IMPORTANCE OF HAVING AN UNDERSTANDING OF THE MANAGEMENT FRAMEWORK

Since many supervisors move into their positions as a reward for job performance and have had little supervisory training, it is not surprising that they do not have a "big picture" perspective or understand the management framework in which they play a

major role. The management framework includes understanding: (1) what an organization is, (2) how it functions as a system, and (3) how it operates through objectives,
organizational structure, and organizational relationships.

WHAT IS AN ORGANIZATION?

An organization is a grouping of human and material resources organized to achieve
one or more specific goals. Human resources include governing boards such as a board
of directors, managers, supervisors, and employees. Material resources include money,
property, equipment, buildings, supplies, and other organization-controlled assets.

Organizations can be described as private or public, profit-making or nonprofit,
and product- or service-oriented. A private organization such as General Motors or a
local shoe store is owned by individuals or groups, while a public organization such
as the Internal Revenue Service, a university, or the city utilities department is owned
by the federal, state, or local government. A profit-making organization has as a goal
earning a profit. Nonprofit organizations may or may not receive money and acquire
additional assets; however, they are not designed to earn a long-run profit. Product
organizations produce products such as toys, clothes, or televisions. A service organization produces a service such as counseling, consulting, or brokering. Some organizations offer both products and services.

A SYSTEMS VIEW OF ORGANIZATIONS

Haynes, Massie, and Wallace define a system as an orderly grouping of different,
interdependent components or combinations with the intention of attaining a planned
goal.[1] They go on to say that any system should have three characteristics: (1) It must
be an orderly grouping; (2) there must be linkages of communication and influence
among components; and (3) the design of a system must be oriented to goal attainment.

The systems concept was introduced by Ludwig von Bertalanffy[2] and further
refined by Norbert Weiner,[3] Kenneth Boulding,[4] Herbert Simon,[5] and others since
these early pioneers developed the systems concept.

The systems approach views organizations as unified and purposeful systems
composed of interrelated parts wherein the activity of one part affects the activities of
every other part. The major parts include *inputs, processes, outputs,* and *feedback.*
Organizational inputs may consist of labor, material, capital, information, knowledge,
and so on. Processes include activities such as managing, supervising, and working.

[1]W. Warren Haynes, Joseph L. Massie, and Marc J. Wallace, *Management: Analysis, Concepts, and Cases,*
3d ed. (Englewood Cliffs, NJ: Prentice-Hall, 1975), p. 440.
[2]Ludwig von Bertalanffy, *General Systems Theory* (New York: Harper & Row, 1968).
[3]Norbert Weiner, *The Human Use of Human Beings: Cybernetics and Society* (Garden City, NY: Doubleday/
Anchor, 1954).
[4]Kenneth E. Boulding, *The Meaning of the 20th Century* (New York: Harper & Row, 1965).
[5]Herbert Simon, *The Science of Management Decisions* (New York: Harper & Row, 1977).

Processes transfer inputs into outputs. Outputs are products or services produced by an organization. Finally, feedback, which could include profit, sales, success or failure, employee satisfaction, consumer satisfaction, among other things, provides information that affects future inputs, processes, and outputs. This process is developed further and illustrated in Chapter 3.

Other important systems terms are *subsystems, synergy,* and *open* and *closed systems.* Subsystems in organizations are the departments, work groups, and organizational functions and activities that are parts of the total system. Synergy means that the whole is greater than the sum of its parts. In organizations, this means that separate subsystems interacting together produce a result greater than that of each individual subsystem acting alone. A system is open if it interacts with its environment, closed if it does not. All organizations are open systems, although some are more open than others. The CIA, for example, would be less open a system than a company that manufactures television sets.

How can a systems view of organizations help a supervisor? Without a systems view, supervisors are likely to view their job from a limited perspective. They can develop tunnel vision, viewing everything in terms of how it affects their group, rather than realizing how their group fits into the big picture and affects other groups.

ORGANIZATIONAL OBJECTIVES

Organizational objectives define the purpose of an organization. Organizational objectives often begin with a general mission statement that briefly describes an organization's overall purpose. An example of a mission statement could be:

> To manufacture high-quality clothes for men and to provide a high quality of work life for employees.

This statement defines the business that a company wants to be in and the type of attitude that it wants to have toward employees.

Organizational objectives can be divided further into strategic objectives. Strategic objectives describe the major, long-range objectives of an organization. Areas for consideration could be:

Growth	Quality of work life
Profitability	Social involvement
Market standing and mix	Working conditions
Productivity	Training
Service	Capital improvements

Organizational objectives are further divided into annual organization, department, work group, and personal objectives. These objectives are discussed further in Chapter 12. Supervisors need to be aware of organizational objectives so that they can assure that the objectives of the group they supervise fit into larger departmental and organizationwide objectives.

Figure 2.1 Organizational hierarchy.

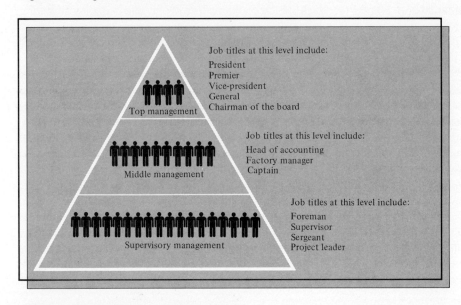

ORGANIZATIONAL STRUCTURE

Organizations accomplish objectives through a structure that includes *organizational functions, hierarchy,* and *centrality.*

Organizational Functions

Organizational functions define the major grouping of activities in an organization. Typical functions could be manufacturing, engineering, marketing, accounting and finance, planning, human-resource management, and public relations.

Organizational Hierarchy

An organization's hierarchy is usually defined in terms of top management, middle management, supervisory management, and employees. Rachman and Mescon show a typical hierarchy in their book *Business Today* (see Figure 2.1).[6]

The responsibilities of each level of management are shown in Figure 2.2. Top management is concerned with overall management policy and strategy and is responsible for the operation of an organization. Middle management may encompass many levels in the organization. Middle managers may direct the activities of other managers and supervisors and, in some cases, even the activities of high-level operating employees. Supervisory management includes the supervisors that manage activities of

[6]David J. Rachman and Michael H. Mescon, *Business Today,* 2d ed. (New York: Random House, 1979), p. 78.

operating employees. They are typically the leaders of work groups that are assigned specific tasks to do.

Centralized versus Decentralized Structure

Another consideration in understanding an organization's structure is whether the organization has a centralized or decentralized structure. In a centralized structure, authority and decisions are concentrated at the top of the organization. A centralized structure has the advantage of improving consistency, uniformity, control, and coordination with regard to major decisions and policies. However, as organizations get larger, it becomes increasingly difficult to control everything from the top and often results in poor decisions and a slowdown in decision making.

In a decentralized organization, authority and decision making are pushed down the organization. A decentralized structure increases autonomy and the ability to make localized decisions without seeking the approval of top management. It is a more developmental structure for people throughout the organization; it makes the organization more spontaneous and adaptable to change, and it improves communication. However, it can also result in lack of control and coordination, overlap in functions and responsibilities, and empire building when strong leaders build departments beyond what is in the best interest of overall organization objectives.

Figure 2.2 Responsibilities of each organizational level.

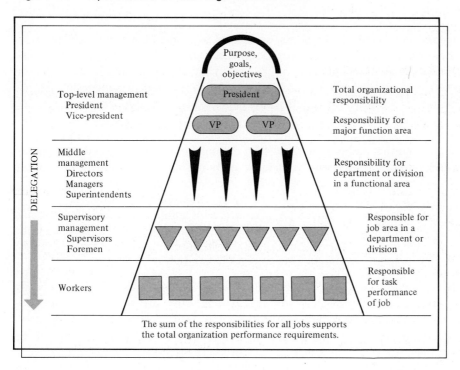

RELATIONSHIPS

Organizational relationships can be defined by the relationship between line and staff functions, how relationships are defined through delegation, and how relationships are defined by authority, responsibility, and accountability.

Line and Staff

Line activities are those activities that contribute directly to an organization's goals. Examples would be production, sales, and purchasing departments. Staff activities refer to those activities that support and facilitate line activities. Personnel, finance, engineering, and quality control departments would be examples of staff functions. Staff functions can also be defined by whether a staff is a personal staff that directly assists a line function or a specialized staff that performs a specialized skill. Line authority carries with it the right to command, while staff authority entails the right to advise and recommend.

    The relationship between line and staff is not always as clear as it may sound and many times results in friction. Line personnel may refuse or dislike staff advice, and staff personnel may feel that line personnel are unknowledgeable and resistant to ideas and change.

Delegation

Delegation is the assignment of responsibilities, authority, and accountability to another person. Delegation enables managers and supervisors to assign work and decision making to subordinates. Responsibilities include duties and results that a person could be held accountable for, such as completing a report or supervising people. *Accountability* suggests that a person will have to answer to the delegator regarding the responsibilities delegated. *Authority* is the power needed to accomplish responsibilities. Authority includes the right to make decisions, take actions, and discipline employees. Formal authority is created by designating an official position in the organization. Informal authority is indirect authority acquired through persuasion, knowledge, expertise, contacts, or a particular relationship between individuals.

    Figure 2.3 shows the relationship between responsibility, authority, and accountability. The ideal is that a person be given sufficient authority to carry out delegated responsibilities. Unfortunately, this rarely happens. Responsibilities often have to be accomplished through informal authority. It should also be pointed out that a delegator still retains ultimate responsibility for tasks delegated.

SUMMARY

Supervisors are often promoted into supervision without an understanding of the management framework in which they perform as supervisors. The first procedure in understanding the management framework is to develop a systems view of organiza-

Figure 2.3 Distribution of responsibility, authority, and accountability.

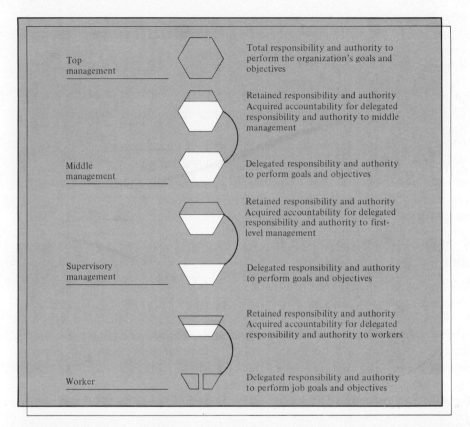

tions. This requires knowledge of an organization's inputs, processes, and outputs. The next procedure is to become aware of an organization's mission and objectives. This should be followed by becoming familiar with an organization's structure in terms of its hierarchy and centralized or decentralized orientation. Finally, knowledge of an organization's relationships is important. Organizational relationships are defined by line and staff functions and the delegation of responsibilities, authority, and accountability.

IMPORTANT TERMS

systems view of organizations
organization mission
strategic objectives
organization structure
centralized structure
decentralized structure
organization hierarchy

organization relationships
line and staff functions
delegation
responsibility
formal authority
informal authority
accountability

REVIEW QUESTIONS

1. Why do supervisors need to understand the management framework?
2. What would a supervisor look for in understanding an organization from a systems viewpoint?
3. Why should organizations have mission statements and strategic objectives?
4. Describe the four levels of hierarchy in most organizations. What general responsibilities do the people at each level have?
5. What are the advantages and disadvantages of centralized and decentralized structures?
6. What are the differences between line and staff functions?
7. What does it mean to delegate responsibility, authority, and accountability?
8. Do supervisors give up responsibility when they delegate? Explain your answer.

EXERCISES

2.1 Supervisor's Responsibility for Subordinates' Satisfaction

Break into groups of five members for approximately 20 minutes and discuss the management concern: "If the organization is designed with functions defined, jobs specialized, and tasks specialized so that a person sometimes feels like a machine, how does job satisfaction evolve for the worker?" Your group should make some conclusions regarding the supervisor's role in providing job satisfaction for subordinates.

2.2 Authority versus Responsibility

Be prepared to give your opinion on the following statement before the class: "A supervisor should make decisions on all matters that come to his or her attention except those for which he or she does not have sufficient authority. Matters for which the supervisor does not have sufficient authority are decided upon by committees or higher management."

CASE

2.1 Queens Burger

Queens Burger is a very profitable fast-food restaurant which is part of a chain of restaurants located in a major city in the western region of the United States. Twenty-five people are employed at this firm, and the supervision consists of a general manager and two assistant managers. The remainder of the employees are food-service personnel who specialize in various products such as french fries, drinks, or hamburgers. Louise Smith, the general manager, is a humanistic manager who is respected and liked by all the employees. One of the assistant managers, Kipp Carol, pushes employees very hard and believes in firm control over the newer employees. He will often shout at or embarrass the newer employees.

Employees receive the minimum wage when they start their employment at Queens Burger; however, seniority raises and fringe benefits are excellent. For example, after one year of employment, workers receive a week's vacation with pay. This is considered very good for the fast-food business.

One evening after working an eight-hour shift, Paul Dale, a new employee with approximately 10 days on the job, was cleaning the french-fry machine after closing time. Because he was a new employee, he was working very hard to impress Kipp Carol, the supervisor for the evening shift. Approximately 10 other employees were also in the process of cleaning various equipment. The 10 employees decided to take a soda break and sat around telling jokes. Paul continued to work. The older employees started to tease Paul, and finally Paul filled a glass with soda and joined them. Just as Paul joined the group of workers, Kipp entered the room and said to Paul, "What —you're not done? Cleaning the french-fry machine should take only a half-hour!" Kipp then went over to the time cards, inserted Paul's card in the machine, and clocked him out for the evening. Paul finished cleaning the french-fry machine and then left for the evening.

Questions

1. Assume you are another shift supervisor and the next morning Paul comes to you for guidance. How would you advise him?
2. Should Paul ask for an appointment with Louise Smith?
3. Discuss the implications of the peer group and Paul's response to their comments.
4. What other supervisory issues do you see in this case?

SUGGESTED ADDITIONAL READINGS

Barnard, Chester I. *The Functions of the Executive.* Cambridge, MA: Harvard University Press, 1938.

DeLong, Thomas. "What Do Middle Managers Really Want from First-Line Supervisors?" *Supervisory Management* (September, 1977).

Fayol, Henri. *General and Industrial Management.* London: Sir Isaac Pitman & Sons, 1949.

George, Claude S., Jr. *The History of Management Thought.* Englewood Cliffs, NJ: Prentice-Hall, 1968.

Lee, James A. "Behavioral Theory vs. Reality." *Harvard Business Review* (March-April, 1971).

Levenson, Harry. "Don't Choose Your Own Successor." *Harvard Business Review* (November-December, 1974).

McGregor, Douglas. *The Human Side of Enterprise.* New York: McGraw-Hill, 1960.

Shetty, Y. K. "There Is No One Best Way to Manage a Business." *Management World* (December, 1974).

Taylor, Frederick W. *Scientific Management.* New York: Harper & Row, 1911.

Viola, Richard W. *Organizations in a Changing Society: Administration and Human Values.* Philadelphia: Saunders, 1977.

White, Harold C. "How the Leader Looks to the Led." *Administrative Management,* March, 1974.

3

Exploring Schools of Management Thought and Developing a Supervisory Philosophy

Human history is in essence a history of ideas.

H. G. Wells

OBJECTIVES

This chapter provides you with the information necessary to:

1. Describe the major schools of supervision and management thought
2. Understand why the early writers emphasized economic skills (specialization) for the supervisor
3. Describe how and why the human-relations writers were in some ways a reaction to early writers
4. Gain an overview of studies and their influence on management thought
5. Elaborate upon the assumptions of Theory X and Theory Y and their implications for supervisors
6. Describe the contribution the management sciences made to supervision and management

7. Understand the contingency nature of supervision in today's organizations
8. Discuss why supervisory philosophy is so important to successful supervision
9. Describe the importance and basics of a sound supervisory philosophy
10. Understand how a supervisory philosophy must be tailored to unique personal skills to get things accomplished

BUILDING A FOUNDATION FOR SUCCESSFUL SUPERVISION

A favorite question asked by both supervisors and managers is "What is the single most important thing a supervisor needs to know to be successful?" Perhaps the answer is to develop a sound supervisory philosophy. Supervisory philosophies, like most carefully thought-out life philosophies, provide us with: (1) a logical basis for behaving and making decisions, (2) a solid foundation to build on, and (3) a frame of reference for building consistency into our actions.

WHY A SUPERVISORY PHILOSOPHY IS IMPORTANT

Supervisors spend a considerable amount of time learning how to supervise. Through trial and error, experience, observing their bosses and other supervisors, and attending training sessions (some good and some bad), supervisors often wander many years trying to understand this phenomenon called management. This time of wandering is often assisted by well-intended "seasoned managers" who all offer different formulas for success and by employees who never act the way the textbooks say they are supposed to. The dilemma of learning how to manage at times seems overwhelming. And yet, there are managers who make it all seem natural. In spite of the apparent confusion that has befallen their counterparts who are struggling to understand supervision, they seem to have logical bases for behaving and making decisions. The reasons are either that they have intuitively developed a supervisory philosophy to guide them —probably a spillover benefit from having taken the time to acquire a life philosophy —or that they have taken time to think carefully through their supervisory philosophy. Without a philosophy, a supervisor will struggle inconsistently with each new decision in evaluating its ethical, behavioral, technological, and organizational implications.

SCHOOLS OF MANAGEMENT THOUGHT

There are many insights and skills that supervisors can learn from studying the early thoughts of management writers and practitioners. Each writer builds upon the experience and principles of previous authors and adds to earlier contributions. Some of the major schools of management thought are shown in Figure 3.1.

Although ideas about supervision and management cannot be dated, Frederick W. Taylor is generally credited with giving the initial impetus to the study and documentation of management thought.

Figure 3.1 Major schools of supervisory and management thought.

Early Supervision and Management—1900s	Improvements—1930s	Supervision Today— 1960s to Present
Scientific Management— 1903 Bureaucratic Theory—1915 Administrative Management Theory— 1916	Human Relations—1930s Management Sciences— 1950s	Systems View Contingency View
Supervisor's Role		
Performance-oriented Economic skills	People-oriented Social skills	See the relationships between all parts of a system. Meet the goals of the organization.
Dependency of the worker	Economic and rational orientation Quantitative skills	Diagnose the situation and apply needed management and supervision tools.

Scientific Management

Some of the leaders in the scientific management approach were:

1. *Frederick W. Taylor,* whose rather narrow approach to supervision stressed planning and standardization of tasks.
2. *Henry L. Gantt,* one of the first persons to emphasize humanizing scientific management.   1st PHD MGMT PROF
3. *Frank and Lillian Gilbreth,* who developed "the one best way" and became known as efficiency experts. America knows them through the book and movie *Cheaper by the Dozen.*

Taylor,[1] who is considered the father of scientific management, was the first recognized American author to develop what can be construed as a theory of supervision and management. Most theories are products of their times, and Taylor's scientific management approach was no exception. He offered his first principal writing in 1903,[2] following the industrial revolution, when organizations were becoming increasingly complex, more diverse in their activities, and much larger in size and influence. His approach included such concepts as division of labor, time and motion studies, efficiency through carefully engineered and organized jobs, clearly defined rules and regulations, motivation through pay incentives, a division between management and the workers, a heavy emphasis on production, and a scientific engineering approach to organizing and simplifying workers' jobs so they would work more efficiently.

Taylor's view of supervision and management was strongly influenced by the

[1]Frederick W. Taylor, *Scientific Management* (New York: Harper & Row, 1911).
[2]Taylor, *Shop Management* (New York: Harper & Row, 1903).

Protestant ethic, emphasizing hard work, loyalty, and doing one's best on a task. This theory of management had a major influence on organizations because it removed the workers' discretion in how they did their jobs. Workers could no longer plan and organize a task; rather, they did exactly as told by the supervisors in order to gain increased individual productivity and financial rewards.

The role of the supervisor in the scientific management approach was clearly performance-oriented. The human side of management was taken for granted, since it was assumed that workers would respond without question to the wishes of management as long as management was able to satisfy their economic self-interests through adequate wages and incentive plans for extra work.

Although scientific management achieved wide popularity and fulfilled a need for a more scientific approach to management, some of the procedures designed to produce efficiency and motivation often accomplished just the opposite. The approach tended to increase conformity at the expense of creativity, made work more impersonal, decreased the status of the person, created a preoccupation with rules, and led employees to think that motivation was the result of higher pay and better working conditions. Consequently, employees often became preoccupied with seeking higher wages, reducing the time spent at work, and acquiring more fringe benefits to compensate for a tedious work environment.

Henry L. Gantt, a coworker of Taylor's, was the first person to question the lack of humanization in scientific management. Although he emphasized production and was most famous for the development of the Gantt chart used in work scheduling, he began to sound the alarm about the need to be concerned with people and their needs.

Bureaucratic Theory

The leader of bureaucratic theory was *Max Weber*. Weber designed organizations around professional managers, a set of rules, fixed salaries, and a merit system.

Although the term *bureaucracy* immediately produces visions of red tape, inefficient government employees, and artificial roadblocks, Max Weber saw bureaucracy as a technique to manage large organizations whereby all people requesting the services of an organization would be treated in the same manner by the employees of the organization. Thus, what he viewed as a major advantage of his theory of management became the major stumbling block of present bureaucracies.

The major parts of Weber's bureaucratic model are:

The right to exercise authority based upon the power of a professional manager
A set of files and rules
Compensation in the form of a fixed salary
Various levels (hierarchy) of authority and responsibility (organizational structure)
Requisite technical qualification of officeholders (supervisors)
Division of labor
Impersonality of interpersonal relations

Although Weber viewed management's role as a professional and fair enforcer of the rules, the role of management eventually evolved into one of almost always following the rules even at the expense of people. Officeholders soon learned that they could not be criticized for following the rules, and therefore creativity and innovation were reduced in bureaucratic organizations.

Henri Fayol provided major contributions to the relationship form of management and developed 14 guidelines for effective supervision. The guidelines were:

1. Division of work. Specialization of labor produces efficiency.
2. Authority and responsibility—the obligation and power to perform a task.
3. Discipline. Discipline is the cornerstone of a smooth running organization.
4. Unity of command. Each subordinate should receive instructions from only one supervisor.
5. Unity of direction—one supervisor and one plan for each group of activities in an organization.
6. Subordination of individual interests to group or organizational interests.
7. Remuneration of people. Rewards should be fair and produce satisfaction.
8. Centralization. This is a natural condition of organizing.
9. Scalar chain—chain of supervisors from the top to the bottom of the organization.
10. Order. All must know their places in the organization.
11. Equity. Justice exists in the organization.
12. Stability of tenure of employees. Time is needed for employees to adjust to their work.
13. Initiative. Zeal and energy are needed at all levels.
14. Esprit de corps. Interpersonal relationships and good working conditions are necessary.[3]

13.14 → Teamwork issues

Although modified through the years, Fayol's 14 principles became the basis for present-day universal principles of management. He further stressed that his 14 principles were not all-inclusive and that newer principles would be discovered. Although he recognized that supervisors and managers must be flexible, he saw their role as basically performance-oriented, with the task of creating an efficient organization structure.

Mary Parker Follett extended the writings of this era by strongly advocating the need for scientific management techniques in government agencies. Through her many speeches, she functioned as a catalyst for change in government. Business executives sought out Follett as she campaigned for more cooperation between labor and capital and stressed professionalism, creativity, participation, and human treatment of workers.

Human Relations

The major contributors to the human relations school of management thought were:

[3]Henri Fayol, *General and Industrial Management,* trans. Constance Storrs (London: Sir Isaac Pitman & Sons, 1949), pp. 19–42.

1. *Elton Mayo*—the father of the human relations movement—who stressed social needs on the job.
2. *George C. Homans,* who introduced the ideas of equity, motivation, and groups.
3. *Kurt Lewin,* who emphasized the importance of democratic group decision making and the effects of participation on motivation, taking into account workers' feelings, attitudes, beliefs, ideas, and sentiments.
4. *Douglas McGregor,* who developed a theory for managing people that is human-relations oriented.
5. *Carl Rogers,* who emphasized open and nondirective communications skills for managers.

Mayo's Western Electric studies prompted the big rush to human relations and the attempt to return dignity to man. Mayo was trying to improve worker productivity by improving light levels in the work areas. As changes were made, regardless of whether the lighting was brighter, dimmer, or constant, production continued to increase during the study in every one of the rooms, while it remained constant in the control groups. Mayo attributed the results to the fact that the experiment groups were receiving special attention, which gave the groups an elite feeling. They also participated in the decision-making process. Other important human relations pioneers were Homans,[4] who demonstrated the effect of groups on motivation; Lewin,[5] who stressed the promise of democratic and group decision making as well as the importance of participation in motivating people; and Rogers,[6] who underscored the need for understanding, empathy, open communication, and nondirective management. Finally, Douglas McGregor[7] made the assumption that some people dislike work and attempt to avoid it (Theory X) while other workers want to do well, seek out additional responsibility, and excel on the job (Theory Y) (see Figure 3.2).

In human relations theory, the supervisor's role is to consider the feelings of workers, to permit them to participate in making decisions, and to allow and even encourage free interaction among the employees. The objective is to keep workers satisfied, strive for harmony, avoid conflict, and be warm and accepting. Such an approach is based on the assumption that people can be motivated to work more productively by meeting their social and psychological needs; that is, when these needs are met, people will automatically be productive.

The human relations movement was instrumental in focusing the attention of management on the importance of recognizing the needs of human beings, who resented being treated like machines. However, keeping employees happy does not necessarily result in higher motivation and productivity. Rensis Likert and Daniel Katz, in their famous University of Michigan studies of the relationship of leadership, motivation, and productivity, found very little relationship between employees' atti-

[4]George C. Homans, *The Human Group* (New York: Harcourt Brace Jovanovich, 1950).
[5]Kurt Lewin, "Frontiers in Group Dynamics," *Human Relations* (June, 1947), pp. 1, 5–41.
[6]Carl R. Rogers and F. J. Roethlisberger, "Barriers and Gateways to Communication," *Harvard Business Review* (July-August, 1952), pp. 28–34.
[7]Douglas McGregor, *The Human Side of Enterprise* (New York: McGraw-Hill, 1960), chap. 4.

Figure 3.2 Theory X and Theory Y.

9 out 10

Theory X	Theory Y
Assumptions about People	**Assumptions about People**
Most people . . .	Most people . . .
Dislike work and want as little as possible to do Are lazy Dislike responsibility Resist change Are indifferent to organizational goals Are self-seeking Are primarily motivated by money Prefer to be directed	Enjoy and want meaningful work Will work hard to accomplish worthwhile goals Like responsibility Will adapt to change Will become committed to meaningful organizational goals Are able to seek team goals Are primarily motivated by challenging work Prefer self-direction
Supervisory Practices	**Supervisory Practices**
A supervisor should . . .	A supervisor should . . .
Plan, organize, direct, and control closely the efforts of people Make most of the important decisions Punish mistakes Not get too close to employees Assume that his or her authority is unquestionable Push people to keep them motivated	Let employees become involved in planning, organizing, and controlling their own efforts Delegate the authority to make decisions Focus on resolving problems, not punishing mistakes Know each employee personally Rely on earned, not formal, authority Motivate people by giving challenging assignments

tudes toward the company and their productivity. In many cases the happy employees tended to do whatever was necessary to get by, and the productive employees often showed little concern for the company.[8] The fact that a company has good working conditions, excellent fringe benefits, recreation facilities for employees, and a company psychologist available for counseling does little to motivate people if jobs are boring or accomplishing organizational goals becomes secondary to having good relationships.

The human relations authors basically proposed a collaborative or consensus style for supervisors, wherein the employees participated in the decision-making process. They did not recognize that there were workers who did not want to participate in the decision process or who lacked the technical skills to give good inputs to management. This general "let them be happy" attitude became a major criticism of the human relations movement.

[8]Robert L. Kahn, "Productivity and Job Satisfaction," in *Management and the Behavioral Sciences: Text and Readings,* ed. Maneck S. Wadia (Boston: Allyn and Bacon, 1968), pp. 134–143.

Management Sciences

While the *people* approach was emphasized in the human relations movement, the *quantitative* approach was stressed in the management sciences. During World War II, there developed a need for quick, quantitative, scientific solving of problems. This demand resulted in greater use of computers in the decision-making process and the introduction of new management techniques, such as operations research, the program evaluation and review technique (PERT), linear programming, input-output analysis, and simulation. The authors in this quantitative school approach problems from the viewpoint of optimization. They analyze all alternatives, usually through a mathematical model, and recommend the alternative or alternatives that will come closest to meeting the supervisor's objectives (the best or optimal decision).

These schools of thought on supervision and management present conflicting views at times, and this conflict may seem confusing to the student of supervision. Rather than becoming disenchanted with the study of supervision, the student should welcome these diverse contributions because each school of thought presents selected techniques of supervision. However, management theorists and practitioners also worried about these divergent and at times polarized views and began to look at the organization as a total system, with supervision and management as subsystems.

SUPERVISION TODAY

Current management thinking has developed two new theories:

1. *Systems theory.* Chester Barnard[9] was one of the first management writers and practitioners to recommend that organizations be viewed as systems. Any change in any subsystem has an effect on the other subsystems.
2. *Contingency theory.* This group of writers recommends that the supervisor begin with a proper diagnosis of the problem. Then, the appropriate management techniques should be used—both quantitative and people approaches.

Chester Barnard was one of the first management writers to view organizations as systems. Any organization viewed as a system (see Figure 3.3) consists of four basic components: (1) inputs, (2) conversion-process activities, (3) outputs, and (4) results of the operating environment. An organization's inputs are human resources, capital resources, and information that it receives from the environment. Resources are converted into outputs through a conversion process. Figure 3.3 presents some examples of the flow of resources through a system.

For purposes of discussion, consider General Motors as a system. Selected examples of organizational inputs are people and investment by the stockholders. The conversion process is the assembly line, and the output is an automobile. Thus, the organization's output is returned to the larger environment (society), where the results are evaluated by the users. In the long run, if the organization's outputs do not meet

[9]Chester I. Barnard, *The Functions of the Executive* (Cambridge, MA: Harvard University Press, 1938).

Figure 3.3 Organization as a system.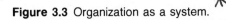

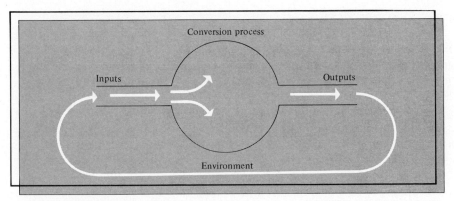

the expectations in the environment (society), the organization's inputs will eventually be restricted or reduced.

Subsystems of the Conversion Process

In Figures 3.3 and 3.4, we diagram the organization as a total system. Within this system, what are the roles of supervisors or managers? Before answering that question, it is necessary to explain further the conversion (activities) process of an organization. The conversion process consists of the following three subsystems (as shown in Figure 3.5):

1. The technological subsystem
2. The human subsystem
3. The structural subsystem

These three subsystems interact in a very complex fashion within the conversion process, and any change made in one subsystem will generally have an impact on the other two subsystems.

In Figure 3.3, energy is represented by the arrows. Energy is the organization's capacity for vigorous activity to achieve. Ideally, managers attempt to reduce the kinks

Figure 3.4 Input-output model for understanding organizations.

Inputs	Conversion Process (Activities)	Outputs	Results
Energy Dollars People Information	Writing reports Engineering Designing Selling Keeping records Accounting Management style and philosophy Organizational structure Organizational technology	Proposals Products Services	Amount of profits Amount of business Amount of dividends Quality Quantity

Figure 3.5 Systems model for understanding organizations.

Technological Subsystems	Human Subsystems	Structural Subsystems	Results of the Interaction of the Three Systems
Computer systems Accounting systems Product of service technology Capital External environment Economic conditions	Management and supervisory practices, philosophies, and styles Informal communication Informal activities, processes, relationships, and norms between groups Informal activities, processes, relationships, and norms among groups Informal recognition and reward systems Informal discipline and punishment systems Employee perceptions Social structures Employee needs Employee influence Informal power relationships Actual decision-making and problem-solving processes Emergent activities Employee background (abilities, values, education, maturity, etc.)	Formal organizational goals, policies, rules, and procedures Formal communication systems Organizational structure Formal job structures Formal personnel policies and practices (pay, fringe benefits, ways of evaluating and rewarding employee performance, discipline procedures, working hours, etc.) Working conditions Selection and training procedures Formal authority and reporting relationships Required work flow within and between groups Physical arrangements of work environments Required activities (selling, engineering, writing reports)	Employee productivity Employee motivation Employee satisfaction Amount of sales Amount of profit Amount of dividends Individual and organizational growth Amount of trust Organizational image Individual and organizational self-renewing capabilities

in the arrows because the kinks are losses of energy in the conversion process. The optimum situation is one represented by straight arrows. Why is energy lost in organizations? The answer lies somewhere in the understanding of the interaction of the three subsystems in the conversion process.

The role of the supervisor in an organization is to be a good diagnostician and recognize the possible results of the interaction among the three subsystems. Assuming a proper diagnosis of the situation, supervisors must then apply one or more of the techniques of management advocated by the various schools of thought on supervision and management.

DEVELOPING YOUR SUPERVISORY PHILOSOPHY

Having evaluated various schools of management thinking, a supervisor should begin to develop a supervisory philosophy. Each person's philosophy may vary, depending on what they want to include in it, but there are at least four major ingredients that should be considered:

1. Basic assumptions about values important to supervision
2. Basic assumptions about human behavior
3. Basic assumptions about group behavior
4. Basic assumptions about what an effective supervisor does

Values Important to Supervision

Supervisors and managers need to take full responsibility for their values, because values permeate every area of a person's actions. Also, there is a tendency for people to imitate the values of their leaders. They may imitate their boss's dress, vocabulary, management style, ethics, personal habits, life-style, even the cars they drive. In one organization, all of the "in" salespeople drive Porsches even though they can't afford them, and the cars are impractical for their work. The higher one goes in an organization, the more influential values become. For example, top-management values concerning degrees of honesty (total honesty, honesty with a few half-truths, honesty unless it is inconvenient, outright misrepresentation of the facts) may affect every phase of an organization, from how employees are treated to the accuracy of financial information.

Although there is no specific chapter pertaining to values, this entire book makes clear the advantages over the long run of strong values of honesty, straightforwardness, genuine caring, and high standards. It may be more convenient in the short run to misrepresent the truth, be a game player, or maintain a constant "looking out for number one" attitude. However, over the long run you will lose credibility and self-respect, and the organizations that reward such behaviors are destined for problems.

Assumptions about Human Behavior

A person's basic assumptions about human behavior are likely to become a self-fulfilling prophecy whether they are accurate or not. Even though we recognize that people are different, we tend to make assumptions about human behavior that affect our interpersonal relationships and, particularly, the way we manage. For example, let's assume that a supervisor believes that most people are lazy, irresponsible, untrustworthy, and basically selfish, and prefer to be told what to do. Under such assumptions, a supervisor will be autocratic, enforce strict rules and procedures, and oversupervise the "untrustworthy" employees. Under such conditions, the employees will do minimal work, avoid responsibility, and resentfully do as they are told—no more and no less (it's safer). The boss will conclude, "Well, people are basically lazy and irresponsible. If you don't believe it, look at my people."

Are people really basically lazy and irresponsible, or did the boss create a situation by his or her assumptions? It is to the supervisor's advantage to believe the best about people, knowing that beliefs tend to create a self-fulfilling prophecy. This is not an advocacy of "blind" trust, but rather an attitude toward people; it would be foolish to trust someone who has proven untrustworthy.

Assumptions about Group Behavior

Even though supervisors spend most of their time trying to accomplish things through groups, perhaps their greatest knowledge gap involves group behavior.

Unfortunately, many supervisors and managers have never had the opportunity to study group dynamics, team-building and conflict-resolution skills, or how to understand and develop large groups such as whole organizations or companies. Their human relations education often stops with the study of individual behavior. This limits their understanding of the work environment, since individual behavior is heavily influenced by group behavior.

Some of the group-behavior basics that should be kept in mind are

Group norms often have a stronger influence on group members than any other factor in the work environment.

The dynamics of a group (structure, social and interpersonal patterns, problem-solving approaches, and decision-making style) and the group norms significantly contribute to effectiveness or ineffectiveness of a group.

Group members should agree that group problems will be confronted openly and constructively and that it is unacceptable for a group member to misuse, disrupt, or divide a group for their own purposes or causes.

Group members who refuse to cooperate with constructive and agreed-upon dynamics and norms should not be kept in the group.

What an Effective Supervisor Does

Supervisors who manage without a plan soon become fire fighters, too busy putting out fires to take the time to decide how to manage effectively. Effective supervisors manage by design, not by crisis. They control their work rather than letting their work control them.

What does an effective supervisor do? Many have options of how they spend their time, and since each job has different requirements, not all spend their time the same way. There are a few basics, however, that most effective supervisors follow which help them to be consistent and successful. The emphasis they place on each item may vary according to their own unique strengths and the specific requirements of each job.

GUIDELINES IN IMPLEMENTING YOUR PHILOSOPHY

Your initial identification of a sound supervisory philosophy will more than likely be changed or supported by the concepts in this book. When you have completed the text and have solidified your philosophy, resist the temptation to make major revisions unless you have substantial evidence that change is needed. Otherwise, temporary circumstances and pressures may control the use of your philosophy. For example, a supervisor who assumes that most people are basically good and honest may get burned by a dishonest employee and become cynical. Establishing a new philosophy to treat all employees with suspicion and distrust because of this would be acting against your basic beliefs.

It is also important to seek occasional feedback on the agreement between your philosophy and your actions. Discrepancies between beliefs and actions will cause you to receive inaccurate information regarding the practical use of your philosophy as well as contribute to confusion among your subordinates. The goal in implementing your philosophy is to be consistent and make your beliefs and your actions agree.

SUMMARY

It was not until the early 1900s that a written body of management knowledge was started. The three major development periods regarding supervision and management are: (1) early supervision and management (1900s), (2) improvements (1930s), and (3) supervision today (1960s to present). This body of knowledge evolved through a series of trials and errors in industry and government. Each succeeding management writer "borrowed" from the preceding writers and then attempted to improve upon the written principles of supervision and management as they existed at that point in time. Present-day supervisors can learn much about management thought by studying the early practitioners and writers.

Early supervision and management consisted of scientific management, bureaucratic theory, and administrative management theory. The creators of these approaches basically believed that workers were motivated by economic returns and that it was management's job to increase productivity through task specialization and work improvement.

During the 1930s the human relations and management science writers improved upon the theories of the early writers by stressing human needs and quantitative skills for supervisors and managers.

Supervision today must view the organization as a complex system of inputs, conversion processes, and outputs that exists in a highly turbulent environment. The present-day supervisor must increase productivity by possessing technical skills, human skills, quantitative skills, and management skills that can reduce the amount of lost human energy in organizations.

A sound supervisory philosophy is one of the most valuable tools that a supervisor can have. Like a sound life philosophy, it provides direction and purpose and builds consistency into our actions. While a person's supervisory philosophy should be tailored to his or her unique skills and style, there are at least four major ingredients that should be considered in developing a sound philosophy:

1. Basic assumptions about values important to supervision
2. Basic assumptions about human behavior
3. Basic assumptions about group behavior
4. Basic assumptions about what an effective supervisor does

Although a management philosophy is a fluid process that may gradually change with experience and exposure to new ideas, the basics should stand the test of time. In implementing a supervisory philosophy, one should: (1) resist the temptation to make major decisions without substantial evidence that a change is needed, and (2) solicit occasional feedback to assure your beliefs and actions are consistent.

You should establish the ingredients of your true philosophy now. As you proceed through this text you will be able to revise your initial thoughts and mold a pattern for success.

IMPORTANT TERMS

management philosophy	Frederick W. Taylor
schools of management	Henry L. Gantt
scientific management	bureaucratic theory
Max Weber	administrative management theory
Henri Fayol	Elton Mayo
human relations	Mary Parker Follett
George C. Homans	systems theory
management science	Kurt Lewin
Theory X and Theory Y	Douglas McGregor
Rensis Likert and Daniel Katz	management values
contingency theory	Frank and Lillian Gilbreth
Chester Barnard	Carl Rogers

REVIEW QUESTIONS

1. List the major schools of supervision and management thought.
2. What contributions did Taylor make to management theory?
3. What was the role of the supervisor in scientific management?
4. What are the major parts of Weber's bureaucratic model?
5. What were Henri Fayol's major contributions to the management framework in organizations?
6. Elton Mayo's studies at Western Electric introduced what new management theories?
7. Why is a sound management philosophy important?
8. What are the basics of a sound management philosophy? Can you think of other areas that could be important?

9. Discuss some important guidelines necessary for implementing a management philosophy.
10. What are some important elements in your management philosophy?

EXERCISE

3.1 Building a Sound Management Philosophy

The purpose of this exercise is to help people develop a sound management philosophy. It is also an excellent exercise for quickly exposing people to what others think about management.

1. Complete Exhibit 3.1 by brainstorming a list under each heading. (Brainstorming means that you should write down whatever comes to your mind without any attempt to evaluate or discuss any of the items.)
2. For each of the lists, quickly refer to any relevant chapters in the book and revise the list by adding, rephrasing, or eliminating items.
3. Meet in small groups and complete step 1 using chart paper and a Magic Marker. Then start with the first list and as a group discuss and rank the most important items. Each group should elect a group leader for this task to assure that it is accomplished within the allotted time period without the group's getting sidetracked.
4. Each group should then tape its philosophy to the wall and the group leader present it to the class. Depending on the amount of time available, other options would be to limit the number of groups that report, let the class members circulate, personally reviewing each list, or have the instructor review each list, mentioning only items that have not been mentioned before.
5. Each person should now develop a revised philosophy (see Exhibit 3.1) by reviewing his or her initial philosophy and the comments from the group and the instructor.

EXHIBIT

3.1 Developing a Management Philosophy

1. Brainstorm a list under each heading.
2. For each list, quickly refer to any relevant chapters in the book and revise the list by adding, rephrasing, or eliminating items.

SUGGESTED ADDITIONAL READINGS

Bedeian, Arthur C. "Superior vs. Subordinate Role Perception." *Personnel Administration/Public Personnel Review* (November-December, 1973).
Fiman, Byron G. "An Investigation of the Relationships among Supervisory Attitudes,

Basic Assumptions about Values Important to Management	Basic Assumptions about Human Behavior	Basic Assumptions about Group Behavior	Basic Assumptions about What an Effective Manager Does

Behaviors and Outputs: An Examination of McGregor's Theory Y." *Personnel Psychology* (May, 1973).

French, Wendell L., Bell, Cecil H., Jr., and Zawacki, Robert A. *Organization Development: Theory, Practice, and Research.* Plano, Tx: BPI, 1983.

Gibson, J. L., Ivancevich, J. M., and Donnelly, J. H., Jr. *Organizations: Behavior, Structure, Processes.* Plano, Tx: BPI, 1982.

Ritti, Richard R., and Funkhouser, Ray. *The Ropes to Skip and the Ropes to Know.* Columbus, OH: Grid, 1977.

PART TWO
Supervising Individuals

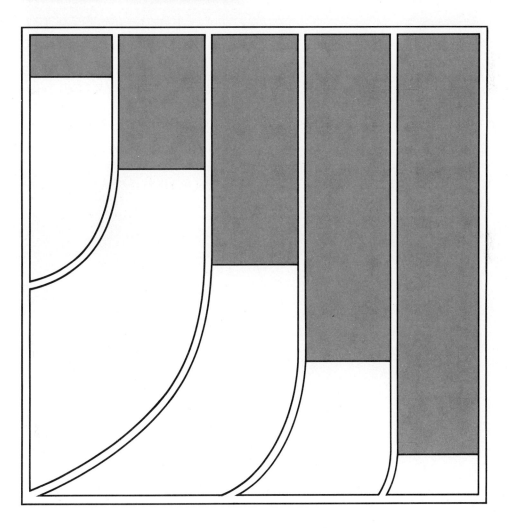

4

Understanding Individual Behavior

You cannot teach a man anything. You can only help him discover it within himself.

Galileo

OBJECTIVES

This chapter provides you with the information necessary to:

1. Understand the self-concept and why employees have a high need to preserve or improve it
2. List and describe the basic defense mechanisms and their effect on individual behavior
3. Describe the Johari Window and explain how it helps supervisors understand employee behavior

---

THE INFLUENCE OF BEHAVIOR

The foremost objective for any manager or supervisor is to be able to create a productive work force. The very essence of productivity, however, is rooted in individual values and attitudes and in how employees perceive themselves in relation to the needs and goals of the organization. Employees who understand how their efforts contribute to the organization can find a real sense of achievement. On the other hand, a person whose opinions are rejected or ignored and whose basic likes and dislikes are not considered important to the organizational process is likely to develop some undesirable attitudes toward the organization.

Personal values give meaning to job performance. They provide the standards by which to judge what is a good job or a poor one, what is right or wrong, good or bad, significant or insignificant. A supervisor needs to know where values come from in order to understand how they contribute to individual behavior.

An employee's individual behavior is a function of his or her personal thoughts, actions, and habits, plus feedback from others. These functions can be divided into two environments. The first is the personal environment of the individual; the second is the social and physical environment (situational context) in which the individual behavior takes place. The various forces are represented schematically in Figure 4.1. Thus an individual's personality represents an integration of some combination of the variables outside the circle in Figure 4.1. The degree of integration or lack of integration of the variables is what leads toward individual differences in behavior.

Supervisors should not act as or pretend to be psychologists involved in deep therapy. They should not overreact to the meaning or intentions of the behavior of their

Figure 4.1 Some influences on individual behavior in the work place.

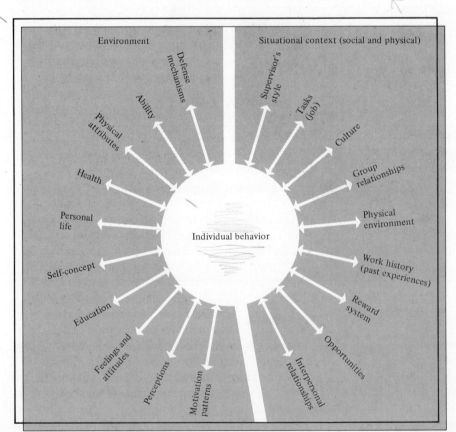

employees. Rather, they should try to understand individual behavior. In reality, the supervisor has to work with "second-hand" individuals. This presents fundamental problems. The work force brings to the organization a variety of values and personal standards that may differ significantly from those of the supervisor. Responsiveness to the supervisor's instructions and his or her perceptions of right and wrong, good and bad, success and lack of success may not be understood by the employee. In some cases, there may be fundamental disagreement with the supervisor's requests. This disagreement should not be automatically interpreted by the supervisor as dislike. Many times it is more a difference in individual values.

Supervisors should develop an awareness of the importance of values to employee performance and learn to adjust their management styles to the situation and people involved. As supervisors gain a better understanding of their own behavior, they can become more responsive as people to the integration of both organizational and subordinate needs and goals.

The key then is that supervisors remember that each employee is a unique individual with a different personality that is shaped by each person's unique personal, social, and physical environment. By using the models of personality described in this chapter, supervisors can become better at understanding the whys of employee behavior.

While most of the variables outside the circle are the subject matter for this book, the variable of self-concept will be discussed at length because of its extreme importance in explaining employees' behavior.

UNDERSTANDING THE SELF-CONCEPT

Each of us has created an image of ourselves—an image variously tagged by behavioral scientists as the self-image, the self-structure, or the self-concept. Regardless of the label used, each of us has a system of ideas and beliefs about ourselves accumulated through many experiences. Simply stated, the self-concept is how we feel about ourselves. Actually, our self-concept can be diagramed as three overlapping circles (see Figure 4.2). The three parts of our self-concept are: (1) how we see ourselves, (2) how others see us, and (3) the ideal self that we strive toward. The more these three circles overlap, the more in touch with reality we are. The area where the three circles (selves) overlap represents balance for the individual. In a highly balanced person, all three circles will overlap completely. Very few people can be represented by completely overlapping circles; most of us are in a state of growing and maturing as real people, contending with daily problems, frustrations, and minor setbacks. Further, many of us see ourselves slightly differently than our peers see us.

There are some important things to remember about a subordinate's self-concept that will directly affect his or her relationship with others: (1) It is a pattern of beliefs developed over a long period of time; (2) people have a deep-seated need to preserve this system of ideas about themselves; and (3) in most cases, they will not only want to preserve it but also to enhance or improve it.[1]

Behavioral researchers have found that people cope with a threat to their self-

[1]Adapted from Robert A. Zawacki and Peter A. LaSota, "The Supervisor as Counselor," *Supervisory Management* (November, 1973), pp. 16–20.

Figure 4.2 Self-concept diagram.

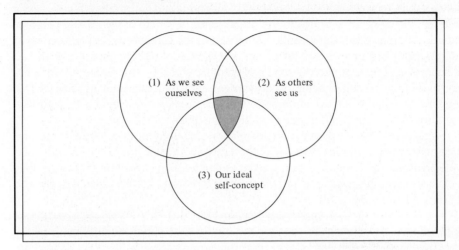

concept by exhibiting defensive behavior or by changing their self-concept and, possibly, their actions. The greater the threat to the person, the more negative the reaction to a supervisor's counseling efforts.

What happens when we use the self-concept and place the person in an organizational context? What are some of the resulting pressures for the worker (see Figure 4.3)? In an organization, our self-concept changes in part from our perceptions of where we see ourselves in relation to events in our lives, the meaning we attach to those events, nonwork demands, and work demands. Nonwork demands might include a disagreement with a spouse before coming to work or a child that is having discipline trouble at school. Work demands are such things as our perception of our skills, abilities, and aptitudes as we compare ourselves to others. Thus, the self-concept is in constant motion or change, and out of this dynamic situation we attempt to achieve a balance. A favorable self-concept usually arises in individuals who perceive themselves as equal to or even better than their peers in terms of skills, abilities, and aptitudes; a negative self-concept, needless to say, comes from perceiving oneself as below average when comparing skills and accomplishments.

PRACTICAL IMPLICATIONS

Now consider that you are a supervisor counseling a subordinate on his or her behavior. The person is a new employee, and the employees with more seniority complain about the newcomer's poor interpersonal skills and lack of tact. When you inform the employee of these shortcomings during the counseling session, your comments may be interpreted as a threat to self-concept because of a need to preserve self-image. In reaction to negative feedback, the employee can: (1) change the behavior, (2) leave the organization, or (3) act defensively by arguing that other employees are to blame.

Figure 4.3 Self-concept and balance. Adapted from Arthur N. Turner and George F. Lombard, *Interpersonal Behavior and Administration* (New York: The Free Press, 1969), p. 151.

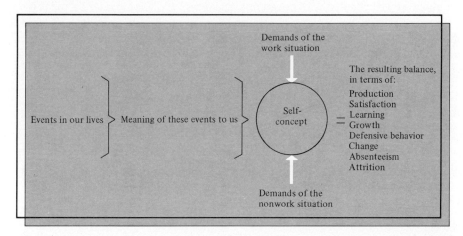

Of the three alternatives, your objective should be to change the behavior through counseling. However, your goal is the employee's least likely option. He or she will prefer to act defensively, or, if possible, leave the organization or counseling situation. While your goal is to change the behavior, the employee's goal is to preserve or even enhance self-concept. Understanding the self-concept and defense mechanisms should permit supervisors to be more effective managers.

We suggest that you complete Exercise 4.1, "Building a Positive Self-Concept," at the end of the chapter before going on to the next section.

DEFENSE MECHANISMS[2]

In attempting to evaluate employee behavior, supervisors should be aware that what they are observing may be an individual defense mechanism instead of a true response.

Defense mechanisms are learned behaviors that usually operate at the unconscious level to help preserve or even enhance the opinions people have of themselves. Although defense mechanisms involve a certain amount of reality denial and distortion, they are only harmful if carried to such an extreme that the people using the defense do not assume responsibility for their behavior. Defense mechanisms help us maintain our self-concept as we move through the daily stresses of personal and organizational life. Persisting in using defensive mechanisms even after receiving counseling from supervisors can become unhealthy because it prevents people from learning from their experiences and growing as balanced personalities.

[2]For a complete explanation of defense mechanisms, see Don E. Hamachek, *Encounters with the Self* (New York: Holt, Rinehart and Winston, 1971), pp. 17–29. The concept of the material in this section was heavily influenced by the writings of Don E. Hamachek.

Rationalization

This is probably the most common defense mechanism. We hear examples of it every day: "I might as well cheat at work; everyone else does." Or "Going over 55 miles per hour (speeding) actually saves gas in my car." Or "It won't hurt to be late for work because it will probably be another boring day." Rationalization helps us invent excuses for something we don't really want to do or helps us hide disappointment when we do not achieve a goal that we set for ourselves.

Repression

Repression is a defense mechanism that helps employees suppress experiences and thoughts that are painful, dangerous, or fearful. Repression keeps a person from thinking about an undesirable experience by blocking that experience out of consciousness. This defense mechanism consumes a lot of energy and hinders healthy personality growth.

Displacement

This defense mechanism shifts blame from the person for whom it was originally intended to a less powerful person. For example, your boss calls you into his or her office and "disciplines" you for something over which you have very little, if any, control. It is near merit-increase time; you do not want to alienate the boss, so you internalize your hurt feelings rather than speak out. That evening as you arrive home, your spouse greets you at the door with good news about how wonderful the garden is growing. Without thinking, you immediately scream at your spouse that you don't care about the darn garden and would rather have a beer and dinner. The spouse now has hurt feelings but internalizes them. Your oldest son comes home from playing at the neighbor's and your spouse scolds him for playing rather than cleaning up his bedroom. The son becomes angry and goes to his bedroom and kicks the dog, who is sleeping on the water bed. The poor animal is confused. If the dog understood individual human behavior, the dog would go and bite the boss!

Denial of Reality

By refusing to discuss unpleasant topics, people tend to deny reality. For example, we may refuse to discuss death and dying, or a poor student may deny his or her lack of mastering a school subject by saying that the people who received high scores on the examination were just lucky. This mechanism can also keep employees from realistically evaluating their situations and learning from past mistakes.

Attrition

This defense mechanism permits employees to leave the situation—either mentally or physically. If they can, they may simply walk away from threatening feedback from peers or supervisors. If they cannot physically leave the situation, then they may mentally tune out the source of the threat.

Projection

This defense mechanism permits employees to transfer their mistakes, shortcomings, and failures to other employees. For example, when a lathe operator has a product rejection rate that is too high compared to standard, he or she may blame the lathe or interference from peers. The real problem may be that the lathe operator is at fault.

Overview of Defense Mechanisms

In summary, defense mechanisms are learned behaviors that normally operate at the unconscious level and permit people to preserve or even improve their self-concept. They also involve a degree of self-deception and distortion of reality. Carried to the extreme, they can be harmful because they can block or interfere with personal growth and development.

INTEGRATION OF THE SELF-CONCEPT

An attempt to integrate the self-concept and work with the individual awareness of attitudes and values as they affect work performance is at best extremely difficult for the typical supervisor. To ease the approach somewhat we ask you to think about some practical points that can be helpful in relating to individual behavior:

1. A subordinate will rarely attempt to change behavior or to perceive a situation from another point of view unless he or she is made to understand that present behavior is not appropriate for job performance.
2. Appropriateness is typically viewed as behavior that supports positive worker performance.
3. The supervisor should start with ensuring that the employee has complete, concise information about company policies, procedures, and rules for the job. clear comm.
4. The supervisor should attempt to find out how the employee feels about the company. ask emp. whats going on.
5. Is the employee interested in the job or bored by it?
6. Does the employee relate well to others?
7. Does the employee cooperate and respond positively to individuals in authority?

We remind you that people do things for a reason. The basis for an employee's performance may be a patterned response formed by his or her values and attitudes or simply an application of his or her perceived self-concept.

The performance of employees is also influenced by their perception of what the supervisors' values and self-concepts are. To be able to influence employees, supervisors must learn about their background. Additionally, the supervisors should try to:

1. Set a positive example and work with enthusiasm.
2. Protect and serve subordinates with trust. Work to develop their skills and potential.

3. Replace habits and attitudes that affect employees negatively by seeking to identify differences in values.
4. Avoid categorizing subordinates' responses as good or bad simply because they agree or disagree with the supervisor's point of view.
5. Remember that the "perfect" subordinate does not exist. The employee who can be made to succeed is the one who can be taught how to adjust behavior to be compatible with the work place.
6. Resist expecting people to change overnight. Behavioral patterns change slowly.
7. Remember that it is difficult for an individual to be enthusiastic about performing a dull, boring job.

Exercises 4.2 and 4.3, at the end of this chapter, help illustrate these points. We suggest that you complete them before going on to the next section.

A FRAMEWORK FOR LOOKING AT YOURSELF

The temperament types exercise (Exercise 4.3) is one way of looking at yourself. Another tool for looking at yourself and understanding other people is the Johari Window. The Johari Window is a concept originated by Joe Luft and Harry Ingram to describe the whole person or groups in relation to other people or groups. The model is based on a categorization of behavior according to what is known and not known by yourself and others:

	Known to Self	Not Known to Self
Known to Others	Public Self (Self known by both you and others)	Blind Self (Self known by others but not yourself)
Not Known to Others	Hidden Self (Self known by you and hidden from others)	Unknown Self (Self that is unknown by both you and others)

Public Self. The public self includes behavior that is known by yourself and others, such as what you do for a living or what your values are. A large public self enables you to have closer contact with reality, to learn more about yourself and others, and to work better with others because of the shared information.

Blind Self. Your blind self is the part of your behavior that others are aware of but you are not. This could be a speech mannerism, gesture, strength, or weakness that is obvious to others but not to you. Having a large blind self comes from protecting yourself from exposure and feedback and limits your effectiveness and ability to learn about yourself.

Hidden Self. The hidden self is the part of your behavior that you know about but will not make known to others because of fear, defensiveness, desire for power, or some other reason. Examples of behaviors kept in the hidden self are feelings about something, something you are ashamed of, and motives that you don't want others to know about (hidden agendas). This protective front is necessary to some extent, but a large hidden self limits the ability of others to know or work with you as well as your own capacity for growth and the full use of your potential.

Unknown Self. The unknown self is not known to you or to others. It is part of your subconscious. A large unknown self is also limiting. The unknown self can become more known as you expose yourself and seek feedback more frequently.

Examples of Different Kinds of People

1. Large public self, small blind, hidden, and unknown selves
2. Small public self, large blind, hidden, and unknown selves

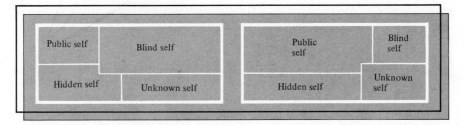

We suggest completing Exercise 4.4, "Your Johari Window," at the end of the chapter before going on to the next section.

Advantages of a Large Public Self

It is much easier for people to work with supervisors with large public selves. Subordinates know better where supervisors stand, can anticipate how they will react, have a reasonably good understanding of their strengths, weaknesses, likes, dislikes, and desires, and know how to communicate with them. There are also personal advantages to having a large public self. By making more of themselves known to others, supervisors will find out how others see them, gain new insights about themselves, and, in general, begin to know themselves and become more congruent with the way others see them and the way they see themselves.

How to Increase the Public Self

You can increase the public self by interacting with others in an open, nondefensive, trusting, and risk-taking manner through two processes:

1. Exposure: open and candid expressions of your feelings, factual knowledge, and guesses in a conscious attempt to share and check out information about yourself with others.
2. Soliciting feedback: actively and nondefensively seeking information about yourself that others may have.

How Large Should the Public Self Be?

There are definite advantages to enlarging the public self in terms of your own personal growth and effectiveness and the ability of others to work and communicate with you. However, judgment should always be used in deciding how much exposure is appropriate and how much of yourself should be kept private. Being open with someone who will abuse openness or is too rigid to deal with openness will not help you or the other person.

SUMMARY

The employee's individual behavior on the job is a function of that person's thoughts, actions, and habits, plus feedback from other people. The environments that the employee performs in are social, physical, and personal. All of these forces influence individual behavior in a unique way for each employee because no two people react to these environments identically. Individual responses are partially conditioned by self-concept. The self-concept is a system of ideas and beliefs that we have about ourselves, accumulated over many years of experiences with life, and we attempt to preserve or even enhance it. When our self-concept is threatened we may change our behavior, leave the organization, or act defensively. Some common defense mechanisms are rationalization, repression, displacement, denial, projection, and attrition. After thoroughly studying the model of personality and individual behavior presented in this chapter, supervisors should remember that each employee is a very special person with unique attitudes, values, and sentiments that are the result of personal experiences and growth processes that have been incorporated into the self-image. Supervisors must attempt to understand "where the employee is at" before they can begin to give the employee effective feedback that will help the employee continue to grow and develop into a productive member of the organization's work force.

IMPORTANT TERMS

situational context	hereditary givens
self-concept	extrovert
defense mechanisms	Johari Window

REVIEW QUESTIONS

1. What are some of the influences on individual behavior in the work place?
2. How can the way we see ourselves differ from how others see us?
3. Why do most people want to preserve or even improve their self-concepts?
4. Why is behavior change the least likely employee response to negative feedback from a supervisor?
5. Does the use of defense mechanisms constitute healthy behavior? Explain your answer.
6. How can you use the Johari Window when counseling a subordinate with a problem?

EXERCISES

4.1 Building a Positive Self-Concept

Your self-concept is the picture you carry in your mind of who you are and what you are capable of doing. It may or may not be accurate, but it tends to be a self-fulfilling prophecy. This exercise is designed to help you develop a positive self-concept that allows you to utilize your full potential.

1. In your mind visualize your ideal self.
2. Begin to act like the person you are visualizing.
3. Write on a piece of paper what you would ideally but realistically like to be. Carry the list with you and look at it when you first get up, during the day, and before you go to bed.
4. As you live your new self-concept, learn from your mistakes, forgive yourself for making mistakes, and move on.

4.2 Understanding Your Behavior

To help you gain a better understanding of all of the factors influencing individual behavior in the work place, complete the following questionnaire on your hereditary givens (such as sex, age, intelligence, and temperament), parents, and environment. Take 20 minutes to complete this part of the exercise.

Hereditary Givens

1. Describe some of your hereditary givens (sex, race, temperament, intelligence, physique, etc.).

2. What givens could you change if you wanted to?

Parents

1. What were your parents or parental figures like (characteristics, mannerisms, shoulds and oughts, values, biases, looks, etc.)?

Mother	Father	Other

2. In what ways are you similar or different?

Similar	Different

Environment

1. What has your environment been like?

	Past	Present
Cultural		
Friends		
Expectations of others		
Rewards		
Experiences		
Physical (Where you lived, etc.)		
Jobs		

2. What could you realistically change in your present environment to make your life more meaningful and productive?

Self-Concept

Describe your present self-concept in terms of how you see yourself, how you think others see you, and the ideal self you want to become.

How You See Yourself	How Others See You	Your Ideal Self

4.3 Understanding Temperament Types

People can be better supervisors and followers if they have a good understanding of how other people see them. Part of our individual behavior is a function of our temperament. The purpose of this exercise is to help you determine and reflect upon your basic temperament type. Further, it should help you analyze the strengths and weaknesses of each temperament type.

Go through the characteristics, strengths, and weaknesses of the different temperament types and list the ones that apply to you in the appropriate spaces in the chart. You have 25 minutes to complete this exercise.

EXTROVERT

Characteristics	Strengths	Weaknesses
warm	enjoys life	insincere
lively	enthusiastic	disorganized
friendly	forgets disappointments	impulsive
spontaneous	positive thinker	restless
emotional	innovative	seldom realizes potential
inspiring	makes others happy	undisciplined

empathic	compassionate	leaves boring tasks
sociable	never gets ulcers	undependable
happy		rationalizes
sincere		weak-willed
extrovert		
lovable		
forgiving		
optimistic		
understanding		
cheerful		

SELF-SUFFICIENT

Characteristics	Strengths	Weaknesses
aggressive	self-disciplined	hot-tempered
strong-willed	self-confident	arrogant
practical	productive	bossy
self-motivated	sets and reaches goals	uncompassionate
goal-oriented	persistent	unsympathetic
plans ahead	dependable	carries grudges
definite	effective leader	revengeful
leader	energetic	prone to get ulcers
organized		won't admit mistakes
domineering		cold
self-sufficient		distrusts others
unemotional		
persuasive		
outspoken		

MELANCHOLY

Characteristics	Strengths	Weaknesses
analytical	artistic	overly introspective
self-sacrificing	good at details	easily depressed
perfectionist	loyal friend	pessimistic
sensitive	excellent behind-	self-centered
introvert	the-scenes person	easily offended
moody	thinks deeply	indecisive
strong feelings	sees through things	critical
temperamental	precise	expects perfection
ecstatic or depressed	sympathetic	of others
highly skeptical	honest and sincere	unpredictable
		often harbors hatred
		unforgiving

EASY-GOING

Characteristics	Strengths	Weaknesses
calm	humorous	slow
cool	good listener	lazy
easy-going	objective	lacks motivation
even-tempered	fulfills obligations	misuse of humor
happy	works well under pressure	resists change
seldom gets ruffled	very patient	stubborn
consistent	practical	selfish
spectator		indecisive
follower		low risk taker
diplomatic		conformist
good sense of humor		
methodical		

	Characteristics	Strengths	Weaknesses
Extrovert			
Self-sufficient			
Melancholy			
Easy-going			

My basic temperament type is _____

Estimate the approximate percentage of each temperament type in your total makeup. (Percentages should add to 100.) Your highest percentage is your predominant style; your next-highest percentage is your backup style.

Extrovert	_____ %
Self-sufficient	_____ %
Melancholy	_____ %
Easy-going	_____ %
Total	100 %

4.4 Your Johari Window

The internal structure of your Johari Window with regard to your public, blind, hidden, and unknown selves will change depending on how well you know people you are interacting with, whether you are in a large or small group, and other factors. However, you will also have a window that represents what you are like *most* of the time and in *most* situations. Fill in the internal structure of the window below with your own estimation of the size of your *public, blind, hidden,* and *unknown selves.*

SUGGESTED ADDITIONAL READINGS

Anderson, John. "Giving and Receiving Feedback." *Personnel Administration* (March-April, 1968). Reprinted in *Organization Development: Managing Change in the Public Sector,* edited by Robert A. Zawacki and D. D. Warrick, pp. 223–229. Chicago: IPMA, 1976.

French, Wendell L.; Bell, Cecil H., Jr.; and Zawacki, Robert A. *Organization Development: Theory, Practice, and Research.* Dallas: Business Publications, Inc., 1983, part 4.

Hamachek, Don E. *Encounters with the Self,* 2d ed. New York: Holt, Rinehart and Winston, 1978.

Sutermeister, Robert A. *People and Productivity,* 3d ed. New York: McGraw-Hill, 1976.

Zawacki, Robert A., and LaSota, Peter E. "The Supervisor as Counselor." *Supervisory Management* (November, 1973), pp. 16–20.

5

Motivation: The Path to Productivity[1]

The healthy man is primarily motivated by his needs to develop and actualize his fullest potentialities and capacities. . . . What man can be, he must be.

Abraham Maslow

The supreme goal of man is to fulfill himself as a creative, unique individual according to his own innate potentialities and within the limits of reality.

Carl Jung

The primary function of any organization, whether religious, political, or industrial, should be to implement the needs for man to enjoy a meaningful existence.

Frederick Herzberg

[1]Adapted from J. Daniel Couger and Robert A. Zawacki, *Motivating and Managing Computer Personnel* (New York: Wiley Interscience, 1980), chap. 5, used with permission, and from the models and concepts of D. D. Warrick.

OBJECTIVES

This chapter provides you with the information necessary to:

1. Define motivation and discuss the motivation concept
2. List two main process theories and two main content theories of motivation and summarize the main points of each theory
3. Explain the relationship between production, time, and rewards or punishment
4. Understand the relationship between Maslow's need theory and Herzberg's motivation-hygiene theory
5. Explain the difference between maintenance factors in Herzberg's theory
6. Explain the difference between internal and external motivation
7. Explain how to motivate your boss
8. Understand the concept necessary to use job enrichment as a motivational tool

---

MOTIVATION

Before discussing motivating specific people in an organization, it is necessary to have a general understanding of the term *motivation*. Supervisors, parents, teachers, and counselors are constantly charged with the responsibility of motivating others. In theory, that sounds like a worthwhile goal, but in practice it is difficult to accomplish because of the elusive nature of the word *motivation*. The word *motivation* is similar to the words *desire, want, need,* and *drive.*

Motivation cannot be seen, felt, heard, or smelled. It is something that simply exists in our society, and academics have labeled those things *concepts*. Motivation is a concept. A diagram of the concept of motivation may be a helpful starting point toward a definition.

Linked to the definition of motivation are three basic assumptions:[2]

1. Human behavior is caused.
2. Human behavior is goal-oriented.
3. Human behavior is motivated.

Needs and Tension Begin the Motivation Process.   People begin the behavior process with a felt need that produces tension within their systems (see Figure 5.1). This tension may be the need for food, sex, power, achievement, or even some object, such as a car. Using the example of a car, people may realize the need because: (1) they ride the bus to work while everyone else drives a personal automobile, or (2) their present car is in need of repairs and has high mileage, or (3) a new automobile is perceived by them as a means of favorably impressing their friends.

We Search the Environment.   Once aware of the need (tension), people begin a search process for ways of satisfying the need. In the car example, the person with

[2]Harold J. Leavitt, *Managerial Psychology* (Chicago: University of Chicago Press, 1964), p. 12.

Figure 5.1 The motivation concept.

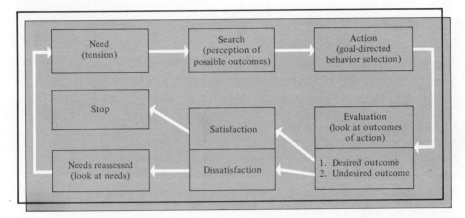

the need can visit a number of new-car showrooms and make some comparisons. They may compare Fords, Buicks, Chryslers, and Volvos. During the search phase, the person will rank the cars according to their perceptions of each car and how each car will meet their perceived needs. An important point is that a motivator must be perceived as a motivator by the person with the need before it is truly a motivator of behavior. All too often, supervisors believe they know what motivates their subordinates when in fact the supervisors' perception is different from the subordinates' perception. The following story emphasizes our point:

Wrong Reward[3]

Dr. Charles H. Hollenberg, physician in chief of Toronto General Hospital, spoke recently to a group of doctors about the use of behavior-modification theory in treating obesity. According to the *Medical Tribune,* Dr. Hollenberg related the incident of a female psychologist who attempted to encourage her overweight husband to slim down by using a reward system. The reward that she decided to use to reinforce his slimming program was her "romantic availability" in the evening.

"One can only hope," Dr. Hollenberg said, "that the therapist retained her scientific objectivity when her husband gained 10 pounds in the next three weeks."

People Take Action.   After searching for solutions for our need, we rank the cars according to our subjectively calculated probability of each car's ability to satisfy our need. Then we select the car with the highest probability of meeting that need. This is goal-directed behavior. Goal-directed behavior is determined by the need with the greatest strength at the time a person is making a decision (see Figure 5.2). For example, the need may be for a car that delivers over 20 miles per gallon of gas, is comfortable to drive, and is perceived by family and friends as a car of above-average status. Subjectively, the buyer ranks this above a vacation, television set, or other possible purchase.

[3]*Prevention* (August, 1975), p. 1.

Figure 5.2 Motive strength.

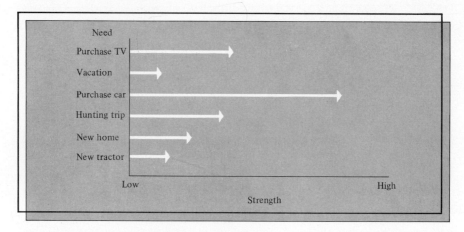

Evaluation of the Choice. After selecting a certain car—a Volvo, for example —the owner constantly evaluates that car to see if it meets his or her expectations. In the evaluation process the owner looks at the performance (mileage, repair costs, luxury, etc.) of the car and subjectively compares it to the performance of other makes of cars. Now a unique process may take place in the owner's mind if he or she begins to believe that the Volvo does not meet his or her expectations. This process is known as *cognitive dissonance*. In the example of the car, the purchaser begins to receive inputs that are in conflict with expectations, and these inputs can create conflict, creating tension in the mind of the purchaser. This tension is psychologically uncomfortable. Leon Festinger has come forth with a theory of how the purchaser may reduce this tension.[4] Because the state of cognitive dissonance is uncomfortable, the purchaser will attempt to reduce dissonance and to achieve more balance in his or her mind (cognitive system). Methods of reducing this cognitive dissonance are:

1. The purchaser can ignore the new inputs that do not agree with original expectations (inputs).
2. The purchaser can recognize the new inputs but rationalize the accuracy of the new inputs. "I am getting only 17 miles per gallon of gas, but almost all of my driving is in the city."
3. The purchaser can blame himself or herself. "I did not check into mileage before I made the decision."
4. The purchaser can blame someone else. "The salesperson did not give me accurate information on gas mileage."
5. The purchaser can accept the inputs as accurate and regret the purchase. "I really didn't want a Volvo anyway—next time I'll purchase an American-built car."

[4]Leon Festinger, *A Theory of Cognitive Dissonance* (Stanford, CA: Stanford University Press, 1957).

All these techniques are methods of coping with uncomfortable perceptions that the purchaser has about himself or herself and what other people in the environment may think.

Satisfaction or Dissatisfaction.   After evaluating the performance of the new car, the purchaser may experience satisfaction or dissatisfaction. For example, if the purchaser ignores inputs that do not agree with expectations, he or she may be satisfied and the original need (a new car) fulfilled. A fulfilled need is no longer a motivator because tension or desire (need) no longer exists.

Reevaluate the Alternatives.   If the performance evaluation process results in dissatisfaction, the purchaser may again evaluate other cars that will satisfy his or her need. Thus, the state of dissatisfaction results in tension which may still be a motivator of behavior. Whether or not the person purchases another car will depend upon the strength of the need.

Work Motivation Basics

After exposing you to a very brief overview of motivation, we now want you to analyze your personal views about motivation. Complete Exercise 5.1 at the end of this chapter.

THEORIES OF MOTIVATION

After a discussion of the model of motivation, it is now proper to introduce theories of motivation that can serve the supervisor as a model when motivating subordinates, their bosses, or even themselves. The two basic categories of motivation theory are process and content (see Figure 5.3).

There are actually many, many theories of motivation. We are presenting only the five main theories of process and content. Our objective is to present the theories in a straightforward manner so that you will be able to remember the overall points of a few theories that have meaning and application in organizations.

Figure 5.3 Motivation outline. TYPOLOGY

I. Process Theories
    A. Stimulus-response theory (Skinner) READING 5.4
    B. Equity theory (Homans, Adams)
        C. Core job theory
        D. Expectancy Theory
II. Content Theories
    A. Need theory (Maslow)
        B. Motivation-hygiene theory (Herzberg)
        C. NEED THEORY DAVID McLELLAND

Process Theories

Process theories are theories that describe motivation as a process or flow of inter-related activities. Figure 5.1 is an example of a process. It may be helpful for the supervisor to remember that the process of motivation is similar to the flow of oil through a refinery. The entire process of a refinery can be described in terms of the flow of the oil from raw inputs through refined gas and oil.

Stimulus-Response Theory.   Theorists of the stimulus-response (S-R) theory argue that behavior can best be understood by studying the relationship between stimuli and responses. They define stimuli as events or activities (internal or external) that modify behavior. They further believe that future responses (new behavior) will depend upon how a person is reinforced for the new response. The leading American psychologist who has been influential in applying the principles of reinforcement is B. F. Skinner. The best known example of his theory that consequences determine future behavior is his novel *Walden Two,* in which he designed a utopian society. In his society, people are placed on a contingency reinforcement schedule whereby desired behavior is rewarded and undesired behavior is punished.

Stimulus-response theory has a potential benefit to supervisors because they are basically interested in when to reward and when to punish people. Simply stated, which is more effective, a reward-centered supervisor or a punishment-centered supervisor?

In Figure 5.4, we have diagrammed the situation wherein we introduce two supervisors to the organization; one is a reward-centered supervisor and one is a punishment-centered supervisor. The punitive supervisor has a more dramatic effect on production in the short run; however, the rewarding supervisor has a more positive effect in the long run. The punitive supervisor increases production in the short run at the expense of people. In the long run, subordinates leave the punitive organization or contribute the minimum effort that does not attract attention to them. Subordinates are simply less committed to the goals of a punitive supervisor and organization.

When the rewarding supervisor is introduced into the organization, employees' productivity may take a slight dip because subordinates may be unsure of the style and

Figure 5.4 Relationship between production, time, and reinforcement.

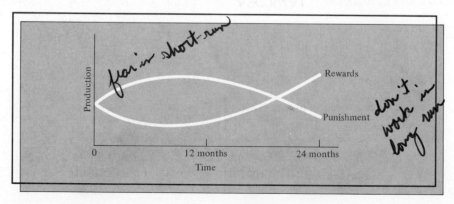

[handwritten margin notes: "view rewards are skeptical. when reading, production increased"]

[handwritten notes on figure: "fear in short-run", "don't work in long run"]

wonder whether the supervisor is for real. After a period of adjustment, productivity under the rewarding supervisor will pass productivity under a punitive supervisor, because employees sense that the rewarding supervisor really is concerned about the task and social relationships, and the consequences are higher organizational commitment, lower turnover, greater satisfaction, and increased productivity.

If rewarding employees is more effective than punishing them, why is punishment so frequently used? First, punishment is easy to apply and quick—supervisors don't have to be creative and think. To use rewards effectively, supervisors *must* think and put forth that little extra effort. Second, supervisors can be rewarded for using punishment because they usually see a quick suppression of undesired behavior and thus assume that they have been effective. But remember the long-run consequences of punishment:

1. It will increase anxiety and tension, which in turn will reduce satisfaction, productivity, and output.
2. Over time the level of punishment must be increased to maintain the continued suppression of undesired behavior. Supervisors soon run out of punishment options.
3. Punishment does not get rid of the undesired behavior; it merely suppresses it.
4. Mild or light punishment may actually reward the subordinates and increase the rate of undesired behavior. For some employees, negative feedback is better than no feedback at all. Some people simply desire attention.
5. In the long run, productivity that is maintained by force will decrease, and workers may leave that organization.

Although there are numerous negative effects from the use of punishment, there are times when a supervisor must use it. However, only about 5 percent or less of the employees in an organization need a kick in the pants once in a while. The other 95 percent want to do well and will do well if they are given the opportunity and leadership. Don't design a punitive control system for all employees when only a small percentage actually need negative motivation.

Equity theory.   This theory is very important to supervisors because it helps them understand the thinking of their subordinates and peers when supervisors are thinking about the allocation of rewards and merit increases in an organization. Specifically, equity theory gives the supervisor a feel for how employees evaluate salaries, merit increases, and fairness.

Equity is always subjective and relative, and it involves more than one person. First, an employee is hired into the organization based upon a ratio of outputs to inputs, which can be diagramed as:

$$\frac{O_a}{I_a}$$

Inputs are experience, education, age, skills, seniority, and sex. Outputs are salary, recognition, opportunity for achievement, danger, boredom, and so forth. For employees to feel equitably treated by the organization, this formula must roughly equal 1.

Remember, this relationship is very subjective and hard to measure. Even if this relationship is in balance, employees do not stop searching for information.

According to George C. Homans, a noted sociologist, they compare themselves to some other person or group (social reference group) and evaluate the equity of that comparison:

$$\frac{O_a}{I_a} = \frac{O_b}{I_b}$$

Notation b may represent a person or a group on or off the job. For example, an assembly line worker at General Motors may compare himself to another worker at GM, or he may compare his job to a like job at Ford Motor Company. Homans suggests that distributive justice is equitable when the ratio of outputs to inputs of person a is equal to the ratio of outputs to inputs of person b. Research evidence indicates that workers within groups, through informal sanctions, try to keep outputs in line with inputs. This is why the "rate buster" can be an outcast in the informal group. The personnel department, through the processes of job evaluation and performance appraisal, tries to measure inputs and keep them in line with outputs. Further, the personnel department should compare salaries of company employees with comparable jobs in the community, the state, and the nation. Supervisors can be certain that employees and union representatives are making these comparisons.

Core Job Theory.[5]   Core job theory is helpful to supervisors in creating conditions for employees' internal motivation through meaningful work. Core job theory identifies the three "critical psychological states" associated with high levels of internal motivation, satisfaction, and quality of performance. These psychological states are the experienced meaningfulness of the work, the experienced responsibility for the outcomes, and the knowledge of actual results. The existence of these psychological states in a job should lead to low absenteeism and turnover and high levels of internal motivation, satisfaction, and quality of performance. The psychological states are the workers' attitudes toward work.

These three critical psychological states are affected by the five core job dimensions. The more of these five core job dimensions that are present in a job, the higher the probability that the person doing the job will experience the personal outcomes in Figure 5.5. The organization benefits from lower turnover and absenteeism and higher productivity.

Each core dimension is defined as follows:

Skill variety: the degree to which a job requires a variety of different activities and involves the use of a number of the employee's different skills and talents
Task identity: the degree to which the job requires the completion of a whole and identifiable piece of work—that is, doing a job from beginning to end with a visible outcome

[5]For the complete background on core job theory, see A. N. Turner and P. R. Lawrence, *Industrial Jobs and the Worker* (Boston: Harvard Graduate School of Business Administration, 1965), and J. Richard Hackman and Greg R. Oldham, *Work Redesign* (Reading, MA: Addison-Wesley, 1980).

Figure 5.5 Core job model.

✱ very important

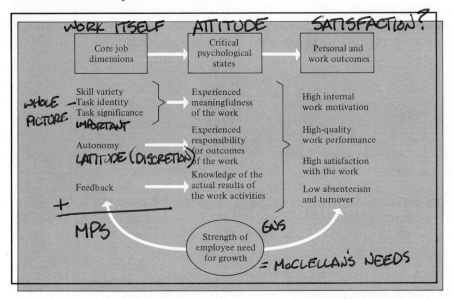

WORK ITSELF   ATTITUDE   SATISFACTION?

WHOLE PICTURE

IMPORTANT

LATITUDE (DISCRETION)

+ ___ MPS   GNS   = McCLELLAN'S NEEDS

Task significance: the degree to which the job has a substantial impact on the lives or work of other people, whether in the immediate organization or in the external environment

Autonomy: the degree to which the job provides substantial freedom, independence, and discretion to the employee in scheduling his or her work and in determining the procedures to be used in carrying it out

Feedback from the job itself: the degree to which carrying out the work activities required by the job results in the employee's obtaining information about the effectiveness of his or her performance.

If the job itself does not provide feedback, then supervisors must provide employees with feedback on job performance in accordance with the guidelines in Chapters 12 and 13 of this book. Examples of jobs that provide good feedback are tool and die work and general accounting. Most people also choose hobbies that provide rapid feedback, such as golf or bowling.

The relationship between the core job dimensions, critical psychological states, and on-the-job outcomes is illustrated in Figure 5.5. When all three are high, internal work motivation, job satisfaction, and work quality should be high and absenteeism and turnover should be low.

We expect that people who have a high need for personal growth and development will respond more positively to a job high in motivating potential than will people with a low need for growth.

Obviously, not everyone is able to become internally motivated, even when the motivating potential of the job is high. Behavioral research has shown that the psychological needs of people determine who can (and cannot) become internally motivated at work. Some people have a strong need for personal accomplishment—for learning and developing beyond their present level, for being stimulated and challenged. These people are high in growth need strength.

The lack of challenge and the low motivating potential of many jobs as currently constituted in our society demand careful consideration for work redesign by managers, for both humanitarian and productivity reasons.

Content Theories

Content theories are theories that describe motivation at a single point in time. If a supervisor could take a snapshot of an employee's behavior, thereby stopping action, the analysis of that behavior is what we call content theory. Of course, in actual organizations it is impossible to stop all action and analyze the content of motivation. However, supervisors can improve their knowledge of human behavior by having a basic understanding of what motivates employees at a specific point in time.

Need Theory.   What is it about a job that motivates workers to produce? Is it money? Supervisors, psychologists, and managers have long debated the relationship between money and productivity. Recently comedian Jackie Mason clarified the argument by stating:

> Some people think the most important thing in life is money. It's not true. Love is the most important thing in life. Personally, I'm very fortunate because I love money.

While this statement was made in a humorous way, we recognize that very few people would work if they were not paid for it. Abraham Maslow was one of the first people to recognize the relationship between money and people's other needs.[6] He did this by developing a hierarchy of needs (see Figure 5.6).

Maslow established that workers are motivated by different things at different times and that workers' needs are in a rough hierarchy from lower-order needs to higher-order needs. He reasoned that workers have a primary need for food and shelter; after that need is met, workers become interested in their financial security, then social needs, then esteem needs, and finally self-fulfillment needs. Tragic evidence of this hierarchy of needs occurred recently in Colorado, when the Big Thompson Canyon flooded in the summer of 1976. Before the flood, many of the residents of the canyon were living at the social or esteem level of needs; after the 30-foot wall of water came down that narrow canyon and destroyed almost all of their homes, their needs were immediately reduced to the basic level—food and shelter. Supervisors should evaluate where their workers are in Maslow's hierarchy of needs and adjust rewards accordingly. Some important points to remember are:

1. A motivator must be perceived as a motivator *by the subordinate* to be effective.
2. It is not necessary for 100 percent of a worker's needs to be met before the worker

[6]Abraham Maslow, *Motivation and Personality* (New York: Harper & Row, 1954).

✳︎ MASLOW'S

Figure 5.6 Hierarchy of needs.

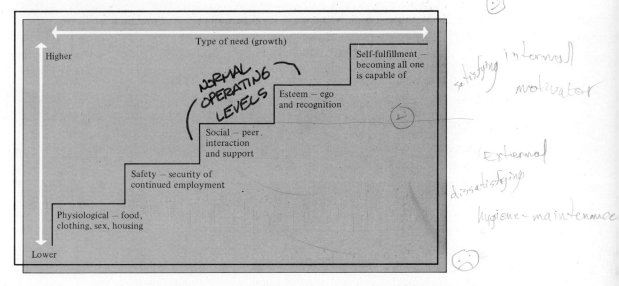

begins to look to satisfy higher-order needs. Workers may look higher when 95 percent of their physiological needs have been met, 80 percent of their security needs, and only 20 percent of their social needs.

3. A satisfied need is not a motivator of behavior.
4. In our society, the lower-order needs are met by and large by society—a private corporation, public agency, or even a welfare program.
5. While money is important as a motivator, other needs should be considered.
6. Lower-level needs must be satisfied before the higher-level needs become motivators. Young workers place a higher priority on lower needs when they are starting their families or trying to purchase a car or home.
7. Very few people in our society are operating at the self-fulfillment level; however, many people are striving toward this ultimate goal.
8. A worker's position in the hierarchy of needs may change with the time and situation, and the worker can move in both directions.

Motivation-Hygiene Theory.   A second content theory of motivation was presented in the 1950s by Frederick Herzberg; his motivation-hygiene theory has also become known as the two-factor or satisfiers-dissatisfiers approach.[7] Herzberg was the first person to say that dissatisfaction and satisfaction are not the end points of a continuous line (see Figure 5.7). He advocated that without certain things at the place of work, workers will be dissatisfied. However, if a supervisor meets the worker's maintenance needs, they will not be *satisfied;* they will only be *not dissatisfied* or not unhappy. To be happy or satisfied, workers basically need jobs that have motivational characteristics or satisfiers.

[7]Frederick Herzberg et al., *The Motivation to Work,* 2d ed. (New York: Wiley, 1969).

Figure 5.7 Satisfaction and dissatisfaction.

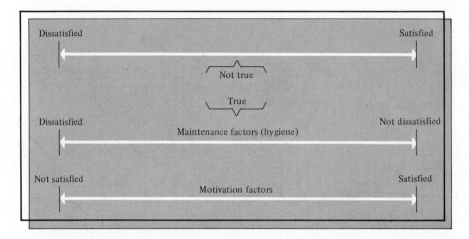

Maintenance Factors (Dissatisfiers)	Motivation Factors (Satisfiers)
Company policy and administration	Achievement
Work conditions	Recognition
Technical supervision	Advancement and growth
Interpersonal relations with peers	Responsibility
Job security	The work itself
Pay	

Without the maintenance factors, workers will be unhappy; but given the maintenance factors they will not necessarily be happy. To motivate people to increase productivity, supervisors must examine the satisfiers of a job after meeting employees' maintenance needs. Further, the maintenance factors are concerned with the surroundings of the job (extrinsic or external factors), while the motivators are concerned with the job itself and how employees feel about the job (intrinsic or internal factors).

Pay is listed as a dissatisfier, and this may puzzle the reader because everyone is willing to accept more pay—no one turns down a pay increase. Herzberg listed pay as a dissatisfier because his industrial research indicated that when salary schedules are perceived by the employees as inequitable, their negative feelings are three times as strong as when pay is considered equitable. Thus, when pay scales are out of balance, workers are *very* unhappy; when they are in balance, workers are only slightly happy. Supervisors can simply get greater returns on effort and investment by concentrating on the satisfiers. Also, Herzberg did the majority of his research in the early 1950s, when yearly inflation was low (under 3 percent). During periods of high inflation, compensation is on most people's minds because money takes on other meanings in our society, such as status, recognition, and the means to at least maintain a standard of living.

A logical concern is one of the relationship between the two theories. Basically, the two theories support each other (see Figure 5.8).

Figure 5.8 Interaction of individual and job motivators.

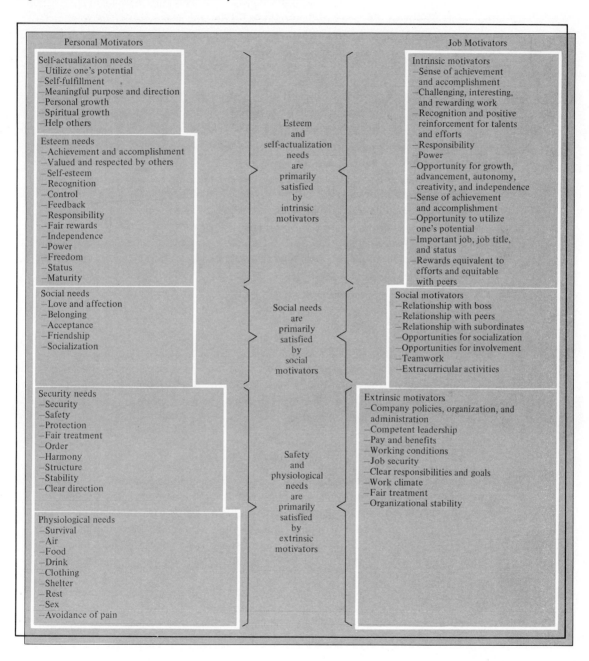

The lower order of needs in Maslow's hierarchy is roughly equivalent to Herzberg's maintenance factors, and Maslow's higher order of needs parallels Herzberg's motivators. Both theories are excellent models for helping supervisors determine what will be motivational for each individual employee. Figure 5.9 summarizes the theories presented in this chapter and indicates how the motivation cycle is related to an employee's self-concept.

EXTERNAL VERSUS INTERNAL MOTIVATION

The process of motivation has a significant effect on the outcome of an individual's efforts to grow as a person and as a good employee. People can have either an internal or external motivation source, or both (see Figure 5.10). In other words, people usually have a dominant source of motivation but probably do some things from internal motives and others from external motives. The source of motivation is very important because the more externally motivated we are, the more we respond from the position of a victim, while the more internally motivated we are, the more we grow from the position of an integrated winner. Victims build their growth on a shaky foundation that can rapidly crumble under changing circumstances; integrated winners build their growth on a solid foundation that is strong enough to withstand changing circumstances.

Motivation Goal

When we are externally motivated, our primary goal is to be *accepted* as worthwhile and capable. Our efforts are directed toward proving ourselves to others and winning their acceptance. When we are internally motivated, our primary goal is to *be* worthwhile and capable. Our efforts are channeled into being worthwhile and capable rather than into proving ourselves to others.

Methods Used to Reach the Primary Goal

When persons are externally motivated, they try to meet their primary goal of being accepted as worthwhile and capable by seeking approval or attention through performance, status, appearance, or role playing. They usually begin trying to be accepted by seeking approval and switch to seeking attention when their approval needs are not met. Approval and attention may be sought first with appropriate behaviors, but a person may turn to inappropriate behaviors if the appropriate behaviors do not get the desired results.

One of the ways to obtain approval or attention is through performance. People may perform by outdoing others, striving for perfection, or trying to meet the expectations of others. On the negative side, they may seek approval from people who condone inappropriate performance (using drugs, lying, etc.) or gain attention through rebellion or lack of performance.

Another way to seek approval or attention is through status. Being the best,

Figure 5.9 Motivation cycle.

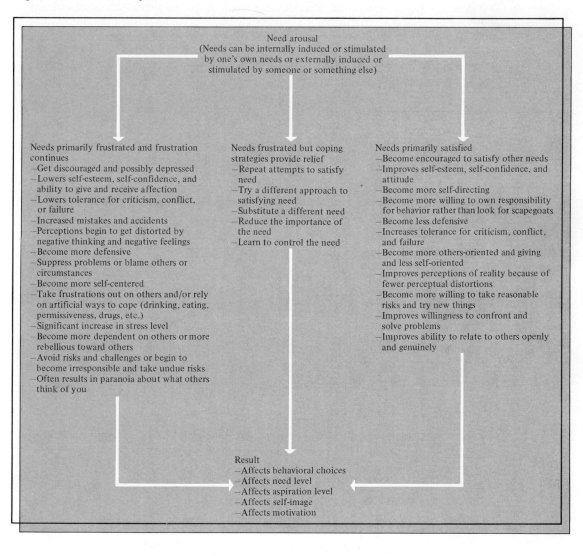

Need arousal
(Needs can be internally induced or stimulated
by one's own needs or externally induced or
stimulated by someone or something else)

Needs primarily frustrated and frustration
continues
—Get discouraged and possibly depressed
—Lowers self-esteem, self-confidence, and
 ability to give and receive affection
—Lowers tolerance for criticism, conflict,
 or failure
—Increased mistakes and accidents
—Perceptions begin to get distorted by
 negative thinking and negative feelings
—Become more defensive
—Suppress problems or blame others or
 circumstances
—Become more self-centered
—Take frustrations out on others and/or rely
 on artificial ways to cope (drinking, eating,
 permissiveness, drugs, etc.)
—Significant increase in stress level
—Become more dependent on others or more
 rebellious toward others
—Avoid risks and challenges or begin to
 become irresponsible and take undue risks
—Often results in paranoia about what others
 think of you

Needs frustrated but coping
strategies provide relief
—Repeat attempts to satisfy
 need
—Try a different approach to
 satisfying need
—Substitute a different need
—Reduce the importance of
 the need
—Learn to control the need

Needs primarily satisfied
—Become encouraged to satisfy other needs
—Improves self-esteem, self-confidence, and
 attitude
—Become more self-directing
—Become more willing to own responsibility
 for behavior rather than look for scapegoats
—Become less defensive
—Increases tolerance for criticism, conflict,
 and failure
—Become more others-oriented and giving
 and less self-oriented
—Improves perceptions of reality because of
 fewer perceptual distortions
—Become more willing to take reasonable
 risks and try new things
—Improves willingness to confront and
 solve problems
—Improves ability to relate to others openly
 and genuinely

Result
—Affects behavioral choices
—Affects need level
—Affects aspiration level
—Affects self-image
—Affects motivation

Figure 5.10 External and internal motivation.

Key Variables	External Motivation	Internal Motivation
Primary Goal	To be accepted as worthwhile and capable	To be worthwhile and capable
Primary Methods for Reaching Goal	Seeking approval or attention through: Performance Status Appearance Role playing	Taking responsibility for your behavior through: Being your best self Developing your unique capabilities
Goal Satisfaction	Satisfaction is controlled by how others react, by circumstances, and by our feelings and is therefore temporary and left to chance.	Satisfaction is controlled by you and can therefore be long-lasting and not left to chance.
Consequences	Insecure, envious of others, and controlled by changing external conditions	Secure, free to accept and give unconditionally to others, and controlled by internal conditions

wearing the latest fashions, using the "in" language, having a fancy car or home, knowing the "right" people, and bragging are all ways of using status to gain approval or attention. Depending on the reference group, status could also come from looking sloppy, working hard to do what is not "in," and trying to be meek. The key is whether status is being used to gain approval or attention, because status itself is neither good nor bad. Wearing nice clothes and driving a big car or wearing sloppy clothes may simply be a matter of choice.

Appearance is also an important way of seeking approval or attention when we are externally motivated. Appearance and status overlap somewhat, but there are some differences. Our appearance is more closely tied to our self-image. The media are very aware of this as they appeal to our vanity, suggesting that if we wear the right clothes or use the right makeup or cologne, people will like us. Our natural as well as external appearance may also have a significant effect on how we feel about ourselves—our approval of ourselves. Not being handsome enough or pretty enough, being too tall, too short, too fat, or too skinny, or having a handicap may all affect our self-image and our motives for behaving.

Externally motivated people may also try to gain approval or attention through role playing. They may be one person at work, another at home, another at church, and still another at parties. They may continually change the way they are, depending on who they are around and what is expected of them or what may gain approval or attention. These changes can be considered role playing if a person changes character in different situations. Responding naturally in different situations when there is no attempt to change character is not role playing. Role playing is self-defeating because it requires considerable game playing as well as mind reading to figure out everyone's expectations, and it tends to produce behaviors that come across as phony and manipulative.

When persons are internally motivated, they seek to reach their goals of being worthwhile and capable by taking responsibility for their behavior, by being their best selves, and by developing their unique capabilities. A person who is internally motivated directs his or her energy toward being and growing rather than toward seeking approval or attention. These persons appreciate approval and attention but are not dependent on them for reaching their goals. In fact, if their needs for approval and attention are not being met, they assume responsibility for finding constructive ways to satisfy their needs. Although some behaviors may be obviously externally motivated, outward appearances may be deceiving. Since internally motivated persons accept responsibility for being their best selves and for developing their unique capabilities, they tend to be high performers and are free to enjoy status or to adapt in a natural, straightforward way to changing environments or situations. The difference is in their motives. While externally motivated persons are seeking approval or attention, internally motivated persons are simply being the best that they can and accepting their best efforts as enough. This approach greatly simplifies life and allows them to devote their efforts to constructive purposes because they do not have to invest time and energy into figuring out how to act, reading minds and expectations, and trying to outdo or outmaneuver others.

Goal Satisfaction

When we are externally motivated, goal satisfaction is controlled by how others react by circumstances, and by our feelings. Satisfaction is therefore temporary and left to chance, since people's reactions, circumstances, and feelings are continuously changing. For example, a person may seek approval by wearing a new outfit to work. If the people at work notice and react in a way that was hoped for, then the goal is satisfied. However, if no one notices or coworkers do not react in the way that was expected, the goal is frustrated. Basing goal satisfaction on circumstances or feelings may be even more tenuous. A person who bases his or her worth on performance may find that self-worth is shattered by an unpredictable change in market conditions or an illness. Feelings that may come from a self-centered or negative attitude, overreacting, or from something in our subconscious may result in dissatisfaction regardless of how high our actual performance or status is.

When internally motivated, satisfaction is internally controlled by an individual and can therefore be long-lasting and not left to chance. While satisfaction may be affected by other people, by circumstances, and by feelings, it is not controlled by them. Internally motivated persons are certainly affected by setbacks or may feel deeply about something that has happened; however, their satisfaction is based on knowing that they did the best they could regardless of how others react, the actual circumstances, or what their feelings happened to be. Even though this approach is not easy to maintain, it does make long-lasting satisfaction possible and does not leave satisfaction in the hands of fate.

Consequences of External and Internal Motivation

Being externally motivated may satisfy our needs temporarily, but it also has some long-range negative consequences. External motivation tends to leave us insecure, envious of others because someone else will always outdo us, and controlled by changing external conditions. It is an unstable, anxiety-filled, up-and-down way to live, an approach that keeps us continuously doubting that we are worthwhile and capable. Nothing we do that is externally motivated will give us lasting satisfaction.

Internal motivation leaves us feeling secure, free to accept and give to others unconditionally, and controlled by internal conditions. It is a stable and adventurous way to live with limited anxiety and stress, an approach that helps us to be and feel worthwhile and capable. Even though people's reactions, circumstances, or feelings may change, it is a life of lasting satisfaction based on well-developed and well-balanced internal resources affected by but not controlled by changing external conditions.

MOTIVATING YOUR BOSS

Most of the theories we have discussed are directed toward supervisors who want to motivate their employees. However, it is not always the employee who presents a motivation problem. Sometimes the problem may rest with managers, and the question is not how supervisors can motivate their employees but rather how supervisors can motivate their bosses.[8]

Now that we have established the possibility that employees can also motivate their bosses, let's examine the various boss-motivation problems that employees may encounter. Some typical problems are:

The boss doesn't boss. The boss doesn't assume the boss responsibilities of planning, organizing, directing, and controlling and leaves employees with little direction regarding their responsibilities and objectives.

The boss bosses too much. The boss performs the duties of a boss with a great flair for giving orders, correcting mistakes, making all the major decisions, and telling people what to do, but with great disregard for delegating authority, involving employees in the decision-making process, and developing a sensitivity for employee needs and capabilities.

The boss keeps you in the dark. The boss does not keep you informed about how the organization is doing, about priorities, about the information you need to perform your job well, or about how well you are doing.

The boss needs a rewind. Bosses, like employees, occasionally need rewinding. This situation occurs when the boss begins to miss deadlines, arrives at work late, stretches out coffee breaks and lunches, misses meetings, acts discouraged, and fails to carry his or her share of the work load.

The boss speaks with a forked tongue. Some bosses unknowingly speak with a forked tongue by giving conflicting orders, frequently reversing their decisions,

[8]This discussion adapted from D. D. Warrick, "How to Motivate Your Boss," *Management World* (July, 1976), pp. 6–8.

giving daily tongue-lashings, and sending double messages in which they say one thing but mean another.

The boss rises to a level of incompetence. One of the more frustrating problems that employees face is a boss who has been promoted beyond his or her capabilities.

When bosses exhibit some or (heaven forbid!) all of these motivation problems, employees may respond in either negative or positive ways, and all too often their response is negative. Employees may develop a bad attitude and do only what they are told. They may stop communicating with the boss; they have a delightful time talking among themselves about the boss's bad habits, and they learn to play manipulative games to their own ends, such as learning how to make the boss think that all ideas are his or hers.

Employees have another choice, however, and that is to motivate the boss positively. Here are some suggestions that may help in solving the delicate problem of how to motivate your boss.

Change the Way You Think about Your Boss.   Many problems with bosses could be solved easily if employees would get rid of certain myths about bosses—for example, the idea that if you were to talk openly about problems with your boss, the boss would strike you dead, mortally wound you, or make life miserable for you for the rest of your days. While some bosses may be capable of such things, most bosses have enough personal investment in wanting to be successful that they would be interested in considering information that could help them. Quite often employees do not receive what they want simply because they do not ask for it.

Motivate Yourself.   Many employees who complain about their boss are just passing the buck because of their own lack of motivation. One of the best ways to motivate a boss is to motivate yourself and set such a good example that your boss feels compelled to stay one step ahead of you. An employee who accepts responsibility, works hard, is open to new ideas, and continues to develop his or her capabilities can be a tremendous motivator to a boss.

Learn How to Confront with Caring.   Most boss problems could be solved easily if employees would learn how to confront with caring. Many of the ideas that employees accumulate about how bosses react to confrontations are based on bad experiences with poorly handled confrontations. Most probably, a boss's inappropriate response is a reaction to the critical, rebellious, or judgmental way in which a confrontation is handled, not to the actual problem involved. When you confront with caring, you present a problem thoughtfully, sticking to specific, objective, honest facts. You show that you care about the other person or persons involved as well as about solving the problem. In the terms of transactional analysis, confronting with caring is leveling in an "I'm OK–You're OK" way.

Search for Points of Resistance.   Employees are sometimes aware that the boss "has it in for them." Yet rather than search for the reason, they waste much of their energy by waiting for the boss to take the initiative to solve the problem or by preparing themselves emotionally for the battles that lie ahead. It would be easier to go to the boss and express a desire to settle any differences and then explore together the problems involved. The boss's resistance may be due to a personality conflict, an annoying mannerism, a rumor, a past mistake, or any number of other things that could be corrected if the problems were brought out into the open.

Practice Upward Communication. It really is amazing how many problems go unresolved because employees wait for the boss to take the initiative to solve problems of which the boss may not even be aware. How often employees are overheard saying, "It's not my job to solve the problem—he's the boss. Besides, any good boss would have resolved the problem long ago." Employees can, in fact, solve many of their problems with their boss by taking the initiative themselves. They can go to the boss and ask for the information they need to perform their work. Then they can schedule a meeting with the boss to receive feedback on how they are doing. They can also ask the boss to delegate more work to them. If they are unclear on their responsibilities and objectives, they can outline their own responsibilities and objectives themselves and set up an appointment to assure that their boss is in agreement.

Enrich the Boss's Job. Most bosses who have received professional management training or have read about professional management are loaded with ideas on how to enrich jobs so that employees can be more motivated. Wouldn't it be great for bosses if the tables were turned and employees were loaded with ideas on how to enrich the boss's job? As a matter of fact, a boss often needs some job enrichment, and employees can play a major role in helping to provide it. They can give the boss credit when he or she does a good job, they can assume responsibility for some of the mundane tasks the boss has to do, or they can help the boss organize the work to make it more challenging. There is almost no limit to what employees could do to enrich their boss's job if they focus their creative minds on the task.

Care! Caring is one of the most powerful facilitators of change. Most problems will eventually be solved if the boss knows that the employees genuinely care and that they have his or her best interests at heart.

Try Other Methods. Even if all these ideas fail, there are still alternatives available to employees for motivating the boss. Sharing information such as articles and books often breaks the ice. This approach is particularly helpful when a procedure is established for both sharing and discussing information. Employees can also suggest that a monthly or quarterly staff meeting be devoted to bringing internal problems out into the open and solving them. Another approach is to interest the boss in some individual training or training for the whole staff. A variation of this is to bring in a speaker several times a year. Finally, the boss could be encouraged to bring in a sympathetic third party to uncover the internal problems and to conduct team-building sessions.

It is important for employees to recognize that bosses also need motivating, that most boss-motivation problems are solvable, and that as employees we often suffer needlessly because we will not accept responsibility for what *we* can do to motivate our boss. Finally, it is important to recognize that trying to motivate your boss through indirect, manipulative methods is very risky and avoids solving the real problems. It may, in fact, compound the problems by undermining the trust between boss and subordinates. It is better for all concerned if problems are approached in a straightforward and caring way.

MOTIVATIONAL STRENGTH THROUGH ENRICHMENT

The supervisor's principal role in developing a motivated work force is to create the working environment which integrates the findings of the motivational theorists. This means that the work place must accommodate the need for satisfaction of individuals and also provide work that contributes to their feelings of self-worth. Most supervisors would find this a formidable task. Cries of anguish heard would probably run from "It's not my problem" to "I only drive the train, someone else lays the track." The possible combinations of task and authority with which supervisors operate is nearly infinite. No single recommended procedure or response would fit all situations. Yet, an understanding of how theory serves as a foundation allows for some premises a supervisor can use to provide a satisfying work environment and thus create a motivated work force. Figure 5.11 lists some factors that contribute to an enhanced motivational work place.

1. Set a clear framework of organization policy, procedure, and measurable standards.
2. Assign complete tasks, not simply parts of tasks.
3. Review the types of tasks involved in a job or assignment. Analyze the level of personal competence needed for these to be accomplished.
4. Recognize extra efforts and high performance.
5. Allow individuals to have more control over their jobs.
6. Assign clear responsibilities and hold people accountable for performing their responsibilities.
7. Let people know where they stand.
8. Establish adequate control procedures to ensure that outcomes are being reached.
9. Communicate thoroughly what you are doing—your intent, goals, and expected outcomes.

Job Enrichment

Areas of the job to concentrate on for possible job enrichment actions are those jobs where you find one or more of the following: (1) low morale, (2) poor attitudes, (3) underutilized people, (4) low worker productivity or work quality. Avoid assigning jobs in which it is impossible to make changes.

Procedures

1. Establish the boundaries within which you want to develop a job enrichment program. How comprehensive will the program be? Which departments, work units, or jobs should be considered in the program?

2. Inform employees of what you are doing and the purpose.
3. Brainstorm a list of changes that can eliminate dissatisfactions and enrich jobs without concern for practicability.
4. Evaluate the list of suggestions in terms of practicability and possible results.
5. Select the best suggestions and screen out generalities such as "give them more responsibility."
6. Whenever possible, steps 4 and 5 should be conducted with those people who would be affected by any changes made in the job enrichment program. For example, a supervisor who was attempting to enrich the jobs of his or her subordinates could meet with them as a group and: (1) explain the job enrichment program goals and boundaries, (2) lead the group in a brainstorming and evaluation session, and (3) take the group's recommendations and decide which ideas should be implemented. A memo should go to the group members ahead of time so that they will be prepared to contribute to the meeting. A variation of this approach is to let the group meet by themselves.
7. Each person involved in implementing parts of the job enrichment program should submit a plan to his or her boss showing what is planned and the target dates for beginning and ending the project.

Job Enrichment Guidelines

1. Be prepared for an initial drop in performance until employees adjust to the new changes.
2. Avoid overdoing job enrichment or implementing programs too fast. Too much change too fast will cause anxiety and suspicion on the part of workers.
3. Remember that people are different and that not everyone wants or needs job enrichment.
4. Make the long-range goals of your job enrichment program to build a work environment in which: (1) people have challenging work, (2) they have a clear understanding of their job responsibilities and objectives, (3) they can measure their work progress, (4) they are held accountable for doing a good job, and (5) they receive positive reinforcement and feedback when they do good work.
5. Remember that job enrichment cannot overcome poor performance because of lack of training or personal incompetence.

SUMMARY

Motivation is a series of events that begins with a felt need (tension) and involves a search process, action (selection), evaluation, and a reassessment of the need. Human behavior is caused, is goal-directed, and is motivated.

There are process and content theories of motivation. The three main process theories are stimulus-response, equity, and core job theory. The two main content theories are need and motivation-hygiene. Process theories describe motivation as a process or flow of interrelated events, whereas content theories describe motivation at a single point in time.

Punishment-centered supervision has a more dramatic effect on productivity in the short run; however, reward-centered supervision is more effective in the long run. Over the long term, subordinates may put forward less than maximum effort because of lack of commitment to the supervisor and the organization.

Frederick Herzberg introduced the idea that dissatisfaction and satisfaction are not the ends of a continuous line. He emphasized that there are indeed two lines, maintenance factors and motivation factors. The maintenance (hygiene) factors are (1) company policy and administration, (2) work conditions, (3) technical supervision, (4) interpersonal relations with peers, (5) job security, and (6) pay. The motivators are: (1) achievement, (2) recognition, (3) advancement and growth, (4) responsibility, and (5) the work itself. The maintenance factors are concerned with the surroundings of the job (extrinsic), while the motivators are concerned with the job itself and how employees feel about the job (intrinsic). The consideration of pay as a maintenance factor is the most controversial part of Herzberg's theory.

Individuals have a dominant source of motivation. The source of motivation is very important because the more externally motivated we are, the more we respond from self-serving values, whereas the more internally motivated we are, the more we grow and develop with the goal of being capable and worthwhile people.

Supervisors must realize that the need to develop motivated subordinates is complemented by the occasional need for subordinates to motivate the boss. The majority of the boss-motivating techniques require analytical and supportive actions by the supervisor.

The principal role of the supervisor in creating a motivated work force is to develop the working environment into one that stimulates the employee's internal motivators, provides for rewarding work, and permits the employee to demonstrate competence.

IMPORTANT TERMS

Motivation
The motivation concept
Motive strengths
Cognitive dissonance
Stimulus-response theory
Equity theory

Core job theory
Need theory
Motivation-hygiene theory
External and internal motivation
Job enrichment

REVIEW QUESTIONS

1. What is motivation?
2. How does a supervisor motivate employees?
3. Can a satisfied need be a motivator of behavior? Explain.
4. What is cognitive dissonance?

5. Define process and content theories of motivation.
6. Why does punishment reduce organizational effectiveness in the long run?
7. What are the inputs that an employee brings to the job?
8. Describe a self-fulfilled person that you know.
9. What are the maintenance factors that Herzberg described?
10. How can you motivate yourself? Your boss?
11. Explain the difference between internal and external motivation.
12. What must be present before job enrichment can be considered?
13. How does job enrichment and motivation tie together as an organizational force?

EXERCISES

5.1 Work Motivation Basics

Read each statement carefully and indicate your degree of agreement or disagreement with each statement. During the next 15 minutes place an X on the line that best expresses your basic views of work motivation. Check only one answer for each statement.

	(a) Strongly agree	(b) Agree	(c) Disagree	(d) Strongly disagree
1. Being nice to people, such as complimenting them on manners or on dress, makes them feel good and is one of the *best* ways to motivate them to work.	_____	_____	_____	_____
2. Coffee breaks and luncheon gatherings of fellow employees help raise morale and are two fairly simple but good means of motivating employees.	_____	_____	_____	_____
3. Giving employees continuing opportunities to test their knowledge and to try their abilities is the strongest factor in motivation.	_____	_____	_____	_____
4. Employees are interested in the paycheck and are				

generally not too inter-
ested in exerting extra
effort for other reasons.　———— ———— ———— ————

5. Lack of motivating factors
in a job will force even the
highly motivated individual
to be more concerned with
the surroundings of the job
(office, parking, etc.).　———— ———— ———— ————

6. Providing employees with
information on the dollar
value of their *fringe benefits* helps them appreciate
their jobs more fully
and should also help them
realize greater job satisfaction.　———— ———— ———— ————

7. Employees on routine jobs
can be motivated through
supervisory recognition of
their *continual diligence*
and *loyalty.*　———— ———— ———— ————

8. When employees find no
satisfaction in a work
situation, it may be a
place to consider automa
tion.　———— ———— ———— ————

9. Strict control, while more
expensive, ensures better
results than making indi-
viduals more respon-
sible and imposing fewer
restrictions upon
them.　———— ———— ———— ————

10. An experienced and well-
performing employee
may find all tasks in his
or her unit to be routine
and chorelike. Through
periodic rotation from
task to task within the
unit for variety, the
employee's work motiva-
tion will be maintained.　———— ———— ———— ————

After all class members have answered all 10 questions, break up into groups of 6 to 10 people each and arrive at a consensus answer for each question.

When your group reaches the point where each person can say, "Well, even though it may not be exactly what I want, at least I can live with the decision and support it," the group has reached consensus. This doesn't mean that all members of the group must agree completely. But all must at least agree minimally. Treat differences of opinion as a way of (1) gathering additional information, (2) clarifying issues, and (3) forcing the group to seek better alternatives. (Check your group answers with those that follow.) After arriving at a group consensus, elect a spokesperson to present the group solution to the other groups.

Answers

1. (d)	2. (d)	3. (a)	4. (d)	5. (a)
6. (d)	7. (d)	8. (a)	9. (d)	10. (d)

Please don't get too excited if you disagree with the experts. The answers are based on Herzberg's two-factor theory. It is not critical if you answered a question (b) when the correct answer is (a). What is important is that your answer is on the correct side of the scale. Stated another way, it does not matter if you answered question 1 (c) or (d), only that you were on the right half of the scale. If you have an incorrect answer and a review of Herzberg's theory does not clarify the issue for you, we suggest that you check with a classmate who answered the question correctly.

5.2 Job Enrichment

This exercise is designed to assist you in understanding the basic operational concerns of a supervisor in integrating the many motivational theories into a practical job enrichment exercise.

Option 1

This exercise may be applied to an existing organizational situation. Students working for the same company may wish to identify an activity, function, or people who, in your opinion, are not performing at peak proficiency. Within the areas you choose as a group, identify one in which you feel motivation is an issue and in which the job itself could be the source of the problems.

Option 2

Dividing the class into small groups of 6 to 10 people, review the following situational case.

The job to enrich is that of janitor.
There are 150 janitors.
There are nine supervisors.
They work in a large central Canadian city, cleaning subways.
There are three shifts.
There is no union.

The yearly salary range for janitors is $9,200 to $14,200 a year. This is a very competitive salary in this city.

Yearly increases are based on longevity, not merit.

Supplies and uniforms are purchased by the city's purchasing department.

The citizens of this metropolitan city are constantly complaining to city hall about dirty subways.

The nine supervisors are the people who have been janitors for the longest period of time.

The city council employs your group as consultants to improve the situation.

Analysis Procedures

1. Specifically identify the concerns.
2. Establish what you think the major tasks are in the activity, function, or people being discussed.
3. Establish your assumptions regarding the types of authority and responsibility the job contains.
4. Using the motivational theory, identify what areas may be contributing to the problem.
5. What new technique would you use to modify the situation to improve motivation?
6. Identify your expectations of changes to organizational structure resulting from your improved motivational methods.
7. What organizational barriers would there be in implementing your change recommendation?
8. Establish strategies to overcome these barriers, or identify barriers that you do not think can be overcome.
9. Finalize your expectations for the problem solution. Be prepared to defend your solution to other groups.
10. Based on the information you have considered in questions 1–9, complete Exhibit 5.1.

EXHIBIT

5.1   Job Enrichment Plan

Name_____ Work Area_____

Date_____ Boss_____

CASE

5.1   Where Do We Start?

Dr. Robert W. Hinkle, dean of a leading eastern college of business and administration, is concerned about the escalation of starting salaries for business faculty members. A case that he has been concerned about for the last two weeks is what salary to offer a candidate for a faculty position in accounting. Donald W. Dittrich, about to receive his Ph.D. from a leading eastern university, interviewed for the position and was rated

Figure 5.11 Motivation-enrichment factor checklist.

Changes to be made to remove dissatisfaction or enrich or improve a job	Reason for making the change	Plan for implementing a change, including target dates

very high in potential by Dean Hinkle's faculty. Dean Hinkle checked with the deans of other leading universities to seek advice on a starting salary for an accounting professor. His quick survey indicated that beginning accounting professors are receiving starting salaries for nine months in the range of $33,000 to $36,500.

These high starting salaries are supported by the marketplace. For example, in 1983 there were five jobs for every Ph.D. graduating in accounting. Dean Hinkle is concerned because his other accounting professors, with many years of productive service, are just barely above the range of starting salaries. Yearly merit increases by the state legislature have not equaled the rate of inflation and have been less than the average yearly increase in starting salaries. For example, Professor Mark Andrew is an above-average performer who came to work at the university seven years ago. His present salary for nine months is $28,500.

As Dean Hinkle ponders these issues, he wonders what his next course of action should be.

Questions

1. What factors have caused this inequitable salary situation?
2. What can Dean Hinkle do to help his present professors?
3. Should the marketplace be a factor in establishing salaries, or should all professors of equal experience at a university, regardless of discipline, be paid about the same?
4. Explain the motivational consequences of this situation for the college faculty.

SUGGESTED ADDITIONAL READINGS

Carrell, M. R., and Dittrich, J. E., "Employee Perceptions of Fair Treatment." *Personnel Journal* (October, 1976), pp. 523–524.

Cascio, Wayne F. *Applied Psychology in Personnel Management.* Reston, Va.: Reston Publishing Co., 1982.

Couger, J. Daniel, and Zawacki, Robert A. "What Motivates DP Professionals?" *Datamation* (September, 1978), pp. 116–123.

French, Wendell L.; Bell, Cecil H., Jr.; and Zawacki, Robert A. *Organization Development: Theory, Practice, and Research.* Dallas: Business Publications, 1983.

Gellerman, S. W. *The Management of Human Resources.* Hinsdale, IL: The Dryden Press, 1976.

Hackman, J. Richard, and Oldham, Greg R. *Work Redesign.* Reading, MA: Addison-Wesley, 1980.

Herzberg, Frederick. "The Motivation-Hygiene Concept and Problems of Manpower." In *Organization Development: Managing Change in the Public Sector,* edited by Robert A. Zawacki and D. D. Warrick, pp. 178–182. Chicago: IPMA, 1976.

Lazer, R. I. "Behavior Modification as a Managerial Technique." *The Conference Board Record* (1975), pp. 22–25.

Maslow, Abraham. *Motivation and Personality.* New York: Harper & Row, 1954.

Maslow, A. H. "The Need for Creative People." In *Organization Development: Managing Change in the Public Sector,* edited by Robert A. Zawacki and D. D. Warrick, pp. 206–209. Chicago: IPMA, 1976.

6

Interpersonal Communication

But let everyone be quick to hear, slow to speak,
and slow to anger.

James I:19

OBJECTIVES

This chapter provides you with the information necessary to:

1. Explain the principal components of a communication model
2. Know the major reasons communication contributes to the success of a supervisor at work
3. Know what to look for to understand the messages you are giving and receiving
4. Explain the impact of barriers and facilitators in communication
5. Understand the need for good listening skills
6. Be able to use assertiveness techniques to assist the communication process

---

THE IMPORTANCE OF COMMUNICATION SKILLS

Our ability to communicate is perhaps the most important skill we have. It will play a major role in our success as a person and in whatever endeavors we become involved in. It is a particularly important skill for supervisors and managers, who must give and receive instructions, evaluate performance, solve problems, listen, communicate ideas and feelings, confront and level with people, and eliminate inappropriate behaviors without alienating people.

Communication is a continuous problem in organizations. It is no small wonder when you consider some of the reasons why an interaction may break down or be misunderstood. The individuals involved may have very different backgrounds culturally, socially, geographically, and experientially. They may also have significant differences in values, beliefs, and education. Add to these factors differences in self-image, position, and power as well as occasional game playing and inconsistencies between a person's verbal and nonverbal messages, and you can understand why perceptions of what was said get distorted and messages are misunderstood.

THE COMMUNICATION PROCESS

The communication process includes six major components: (1) the source, (2) coding, (3) transmission, (4) decoding, (5) receiving, and (6) feedback.

Figure 6.1 illustrates the communication model that is fundamental for supporting the direction of people at work.

The Source

The source of the message is the individual who has initiated an interaction. Since the supervisor is a key source in initiating messages, it is imperative that he or she understand the initiator's role. Too many times the source person initiates a message using only himself or herself as a frame of reference. Unfortunately, the receiver of the message is likely to receive the message using his or her own frame of reference, resulting in misunderstanding.

The supervisor's perception of the problem, background experience, and capability to use the technical language of the operation are seldom the same as those of the subordinate for whom the message is intended. Yet the action directed by the communication must be performed by the individual receiving the message; thus it is important that the source of the interaction assure that the message is understood. This can be accomplished by being sensitive to the feelings and background of the receiver, developing good listening skills, and learning to check out what has been heard.

Figure 6.1 The communication process.

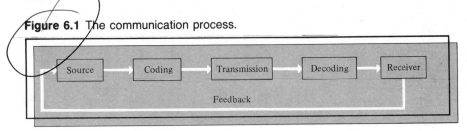

Coding

Coding is the process of selecting the appropriate words, phrases, sentences, and other word structures to convey a particular message. The key to successful coding is to learn to be concise and use words and phrases that are understandable to the receiver.

Transmission

In addition to conventional oral and written forms of communicating, modern communications capabilities in organizations have far outstripped the classical "telephone, telegraph, tell-a-secretary" models. There are many new methods, such as television remote-access computer terminals, modern paging systems, and conference calls. The method of transmission needs to be carefully chosen to be appropriate to the message being sent. Messages that require action, contain important information that needs to be retained, or require accuracy should be communicated orally and then followed by a written message. Emergency messages should be passed personally.

Care should also be taken to eliminate any source of distortion when the message is transmitted. Noise, interruptions, and other environmental events that would cause distraction must be taken into account. If a personal conversation is used, consider the environment, the formal or informal setting, and the need for face-to-face interaction.

Decoding

If the choice of language is at too technical a level for the receiver, the message may become garbled in the execution. The decoding function is essentially one in which the receiver uses personal ability to recognize the code provided by the source. There is always the possibility of double or garbled meanings. Psychological blocks can also cause misinterpretation.

Receiving

It is important to assure that limitations in experience, knowledge, or expectations are overcome before action on the message commences. The sender should check to ensure that the communication is consistent with the receiver's ability to interpret. The message content is in the receiver's perception of reality. A safe technique for checking this is simply to ask for verification of action to be taken.

Feedback

The only meaningful feedback is the review of the action actually taken as compared with what was intended. "The proof of the pudding is in the tasting," and the objective achieved is organizational reality. Once the action taken is known, the source would be required either to continue operations or to correct deficiencies under previously cited control concepts in Chapter 2.

UNDERSTANDING THE MESSAGE

When people think of interpersonal communication, they usually think of words exchanged between two or more persons. However, words comprise only a small part of the message that is sent and received. Some of the factors that affect the message are:

Attitude
Verbal messages
Nonverbal messages
Appearance
Backgrounds of the communicators
Expectations of the communicators
Setting

In interacting with people, all these factors need to be kept in mind in interpreting what is being said and assuring that you are giving clear and consistent messages. For example, if your verbal messages (words) and nonverbal messages (body language) are incongruent, you will send confusing and conflicting messages. You don't need to be a mind reader to interpret what is being said. Simply be aware of the different components of the message, and when any part of the message is unclear, ask questions and check out the intent. If you still can't get straight answers, it is to your advantage to react to the verbal message to eliminate game playing and manipulation.

Attitude

The greatest key to successful communication is having an attitude that encourages open and supportive communication! If our attitude communicates that we value and accept the person with whom we are communicating, communication is almost always possible. The major exception is when the other person is unwilling to communicate. Otherwise, a caring attitude tends to create rapport, openness, acceptance, understanding, honesty, trust, and a willingness to solve problems.

A condescending or negative attitude makes it difficult to communicate regardless of the communication skills a person possesses. Such an attitude generates distrust, reluctance to cooperate, and retaliation.

The importance of attitude should not be overlooked in communicating. Your attitude speaks much louder than your actions or words! Therefore, it is counterproductive to communicate from a negative attitude.

Verbal Messages

The words that we choose are an important part of the message that we are trying to communicate. In choosing your words, it is best to use understandable and supportive words (don't try to impress people with your vocabulary), to avoid loaded words (emotionally charged words or profanity) since they tend to be misinterpreted, and to be concise (information overkill will kill the message). It is also important to keep in mind that words have different meanings to different people and that a person's mood or mind-set may affect the interpretation of words. Therefore, it is helpful to check to see if you are being heard correctly and to ask for occasional clarification to assure that you are interpreting correctly words that are being communicated to you.

Nonverbal Messages

It isn't so much what is said but how it is said that determines how the message is received. Our nonverbal messages often speak much louder than our words. Our nonverbal messages include:

Tone of voice
Gestures
Facial expressions
Posture
Eye contact
Body movements

Nonverbal messages are often difficult to interpret and should be viewed as an important part of the message that give us not facts but *clues* that we may need to check out. Never assume the role of mind reader! If you are unsure of the body signals you are receiving, ask questions to check out what a person is really saying, and remember that if you still cannot get straight answers, it is to your advantage to respond to the verbal message to remove any payoffs for game playing. Also, make sure that your nonverbal messages are consistent with your verbal messages or you will be sending confusing messages. Using compassionate words, for example, with an un-compassionate tone of voice or indifferent facial expressions will send a confusing message, just as expressing anger with a smile on your face will probably cause people to discount your anger.

Appearance

Clothes, cleanliness, hairstyle, shoes, adornments such as jewelry or pins, and even something you have in your hand, such as a cigarette or a drink, may have a significant effect on the message. Flashy clothes, for example, may communicate lack of trust worthiness and that a wheeler-dealer is on the loose. Slovenly dress may communicate a liberal and irresponsible life-style and cause people to discount or misinterpret what you have to say. Anything extreme in your appearance, such as an excess of makeup or jewelry or a highly unusual hairstyle, may communicate the need for attention and lead people to believe that you are insecure. The same person may get a different response when dressed smartly for the job than when wearing a pair of torn jeans for yard work. Cigarette smoking or heavy drinking may be a sign of weakness or low values to some people and may lessen your credibility as a communicator. Overly sexy clothing may cause a genuine compliment to be interpreted as a come-on.

We don't have any sage advice to offer on appearance other than to recognize that it certainly influences the messages that you send. While other parts of the messages may overcome your appearance drawbacks, it is to your advantage to evaluate your appearance and assure that it is consistent with the messages you are trying to send.

Backgrounds of the Communicators

Education, position, gender, race, socioeconomic heritage, status, life-style, and reputation may also affect the message. For instance, a person in a supervisory or management position should be aware that the position itself may result in employees' exaggerating what is said. A casual comment about cutting costs may be interpreted as meaning that layoffs may be imminent. A frown may be interpreted as meaning "the boss doesn't like me."

Backgrounds can be advantageous or disadvantageous in an interaction. For example, credentials, such as a college degree, could lend credibility to what you have to say. On the other hand, if you have a reputation as a manipulator, people may not believe you even when you are telling the truth.

An awareness of the effect of backgrounds on the message can be helpful in assuring that they do not cause you to lose your objectivity in interpreting the message. You can also learn to put people at ease by being warm, friendly, and supportive, so that your background factors are not likely to distort what they are hearing.

Expectations of the Communicators

Expectations tend to create a self-fulfilling prophecy. For example, if you expect a person not to value you, you will tend to read put-down messages into an interaction whether they are in fact there or not. Expectations can also result in disappointments if they are not fulfilled. Assume that you have been doing an excellent job and that you are expecting your boss to shower you with praise. If your boss doesn't know how well you are doing or just assumes that you understand how proud he or she is of you, your expectation is not likely to be fulfilled, and you will be disappointed and may start storing up feelings of anger.

If you have an expectation that you are going to hold people accountable for, you should communicate it or realize that they were not aware of the expectation and did not intentionally overlook it. Supervisors often expect things of employees that have never been communicated. If you have reason to believe that another person's expectations of you are causing a problem, make some inquiries to try to identify the problem.

Setting

If you have ever sat in front of an overpowering desk with a boss or authority figure behind it or have had a boss conduct a performance appraisal with phones ringing and people coming in and out, you know how important the setting can be to an interaction. Room layout, size, decor, traffic flow, and noise can all affect communication.

Trying to communicate something important in a busy lunchroom or a public setting can be very detrimental to an interaction. Bosses, for example, sometimes make the mistake of disciplining someone in front of other employees. Meetings may be held in a setting that discourages open communication or may even encourage dissension by putting one group on one side of the table and another group on the other side.

The setting may not contribute as much to the success or failure of an interaction as the other part of the message, but it definitely should not be overlooked. As much as possible, offices should be arranged and chosen so that they will contribute to the desired communication goal.

The best way to overcome this barrier is to plan for the delivering of the message. Use private, quiet areas, if necessary. Make the receiver sufficiently comfortable that feedback and questioning can take place.

COMMUNICATION BARRIERS AND FACILITATORS

Your use of communication barriers or facilitators will have a significant effect on your ability to interact successfully with people. Communication barriers close off communication, while communication facilitators encourage open, two-way communication. For the supervisor, this can mean the difference between success and failure, since communication is so essential to getting the job done. A supervisor who, knowingly or not, uses communication barriers causes employees to be closed and uncommunicative and often to give inaccurate information so as to avoid saying something the boss doesn't want to hear. Thus, the boss or person who frequently uses communication barriers tends to have an inaccurate view of reality, based on insufficient or distorted information.

Communication Barriers

Communication barriers occur when one or more persons in the interaction feel discounted. A discount is the devaluation of another person or yourself and can come from another person, yourself, or events. Frequent discounting can thwart the healthy development of a person. When people feel discounted, they tend to respond in inappropriate ways by getting defensive, retaliating, rationalizing their position, and so on. (Figure 6.2 includes a list of communication barriers and the types of inappropriate responses they provoke.)

If discounting another person or yourself increases the likelihood of an inappropriate response, it follows that using discounts is self-defeating even if someone in your estimation deserves to be discounted. Creating ill feelings, damaging egos, or provoking anger and resentment are simply not conducive to communicating. For example, if an employee does something that upsets his or her supervisor, belittling, scolding, threatening, or embarrassing the employee in front of other employees increases the likelihood of an inappropriate response. The employee may retaliate by rationalizing his or her position, pointing out that if you had given better instructions the problem would never have occurred, or by reluctantly apologizing and then becoming a morale

Figure 6.2 Communication barriers.

Communication barriers occur when one or more persons in an interaction feel discounted. A discount is a devaluation of another person or yourself. Discounts *decrease* the likelihood of successful communication and *increase* the likelihood of an inappropriate response.

Barriers	Typical Inappropriate Responses
Judging, condemning, advising, instructing, or moralizing from a critical position	Triggers almost all the inappropriate responses described below and may get a critical response in return
Attacking people rather than problems	Provokes anger, resentment, resistance, rebellion, and stubbornness
Being autocratic or intimidating	Gets temporary results but may encourage defensiveness and retaliation
Blaming, scapegoating, and belittling	Encourages lying, rationalizing, and distortion of the truth
Using killer glances (put-down looks)	Produces guilt and rage
Motive raping (attributing motives to the acts of another person)	Stimulates feelings of helplessness and frustration
Explaining away the feelings or ideas of others	Results in the suppression of ideas or feelings
Using loaded (emotionally charged) words or sarcasm	Increases the likelihood of overreactions or misinterpretations
Making absolute or exaggerated statements	Undermines credibility and often results in people tuning out
Overreacting to the words or actions of another person	Blows things out of proportion
Sending double messages (verbal and nonverbal messages that are different)	Reduces the interaction to confusion, mind reading, and misinterpretation
Indifference	Destroys self-confidence and frustrates needs for acceptance
Not listening	Devalues self-worth, increases frustration
Nagging	Creates resistance and hostility
Sidetracking	Inhibits problem solving
Shotgunning (continuously putting down ideas)	Blocks creativity and openness
Negativism	Undermines morale
Interrogating	Implies lack of trust and presumes guilt
Stereotyping	Often results in inaccurate perceptions
Labeling	Causes resentment and may produce self-fulfilling prophecies
Interrupting	Causes frustration and clamming up

problem that will require an excess of supervisory attention. There are certainly times when supervisors need to be firm or even need to discipline employees. However, such actions should be taken without the need to use discounts.

In developing an understanding of communication barriers, it is important to be aware of different ways that we discount people and to realize that the emphasis should be on recognizing when one *feels* discounted. Whether you in fact discount a person or not is irrelevant if the person feels discounted. People can feel discounted because of something the communicator does or says; because of devaluing they do to themselves, such as sending put-down messages to themselves; or because of something that occurred outside of the interaction, such as an argument with another person. The wise communicator tries to be alert enough to pick up discount clues. For example, when people feel discounted, they tend to respond by:

Doing nothing (withdrawing, procrastinating, becoming silent)
Overadapting (adapting behavior to what you think is expected)
Becoming agitated (showing signs of nervousness, agitation, resistance, stubbornness, etc.)
Becoming incapacitated or violent (a person who is often discounted may become helpless, become a drug addict or alcoholic, throw temper tantrums, or do something violent)

When you become aware of a possible discount blocking communication, you should try to remove it: eliminate a discount that you may be sending; ignore or confront gently a discount you are receiving; probe for the source of the discount, if appropriate; treat a person with value and respect to help overcome the discount the person is feeling; remove any payoffs for discounting by not responding to the discount or having reasonable consequences for the discounts.

Communication Facilitators

Communication facilitators are present when one or more persons in the interaction feel valued. Thus, communication facilitators include anything in the interaction that adds value to the communicators. Facilitators could include verbal or nonverbal messages that show genuine interest and caring, or they could include active listening, a smile, good eye contact, being understanding and helpful, attacking problems rather than people, or being willing to be rational and solve problems. Communication facilitators increase the likelihood of effective communication and decrease the likelihood of an inappropriate response. A list of communication facilitators and typical responses they elicit is shown in Figure 6.3.

Supervisors need to learn to develop and use facilitators from the perspective that they will significantly increase the ability to communicate. Without this perspective, supervisors often succumb to discounting people because "they deserve it," retaliating instead of trying to solve problems, or stubbornly defending their position. At best, they may win the battle and lose the war. Winning an argument or being heard at the expense of another person usually results in everyone involved losing over the long

Figure 6.3 Communication facilitators.

Communication facilitators are present when one or more persons in the interaction feel valued. Valuing a person *increases* the likelihood of successful communication and *decreases* the likelihood of an inappropriate response.

Facilitators	Typical Appropriate Responses
An attitude of genuine caring	Establishes rapport and a willingness to communicate and frees people to be themselves, drop their defense mechanisms and facades, and express their real feelings
Active listening (demonstrating interest, drawing people out, being understanding, checking perceptions, and exercising self-control)	Frees people to communicate, cooperate, and solve problems knowing that they have been heard and understood
Attacking problems, not people	Keeps the focus on solving problems without getting sidetracked into attacking people
Leveling and confronting with caring (with no attempt to devalue another person)	Makes it possible to be direct, to level with people, and to talk about negative issues without being demeaning
Honesty	Frees people to listen without having to interpret what you are really saying
Trust (assuming the best about people whether they deserve it or not unless to do so would be foolish)	Increases the probability that a person will act trustworthily and frees people of the need to manipulate and play games
Calmness, patience, and self-control	Cools down an emotionally charged climate, allows people to calm down, and frees people to be more objective and less emotional
Assertiveness with caring (knowing and expressing opinions, needs, and feelings in a caring and constructive way)	Increases the likelihood of need satisfaction and of making things happen
Reflecting feelings (constructively expressing your feelings or what you believe to be the feelings of others)	Helps put all parties involved in touch with their real feelings and allows them to continue communicating knowing that their feelings have been recognized
Giving specific rather than general feedback	Enables the communicators to deal with the real issues without having to rely on trying to interpret generalizations
Using descriptive rather than evaluative words (describing what you observed or the effect something had on you in a nonjudgmental way rather than evaluating the goodness or badness of what a person said or did)	Enables you to talk about issues without provoking defensiveness or overreactions in others
Using "I" messages (messages that describe how you feel or how something has affected you)	Allows you to express feelings and opinions without passing judgment on another person or making another person responsible for your feelings

run. Using facilitators when others may be using barriers is very difficult to do. However, it is worth the price and self-sacrifice if your goal is to be an effective communicator.

Active Listening

The most important facilitator, as mentioned previously, is a caring attitude. A caring attitude quickly establishes rapport and a willingness to communicate. The second most important facilitator is active listening. Active listening is a difficult but necessary skill for supervisors to develop. Unfortunately, we have a tendency to focus more on our own messages than on the messages we are receiving. Active listening reverses this process and places the focus on hearing what another person is saying and feeling.

There are five basic skills involved in active listening:

1. Demonstrating genuine interest
2. Drawing people out
3. Being understanding
4. Perception checking
5. Exercising self-control

Demonstrating Genuine Interest. Genuine interest can be demonstrated through a caring attitude, good eye contact, attentive body language such as leaning forward and being alert instead of looking bored, and showing enthusiasm or empathy toward what is being communicated. It is also important to eliminate as many distractions as possible, such as phone calls, interruptions, or conflicting activities such as reading your mail while you are supposedly listening.

Drawing People Out. This skill implies focusing on getting another person to communicate rather than dominating an interaction yourself. One of the best skills for drawing people out is to ask open-ended questions. Closed questions are questions that can be responded to with a yes or no answer. An example would be "Are you happy with your job?" The respondent can end the conversation with a yes or no answer. Open-ended questions cannot be answered with *yes* or *no.* An example would be "What do you like best and least about your job?" People can also be drawn out by asking for more information or clarification or by reflecting feelings. Reflecting feelings is accomplished by expressing to another person the feelings that you think they are experiencing. For example, you might say, "Are you feeling that your performance review was unfair?" If they insist that you are not accurately portraying their feelings, apologize and move on. However, if you are right, the person may begin to express what is really on his or her mind.

Being Understanding. We cannot always fully understand another person, since our experiences differ. We can, however, learn to be understanding. Being understanding means putting aside our own biases and needs and concentrating on what another person is saying and feeling. You do not have to agree with a person or even like the person to be understanding. The goal is to understand things from that person's perspective. When people feel that they are not understood, they have a tendency to keep repeating their position or to withdraw. On the other hand, when people feel understood, they are more willing to cooperate, solve problems, and receive feedback.

　　Perception Checking.   Perception checking is a skill in checking out what you have heard and assuring that what you have said has been accurately received. You can check out what you have heard by summarizing or repeating what you think has been said or decided. In addition, you can ask others their interpretation of what you have communicated. For example, after giving an assignment, a supervisor may want to say, "Why don't you explain to me what you think your assignment is so I can make sure I communicated accurately what I want you to do."

　　Exercising Self-Control.   Perhaps the most difficult part of active listening is exercising self-control during the listening process. We may be tempted to interrupt, complete sentences started by others, argue, justify our own position, react to discounts being sent our way, or impress another person with our knowledge or who we are. Resist! Considerable self-control is required of a good listener.

TRANSACTIONAL ANALYSIS: A MODEL FOR MONITORING HOW YOU COMMUNICATE

Transactional analysis (TA) is a method developed by the late Eric Berne that was designed to analyze human behavior and interpersonal interactions.[1] It was originally developed as a method of psychotherapy and is still used in this capacity by certified TA practitioners. It was simplified for lay persons by Thomas Harris in his best-seller *I'm OK—You're OK*[2] and by Muriel James and Dorothy Jongeward in their best-seller *Born to Win.*[3] Now there are numerous TA books out, many of which are oriented toward business. In organizations, TA can become a very valuable skill when it is used as an awareness tool that can be used by people (especially supervisors and managers) to: (1) monitor the way they communicate; (2) evaluate organizational objectives, policies, leadership styles, and life scripts. It should not be used for "analyzing" others! Unfortunately, some people see TA as a quick way to become an overnight psychologist. They throw around TA buzzwords and tell people why they do what they do. Don't! Use it primarily as an awareness tool to monitor your own behavior and to better understand (not analyze) the behavior of others.

Major TA Areas of Study

Transactional analysis is concerned with four kinds of analysis:

1. *Structural analysis:* the analysis of an individual's Parent, Adult, and Child ego states.

[1]Eric Berne, *Games People Play* (New York: Grove Press, 1964).
[2]Thomas A. Harris, *I'm OK—You're OK* (New York: Avon Books, 1967).
[3]Muriel James and Dorothy Jongeward, *Born to Win* (Reading, MA: Addison-Wesley, 1971).

2. *Transactional analysis:* the analysis of interpersonal communication patterns by classifying transactions between ego states as:
   a. *Complementary transactions:* when a message is sent from a specific ego state and gets an expected and appropriate response from a specific ego state in another person. Complementary transactions can continue indefinitely.
   b. *Crossed transactions:* when a message that is sent receives an unexpected or inappropriate response. Crossed transactions usually result in a communication breakdown.
   c. *Ulterior transactions:* when someone says one thing and means another. Ulterior transactions are also often called *double messages.* In an ulterior transaction, the verbal and nonverbal message are incongruent. They are basically dishonest and make it difficult for the receiver to determine which message to believe.
3. *Game analysis:* the analysis of psychological games played between people. A psychological game occurs when an interaction between people includes ulterior motives housed in seemingly rational messages.
4. *Script analysis:* the analysis of the recurring themes or patterns of behavior that occur in the lives of people and organizations. Scripts result in people (and organizations) assuming psychological positions regarding themselves and others. The psychological positions fall into four basic patterns:
   a. *I'm OK—You're OK.* This is a healthy, winner's position that assumes I am worthwhile and valuable and so are you. A person in this position accepts others and himself or herself. Being OK is not a statement of fact but rather an attitude toward others and self.
   b. *I'm Not OK—You're OK.* This is the position of the person who usually feels unworthy, powerless, weak, helpless, and unloved. People in this position tend to be passive, withdrawn, and often depressed. Employees sometimes relate to their supervisors from this position.
   c. *I'm OK—You're Not OK.* A person in this position looks down on others, blames them for his or her mistakes, tries to control others, and becomes defensive when questioned. An "I'm OK–You're Not OK" attitude is often a cover-up for inner insecurities and a lack of self-worth.
   d. *I'm Not OK—You're Not OK.* This is the position of a person who does not value himself or others and has more or less given up.

Ego States

The major concept in TA is the notion that we interact from *ego states* and that each person has three ego states: a Parent ego state, an Adult ego state, and a Child ego state. The ego states refer to feelings and behaviors, not chronological development. Figure 6.4 shows the three ego states and their subcomponents. Each individual has a different configuration.

The Parent Ego State. You are in your Parent ego state when you are thinking, feeling, and acting like your own parents or parental figures. There are two sides to

Figure 6.4 Transactional Analysis ego states.

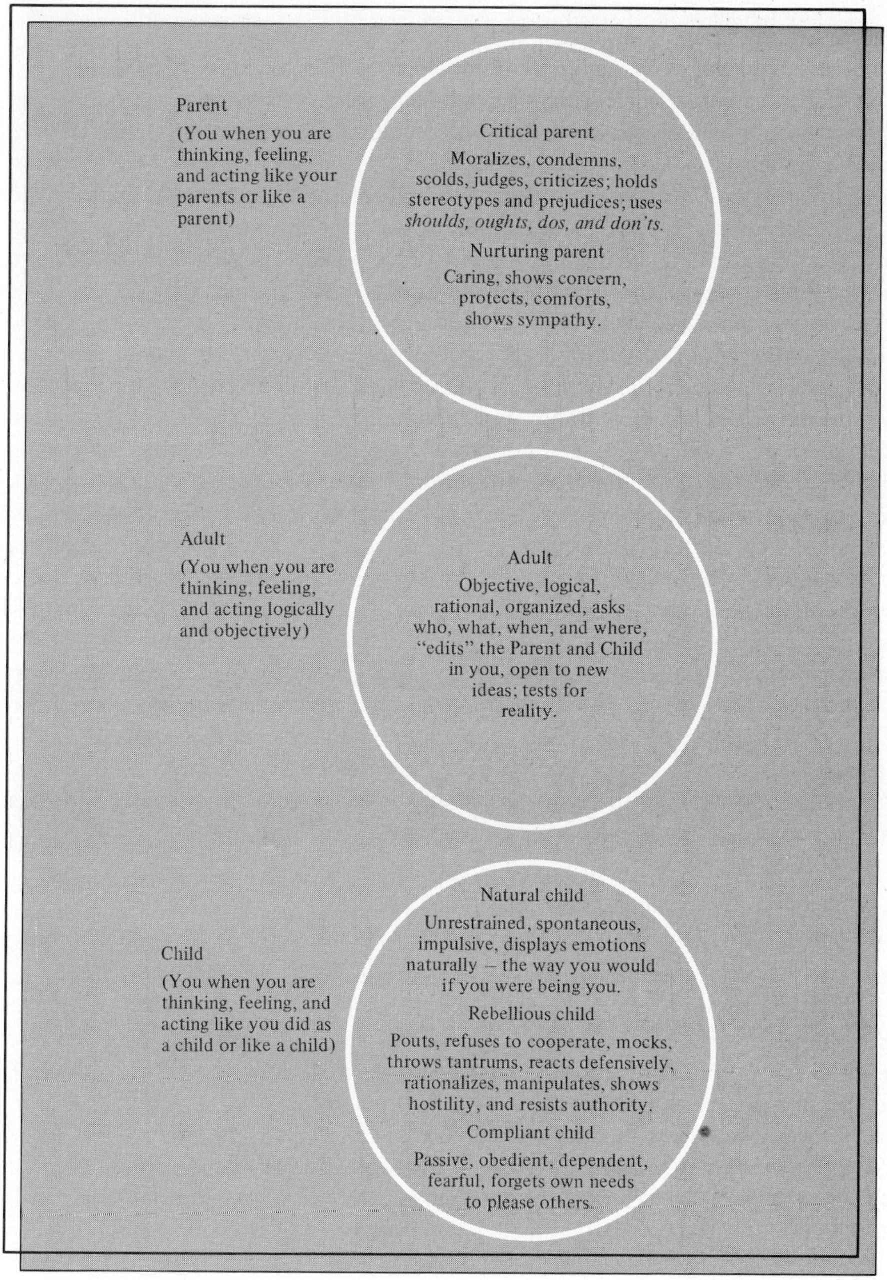

Parent

(You when you are thinking, feeling, and acting like your parents or like a parent)

Critical parent

Moralizes, condemns, scolds, judges, criticizes; holds stereotypes and prejudices; uses *shoulds, oughts, dos, and don'ts.*

Nurturing parent

Caring, shows concern, protects, comforts, shows sympathy.

Adult

(You when you are thinking, feeling, and acting logically and objectively)

Adult

Objective, logical, rational, organized, asks who, what, when, and where, "edits" the Parent and Child in you, open to new ideas; tests for reality.

Child

(You when you are thinking, feeling, and acting like you did as a child or like a child)

Natural child

Unrestrained, spontaneous, impulsive, displays emotions naturally — the way you would if you were being you.

Rebellious child

Pouts, refuses to cooperate, mocks, throws tantrums, reacts defensively, rationalizes, manipulates, shows hostility, and resists authority.

Compliant child

Passive, obedient, dependent, fearful, forgets own needs to please others.

the Parent in you: (1) the Critical Parent and (2) the Nurturing Parent. The Critical Parent will usually trigger unhealthy or unconstructive feelings that result in defensiveness, hostility, rebellion, and feelings of inadequacy and lack of self-worth, while the Nurturing Parent tends to generate warmth, caring, acceptance, and feelings of worth.

1. *Critical Parent.* The Critical Parent is filled with prejudices, stereotypes, and strong opinions about religion, politics, life-styles, child rearing, proper dress, and so forth, that have been accepted as truth but not logically checked out. It moralizes, scolds, judges, condemns, domineers, makes absolute statements, lays down the law, and sets standards. Your Critical Parent uses words such as *always, never, should, ought,* and particularly evaluative or value-loaded words such as *stupid, ridiculous, absurd, asinine,* and *lousy.* Typical Critical Parent phrases are: "What you should do is . . . ," "Don't tell me what to do," "That is the dumbest idea I ever heard." Some physical clues that the Critical Parent displays are: pointing index fingers, furrowed brow, looks of disgust, foot tapping, hands on hips, horrified looks, sighing, patting another on the head, arms folded across the chest, and killer glances. Using the Critical Parent, especially as a supervisor or manager, is almost always self-defeating, since it tends to stimulate inappropriate responses.

2. *Nurturing Parent.* The Nurturing Parent also displays learned parental behaviors. However, most nurturing behaviors are healthy and get a positive response. They include such behaviors as showing caring, being sympathetic, being protective, and comforting others. The Nurturing Parent may say things such as "Everything will be OK," "Is there anything I can do to help?" "Be sure you look both ways before you cross the street." The Nurturing Parent may use physical gestures such as understanding looks, a sympathetic tone of voice, or an arm around a shoulder. When unmonitored by the Adult, the Nurturing Parent can be misused. It can become a constant rescuer, a person who "nurtures people to death" and relieves them of responsibility for their actions. A supervisor who becomes overly nurturing keeps employees immature and irresponsible.

The Adult Ego State.   You are in your Adult ego state when you are thinking, feeling, and acting rationally and objectively. Your Adult bases its behavior on logic and reasoning rather than on memories or "tapes" from the past. It is oriented toward current reality (the here and now) and objective processing of information. It is organized, adaptable, cooperative, and open to new ideas. It functions by testing out reality, checking out perceptions, and estimating probabilities. The Adult ego state can also be used to edit out inappropriate Parent and Child behaviors as well as to develop more appropriate behaviors.

The basic vocabulary of the Adult consists of *who, what, when, where, how,* and *why.* Other terms used by the Adult are: "In my opinion," "What is your side of the story?" "Could you be more specific about what you mean?" The Adult also uses words to make people feel accepted, to draw them out, and to enable them to communicate openly. The Adult listens actively and communicates by using good eye contact, employing congruent physical expressions and words, and being aware of the messages that are being sent out and received.

The Child Ego State.   You are in your Child ego state when you are thinking, feeling, and acting primarily from your emotions in a childlike and often immature manner. Your Child uses such words and phrases as: "I wish," "I want," "I could care less," "I refuse," "I can do whatever I want to do," "You're not so hot, either," "You're so big and strong," "My new car is bigger than your new car." Some physical expressions of the Child ego state are crying, laughing, quivering lip, pouting, showing affections, temper tantrums, high-pitched whining, shrugging shoulders, teasing, giggling, baby talk, withdrawing, and acting hurt. TA experts disagree on the components of the Child. The components that are most frequently mentioned are:

1. *Natural Child.* The Natural Child is the unrestrained, spontaneous, impulsive, pleasure-seeking side of you. It is the part of you that is genuinely affectionate, shows curiosity, is sensuous, and is in essence uncensored. It laughs, cries, jokes, or gets angry at a given moment because that is the most natural response based on what you are feeling. The Natural Child can be a healthy and likable part of our personality if it is monitored by our Adult. A person without a well-developed Natural Child tends to be cold, unfeeling, and unspontaneous. However, the Natural Child can get out of control and make spontaneous but immature choices if it is not controlled by the Adult.

2. *Adapted Child.* The Adapted Child is you when you adapt your behaviors rather than do what you would do naturally. Adaptation starts prior to childbirth when the natural responses of the fetus must adapt to the mother's emotions, chemical makeup, habits (smoking, drinking, using drugs), nutrition, and daily routine. Then, all through life we have to make decisions about adapting to parental demands, authority, rules, regulations, circumstances, expectations, and so forth. You are operating from your Adapted Child when you adapt by being rebellious or compliant. For example, when a person in authority tells you to do something, you might obediently do it or rebel by refusing to do it.

3. *Rebellious Child.* You are reacting from your Rebellious Child when you are acting out of a sense of rebellion by resisting authority, refusing to listen or cooperate, pouting, being stubborn, crying to get your way, throwing a temper tantrum, doing the opposite of what people want you to do, reacting defensively, purposely breaking rules, spreading rumors, giving people the silent treatment, reacting from a position of hostility, or manipulating others as opposed to being straightforward.

4. *Compliant Child.* There are times when it is logical to be compliant. We all have to follow certain rules, laws, and procedures to function successfully in society. However, when overdone, operating from a position of compliance can be unproductive and can also inhibit growth. You are operating from your Compliant Child when you obediently obey what others tell you to do or try to adapt your behavior to the expectations of others without considering your own needs or what is best. A large Compliant Child comes from having to adapt one's behavior to please others, to be loved or accepted, or to avoid pain. When overdone, it causes a person to lose a sense of identity, self-esteem (since no one is accepted without having to adapt), and the incentive to utilize his or her full potential.

5. *Little Professor.* The Little Professor is innately intuitive, cunning, manipulative, and wise in a childlike, unschooled, and basically self-centered way. The Little Professor in you reads nonverbal responses, sizes up people and situations, and intuitively responds to his or her best advantage. A major controversy exists over the inclusion of the Little Professor. Some TA experts include it; others leave it out; others say that it is part of the Adapted Child; and others feel that it belongs to a different construct altogether.

For use in organizations, we have chosen to drop the Adapted Child and Little Professor and include the Natural Child, the Rebellious Child, and the Compliant Child. Rebellious Child and Compliant Child responses are usually learned responses that are used with certain people to get your way because they work. Little Professor activities could also be Natural Child responses—innocent and intuitive. Thus, Rebellious and Compliant behaviors are not always Adapted, and Little Professor activities may be Natural, Rebellious, or Compliant.

The Integrated Adult

A person operating from the Adult without integrating appropriate Parent and Child ego states would act like an unemotional, computerlike robot. The goal of the Integrated Adult is to develop a healthy personality with an "I'm OK–You're OK" attitude that has learned to develop and integrate Adult, Nurturing Parent, Natural Child, and, when appropriate, Compliant Child behaviors. The major functions of the Integrated Adult are:

1. To develop an integrated balance between the ego states by objectively *editing out* inappropriate responses from the Critical Parent, Rebellious Child, and the overused Compliant Child, and by *editing in* or learning appropriate responses from the Nurturing Parent, Adult, Natural Child, and Compliant Child.
2. To learn to *think before acting.* An Integrated Adult can learn to *deal* with inappropriate ego states before they come out, *catch* them when they come out and improve an interaction while it is in process, or *learn* from inappropriate interaction after the fact. An Integrated Adult can also learn to choose when to use each ego state. The goal is to build good interaction habits so that interactions will become increasingly effortless and spontaneous.
3. To monitor internal as well as external interactions and feelings. For example, a person may wish to ask a question, but his Critical Parent, unless monitored by his Adult, may tell him, "Don't ask a question, you may appear stupid." We carry on many conversations in our head, and these conversations also need to be monitored by the Adult. The Adult can also learn to monitor feelings so that they can be identified and dealt with or expressed in constructive ways.
4. To recognize and eliminate Adult contamination. Contamination occurs when Adult thinking is influenced by internalized Parent or Child messages or "tapes." For example, a person operating from the Adult may hold Parent prejudices and biases that cause him or her to discriminate "rationally." An extreme example is the

Nazis' "logical" persecution of the Jews during World War II. They rationally carried out irrational orders. Child contamination can occur, for example, when unfounded fears or an inaccurate self-image (being told we are stupid when we are not, for instance) are internalized and prevent us from utilizing our full potential because our Adult assumes that these perceptions are accurate (see Figure 6.5).

5. To develop constructive, well-based *values* and *thinking processes.* This function of the Integrated Adult is extremely important! The amoral Adult, or an Adult with continuously fluctuating values, can be dangerous to himself or herself and others and will have difficulty making choices involving values. Since the way we think about things determines what we see, it is also important to develop thinking patterns that enable us to see the world objectively and constructively.

Major TA Principles

Some of the major principles of TA are summarized as follows:

1. Perhaps the most important TA concept is the notion that interactions are most productive when conducted from an "I'm OK–You're OK" position. Another way of saying the same thing is "Love your neighbor as yourself" or "Do unto others as you would have them do unto you." These principles sum up all of the TA concepts because an "I'm OK–You're OK" position produces, with few exceptions, openness, honesty, a willingness to confront and solve problems constructively, and the freedom to be oneself and grow. Interaction problems usually develop when a person interacts from an "I'm OK–You're Not OK," "I'm Not OK–You're OK," or "I'm Not OK–You're Not OK" position.

2. The most effective ego states to interact from are the Adult (objective), the Nurturing Parent (understanding), and the Natural Child (uninhibited). The most ineffective ego states are the Critical Parent (judgmental), the Rebellious Child (uncooperative), and the Compliant Child (passive) when it is overused. Interactions from the

Figure 6.5 Adult contamination.

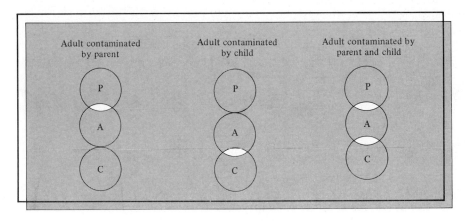

Adult contaminated by parent   Adult contaminated by child   Adult contaminated by parent and child

P

A

C

Critical Parent or Rebellious Child generate responses of defensiveness, anger, compliance, resentment, and "Not OK" feelings and will usually trigger an inappropriate response.

3. *Stamp collecting* is a phrase borrowed from the practice of collecting trading stamps when making purchases and redeeming them later for merchandise. People tend to collect psychological trading stamps, feelings they have about themselves. When they have enough stamps (feelings), they cash them in for a psychological prize. Good feelings are called gold stamps and bad feelings brown stamps. Gold stamps are collected to support an "I'm OK" view of yourself and can be very valuable if you need to cash them in at a time when you are discouraged. Brown stamps are collected to support a "Not OK" view of yourself and almost always have a destructive outcome when they are cashed in.

    People play a lot of games to collect the kinds of stamps they are after. For example, a person can collect brown stamps to support a "Not OK" view of himself or herself by playing such games as "I'm stupid," "See what you made me do," "Uproar," or "Ain't everything awful" to get negative feelings, which will eventually be cashed in by blaming others, getting violent, exploding in anger, copping out, getting even, or the like.

4. *Hooking* is a concept used to describe a transaction in which one person "hooks" an ego state of another person. For example, Critical Parent transactions will tend to hook the Critical Parent, Rebellious Child, or Compliant Child in another person and result in problems. Adult transactions will tend to hook the Adult in others. It is important to learn to hook *effective* ego states in others and learn to avoid getting hooked into ineffective ego states of your own.

5. *Life scripts* are recurring patterns of behavior that people and organizations follow and continue to follow with only minor deviations unless the scripts are changed. Typical scripts are "Leader," "Follower," "Martyr," "Success," "Failure," "Turn Misfortunes to Advantages," and "Create Problems." Once the patterns are identified, it is usually possible to reinforce the good parts of the script, eliminate unproductive parts, and add new parts. In other words, scripts are changeable!

6. *Games* occur when one or more persons involved in a conversation or activity are not straight with each other and use indirect means to get their needs met. People play games to support their life positions ("I'm OK—You're Not OK," etc.), to get strokes (see next paragraph), or because conditions (closed communications, lack of trust and openness, fear, etc.) encourage game playing. Games tend to result in wasted time, bad feelings, lower productivity, backstabbing, lack of trust, confusion, and misunderstandings. The fact is that game playing is manipulative and dishonest! Games can be stopped or minimized by the same procedures used for dealing with discounts.

7. *Strokes* are units of attention or recognition, and they are a matter of survival. Strokes are so important to our needs that in the absence of *positive strokes* (compliments, smiles, etc.) people will seek *negative strokes* (severe criticism, frowns, etc.) rather than try to exist in an environment where they get no strokes at all. When people are acting in ineffective ways, it is often the result of not getting

enough positive strokes or getting too many negative strokes. Positive strokes make people feel OK and help them grow and develop. Negative strokes make people feel not OK and tend to inhibit growth. Strokes can be conditional, unconditional, genuine, or plastic. Conditional strokes have strings attached while unconditional strokes are free. Genuine strokes are sincere, and plastic strokes are insincere and can be very misleading. The best strokes are positive, unconditional, sincere strokes. They could very well be the most effective way to motivate people and help them change, grow, and improve! Some people seem to feel that they were born with 100 positive strokes for use during their lifetime, and they give them out sparingly so they won't run out! If you operate this way, your Adult is contaminated, because the truth is that we have an unlimited supply of strokes to give out. We encourage you to start giving them away right now!

TA Guidelines

Some guidelines for applying TA effectively are:

1. Avoid using TA buzzwords on people unless they are familiar with the field and find it helpful to use TA terminology. The best way to turn someone off on transactional analysis is to barrage them with a lot of TA buzzwords.
2. TA is best used to monitor your own behavior rather than to psychoanalyze everyone else's behavior.
3. TA becomes *misused* when: (1) It is used as a technical tool to give a detailed analysis of which ego state a person is transacting from (sometimes ego states look very similar, but it really doesn't matter if you can accurately diagnose the ego state as long as you know if it is appropriate or inappropriate); (2) a person becomes overly conscious of his or her behavior; or (3) a person uses this increased awareness to become resentful of past influences.
4. In understanding a transaction, it is the message that is *received* that is important, not the specific words or nonverbal communication used. If a person received a message as a Critical Parent message, it doesn't matter if you insist that it was an Adult message.
5. TA is also useful for analyzing company policies and procedures, leadership styles, written communications, meetings, employee manuals, organizational structure, recurring patterns of behavior, and any form of formal communication.
6. Focus on creating "I'm OK–You're OK" communications, on being willing to give away positive strokes, and on developing constructive values as a sound basis for making adult decisions, and you are likely to be very successful at interpersonal communication.

ASSERTIVENESS WITH CARING: A COMMUNICATION SKILL FOR EXPRESSING YOUR NEEDS

The general manager of one of Digital Electronic Corporation's largest facilities declared, "Assertiveness training is the most important behavioral skill breakthrough that we have had in the last decade!" Assertiveness is a skill in expressing ideas, opinions, feelings, and needs in a constructive, genuine, and authoritative way. For supervisors and managers, assertiveness training can significantly increase their ability to get things accomplished upward, downward, and with peers without playing games or tiptoeing around issues.

Originally, assertiveness training was designed for women on their way up who were faced with the dilemma of coming from a culture that rewarded them for being passive, manipulative, and nonaggressive while having to compete in a primarily male-oriented culture that rewards aggressiveness and self-actualization. Today, how-ever, assertiveness training is recognized as a people skill for both men and women who would like to be more successful in getting their needs met.

We call our approach to assertiveness training "assertiveness with caring" to describe a constructive approach to assertiveness training that avoids misuse. Some people use assertiveness training as a license for becoming selfish, insensitive, and demanding or for insisting on their rights and venting hostile feelings without having to be responsible for the consequences on others. Some assertiveness training encour-ages this kind of thinking by starting the training with a "bill of rights." While the intent is good, the bill-of-rights approach tends to encourage people to think that the world owes them something and that it is their job to get what is theirs. With this attitude, they become takers in life rather than givers. On the other hand, you can learn to be assertive in a caring way that significantly increases your probability of getting your needs met without having to carry a bill of rights or becoming insensitive to others.

Advantages of Assertiveness

If you have not been assertive in the past, being assertive will seem awkward at first. However, with practice it will become increasingly comfortable, and you will be sur-prised and even amazed at how many needs you can meet. Some of the things that you should be able to do as you become more assertive are:

1. Increase the probability that you will be able to get your needs met by being able to express them without beating around the bush or feeling intimidated.
2. Express your feelings and opinions, whether they are positive or negative, in a constructive way.
3. Give and receive compliments or constructive criticism. This is especially important to supervisors and managers.
4. Acknowledge and solve problems that you have been living with because you were afraid to bring them up.
5. Give yourself permission to communicate openly with authority figures (bosses, parents, doctors, etc.) without being intimidated.
6. Learn to say *no* without being offensive.
7. Learn to be persistent without being obnoxious.
8. Give yourself permission to ask questions or ask for clarification.

Learning to Be Assertive

In learning assertiveness with caring, you need to: (1) develop an awareness of when you are being aggressive, manipulative, passive, or assertive, and then (2) practice being assertive and learn to weed out inappropriate aggressive, manipulative, or passive behaviors.

Most people use all these behaviors at different times. However, aggressive, manipulative, and passive behaviors tend to be self-defeating (Figure 6.6 discusses the definition, characteristics, and typical consequences of each behavior). They are self-defeating because they have the potential to alienate people, to undermine trust and credibility, and even to damage one's own self-worth by knowing that devious rather than straightforward methods must be used to meet one's needs. The dilemma that people often fall victim to is that because aggressive, manipulative, and passive behaviors may be effective in getting needs met, they are presumed to be appropriate.

Aggressive Behavior

People are being aggressive when they take care of their needs, feelings, and rights by forcefully doing things their way no matter what the costs. People that operate primarily from an aggressive position tend to be demanding, pushy, and domineering and often try to intimidate and manipulate people. Some of the internal symptoms of aggressive behavior are feelings of hostility, a high need to control others, insecurity, selfishness, and a win-lose attitude. Some aggressive behaviors are simply learned behaviors that are not motivated by ulterior motives. The consequences of aggressive behaviors are that they alienate people and undermine the ability to relate to people openly and affectionately.

Manipulative Behavior

People are being manipulative when they take care of their needs, feelings, and rights by being indirect, cunning, and crafty. People who operate primarily from a manipulative position tend to play games, drop hints, hide their real feelings and intentions, try to maneuver people to do what they want them to, tell half-truths and lies if it is to their advantage, give or withhold affection and attention in order to control others, use emotions such as pouting or looking hurt to achieve their goals, send double messages, and, in general, do most things with an ulterior motive. Some of the external symptoms of manipulative behavior are being temperamental, distrusting others (since they know they can't be trusted), being slightly out of touch with one's real feelings (the ability to turn feelings on and off to get their way causes manipulative people to lose touch with their real feelings), being insecure though one may try to appear highly self-confident, feeling unloved, and getting defensive to avoid exposing one's games. Many of these behaviors are simply learned behaviors. Nevertheless, they are basically dishonest and self-defeating, even though it is often true that "everyone else uses them." They are self-defeating because they undermine credibility along with self-image. You

Figure 6.6 Assertiveness model.

Definitions	Characteristics		Major Consequences
Aggressive Behavior Needs and wants are taken care of in a forceful and self-serving way.	Self-serving Demanding Dogmatic Competitive Pushy Use intimidation, power, and status	Insensitive Strong need to control and dominate others Fear rejection Impatient Temperamental	May accomplish personal desires and goals but tends to alienate people, create distrust and tension, and undermine the ability to establish lasting and healthy relationships
Manipulative Behavior Needs and wants are taken care of in an indirect, cunning, deceptive, and crafty way with ulterior motives in mind.	Game player (use pouting, looking hurt, silence, dropping hints, flirting, giving or withholding attention or caring, and other indirect methods to maneuver people) Use double messages (say one thing and mean another) Hide real feelings and intentions	Inward feelings and outward expressions often incongruent Rebellious Get defensive and angry when caught manipulating Strong need for approval and attention Insecure but wear facade Distrust others	May be successful in maneuvering others in indirect ways, but also undermines credibility and trust and causes self to lose touch with real self and real feelings
Passive Behavior Needs and wants are taken care of by suppressing them or maneuvering others to take care of them. Passive people use manipulative behaviors in getting others to take care of them.	Deny needs, subordinate them to others, or manipulate others to take care of them Often play martyr role Create conditions in which others will take the lead or make decisions Follower Try to do what they think others expect of them	Lack self-confidence Easily intimidated and controlled by others Indecisive Moody Occasionally cash in on stored-up anger and feelings Uncertain about who they are	May result in some needs getting met but often results in sacrificing needs, getting them met in inappropriate ways, and the loss of identity and ability to take care of self
Assertive Behavior Needs and wants are taken care of by knowing, accepting, and acting on them in constructive, straightforward, and authentic ways.	Caring Genuine Sensitive to the needs and feelings of others Unselfish Express needs and feelings in constructive and straightforward ways Persistent without being offensive	Level and confront from caring and reasonable position Good sense of timing and judgment about when to assert themselves Self-confident Calm in a crisis	Able to know and take care of needs in a constructive way without doing so at the expense of others

never know when to trust or believe manipulative people; even when they are telling the truth, you doubt their intentions. This is self-defeating for the manipulators because they have to manipulate their own feelings to be able to feel good about being deceptive and using people, and that makes it difficult for them and for others to know who they really are. Excessive manipulative behavior can cause one to gradually become more and more out of touch with reality, since one begins to lose track of which stories are true and which are not.

Passive Behavior

People are being passive when they take care of their needs by suppressing them or getting someone else to take care of them. When operating primarily from this position, people tend to deny, hide, or distort feelings, subordinate important needs to the needs of others, and create conditions in which they can be followers and let others take care of them and make decisions for them. Some external symptoms of being passive are a martyr complex, depression, nervous habits such as nail biting, overeating, heavy smoking, excessive drinking or the use of drugs, frequent headaches and illnesses, insomnia, and a lack of self-confidence. If passive people's solution for taking care of their needs is to get other people to take care of them, they may be reasonably successful in getting their needs met. However, the major consequences are that they become increasingly helpless when left on their own, and they sometimes learn to be devious in getting others to take care of them. Suppression has greater consequences as it pushes more and more needs into the subconscious, where they are not dealt with rationally. People who suppress needs don't get rid of them. The suppressed needs that have been building up may be cashed in on an innocent victim who just happened to be present at the wrong time! A boss, for instance, may cash in on an employee who makes an innocent mistake because of problems at home that have been building up. The biggest cost of passive behavior is the possibility of sacrificing not only one's needs but also one's identity, since the passive person becomes a combination of everyone else's expectations and may not be sure who he or she really is.

Assertive Behavior

People are being assertive with caring when they know, accept, and act on their needs with an "I'm OK–You're OK" attitude. When people operate primarily from this position, they know themselves and their needs well and are willing to express them and take care of them in caring, genuine, straightforward, and constructive ways. Interestingly enough, by taking responsibility for getting their needs met in constructive ways, they are very efficient in meeting their needs and are therefore not preoccupied with the fulfillment of personal needs. Also, since most of their needs are fairly well satisfied, they have more time to devote to others and to concentrate on productive activities. Some of the external symptoms of assertiveness are self-confidence, a good self-image, a relaxed and gentle manner, and a genuinely caring attitude. The greatest benefit is that needs can be met in constructive ways that are not at the expense of others.

Behavior Combinations

While most people will have a predominant behavioral profile, they may also react from a combination of characteristics. For example, their pattern may be some combination of aggressive, manipulative, passive, and assertive behaviors. A typical pattern might be passive-aggressive behaviors, where a person switches from getting their needs met in passive ways to becoming very aggressive.

Assertiveness Principles

Learning to be assertive will probably be awkward at first, but with practice it will become more and more natural. Some principles that will help you become assertive are:

1. You need to know yourself and your needs and to develop a positive self-image that allows you to be assertive. Asserting yourself from a negative self-image or when you aren't sure who you are or what you want by misreading your needs can produce behaviors that appear phony and lack authority.
2. Be selective about which needs or opinions you assert yourself about. You could make assertiveness a full-time, nonproductive occupation if you assert yourself for *every* need and opinion you have!
3. Learn to feel and to express your feelings in constructive ways. With practice, you can learn to express happiness, pain, affection, anger, and other emotions. It is sometimes a helpful exercise to write down or try to communicate to someone what different emotions feel like as they develop inside you. Then practice different alternatives for expressing your feelings in constructive ways that help you deal with your feelings without putting others on the defensive.
4. Learn to ask for what you want without beating around the bush. You will be amazed how often you can get your needs met simply by asking for what you want or by telling people what you need or how you feel.
5. Realize that persistence significantly increases your probability of need satisfaction. Avoid being obnoxious and gently and kindly persist by attacking the issue and not another person and by continuing to focus on the problem without getting side-tracked.
6. Practice confronting and leveling with people from a position of caring without having a need to judge them or put them down for their behaviors or views.
7. Make assertiveness a two-way street. When asserting yourself, also listen to the needs of others and be willing to make adjustments if new information or understanding warrants it.
8. Lead a life worthy of assertiveness. A person's ability to be assertive has a great deal to do with his or her life-style. A respected life-style makes you feel good about

yourself, helps you speak with authority, and increases your credibility. On the other hand, a questionable life-style undermines your self-image, your authority, and your credibility.

Guidelines in Applying Assertiveness

Feeling natural being assertive comes with developing an awareness of assertive and nonassertive behaviors and practicing the assertiveness principles. In becoming an assertive person, considering the following guidelines may be helpful:

1. Integrate your assertiveness into yourself. Trying to express your assertiveness like someone else, in the way you think an assertive person should be, will come across phony. Assertive people come in all sizes, shapes, and personalities. Some are quiet, some are extroverts, some are leaders, and some are followers. What they have in common is that they are able to express and take care of their needs in straightforward and constructive ways.
2. Part of being assertive is developing the maturity to use good judgment in choosing when to assert yourself and when not to assert yourself.
3. In becoming more assertive, invest your energy and time in practicing assertiveness rather than in analyzing why you are not more assertive or in feeling guilty every time you make a mistake in your efforts to become more assertive.
4. As much as possible, be prepared with sound and logical information and facts and believe in what you are doing when asserting yourself so you can speak with authority.
5. Recognize that assertiveness is a result of the total message—attitude, words, body language, appearance, backgrounds of the communicators, expectations of the communicators, and setting.
6. Practice staying in charge of your emotions and in constructively managing the stress and fear sometimes associated with being assertive. It may help to try to identify the source of your anxiety and fears so you can deal with them rationally; or try to put them into proper perspective, since few of our fears ever come true; or try to express what you are feeling as part of being assertive. For example, you may want to say something like, "It scares me to death to bring up this subject, but I would be doing both of us a disservice if I didn't."
7. If you change overnight without letting anyone know what you are up to, you will frighten people! Let the people you are close to know what you are trying to learn and assure them that you have no intentions of learning and growing at their expense.

HANDLING COMMUNICATION BREAKDOWNS

A communication breakdown occurs when one or more persons in an interaction ceases to communicate. Communication breakdowns can be the result of misunderstanding, personal communication barriers, or an unwillingness to cooperate and solve problems in a mature and constructive manner. Communication breakdowns can be minimized by the use of the communication skills previously mentioned. However, when they do occur, supervisors need to be prepared to deal with them. Most breakdowns can, in fact, be overcome if supervisors learn to be aware of the type of situation they are dealing with and are equipped with the appropriate skills to handle the breakdowns. To repair a communication breakdown, you must be able to deal with three kinds of personalities: the problem solvers, the resisters, and the hard-core resisters. The two basic skills that can be used in overcoming communication breakdowns are problem-solving skills and conflict-resolution skills.

Problem Solvers

Problem solvers are reasonable, fair, and rational people whose primary emphasis is on solving, not making, problems regardless of who or what caused the problem or where the fault lies. If a communication breakdown is made known to them, they are eager to seek a resolution. Thus, when communication breakdowns occur with problem solvers, it can be rectified by making known the problem and using problem-solving skills to achieve resolution.

A variety of approaches to problem solving can be used. What is important is for supervisors to develop a problem-solving strategy so that problem solving will become a natural part of their supervisory behavior. A possible problem-solving strategy would be the following:

1. Whenever possible, prepare yourself for problem solving by clearing your mind of any anger, contempt, or resentment, developing a problem-solving attitude with a sincere desire to be helpful and cooperative, and by doing any homework necessary for problem solving.
2. Express your sincere desire to resolve any problems.
3. Try to define the problem by sharing your perceptions and listening to and trying to understand the perceptions and feelings of whomever you are communicating with.
4. Discuss any relevant information by attacking problems and not people; identifying and sticking to the key issues without getting sidetracked; sharing information in a caring and accurate way without arguing, exaggerating, or being critical or judgmental; and checking perceptions of what is being said, heard, and felt.
5. Explore constructive alternatives given the realities of the situation without forcing or demanding a particular alternative and then evaluate the advantages, disadvantages, and possible consequences of each alternative.
6. Agree on the best alternative and on any actions to be taken.

Resisters

Resisters are people who give you a difficult time when you try to solve problems with them. They may be angry or resentful over the communication breakdown and therefore resort to resisting your efforts. They may also be resisting because resisting has become a learned behavior—a habitual response. Resistance can also result from being misinformed, from not being kept informed, or from fears (that they might be mistreated, manipulated, taken advantage of, etc.). Resistance may or may not be justified. Either way, it is a deterrent to communication.

In most cases, resistance can be overcome with persistent problem solving. Therefore, the first procedure with a resister is to persistently follow the problem-solving strategy suggested for dealing with problem solvers. If a problem-solving strategy does not work, other alternatives are:

1. Agree on guidelines or ground rules for discussing and resolving problems. For example, you may want to agree on what you would ideally like to accomplish, to stick to the subject, to attack problems and not each other, to confront sidetracking or put-downs, and to agree on how to disagree.
2. If resistance continues, you may want to confront what you see happening or level about how you are feeling about the resistance. Sometimes people continue resisting because no one holds them accountable for the consequences of their resistance.
3. Listen to the resister, try to understand his or her position, and, if necessary, let the resister blow off steam in the hope that he or she will calm down and be willing to solve problems once he or she is understood. A good listener learns to listen without having to agree and without empathizing so much that listening provides reinforcement for inappropriate responses or choices.
4. Remove any payoffs for resistance by *not* playing the complimentary hand and responding to discounts or game playing such as put-downs, pouting, or intimidation. You are playing the complimentary hand when you play into the discounts of the other party by getting defensive, striking back, or losing control.
5. If double messages (incongruent verbal and nonverbal messages) are sent, probe for the real meaning without relying on mind reading. If the double messages continue, respond to the verbal message to avoid rewarding manipulation.
6. If another person gets upset or angry, allow the person to calm down without overreacting to or calling attention to his or her actions. If the person begins to cry, offer some Kleenex or ask if he or she would like some time to be alone before continuing.
7. If resolution has still not been achieved, express your frustration with what is happening, suggest that you have run out of options, and ask for suggestions on how to proceed or how you could successfully communicate with the other person.

Hard-Core Resisters

It is important to realize that while you can substantially increase the probability of being able to communicate successfully and of being able to overcome resistance, there will be a few situations in which communication is impossible. This occurs when one or more persons in the interaction become "hard-core resisters" and in essence refuse to communicate. They may resist through making you, someone else, or something else responsible for their behavior, or through silence, rebellion, rationalization, anger, stubbornness, the need to be right, twisting meanings or nitpicking at words, game playing, power plays, or developing a win-lose attitude. They may even sound like they are trying to be cooperative. However, the long-run pattern is that they make sure that nothing that you try will work and that the responsibility for problems does not rest on their shoulders. If you are not aware that you are dealing with a hard-core resister, you will try to work the problem out rationally, and it won't work, because at that point in time you are trying to deal rationally with an irrational situation. The hard-core resister will use irrational logic by twisting facts and using inaccurate or contrived information to turn the tables on you and make you think that you are wrong and he or she is right. You will probably leave the interaction confused and feeling that you are at fault for the problem or for the resister's problems.

You can recognize hard-core resisters by observing some of the following patterns of behavior:

1. They make others or circumstances responsible for their behaviors, feelings, and choices.
2. They make sure that all your efforts to solve problems will fail. They may confuse you by sounding logical or occasionally throwing in a "lunch trick." The lunch trick is a technique used to throw people off guard by *occasionally* taking them to lunch and telling them how great they are, being willing to cooperate on a minor issue, or doing something nice for them.
3. They will tend to have double standards, according to which they expect others to do all the things that they refuse to do.
4. Change is almost always based on what someone else can do. Rarely do hard-core resisters accept responsibility for making changes themselves. If others fulfill all the changes requested of them, hard-core resisters will find fault with the changes or provide a new list.

Rather than resent people when they get into a hard-core resister position, we need to try to understand what is happening. When any of us is unwilling to be responsible for our behavior, it creates an inner tension that we tend to deal with by *suppressing* problems or *projecting* them onto others or circumstances. The latter is what usually happens when you are trying to communicate with hard-core resisters. Rather than accept responsibility for their behavior, they project their problems onto you and make you feel guilty and responsible for their problems. By attributing their problems to you or circumstances, they feel justified in their actions and relieved that they have escaped having to be responsible for their inappropriate behaviors.

Although getting hard-core resisters out of their position so they can communicate is very difficult, here are a few constructive things that you can try:

1. Try to use the suggestions offered for dealing with problem solvers and resisters. If it becomes clear that they will not work, move to step 2 below.
2. Confront the patterns of behavior that you see kindly and in a nonjudgmental way. Use specific examples as much as possible, and try to get the hard-core resister to agree to some guidelines for communicating.

3. Offer to resolve any part of the problem over which you have control and coach the person to take responsibility for what he or she can do. You are likely to meet resistance at this point because a hard-core resister will try to manipulate or rationalize his or her way out of being responsible.

4. If the other person is rebelling, being belligerent, or getting angry, *do not* argue or respond to his or her discounts. Instead, try to get the person into the Adult ego state by sticking to the issues and being rational, objective, and calm. If this does not work, it may be best to explain that the conversation is going nowhere and end the interaction. It is sometimes helpful to agree on another time to continue the interaction or to offer to continue whenever the other person is willing to focus on the issues and work toward resolution.

5. If you are in an authoritative position, as in a supervisor-to-employee relationship, it may be best at this point to take charge. Explain that the other person may not agree with you or your perceptions, but that since you have been placed in a supervisory position, your best judgment is going to take precedence. Options could be to explain what you are willing to do, tell the person what he or she must do, and establish consequences for being unwilling to cooperate. Reasonable consequences for not cooperating could be taking disciplinary action or laying down specific changes that must be made in a specified time period or risk being "let go." The required changes should include attitudinal as well as behavioral changes; otherwise, the resister may change to meet your conditions but still defy you in attitude. Hard-core resisters take their toll on any relationship. At work, they should not be kept if they manage to escape all responsibility for change.

6. Another alternative is to bring in an objective and fair third person to arbitrate or provide counsel in an attempt to resolve differences. A hard-core resister will often become reasonable and cooperative with a third person present. In a one-to-one interaction, a hard-core resister can resist and then deny it if confronted. However, with two other persons present, the resister's credibility would be questioned if he or she tried to deny the inappropriate behaviors under discussion. The disadvantage of this approach is that a hard-core resister may use it as an opportunity to appear cooperative and then later continue in his or her usual practices.

7. If at this stage resolution has still not been achieved and continued contact is necessary or desirable, several alternatives are available:

    a. Determine to do the best you can to take care of your part of any problems even though this is not likely to cause any change in the situation. This choice is primarily for your own benefit so that you will have peace of mind and not become bitter or resentful and become a hard-core resister yourself. There is also a possibility that your persistent willingness to solve problems will eventually win over a hard-core resister.

    b. Try not to personalize guilt messages and manipulative efforts directed at you by a hard-core resister. Attempt to sort out legitimate from unfounded statements or requests and realize that making you responsible is the resister's way of avoiding responsibility.

    c. Consider minimizing contact.

     d. Try to view the situation as an opportunity for sharpening your communication and problem-solving skills and for remaining strong and healthy under very difficult circumstances.

SUMMARY

Our ability to communicate is perhaps our most important skill as human beings. This skill will play a major role in our success as people and as supervisors. We can improve our ability to communicate by learning to understand the communication process, by tuning in to the verbal and nonverbal components of the messages being sent and received, and by minimizing communication barriers and increasing the use of communication facilitators.

     A communication skill that can be used to increase one's ability to express ideas, requests, feelings, and needs in a constructive way is assertiveness with caring. Assertiveness, when used constructively and unselfishly, can significantly increase a supervisor's ability to communicate and get results. Another communication skill that can be used to improve communication is transactional analysis. TA is best used as an awareness tool to monitor one's own communication skills and behavior, not to analyze others.

     Communication breakdowns are inevitable but can usually be managed with the appropriate skills. When communication breakdowns occur, a supervisor should determine if he or she is dealing with a problem solver, a resister, or a hard-core resister. The type of person one is dealing with will determine if problem-solving or conflict-resolution skills are most appropriate.

IMPORTANT TERMS

communication process	strokes
communication message	game playing
communication barriers	assertiveness
communication facilitators	aggressiveness
transactional analysis (TA)	passiveness
Critical Parent	manipulation
Nurturing Parent	problem solver
Adult	resister
Natural Child	hard-core resister
Rebellious Child	problem-solving skills
Compliant Child	conflict-resolution skills
Integrated Adult	

REVIEW QUESTIONS

1. What are the major components of the communication process?
2. What are the major components of the message? Which is the most important? Why?

3. Why are communication barriers self-defeating? What are some of the major communication barriers?

4. Why do communication facilitators increase the probability of communication and decrease the probability of receiving an inappropriate message?

5. What are aggressive, passive, manipulative, and assertive behaviors and what are their typical consequences? How can supervisors use assertiveness training?

6. How can transactional analysis be used by supervisors?

7. In dealing with communication breakdowns, what do the terms *problem solver, resister,* and *hard-core resister* mean? How would you respond to each?

EXERCISES

6.1   Understanding the Message

Evaluate yourself in terms of the positive and negative messages that you send by making notes on each of the items listed below. Allow for the possibility that you may send different messages in different settings.

>   Attitude
>   Words
>   Body language
>   Appearance
>   Background
>   Expectations you have of yourself
>   Expectations others have of you
>   Settings

If you have some friends whose judgment you value and who would be honest with you, you may want to ask for their impressions on each item. Based on what you learned, would you like to make any changes? This exercise would be a good one to debrief in small groups if the group members know each other fairly well. Each member simply discusses what he or she learned and if he or she plans to make any changes.

6.2   Communication Barriers and Facilitators

Six to 10 volunteers choose a discussion topic and have an actual meeting during which they try to reach some specific conclusions. However, half of the volunteers should concentrate on using communication barriers and half on using communication facilitators. (Each volunteer can draw a piece of paper that states whether to use barriers or facilitators.) The volunteers hold their meeting in front of the class, which is to make notes on the barriers and facilitators that they observe and their consequences. Figures 4.2 and 4.3 should be used in making notes and can also be reviewed by the role players before starting the meeting. The group has 15 minutes to conduct their meeting. They should begin by choosing a group leader and a topic followed by a discussion to try to reach some specific conclusions regarding the topic.

Following the meeting, the class should discuss the barriers and facilitators that each person in the meeting used and their consequences. Before ending the exercise, the role players might give their own observations of the meeting.

6.3 Evaluating Your Communication Barriers and Facilitators

Each class member should use Figures 4.2 and 4.3 to evaluate the communication barriers and facilitators they use by checking the appropriate ones and adding any relevant ones that are not on the list. Then they should write a paragraph on the typical consequences they are aware of when they use barriers and a paragraph on the consequences when they use facilitators. If the class members meet regularly in groups and know each other fairly well, they could also meet with their group to share some of their individual barriers and facilitators and their consequences and solicit feedback from the group.

6.4 Demonstrating Ego States

The class should break into small groups, and each group develops two or more role-playing situations that illustrate successful and unsuccessful interactions between ego states. For example, if there are six groups, each group could be assigned one of the six ego states (Critical Parent, Nurturing Parent, Adult, Natural Child, Rebellious Child, and Compliant Child) and have them develop one role-playing situation in which the ego state was used inappropriately and a second role-playing situation in which the Integrated Adult is able to get a person or group out of the inappropriate ego state assigned to the group. For example, the first situation could show a supervisor interacting with an employee from his or her Critical Parent about a mistake that the employee has made. The second situation could show two people trying to solve a problem in which one is interacting from a Critical Parent position and the other from an Integrated Adult until the Critical Parent person finally also gets into his or her Adult.

The groups should have about 10 minutes to prepare their role-playing situations (not everyone in the groups needs to be a role player). They should then meet together as a class and take turns presenting their situations. Using actual experiences may be a convenient way to choose the role-playing situations. Each role-playing situation should last approximately two to five minutes. Following each situation, the class should be asked to discuss what they observed by focusing on the following questions:

1. What ego states did you see in the interaction? (Include observations on all persons involved.)
2. What were the consequences of interacting from the ego states that you observed?

6.5 Applying Transactional Analysis

Complete the information requested below. It may also be helpful to discuss your observations with a few other people who know you well and ask for their observations.

Ego States	Sub-categories	Me Now (describe yourself.)	Edit Out (List things you would like to edit out.	Edit In (List things you would like to edit in.)	Ideal Self (Describe the way you would ideally like to be.)
Parent	Critical Parent				
	Nurturing Parent				
Adult					
Child	Natural Child				
	Compliant Child				
	Rebellious Child				

Estimate the % of you that occupies each ego state:

Parent	Critical Parent	_____
	Nurturing Parent	_____
Adult	Adult	_____
Child	Natural Child	_____
	Compliant Child	_____
	Rebellious Child	_____
Total		100%

6.6   Giving and Receiving Positive Strokes

This is a strength-building exercise that teaches people how to give and receive strokes. Meet in small groups with people you know. Start with one person and have the other group members "spontaneously" call off anything they like about the person (strengths, skills, talents, interpersonal skills, etc.). Do not take turns calling off strengths—do it spontaneously and genuinely and focus on one person at a time. The person receiving the strokes should write them down. The exercise takes about two or three minutes for each person. Don't miss this one!

6.7   Learning to Be Assertive

Break into small groups and have a person volunteer to describe briefly a situation in which he or she would like to be assertive. Then have the group explore ways in which a person would approach the situation from aggressive, manipulative, passive, and assertive positions. Choose only situations that are very important to you. Go through the same procedure for each person in the group. If time permits, the group can continue with additional situations. The purpose of the exercise is to help people learn specific alternatives for being assertive in situations important to them.

SUGGESTED ADDITIONAL READINGS

Berne, Eric. *Games People Play.* New York: Grove Press, 1964.

Bower, Sharon Anthony, and Bower, Gordon. *Asserting Your Self.* Reading, MA: Addison-Wesley, 1976.

Faurnies, Ferdinand F. *Coaching for Improved Work Performance.* New York: Van Nostrand Reinhold, 1978.

Fisher, Dalmar, *Communications in Organizations,* St. Paul, Minn.: West Publishing Co., 1981.

Harris, Thomas A. *I'm OK—You're OK.* New York: Avon Books, 1967.

James, Muriel. *The OK Boss.* Reading, MA: Addison-Wesley, 1975.

Level, Dale A., Jr., and Galle, William P., Jr., *Business Communications: Theory and Practice.* Dallas: Business Publications, Inc., 1980.

Rendero, Thomasine. *Communicating with Subordinates.* New York: AMACOM, 1974.

Villere, Maurice, *Transactional Analysis At Work,* Englewood Cliffs, N.J.: Prentice-Hall Inc., 1981.

Wagner, Abe. *The Transactional Manager.* Englewood Cliffs, NJ: Prentice-Hall, 1981.

Wenburg, John R., and Wilmot, William W., *The Personal Communication Process.* New York: John Wiley and Sons, Inc., 1973.

Wenburg, Wilmot. *The Personal Communication Process.* New York: Wiley, 1973.

7

Developing Your Personal and Supervisory Potential

People can be divided into three groups: Those who make things happen, those who watch things happen, and those who wonder what happened.

John W. Newbern

Sow a thought and reap an act,
Sow an act and reap a habit,
Sow a habit and reap a character,
Sow a character and reap a destiny.

Anonymous

God grant me the serenity to accept the things I cannot change, the courage to change the things I can, and the wisdom to know the difference.

Francis of Assisi

OBJECTIVES

This chapter provides you with the information necessary to:

1. Understand why it is so important for managers to continue growing
2. Know why a sound philosophical basis for growing is important
3. Understand the advantages of developing your potential and the reasons why more people aren't utilizing their potential
4. Understand the greatest key to growth and how you can do almost anything that you are willing to do regardless of how you got the way you are
5. Know how to understand and change your behavior
6. Know how to set worthwhile goals, evaluate the consequences of your growth, win your struggles, stay motivated, and become increasingly internally motivated
7. Substantially increase your potential!

THE EXCITING ADVENTURE OF DISCOVERING AND DEVELOPING YOUR POTENTIAL

Few people realize how much potential they have, and even fewer fully utilize their potential. The fact is that we each have capabilities far beyond what we can imagine, and we also have the potential to be unique, special, successful, and happy. Sometimes we forget just how unique and special we already are. What a marvelous creation a person is! We are equipped with 263 bones and 500 muscles enclosed in a shell of skin that serves as a life-supporting environment for millions of living microscopic inhabitants. The control center for this unique creation is a brain that contains billions of cells and working parts, that can store information equivalent to over 100 trillion words, and that is utilized to only a small fraction of what it is capable of. Add to this a life-supporting heart that beats 70 times a minute, 36,792,000 times a year, and pumps 7¾ tons of blood a day. Many other examples of our uniqueness could be given, but the point is that we are unique and we do have considerable potential!

While we each have considerable potential, choosing to develop our potential is not an easy task. It takes discipline and self-control and a willingness to learn from the mistakes and failures that come with taking the risk to be special. It is also sometimes accompanied by resistance, since, unfortunately, not everyone may want us to grow. However, the exciting adventure of discovering and developing your potential is well worth the price, and, fortunately, the victory is in the process. The willingness to grow and learn brings immediate satisfaction without having to wait for the actual accomplishment. Some of the major payoffs of responsible personal growth are:

1. You have the satisfaction and security of knowing that you did the best that you could with your unique capabilities, regardless of the expectations or reactions of others.
2. You can learn to value and accept yourself and others.
3. You can learn to control most of your circumstances, and for those you cannot

control, you can control your response by turning difficulties into opportunities and by not becoming a victim of circumstances.

4. Your personal security and self-worth will give you the freedom to go through life being a giver and not a taker and to be in a position to help others.
5. You can have a life of direction and purpose in which you learn to make things happen and do almost anything you are willing to do.
6. By accepting responsibility for your behavior and its consequences, you can be the person you are willing to be regardless of how you got the way you are or who is to be credited or blamed.
7. You can learn how to live the balanced life of a whole person mentally, emotionally, physically, and spiritually, a life with a solid foundation that is not likely to crumble under difficulties.
8. You will be able to devote your life to meaningful, constructive, self-developing activities without wasting time and energy on meaningless, unconstructive, self-defeating activities.
9. You are likely to be successful in whatever is important to you in life.
10. You have the potential to take charge of your life and turn it into an exciting adventure.

WHY SUPERVISORS NEED TO GROW

In many ways the most effective and inspiring supervisor is one who is simply a healthy, integrated, and growing person who has acquired specialized knowledge and skills in supervision. We all have tremendous potential in life if we are willing to search for it, develop it, and use it; effective supervisors have decided to go for it in life and take as many people with them as they can! They have also realized that by choosing to be in a supervisory position, they influence many other people and therefore bear some responsibility for the type of example that they make. Thus, supervisors need to grow and keep growing. Their potential for expanding their own capabilities, as well as for motivating others to reach for what is possible, is considerable.

THE IMPORTANCE OF A SUPERVISOR'S EXAMPLE

Managers are taught to lead by example, and yet, as one highly motivated employee remarked about her manager, "If we all follow his example, we haven't much to look forward to in life." Her boss was fairly typical. He worked long hours and was reasonably competent and effective. He showed flashes of creativity and exciting thinking, but more often than not played it safe. He tried to act OK and together, but most people knew that underneath his facade he was insecure and inconsistent and lacked purpose and direction in his life other than a few career goals. He was successful in terms of external trappings—money, prestige, and material possessions. However, those who knew him were aware that he was not very successful in holding his personal life together. He was slightly overweight and more than slightly out of shape, but he really didn't have time for nutritious eating and physical conditioning. He was quite good at fitting in with "the crowd." He wore the right clothes and used the right language (slightly off-color), and he could outdrink the best of them—without going too far— because he also had a religious side which he had also learned to practice without going too far so as not to be seen as too religious to be "in." The problem, though, was that it was difficult to cut through all of his roles to find the real person that we were to know and follow. It seemed that he had learned the art of making a living and faking living, but never really learned how to live.

The supervisor just portrayed may be an extreme example. Ideally, we would all like to work for a supervisor who inspires us to realize our potential and who sets a good example for us to follow. Our point is that a supervisor's example can have a significant positive or negative influence on subordinates. Therefore, it is to a supervisor's advantage to multiply his or her example in a positive way by taking responsibility for continuously learning and growing.

BEING YOUR BEST SELF

Before making a commitment to personal growth, a worthwhile goal needs to be established to channel your growth in a positive and responsible direction.[1] Otherwise, you may grow in ways that have unnecessary costs to you and others as well. Perhaps the most worthwhile goal of personal growth should be to learn to be "your best self" and to help others to do the same. Being at your best as a person and supervisor is very different from simply being yourself. Saying "That's me, you will just have to accept me as I am" is a static and self-centered process. It implies that you are going to stay the way you are and therefore others will have to adjust. Being your best self is a dynamic process based on accepting who you are, accepting responsibility for being you at your best and for the consequences of your behaviors, and for continuously growing and improving and being willing to help others grow as well. It is a no-games, no-gimmicks approach to personal growth that helps you grow in a positive and responsible way without losing your genuine concern for and responsibility toward others.

WHY AREN'T MORE PEOPLE UTILIZING THEIR POTENTIAL? ⊀

If we have so much potential and the payoffs are so great, why aren't more people utilizing their potential? Why aren't more supervisors an inspiration to their employees? Some of the reasons people don't utilize more of their potential are:

1. *Lack of awareness, knowledge, or motivation.* Some people underutilize their potential because they are unaware of the tremendous amount of potential that they possess, or they lack the knowledge of how to develop their potential, or they lack the motivation to do anything with their potential.
2. *Fear of failure.* The fear of failure is one of the primary causes of potential underutil-

[1]Len Sperry, Douglas J. Mickelson, and Phillip L. Hunsaker, *You Can Make It Happen: A Guide to Self-Actualization and Organizational Change* (Reading, MA: Addison-Wesley, 1977), p. 64.

ization. A fear of failure usually comes from a low self-image or a need to be perfect.

3. *Fear of success.* Success creates many responsibilities and expectations. What if people found out how competent you are? They would expect more. What if they found out you could improve your temperament or learn to handle problems constructively? You would have to give up many of your excuses, your defense mechanisms, and your emotional crutches. Some people may not like operating below their potential, but they prefer the security of underutilizing their potential to risking success and the responsibility that goes with it.

4. *Lack of purpose.* Without a sense of direction and purpose, people cannot hope to utilize their potential. When we lack purpose, we waste time and energy or invest our time and energy into self-defeating or unproductive activities. With a sense of purpose, people are motivated and filled with hope. Without it, life eventually loses meaning and value. Purpose comes from first looking at life on a large scale and evaluating why we are here and what we can contribute and then becomes actualized by having goals and deciding how we can best live each day.

5. *Becoming a victim of circumstances.* A victim of circumstances is a person whose life is controlled by past, present, or future circumstances. Such people have in effect made circumstances responsible for the way they are and for their life. Their life is controlled by past events, by what others expect, think, or do, by their feelings, and by the breaks of the day. By making circumstances responsible for their life, they are not in a position to develop their potential.

6. *Lack of deep roots.* People often get very enthused about utilizing more of their potential. Then they get sidetracked or run into difficulties and revert to their old habits. Why does this happen? It happens because we don't practice new behaviors long enough for them to become habits and part of our character. The parable of the sowing of the seeds explains this process very well. A farmer was sowing grain in his fields, and as he scattered the seeds, some fell beside a path and the birds ate it before it could grow. Some fell on rocky soil where there was little depth of earth, and the plants sprang up quickly in the shallow soil, but the hot sun scorched them and they withered and died because they had so little root. Other seeds fell among thorns, and the thorns choked out the tender blades. However, some of the seeds fell on good soil and produced a crop that was 30, 60, and even 100 times what had been planted. In terms of personal growth, the seeds that fell beside the path describe the person who hears about how to develop his or her potential but refuses to do anything about it. The seeds that fell on rocky soil describes the person who starts to grow but gives up as soon as difficulties occur. The seeds that fell among thorns describe the person who starts to grow but whose growth gets choked out by unhealthy relationships, a self-centered attitude, materialism, or anything that gets the person sidetracked. Lasting growth that can weather difficulties and circumstances comes only from developing new habits that are rooted deep in our character.

7. *Resistance.* The discovery that not everyone cheers when you grow and the resistance that may accompany growth may eventually wear people down and convince them to coast through life and settle for second best.

THE KEY TO GROWTH: TAKING RESPONSIBILITY FOR YOUR BEHAVIOR

Some people spend a lifetime trying to understand their past, discover who they are, and figure out why they do what they do. As the humorous song by Anna Russell suggests, this approach to growth can be a long and painful road.

> *I went to my psychiatrist*
>   *to be psychoanalyzed,*
> *To find out why I killed the cat*
>   *and blackened my wife's eyes.*
>
> *He put me on a downy couch*
>   *to see what he could find,*
> *And this is what he dredged up*
>   *from my subconscious mind:*
>
> *When I was one, my mommy*
>   *hid my dolly in the trunk,*
> *And so it follows naturally,*
>   *that I am always drunk.*
>
> *When I was two, I saw my father*
>   *kiss the maid one day,*
> *And that is why I suffer now—*
>   *from kleptomania.*
>
> *When I was three, I suffered from*
>   *ambivalence toward my brothers,*
> *So it follows naturally,*
>   *I poisoned all my lovers.*
>
> *I'm so glad that I have learned*
>   *the lesson it has taught,*
> *That everything I do that's wrong*
>   *is someone else's fault.*

Today we are so aware and have so many labels and theories for why we do what we do that it provides a perfect escape clause for those who want to be irresponsible. We can blame something or someone for almost everything we do. Accepting our behaviors and taking responsibility for them regardless of how we got the way we are is essential to change. Denying behaviors or blaming them on someone or something else, regardless of how justified we are or how valid our excuses are, makes change impossible or at best very difficult.[2] For example, if you have a bad temper and you deny it or blame your temper on your circumstances, even though you may be justified, you will still have a bad temper. However, you *can* say, "I have a bad temper and I

[2]William Glasser, *Reality Therapy: A New Approach to Psychiatry* (New York: Harper & Row, 1965), p. 40.

want to do something about it regardless of how I got it or why I keep it"; then you are in a position to do something about your temper. The focus is on *present behaviors* and *present choices,* not the past. Emphasizing the present does not ignore the past. Your past has made you what you are, and exploring past background information may improve your understanding of your present behaviors and provide insights into patterns of appropriate and inappropriate behavior that need to be maintained or changed. However, understanding does not cause change. Change will only occur when people decide to think and behave differently regardless of why they do what they do. Therefore, the primary emphasis needs to be on the present.

For persons who decide to accept responsibility for their behavior, almost anything is possible. What is most important is accepting the way you are (both strengths and weaknesses), deciding how you want to be, and accepting responsibility for getting there, step by step.

THE BEHAVIORAL CHAIN REACTION

For persons who decide to accept responsibility for their behavior regardless of how they got the way they are, understanding and changing behavior does not have to be overly complicated. Figure 7.1 presents a model for understanding behavior. In the model, a *stimulus* starts the behavioral chain reaction that begins with an interaction among our *thoughts, emotions,* and *physical systems* to produce *actions. Thoughts, emotions,* and *actions* that are practiced become *habits.* Our *habits* shape our *character* and our *character* shapes our *life path.* Any *end results* of the behavioral chain reaction provide feedback that may affect future stimuli or thinking, feeling, and acting responses.

A stimulus is anything that causes a response. A stimulus could be an event, something someone says, our environment, another person, a problem, the weather, or anything that starts the behavioral chain reaction. Our thoughts include our conscious and subconscious mind, which in turn includes our intellect, will, memory, self-image, attitude, and perceptions. Our thoughts are like a computer that processes data according to the way it has been programmed. A negative program, for example, will process the same data much differently than a positive program. Our thoughts interact with our emotions and physical systems (such as the autonomous nervous system, which controls our involuntary reactions) to produce actions. Emotions are primarily caused by thoughts, although they can also be chemically induced. For example, you don't tend to feel "Not OK" unless you dwell in your thinking on how "Not OK" you are. You don't tend to feel dislike toward another person unless you think of things that you dislike about that person. And you don't tend to feel depressed unless you dwell on negative things.

Actions are our outward expressions of our inner choices and reactions. Actions could be stimulated by our conscious mind, subconscious mind, emotions, or physiological reactions, depending on which function dominates, or they could be a result of some combination of functions.

Thoughts, feelings, and actions that are frequently repeated become habits. In

Figure 7.1 The behavioral chain reaction.

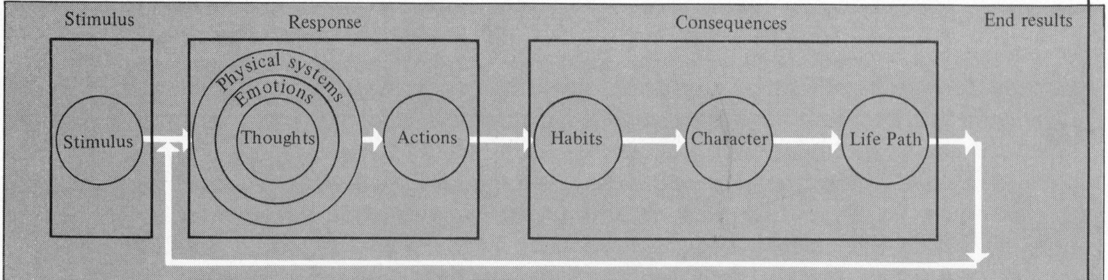

Stimulus | Response | Consequences | End results

Stimulus → Thoughts (Physical systems / Emotions) → Actions → Habits → Character → Life Path

Behavioral components

	Stimulus	Response		Consequences			End results
		Thoughts	Actions	Habits	Character	Life path	
Definitions	Anything that causes a response.	Our mental center consisting of our conscious and subconscious mind. Our thoughts contain our beliefs, values, attitude, knowledge, memory, perceptual processes, common sense, wisdom, and self-image.	Specific behavioral responses to stimuli. Examples would be talking, walking, exercising self-control, or throwing a temper tantrum.	Practiced thoughts, feelings, and actions.	Our mental, emotional, physical, and spiritual characteristics as a whole person.	Long-term behavioral patterns, our life style including our priorities, goals, and activities, and our evolving destiny.	Outcomes in terms of need satisfaction, feelings, performance, growth, change, and success.
Behavioral process	A stimulus produces a response.	Our thoughts interact with our emotions and physical system to produce actions. Constructive thoughts lead to constructive actions. *In this context constructive means responsible, self-developing and mature. The word unconstructive means irresponsible self-defeating, and immature.*	Our actions tend to be consistent with our thoughts. Inconsistencies may be controlled by subconscious thoughts, our emotions, or our physical system and tend to result in inner tension.	Thoughts, feelings, and actions that are practiced become habits.	Our habits shape our character as a whole person. Constructive habits build character while unconstructive habits weaken character.	Our character shapes our life path by determining our behavioral and life style choices and how we cause and respond to circumstances.	Our responses and the constructive, unconstruc- tive, or neutral consequences that they have on our habits, character, and life path result in outcomes that affect future stimuli and responses.

essence, we do what we do because we have been practicing particular responses for so long that they have become habits. Whether habits are good or bad, healthy or unhealthy, they become a normal way for us to behave. Whether we like a habit or not, it is more comfortable for us to behave consistently with the habit than to choose a different response. For example, you may not feel good about throwing temper tantrums, but if you practice throwing temper tantrums long enough, they will become a habit that becomes a more natural and comfortable choice than not throwing temper tantrums.

Our habits shape our character, which consists of self as a whole person (the mental, emotional, physical, and spiritual self). The whole-person concept will be discussed in detail later in this chapter. Character development is important to our present and future success and happiness because it provides the foundation that our life and choices are built on. A strong and sound foundation results in responsible choices and a life that is not easily swayed by changing circumstances. However, a weak foundation creates a potential victim of circumstances whose life is controlled by others or by circumstances.

A person's character shapes his or her life path. The term *life path* describes our long-term behavioral patterns. Based on our character, our life path can be a *growth path* (a responsible and fulfilling life characterized primarily by continuous learning, growing, and improving), a *roller-coaster path* (an up-and-down life controlled by circumstances), or a *regression path* (a life characterized by defeat and discouragement). Our present life path tends to become a self-fulfilling prophecy, since most of our behaviors are oriented toward perpetuating our habitual responses. If we are on a growth path, this can be to our advantage, since deviations are not likely to last unless they are practiced for sustained periods of time and change our habits and character. Fortunately, even patterns that would place us on a roller-coaster or regression path can be changed.

Although we tend to follow one overall life path, we may also take several side paths in different parts of our life. For example, a person may be on an overall roller-coaster path but may be on a growth path at work and a regression path at home. It is important that we take a periodic inventory of our life path or paths so that we don't slip into a roller-coaster or regression path.

Our responses and their possible consequences in terms of changes in our habits, character, and life path lead to end results that may provide feedback that affects future stimuli or responses. Outcomes could include such things as need satisfaction or frustration, success, failure, acceptance, rejection, a sense of accomplishment, and positive or negative changes. It is helpful to consider the present end result in evaluating if change is needed and the desired end result in exploring what needs to be done to accomplish desirable changes.

CHANGING BEHAVIOR

To change a behavior, we need to change the way we think and to practice acting consistently with our change in thoughts until we develop a new habit that becomes integrated into our character and may affect our life path. An understanding of this process makes it possible to change almost anything that we are willing to change. It places the responsibility for behavior and behavioral change squarely upon our own shoulders rather than making others or circumstances responsible and therefore makes it possible to exercise considerable self-control over our lives. A supervisor, for example, may want to learn to listen more to employees and to be less temperamental. By practicing thinking of himself or herself as a good listener or being even-tempered, the supervisor will be reprogramming the way he or she thinks and increasing the likelihood of a change in actions. By practicing listening skills and being even-tempered (a change in actions), the new behaviors are likely to become habits—a normal way to behave. Even though the supervisor may slip back into old habits occasionally, he or she is most likely to return to the new behaviors unless the supervisor practices the old behaviors long enough that they once again become habits. The change process is shown in Figure 7.2.

INTEGRATING THE PAST, LIVING IN THE PRESENT, AND PLANNING FOR THE FUTURE

It is impossible to operate at full potential if too much time and energy is being invested in the past or the future. A fully functioning person has learned to integrate the past, live in the present, and plan for the future.

Figure 7.2 The change process.

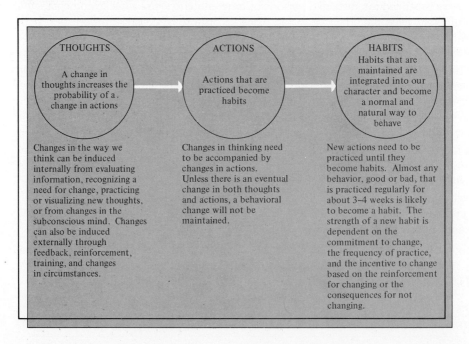

Integrating the Past

Our past can be a liability or an asset. In most cases it is probably some of both. Our liabilities from the past include past occurrences that continue to have a significant negative effect on our present behavior (traumas, failures, relationships, environment, etc.). Our assets from the past include all the occurrences from the past, both positive and negative, that have helped us to live more effectively in the present. Integrating the past is a process of dealing constructively with past liabilities and accepting and utilizing past assets. Dealing constructively with past liabilities can be accomplished in many ways:

1. Forget the past. Dragging past liabilities into our present is like carrying a garbage bag on our back that is full of past traumas, resentments, bitterness, and anger. The more garbage we collect, the heavier the bag gets and the more difficult it is to carry. Yet some people treat their garbage like a prized possession, unwilling to give it up. Depression, discouragement, and emotional problems are often the result of such a garbage bag that gets too full. We are determined to cling to our garbage even though it is causing us emotional, physical, and interpersonal problems! One way to deal with past liabilities is simply to leave the past behind and give up our garbage bag.
2. Learn from the past and reprogram it. Our memory records both events and feelings. That is one of the reasons why dwelling on past liabilities causes us so many problems. In essence, we relive our traumas each time we recall them. It is possible, however, to reprogram many of our past liabilities by taking a new look at them and attempting to learn from them. Actually, difficulties provide some of the best opportunities for constructive learning and growth, and when we turn past liabilities into constructive learning experiences, we tend to reprogram the events and feelings into a more positive or valuable experience.
3. Redo the past. One of the ways to release the past is to redo it. Mending broken relationships, apologizing for or rectifying past mistakes, or forgiving someone who has wronged you often will free you from the past.
4. Seek wise counsel. If you cannot integrate your past, it may be wise to seek wise counsel. Wise counsel could come from a healthy, integrated friend or a professional counselor. Make sure, however, that you choose someone who is known for wise advice, does not dwell on the past, and helps you focus on accepting responsibility for making better choices in the present.

Living in the Present

Living in the present means being able to live and give your best in the present without being drained by the past or worrying about or living in the future. It makes it possible to concentrate your energy without draining it and to operate at a higher level of potential. Living life to the fullest each day is a logical way to live. After all, there are no guarantees on tomorrow. Today is the only day you have right now, so why not make the best of it?

Planning for the Future

Planning for the future means deciding what you want your future to be like and planning how you can get there. It is a way of being more in control of your future and of being able to make things happen in life rather than going through life as a victim of circumstances. Some people live in the future. They worry constantly about the future or postpone present good feelings for future events instead of living in the present: "When I get my degree, life will be great" or "When I get the right job, life will be great."

CHOOSING CONSTRUCTIVE BEHAVIORS

We are in a position to grow and develop our potential when we begin accepting responsibility for our thinking, feeling, and acting choices and their consequences and are willing to make constructive choices. The word *constructive* in a behavioral context describes any behavior that is responsible, mature, and self-developing. The word *unconstructive* describes any behavior that is irresponsible, immature, and self-defeating. Let's say that a supervisor is very angry with a subordinate for not completing an assignment on time. A constructive choice might be to take time to cool off, plan a strategy for helping the employee accomplish tasks on time, and then calling in the employee to discuss the issue and agree on any actions to be taken. This response would be responsible, mature, and self-developing. An unconstructive choice could be to throw a temper tantrum, criticize the employee in front of his or her peers, and dwell on how upset you are for several days. Such a choice would be irresponsible, immature, and self-defeating.

The goal of making constructive choices is to practice constructive responses until they become habitual, normal new responses or replace old unconstructive responses.

THE POWER OF CONSTRUCTIVE THINKING AND ACTING

The Power of Positive Thinking, by Norman Vincent Peale, has become a classic in motivational literature. By thinking positively, we increase the probability of acting positively. This concept can be strengthened when constructive thinking is accompanied by practicing constructive actions. The phrase *constructive thinking* is used to broaden the concept of positive thinking. While positive thinking often gives the impression that a person must always be enthusiastic and psyched up, constructive thinking describes thinking that is responsible, mature, and self-developing and allows for processing negative as well as positive information and feelings. A constructive thinker dwells on the positive but can also hurt and experience anger, pain, and discouragement as well as positive feelings. Such people recognize that negative thinking leads to negative and often self-defeating feelings and actions, so they work through problems quickly so that they can turn difficulties into opportunities.

Changing Our Thinking Habits

Our thoughts determine the way we perceive and interpret reality and heavily influence our actions, our feelings, how much of our potential we use, and even our life experience. Two people can experience exactly the same events in a totally different way just because of the way they think. One person loves life and the other abhors it. One person sees difficulties as opportunities for growth and the other sees them as traumas. One person enjoys a compliment and the other is suspicious of the reason behind it. One person can find something good in almost anything while the other can find something wrong with the best of persons or events. It is all a matter of the way we think!

In order to accelerate the change process, we need to develop new thinking habits. Thinking habits are thoughts that are practiced until they become habits. They can be accurate or erroneous (for example, we may discount our abilities even though we are in fact very talented). They function much like a computer program that processes and interprets data. A faulty program will give a faulty result regardless of the data. To change the program, we need to purge it of inappropriate thoughts, replace them with more appropriate thoughts, and practice the new program until it is learned sufficiently to become a habit. For example, a person who looks for the worst in others needs to start focusing on others' strengths. Without a change of thoughts, even changed actions will usually become impossible or at best short-lived. A person who is trying to lose weight and still has an overweight self-image will have great difficulty losing weight and will probably gain back any weight lost.

Developing Your Ideal Self-Image

One of the quickest ways to reprogram one's thinking is to develop an ideal self-image.

Your self-image is the picture you carry in your mind of what you are like. It contains images of your intelligence, appearance, interpersonal skills, potential, capabilities and talents, ways of relating to members of the opposite sex, temperament, personality, and all other aspects of the way you are as a person. It may or may not be accurate and may change at times with circumstances or new data, but whatever it is, it tends to be self-fulfilling and heavily influences the way you see, experience, and interpret things. For example, a person with a genius IQ and a poor self-image will tend to do poorly in school. A beautiful woman with a poor image of herself will see herself as unattractive regardless of how beautiful she in fact may be. Our actions are consistent with our self-image most of the time because the most comfortable and secure way for us to act is consistent with our image, even if it is not a positive image. When our actions are better or worse than our self-image, we eventually bring them back to our image, experience considerable dissonance, or change our image to fit our new actions.

Since our self-image tends to be self-fulfilling and either allows us to utilize our potential or assures that we cannot, it is to our advantage to develop a positive self-image. This can be done through a four-step process:

1. Decide what you would ideally like to be like and write it down on something that you can carry with you, such as a 3- by 5-inch card. Include in your ideal self-image the things you presently like about yourself and desired characteristics.
2. *Review and visualize* your ideal self when you first get up, several times during the day, and when you go to bed, and *practice* being your ideal self. As your new thoughts and actions become consistent and become habits, your new self-image will stabilize and become a new self-fulfilling prophecy. It may be best to review all the items on your list daily but to visualize and practice one item at a time until it becomes a habit.
3. If you get discouraged or make mistakes, start over on the process stated in step 2 without running yourself down. Accept mistakes as a normal part of learning and realize that putting yourself down is self-defeating. If your subconscious mind begins to believe the put-downs, it will create a new self-defeating, self-fulfilling attitude.
4. As much as possible, choose friends, jobs, and activities that will reinforce your ideal self-image.

The power behind this plan is tremendous! If you begin to program your mind to allow you to utilize your capabilities and practice being more capable, you can substantially increase your potential. In order to comprehend what is possible with this approach, you may want to consider that most people include approximately 25 items on their ideal self-image list, of which about half are already accurate. If for each of the remaining items they would devote one month's time to practicing new thoughts and actions, they could be through the entire list in about one year's time! Some behaviors may take more or less time to develop into habits, and some may be unchangeable at the moment, but it is clear that persons who want to be responsible for the way they think and act can change almost anything that they are willing to change.

Changing Our Actions

Changing thoughts substantially increases the potential for being able to change behavior. It accelerates the change process and often makes change possible, but without an eventual change in actions, efforts at self-improvement become efforts in self-deception. To begin to think of yourself as more successful, more even-tempered, or more organized is self-defeating if you do not begin to act more consistently with your new thoughts.

Likewise, accepting responsibility for your behavior does not cause change—it simply makes change possible. For example, you may accept full responsibility for being a procrastinator without blaming your procrastination on others or on circumstances, but still do nothing about it. Change occurs when we act on our wants and desires and begin practicing new behaviors until they become habits. If you wanted to learn how to play the piano or tennis, it would be ludicrous to think that you could immediately become an expert pianist or tennis player without considerable practice. Practice is not easy. We make mistakes and get discouraged, but if we practice the right things enough, we can learn to do almost anything, including changing our behavior. A person with a bad temper who practices being more even-tempered will eventually become more even-tempered.

The key, then, is to practice constructive actions until they become habits. For example, if you wanted to learn to quit interrupting people and become a better listener, you would take advantage of every opportunity to practice listening and to avoid interrupting. It may also be helpful to let several people know what you are trying to accomplish so that you could occasionally solicit feedback on your progress.

THE WHOLE-PERSON APPROACH TO CHARACTER BUILDING

Our character as a whole person (see Figure 7.3) consists of our mental, emotional, physical, and spiritual characteristics. Our character is strongest when we are doing the best that we can to keep our life in balance. It is unlikely that we could ever achieve complete balance. However, it is the willingness to strive for balance that makes one feel worthwhile and builds character.

The Whole-Person Approach

Most of our problems in life, as well as the fact that we function far below our potential, can be explained by the fact that we may not be approaching life as a balanced, whole person. Our inconsistencies, bad decisions, lack of peace, purpose, and happiness, and most of our interpersonal, emotional, and physical problems are all the result of being

Figure 7.3 Our character as a whole person. Our character as a whole person includes our constructive (responsible, mature, and self-developing) and unconstructive (irresponsible, immature, and self-defeating) mental, emotional, physical, and spiritual characteristics. In applying the model to yourself, the dotted line could move upward or downward depending on how constructive or unconstructive your characteristics are.

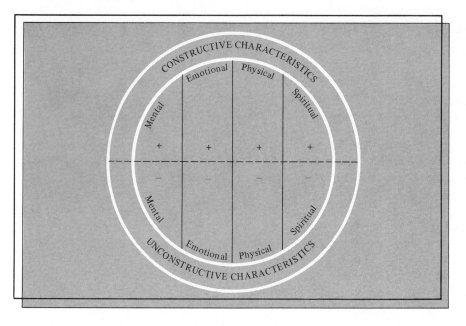

out of balance mentally, emotionally, physically, and spiritually. Like a beautiful, fine automobile that is not properly tuned, we function far below our capacity when we are out of balance. We also fail to realize that when one part of us is out of balance, it begins to affect other parts as well. For example, persons who are out shape physically won't have the energy to stay in balance mentally or emotionally or may simply wear themselves out physically, which will then cause malfunctions in other parts of the whole person.

On the other hand, a person who assumes responsibility for keeping in reasonably good balance can look forward to a life of success, happiness, and purpose.

The whole-person approach allows us to be our authentic, genuine best self without needing to play games, manipulate, figure people out, and constantly change roles in our external activities. It also equips us with an awareness of how we can grow from an integrated, balanced position and shows us how to identify quickly and solve problems that are inhibiting growth. Rather than getting sidetracked with symptoms, we can go quickly to the root cause of our personal problems, a lack of internal balance. In addition, the whole-person approach frees a person to operate at his or her best without unnecessary energy drains and allows for more time for others, since a person's own needs are likely to be reasonably well satisfied.

Mental Balance

You can keep in balance mentally by:

1. Making constructive thinking a habit and being willing to replace or work through unconstructive thinking when it occurs
2. Being selective about what you expose your mind to
3. Continuously developing and improving your mind

To stay in mental balance, constructive thinking needs to be practiced so that it will become a habit. We also need to be willing to wage an all-out war against unconstructive thinking by giving up negative thoughts or working through them. Being selective about what we expose our minds to is also important to mental balance. Filling our minds with unnecessary or detrimental information can result in the old garbage-in, garbage-out concept in terms of our thoughts and actions. Finally, continuously developing and improving our mind is important to mental balance. A mind has the capacity to continue improving throughout life. Senility and loss of memory or mental capabilities occur primarily from not using and developing one's mind, not from age, and can occur early as well as late in a person's life.

Emotional Balance

Our emotions are controlled by our conscious and subconscious thoughts and our body chemistry. However, the primary cause of emotions is our thoughts. We actually cause most of our emotions by the way we think. A negative thinker is sure to experience negative emotions. Thinking about how bad everything is naturally generates feelings of anger, discouragement, or depression. Likewise, positive thinking results in positive emotions. Thinking about good things naturally produces good feelings. The major exception to the relationship between thoughts and actions is when emotions are organically stimulated by the physical system. A chemical imbalance or other physical malfunction can affect emotions.

Emotional balance comes primarily from:

1. Mental and physical balance
2. Taking responsibility for our emotions and recognizing and accepting them and being willing to process them through our constructive thoughts

Thus, we need to be aware of our feelings, accept them whether they are positive or negative rather than denying them or making others responsible for them, and be willing to process them rationally. Processing may include evaluating what is causing our feelings and deciding how to act on them. Decisions should be based on whether our actions would be constructive—responsible, self-developing, and mature. A constructive response could include accepting and working through negative as well as positive feelings. If acting on our feelings would produce unconstructive actions—irresponsible, self-defeating, and immature—then we should make every effort to choose a constructive response. Being insensitive to feelings makes it impossible to operate at your best. However, acting on all your feelings will result in little self-control and immature choices. Feelings may be based on inaccurate perceptions or information, on irrational processing, or on subconscious past memories, so following your feelings, as some experts suggest, is self-defeating without rational processing.

Physical Balance

Even though our body is one of our greatest and most important resources and is essential to our balance as a whole person, we often take better care of our car or other prized possession. Yet our physical balance affects our health, our energy, our ability to handle stress, our self-image, and even our mental and emotional health.

Physical balance is a result of:

1. Good health
2. Physical fitness
3. A nutritious diet

Good health provides the energy necessary to develop our potential. When a person is ill, potential is significantly reduced. Physical fitness provides energy and affects our self-image as well. It takes energy to think positively, to feel good, to act appropriately, to change habits, to care, to stay motivated, and so forth. A physically fit, fine-tuned body is therefore a key ingredient to personal growth. It is not uncommon for people to increase their performance substantially by becoming physically fit and gaining more energy. A nutritious diet is one of the most overlooked aspects of physical balance. It is also a major source of energy and affects our mental, emotional, and physical health. Our diet includes anything that we introduce into our physical system, including drugs and tobacco as well as food and drink. Recent studies show remarkable results in treating physical, psychological, and performance problems with nutrition. Some schools and companies are now developing more nutritious diets in their cafeterias and are also beginning to replace junk food in vending machines with nutritious food because of these findings. An excellent book on nutrition is *Psychodietetics,* by Drs. G. Cheraskin, William Ringsdorf, and Arline Brecher.[3]

The importance of physical balance cannot be taken lightly. It is a necessity for continued healthy growth. If a person is energized but not in physical balance, that person is likely to wear his or her body out too quickly, much like a race car that is not properly tuned for high performance.

Spiritual Balance

The spiritual side of our character includes the guiding force in our life known as the spirit or soul that is based on a relationship with a higher or supreme being. Some people feel that the spiritual side of our character is the most important part of man. It gives meaning and purpose to life and affects our beliefs, values, ethics, morals, life-style, relationships, and as most religions believe, our destiny. There are those who reject the spiritual side of man as being relevant or claim it to be relevant but live as if it is not. We are including it in our whole-person approach because it has been acknowledged throughout history and is the driving life force in many lives throughout the world. In addition, in recent years scientific discoveries and studies have contributed so significantly to substantiating many spiritual teachings that it could be claimed that, for one who is willing to investigate the available evidence, it takes far more faith not to believe than it does to believe.

How does one keep his or her spiritual self in balance? The answer to this important question obviously depends on who is answering the question and the validity of the source they are basing their answers on. Validity is an important issue because being sincerely wrong about one's beliefs is hardly a sound basis on which to give direction to one's life. We can, of course, only express our own opinions about how to achieve spiritual balance, and beyond that simply point out the importance of spiritual balance and encourage our readers to investigate this area for themselves. In our opinion, spiritual balance comes from:

1. Love of God and living one's life to glorify God rather than self
2. Learning to love others and to love unconditionally
3. Diligently seeking truth and wisdom

Some people question whether a supervisor can be caring. The word *love* is probably one of the most misinterpreted words in the English language. In a spiritual context, *love* can be defined as selfless actions that help and edify others, rather than a feeling. With this definition in mind, supervisors can demonstrate caring through behaviors such as patience, kindness, forgiveness, believing the best of others, leveling with others, confronting and disciplining from a position of caring and respect, and not

---

[3]G. Cheraskin; William Ringsdorf, Jr.; and Arline Brecker, *Psychodietetics* (New York: Stein & Day, 1974).

being selfish, rude, rigid, or touchy. Now back to the question of whether a supervisor can be caring. Certainly, caring actions are very appropriate for supervisors. They build trust, openness, and self-confidence and do not limit a supervisor's ability to take decisive actions. They in fact remove the punitive nature of discipline and confronting.

Starting the Day in Balance

For the person who is interested in a whole-person life-style, it is very important to start the day in balance. Starting the day out of balance usually means ending the day out of balance. Daily balance can be achieved by allowing approximately 45 minutes to one hour for preparing for the day. We are taught throughout our lives about the importance of preparation, yet little is said about preparing for each day.

Preparation could, for example, consist of:

1. Reviewing our ideal self-image and planning our priorities for the day (mental and emotional balance)
2. Exercising and having a nutritious breakfast (physical balance)
3. Having a devotion (spiritual balance)

The time spent preparing for the day may be the most important part of the day in helping us to operate at full potential.

BALANCING YOUR LIFE-STYLE

Another important aspect of developing our potential is to keep our life-style in reasonably good balance. Our life-style describes the activities that we include in our life and how we approach these activities. Balance is achieved by:

1. Accepting responsibility for doing the best we can to keep our external activities in balance
2. Leading a constructive life-style

Our external activities include all the activities in our life, such as family, work, play, finances, relationships, and hobbies. This is a very difficult task, considering the complexity of most people's lives today. However, when our external activities get out of balance, we get out of control and underutilize our potential.

Our life-style also describes how we approach the various activities in our life. Numerous approaches are described in Exercise 7.1, "Life-Styles," which we suggest you complete at this point. The most rewarding and satisfying life-style is that of an integrated winner. The other life-styles are common and normal for most of us, but they limit our ability to develop our potential.

SETTING REALISTIC GOALS

It is rare for a person to soar consistently in life without goals. Realistic goals provide direction, purpose, motivation, and hope. Persons who aim for nothing usually find exactly that. Persons who have clear and realistic goals learn to make things happen.

Meaningful and valuable goals should not be established in a vacuum. Ideally, in setting goals we should consider our overriding purpose in life (why we are here, what we hope to accomplish, etc.), as well as our values and priorities. These important issues provide a frame of reference for establishing and evaluating long-range, short-range, and daily goals.

Many times resistance to setting goals comes from not knowing what goals to pursue. Finding worthwhile goals is not a simple task. Therefore, some people wait and wait and wait for the day to come when suddenly their goals become crystal-clear and they can begin life at its best. Most goals are in fact established by people who decide to grind them out, whether they are inspired or not, and who pursue them enthusiastically until they find new goals or discover that the goals were not worthy ones. If the goals do turn out to be unworthy, they try new ones until they find ones that they can commit themselves to.

Goals add direction and purpose to life and significantly increase the possibility of utilizing our potential. Persons without goals waste considerable time and energy and tend to have little to show for their efforts and life. Persons with goals quickly learn how to make things happen in life. Ideally, goals should be written down and should include a goal plan and target dates. They should cover all aspects of life—career, family, health, finances, personal development, spiritual development, recreation, and so on. The method is unimportant as long as it works.

OVERCOMING RESISTANCE TO GROWTH

Unfortunately, not everyone will join your parade when you are growing. Your growth may intimidate them, make them jealous or resentful, or make them feel insecure or even angry. You can detect resistance when people begin telling you that "you aren't being realistic" or "you are too idealistic" or when they become very critical of your behavior, values, or motives. Some of the resistance may be a normal reaction to wondering what you are up to or wondering how your changes will affect your relationship with them. You also may find temporary resistance from persons who are cashing in on all the bad feelings they have been collecting but were afraid to express in the past because they were afraid you couldn't handle it! Pay close attention to resistance that continues regardless of the adjustments you make.

What do you do when someone is resisting your growth? There are several alternatives:

1. Check and see if the resistance is justified. You may be growing at the expense of others without knowing it or may be changing in inappropriate directions.
2. Confront the resistance and try to resolve it.
3. Involve the resister in helping you change.
4. Ignore or stay away from the resistance and keep growing.
5. Be wise and cautious with resisters but continue to treat them with respect in spite of the injustice of what they are doing. Fighting the resistance is a misuse of your

time and energy, and becoming bitter, resentful, or hostile is almost certain to channel your energy and growth in unconstructive directions.

HOW TO STAY MOTIVATED

It is easy to look at successful people with envy—as if being successful is luck! Lasting success isn't luck. It takes a great deal of motivation and continuous growth to be successful. When our motivation and growth begin to slow down or stop, our internal success as a person will soon follow suit, and our external success (material, performance, etc.) in most cases will eventually also be affected.

It is not possible to rest solely on past achievements for present satisfaction. Continuous growth is a necessity for present satisfaction. It is not uncommon for a person who is presently coasting because of past achievement to feel frustrated and dissatisfied. A company president who has amassed considerable wealth but now has little to do and faces few challenges can feel highly dissatisfied without understanding why. When we stop growing, dissatisfaction begins to set in, regardless of how favorable our circumstances are.

The problem, then, is how to stay motivated. Few people stay motivated all the time. Circumstances, transitions, and feelings can steal away our motivation. However, if we could learn to increase the amount of time that we are motivated, we could significantly increase our potential. It is not uncommon for people to double their productivity when they are highly motivated or to reduce their productivity by half when they are demotivated. Thus, staying motivated can considerably improve performance and possibilities for success. Some things you can do to stay motivated are

1. *Think, act, and talk like a motivated person.* This is another way of saying that you should make motivation a habit. Think positive, act in responsible ways, and talk as much as possible about positive and constructive things.
2. *Build on your strengths and develop new ones.* Motivated people find out what they do well, find opportunities and places to utilize their strengths, and continue developing new strengths. They don't ignore weaknesses, but they aren't preoccupied with them either, knowing that dwelling on weaknesses and constantly thinking about them and analyzing them tends to make a person weaker, not stronger. Placing the major emphasis on building on and developing strengths makes growth a positive experience and increases our chances for success and happiness and for having a stronger self-image. This in turn eliminates many of our weaknesses and makes it possible to deal with our remaining weaknesses from a position of strength.
3. *Surround yourself with motivated people.* Motivated people lift you up, inspire you, and give you encouragement. Unmotivated people have a tendency to drag you down and demoralize you if you spend too much time around them. So, it makes sense to associate as much as possible with motivated people who have a positive effect on you and to be careful not to let unmotivated people or people who are motivated in the wrong direction have a negative effect on you. Choose

your close associates very carefully. If some relationships that demotivate you cannot be minimized or avoided, take responsibility for developing sufficient positive relationships and activities to permit you to survive the negative drains on your motivation.

4. *Get involved in activities that keep you motivated.* To stay motivated, you need to get involved in activities that motivate you. Motivated people sometimes get burned out because they lose interest in what they are doing or overwork themselves without getting involved in other activities that keep them motivated. Hobbies, sports, socializing, games, vacations, and other activities that we enjoy can add life to our lives and keep us motivated without getting burned out.

5. *Reevaluate activities that demotivate you.* Like bureaucracies that have a propensity for growing bigger, our lives seem to have a propensity for becoming increasingly cluttered with activities. We need occasionally to reevaluate the activities that collect around our lives and eliminate or minimize any unnecessary ones that demotivate us. Perhaps some of our activities could be delegated, given up altogether, or changed to minimize any demotivating effects. It is useful sometimes to consider all the things that demotivate you in life, including your own attitude and habits, and to begin exploring constructive ways to do something about the ones that you have the capacity to change.

6. *Find constructive ways to get the positive reinforcement, support, and encouragement that you need to stay motivated.* Few people can stay motivated without occasional positive reinforcement, support, and encouragement. Rather than leaving these important motivators to chance, we need to take responsibility for finding constructive ways to get our needs met. The alternatives may be to find supportive friends, to engage in constructive activities during or after work that result in positive reinforcement, to express our needs to our boss or friends, to attend motivational talks, workshops, or retreats, or listen to or read things that motivate us.

7. *Reward your successes.* Setting up rewards for successful accomplishments can often keep you motivated. The rewards can be minor (an hour of window-shopping, treating yourself to a hot fudge sundae, purchasing something that you have been wanting) or major, but they can provide the incentive to stay motivated and make motivation fun.

8. *Make motivation contracts.* When you are having difficulty getting a task done, it is sometimes helpful to make an informal contract with someone for the completion of the task. You can even ask the person to call you to see if you met your deadline. In addition, you might tell the person that you are having difficulty getting motivated and that you really need a push.

9. *Build into your schedule ways to keep motivated.* In areas where you cannot keep yourself motivated, it may be helpful to commit yourself to activities that assure that the task will get accomplished. For example, if you have difficulty getting motivated to exercise daily, you may want to commit yourself to an exercise class or to racquetball several times a week to keep in shape. Or, if you have been

wanting to pursue a hobby such as learning how to play the guitar but never seem to get started, you may want to sign up for guitar lessons.

10. *Take a periodic inventory of your needs and goals.* It is possible that a lack of motivation is coming from frustrated needs, lack of goals, or goals that you are not committed to. By accepting responsibility for our behavior, we can identify needs that are being frustrated and take corrective actions. Likewise, by being responsible, we can establish realistic and meaningful goals and evaluate any present goals to consider if they are worth pursuing. Take the case of the student who had selected a major because jobs in the major were plentiful and later wondered why she was so demotivated. Further probing determined that she didn't really like the field she was preparing for. When she changed to a major that she was enthusiastic about, she became highly motivated.

11. *Take time for self-renewal.* Some people assume incorrectly that staying motivated means continuous hard work and high performance. On the contrary, one of the most important ingredients of sustained motivation is ample time for self-renewal. Play time and learning time are as important as work time. A person who wants to stay motivated needs to learn to relax, to find stimulating and fun things to do, and to take the time to continue learning, growing, and living.

GROWTH GUIDELINES

Change can be painful, frustrating, and discouraging at times. However, the payoff is well worth the effort. Continuous growth makes it possible to have an adventurous, rewarding, and satisfying life that benefits others as well as yourself. Interestingly enough, the satisfaction comes from the process of growth, not from having arrived. In fact, so much growth is possible that there is no such thing as having arrived. For supervisors, growth is especially rewarding because it may inspire subordinates also to discover and develop their potential.

Several guidelines should be followed in developing your potential:

1. *Take one step at a time.* Start with one or two changes that you have a high probability of achieving. As your success and self-confidence grow, take on more difficult tasks.

2. *Change things that are changeable.* Devote your time and energy to things that can be changed. Don't worry about things that you can do little or nothing about.

3. *Learn from your mistakes and move on.* Don't dwell on failures. When you make a mistake, learn from it and move on. Collecting bad feelings and guilt over mistakes is counterproductive.

4. *Let people know what you are doing.* Resistance to your growth often comes from a fear of the possible consequences of your growth on those who are affected by it. Keeping people informed about what you are up to may eliminate or reduce some of the resistance.

5. *Grow from a position of humility.* Enjoy your growth and accept your strengths,

but wear them with a sense of humility. When growth turns to arrogance, it will begin to backfire.

6. *Be available to help others change, but don't force your growth on others.* Share with others how they can grow, and provide a supportive climate for them to grow in—if they are interested. Trying to force growth will usually meet with resistance.

7. *Periodically evaluate the consequences of your growth.* The consequences of your growth to others as well as yourself should be periodically evaluated to make sure that your growth is being channeled into positive and responsible directions.

8. *Don't waste time overanalyzing your behavior.* Decide what you need to do to be your best self and go after it. Don't waste time worrying about what you don't do and analyzing everything that you do. Occasional introspection is valuable if channeled into positive changes, but continuous analysis tends to be counterproductive and inhibits growth, since the predominant focus tends to be on your weaknesses rather than your strengths.

9. *Surround yourself with growth-oriented people who will encourage and support your growth.* Negative people can quickly erode your growth, but positive people can inspire you to new heights.

10. *Work toward being your best self as a balanced, whole person.* Wearing facades, role playing, and game playing are self-defeating, waste time, and drain energy. Being you at your best and as a balanced, whole person is self-developing and frees valuable time and energy for worthwhile endeavors.

ARE YOU WILLING TO DEVELOP YOUR PERSONAL AND SUPERVISORY POTENTIAL?

Deep down, everyone wants to be and feel worthwhile and capable and to be an integrated winner in life who has a happy, successful, and adventurous life of direction and purpose. You are in a position to have a special and purposeful life if you are *willing* to take responsibility for your behavior, avoid blaming others or circumstances, and begin the step-by-step process of developing your potential. It won't be easy. Not everyone will understand such a positive life-style, and some people will resist your continued growth. You will make mistakes, fail, and wonder at times why you shouldn't just be irresponsible and coast through life like many others. You may even wish that you had never read this chapter! But once you get a taste of what it is like to be an integrated winner who is in charge of his or her life, you won't want to turn back. The satisfaction, the feeling of self-control, and the awareness that you can do almost anything that you are willing to do are well worth the price.

SUMMARY

The most effective supervisor is a healthy, integrated, well-balanced, and growing person who has acquired specialized knowledge and skills in supervision. In other words, the most successful supervisors are first of all successful persons. They are aware of the considerable constructive or unconstructive influence that their example can have on others and have accepted the challenge of setting a positive example and continuing to develop their potential.

Few people realize how much potential they have or are willing to reach for what is possible. It may be easier to coast through life, playing it safe, but the exciting adventure of discovering and developing your potential is well worth the effort in terms of the happiness, inner strength, and success that it can bring.

The major key to personal development is taking responsibility for your behavior regardless of how you got the way you are or how justified you are in making others or circumstances responsible for your behavior. No matter how aware you are or how much you understand yourself or know why you do what you do, nothing changes until you decide to accept responsibility for making the necessary changes. Once you decide to be responsible, your behavior is a function of your thoughts, which interact with your emotions and physical systems to produce actions. Thoughts, emotions, and actions that are practiced become constructive (responsible, self-developing, and mature) habits or unconstructive (irresponsible, self-defeating, and immature) habits. Our habits shape our character and our character shapes our life path (long-range, recurring life patterns). To change our behavior, we need to change the way we think and practice new actions until they become habits. Most changes can be made in a relatively short time with continued practice.

To maintain our growth and assure that we are growing in responsible directions, we need to learn how to grow as a balanced, whole person and to take responsibility for leading a constructive life-style. We can also establish realistic goals and plan ways to overcome resistance to growth and stay motivated.

IMPORTANT TERMS

best self	constructive
stimulus	unconstructive
thoughts	growth path
emotions	roller-coaster path
physical system	regression path
habits	ideal self-image
character	whole person
life path	life-style

REVIEW QUESTIONS

1. Why is it so important for supervisors to set a good example and to continue growing?
2. What are some of the major benefits of developing your potential?
3. Why don't some people develop their potential?
4. Why is it important to have a worthwhile goal for growing?
5. Explain what it means to take responsibility for your behavior. Why is taking responsibility so important to growth?

6. What are some specific things that a person can do to integrate the past, live in the present, and plan for the future?
7. Explain each step of the behavioral chain reaction.
8. How can a person change his or her behavior using the behavioral process?
9. Discuss the whole-person concept in terms of its components and what a person needs to do to keep each component in balance. Is it possible for a supervisor to be successful as an integrated whole person? Please explain.
10. What effect do goals have on growth? How do you find the right goals?
11. What are some ways in which a person can respond to resistance to change?
12. What are some things a person can do to stay motivated?
13. What are some guidelines a person should consider in growing, changing, and developing potential?
14. What were your major insights from this chapter?

EXERCISES

7.1 Life-Styles

The descriptions below describe a variety of life-styles. To evaluate which life-styles are characteristic of your life, make a check beside each item that describes you.

7.2 Learning Integration

Divide the preceding review questions among small groups so that each group has three or four questions. Have the groups meet for about 30 minutes to prepare answers to the questions and elect a spokesperson. Meet again as a class and have the group spokespersons spend about five minutes each sharing the conclusions of their groups.

7.3 Self-Interview Questionnaire

The purpose of this exercise is for you to introduce yourself to you. Who are you? What are you like? What is important to you in life? It can also be used to share in groups so that the group members can get to know each other. Feel free to omit any information that you prefer not to share.

1. My name is _____.

   I have lived in _____.

2. My hobbies and interests include: _____

   _____.

3. Something interesting about me from my past, present, or future that most people don't know is _____

   _____.

4. The animal or object that best describes what I am like is _____.

Integrated Winner

1. Take responsibility for my behavior and its consequences ____
2. Take responsibility for being my best self ____
3. Accept responsibility for constructively taking care of my needs and responsibilities ____
4. Genuine ____
5. Positive thinker ____
6. Positive attitude ____
7. Good self-image ____
8. Fill mind with constructive information ____
9. Continuously developing mind ____
10. Process and express emotions responsibly ____
11. Even-tempered ____
12. Good physical condition ____
13. Nutritious diet ____
14. Spiritually in balance ____
15. Accept and value self ____
16. Accept and value others ____
17. Freely give and receive love ____
18. Forgiving ____
19. Have a sense of direction and purpose ____
20. Well-developed and responsible values ____
21. Honest and straightforward ____
22. High morals and ethics ____
23. Clear and responsible priorities ____
24. Goal-oriented ____
25. Internally motivated ____
26. Self-motivated ____
27. Self-confident ____
28. Independent ____
29. Humble ____
30. Unselfish ____
31. Allow others to be themselves ____
32. Believe the best of others ____
33. Freely give to others ____
34. Generous ____
35. Sensitive to the needs and feelings of others ____
36. Successful as a person ____
37. Continuously learning and growing ____
38. Admit and learn from mistakes ____
39. Enthused about life ____
40. Happy ____

Plastic Winner

41. Believe success is more show than fact ____
42. Boast about successes ____
43. Use hypocritical words and actions ____
44. Use success to cover up insecurities ____
45. Successful on the outside but unsuccessful on the inside ____

Phony

46. Game player ____
47. Manipulate to get needs met ____
48. Superficial values ____
49. Wear facades ____
50. Hide true feelings ____

"Me" Attitude

51. Self-centered ____
52. Look out for number one ____
53. Taker ____
54. Do things my way ____
55. Insensitive to others ____

Victim

56. Blame others or circumstances for problems ____
57. Thoughts, feelings, and actions controlled by circumstances ____
58. Do self-defeating things ____
59. Seldom learn from mistakes ____
60. Hope others or circumstances will take care of my needs ____

Crowd Pleaser

61. Follow the crowd ____
62. Do whatever is "in" ____
63. Live according to expectations of others ____
64. Constantly seeking approval or attention ____
65. Controlled by what others think ____

Survivor

66. Do only enough to get by ____
67. Coast through life settling for second best ____
68. Unambitious ____
69. Spend considerable energy avoiding responsibility ____
70. Operate below potential ____

Rebel

71. Resist authority ____
72. Problem maker ____
73. Make stands for shallow reasons ____
74. Hostile ____
75. Stubborn and determined to do things my way ____

Persecutor

76. Spread my misery to others ____
77. Put others down ____
78. Unforgiving ____
79. Cynical ____
80. Bitter and resentful ____

Estimate below the percentage of each life-style that is characteristic of your life. Base your conclusions on the overall control each life-style has on your life rather than the number of items checked. In evaluating the results, it might be interesting to subtract your Integrated Winner percentage from 100%. The result is the percentage of your life-style that may be self-defeating and may be keeping you from being an integrated, happy, and successful person.

Integrated Winner	____	%
Plastic Winner	____	%
Phony	____	%
"Me" Attitude	____	%
Victim	____	%
Crowd Pleaser	____	%
Survivor	____	%
Rebel	____	%
Persecutor	____	%
Total	100	%

(Please explain.) _____

_____

_____

5. The 10 words or phrases that best describe me are _____

_____

_____

_____.

6. The things that I value most in life or that are most important to me are

_____

_____

_____.

7. If I had a magic wand and were free to do anything that I wanted to with no constraints or responsibilities, some things that I would want to do are

_____

_____

_____

_____.

8. Some of the people, events, ideas, books, movies, or other things that have influenced me most in life are _____

_____

_____

_____.

9. My biggest weaknesses or faults that I would admit to are _____

_____

_____

_____

10. My greatest strengths are (include, for example, what you like about yourself, interpersonal skills, education and training, technical skills, creative skills, athletic abilities, experience, health, problem-solving skills, emotional strengths, valuable relationships or contacts, anything that you do well): _____

_____

_____

_____

_____

_____.

11. In becoming my best or ideal self, the things that I am most interested in changing about me or adding to the way I am are _____

_____

_____

_____.

12. The three words that I would use to describe my past, present, and ideal future are

    Past: _____.

    Present: _____.

    Ideal future: _____.

7.4   Discovering and Developing Your Potential

This worksheet is designed for personal use to help you discover and develop your potential. It may be desirable to share some of the information in small groups to check out your observations and stimulate further thinking.

Finding Out What Is Possible

Describe what you think your life would be like if you were utilizing your full potential.

Growth Goal

Write a sentence or paragraph describing a worthwhile growth goal to keep in mind as you grow so you will grow in a positive and responsible direction.

Barriers to Utilizing Your Potential

1. List anything that is keeping you from utilizing your potential now.
2. Make a check by any of the items that you could constructively and realistically do something about.

Accepting Responsibility for Your Behavior

1. Make a list of everything that is affecting your present behavior or that you would like to do or accomplish now or in the future for which you have not accepted responsibility or have blamed on other people or circumstances.

2. Make a check by any of the items that you would be willing to do something about.

Integrating the Past, Living in the Present, and Planning for the Future

1. In two columns, headed *Positive* and *Negative,* list anything from your past that has had a major positive or negative effect on your present behavior.

Positive Effect   *Negative Effect*

2. You can integrate your past by recognizing the positives from your past that are helping your present behavior and by dealing with any negatives by: (a) forgetting them and giving them up; (b) learning from them and re-remembering them based on your learning insights; (c) redoing them by taking responsible corrective actions; or (d) seeking wise counsel that will help you take positive and constructive steps to forget or will help you hunt for problems. What actions would you be willing to take now to integrate your past?
3. What could you do *now* to live more in the present by making your present more enjoyable, exciting, meaningful, and purposeful?
4. List anything that you could do *now* to start planning for an adventurous and successful future.

Understanding and Changing Your Behavior

1. Our behavior is a function of our thoughts, which interact with our emotions and physical system to produce actions, thoughts, emotions, and actions that are practiced and become habits. Our habits shape our character and our character shapes our life path. In evaluating our behavior, we need to consider what we are doing that is constructive (responsible, self-developing, and mature) and unconstructive (irresponsible, self-defeating, and immature). List some of your major constructive and unconstructive behaviors below.
2. Take a look at your life from a whole-person perspective and evaluate which parts are in balance and which parts may be out of balance by circling the appropriate numbers.

Internal Balance

Mental	Out of balance	1 2 3 4 5	In balance
Emotional	Out of balance	1 2 3 4 5	In balance
Physical	Out of balance	1 2 3 4 5	In balance
Spiritual	Out of balance	1 2 3 4 5	In balance

Behavior	Constructive	Unconstructive
Thoughts Both conscious and subconscious, including how we think, our intellect, will, attitude, self-image, memory, and perceptions.		
Emotions Feeling patterns that have become habits: being even-tempered, temperamental, affectionate, cold, calm, overreacting, etc.		
Actions Action-oriented behaviors such as self-control, being helpful, making decisions, solving problems.		
Habits Practiced thoughts, emotions, and actions.		
Character Mental, emotional, physical, and spiritual characteristics and the activities in our life.		
Life Path Long-term recurring behaviors that cause us to be on a growth path, regression path, or roller-coaster path.		

External Balance

Family	Out of balance	1 2 3 4 5	In balance
Work	Out of balance	1 2 3 4 5	In balance
Play	Out of balance	1 2 3 4 5	In balance
Relationships	Out of balance	1 2 3 4 5	In balance
Social life	Out of balance	1 2 3 4 5	In balance
Finances	Out of balance	1 2 3 4 5	In balance
Activities	Out of balance	1 2 3 4 5	In balance

3. Behavior can be learned or changed by identifying the desired end result, changing the way you think about the behavior (see yourself accomplishing the desired behavior), and practicing the behavior until it becomes a habit. List below anything that you would be willing to change or improve in your life.

Developing Your Ideal Self-Image

Describe your present self-image in terms of how you see yourself now, how you think others see you, and how you would ideally like to be. Consider all aspects of your life, including work, play, family, looks, interpersonal skills, technical skills, and so forth.

Present as Seen by You	Present as Seen by Others	Ideal Self-Image

Overcoming Resistance to Growth

Recognizing that not everyone may want you to grow and that you may encounter some resistance to your growth, what are some constructive actions that you could take to overcome this resistance?

Staying Motivated

What are some things that you could do to get yourself motivated? What are some things that you could do to stay motivated?

Setting Realistic Goals

Now you are ready to put it all together by: (1) evaluating the information you have completed in the worksheet; (2) identifying your major strengths and weaknesses; and (3) selecting a few goals for changing your behavior by building on your strengths, changing your weaknesses, or adding new constructive behaviors. Set realistic goals, preferably by starting with easily attainable goals and working up to more challenging goals. Include with each goal a plan for achieving the goal and an estimated target date for completion. Remember that growth should be accomplished one step at a time. Make it fun and achievable by establishing realistic goals.

1. What are my major strengths (interpersonal, technical, talents, human and material resources, education, experience, training, etc.)?

    1. _____   11. _____

    2. _____   12. _____

    3. _____   13. _____

    4. _____   14. _____

5. _____   15. _____
6. _____   16. _____
7. _____   17. _____
8. _____   18. _____
9. _____   19. _____
10. _____   20. _____

2. What major weaknesses could I change if I were willing to do so?

1. _____   11. _____
2. _____   12. _____
3. _____   13. _____
4. _____   14. _____
5. _____   15. _____
6. _____   16. _____
7. _____   17. _____
8. _____   18. _____
9. _____   19. _____
10. _____   20. _____

3. What goals could I set so as better to develop my potential?

Goal	Plan for Reaching Goal	Target Date for Completion

7.5 Personal Awareness Questionnaire

The personal awareness questionnaire provides a structured feedback exercise for helping you compare how you see yourself with the way others see you.

1. Make a check in the column marked S (self) beside each word below that describes how you see yourself. *It is OK to check opposite words if both describe you.*
2. Then meet in a small group of people who know each other and who have also completed their own questionnaires.
3. One group member at a time is selected for feedback. The other group members

Descriptive Words	S	O	Descriptive Words	S	O	Descriptive Words	S	O
1. Positive attitude			53. Calm			104. Closed		
2. Stubborn			54. Frequent complainer			105. Diplomatic		
3. Responsible for behavior			55. Handles problems well			106. Undiplomatic		
4. Self-control			56. Inflexible			107. Allows others to be themselves		
5. Genuine			57. Organized			108. Doesn't listen		
6. Controlled by circumstances			58. Underutilizes potential			109. Good team member		
7. Enthusiastic			59. Self-motivated			110. Domineering in groups		
8. Victim			60. Procrastinates			111. Helps others		
9. Together			61. Consistent			112. Disruptive		
10. Arrogant			62. Not always truthful			113. Patient		
11. Optimistic			63. Generous			114. Closed-minded		
12. Temperamental			64. Negative attitude			115. Eager to learn from mistakes		
13. High concern for others			65. Independent			116. Blames others or circumstances		
14. Low concern for others			66. Irresponsible			117. Gets results		
15. Warm and friendly			67. Loyal			118. Doesn't plan ahead		
16. Cool and unfriendly			68. Game player			119. High achiever		
17. Kind			69. Happy			120. Disorganized		
18. Uses offensive language			70. Moody			121. Spiritual		
19. Leader			71. Fun			122. Selfish		
20. Uncooperative			72. Out of balance			123. Loving		
21. Builds others up			73. Compassionate			124. Inconsistent		
22. Discounts others			74. Uncompassionate			125. Good self-image		
23. Problem solver			75. Expresses real feelings			126. Greedy		
24. Overreacts			76. Hides real feelings			127. Self-confident		
25. Open-minded			77. Makes others feel good			128. Dependent		
26. Impatient			78. Critical of others			129. Sharp dresser		
27. Goal-oriented			79. Sociable			130. Hard to trust		
28. Undisciplined			80. Undependable group member			131. Honest		
29. Plans ahead			81. Trustworthy			132. Unhappy		
30. Too many activity traps			82. Follower			133. Straightforward		
31. Stable			83. Realistic			134. Sends double messages		
32. Insecure			84. Nervous			135. Treats others with respect		
33. Reliable			85. Objective			136. Overly aggressive		
34. Wild			86. Problem maker			137. Assertive		
35. Inspiring			87. Competent			138. Passive		
36. Rebellious			88. Wastes time			139. Supportive group member		
37. Bright			89. Disciplined			140. Sidetracker		
38. Low self-image			90. Lacks worthwhile goals			141. Dependable group member		
39. Internally motivated			91. Good sense of humor			142. Unsociable		
40. Lacks self-confidence			92. Pessimistic			143. Flexible		
41. Unselfish			93. Solid values			144. Does not handle problems well		
42. Sloppy dresser			94. Unstable			145. Resolves conflicts		
43. Polite			95. Attractive			146. Unrealistic		
44. Impolite			96. Unreliable			147. Utilizes potential		
45. Understanding			97. Humble			148. Demotivated		
46. Intimidating			98. Critical			149. High performer		
47. Good listener			99. Even-tempered			150. Erratic performer		
48. Interrupts			100. Manipulative					
49. Democratic			101. Secure					
50. Autocratic			102. Externally motivated					
51. Cooperative			103. Open					
52. Withdrawn in groups								

look through the words and call off any words that *in their opinion* describe the person receiving feedback. The person receiving the feedback should make a check in the column marked O (others) beside each word that is called off. Clarifying questions may be asked. If the group members disagree on a word, a question mark should be used instead of a check. *Group members should only call off words that they believe to be accurate. It is not helpful to share misleading information.* When the feedback is completed, the person receiving feedback should comment on the similarities and differences in the two columns on his or her list.

4. For an analysis of the results, see the chart that follows. (S = self O = others)

Analysis

The words used in the personal awareness questionnaire describe five important aspects of behavior: (1) character (60 items), (2) interpersonal relations (30 items), (3) group relations (20 items), (4) approach to problem solving (20 items), and (5) performance (20 items). Refer to your questionnaire and record below all words that were checked by placing the words under the proper categories. Under *Self* write the words you used to describe yourself, and under *Others* write the words called off by your group.

Character		Interpersonal Relations		Group Relations		Approach to Problem Solving		Performance	
Words 1-12, 31-42, 61-72, 91-102, 121-132.		Words 13-18, 43-48, 73-78, 103-108, 133-138.		Words 19-22, 49-52, 79-82, 109-112, 139-142.		Words 23-26, 53-56, 83-86, 113-116, 143-146.		Words 27-30, 57-60, 87-90, 117-120, 147-150.	
Self	Others	Self	Others	Self	Others	Self	Others	Self	Others

SUGGESTED ADDITIONAL READINGS

Branden, Nathaniel. *The Psychology of Self-Esteem.* New York: Bantam Books, 1967.
Cooper, Kenneth. *The Aerobics Way.* New York: Bantam Books, 1977.
Dyer, Wayne W. *Pulling Your Own Strings.* New York: Funk & Wagnalls, 1978.

————. *Your Erroneous Zones.* New York: Funk & Wagnalls, 1976.

Ellis, Albert, and Harper, Robert A., *A New Guide to Rational Living.* Hollywood, Ca: Wilshire Book Co., 1975.

Hamachek, Don E., *Encounters With the Self.* New York: Holt, Rinehart, and Winston, 1978.

McMiller, S. I. *None of These Diseases.* Old Tappan, NJ: Spire Books, 1976.

Maltz, Maxwell. *Psycho-Cybernetics.* Englewood Cliffs, NJ: Prentice-Hall, 1960.

Parloff, Morris B. "The Me Generation," *Psychology Today,* December, 1979, pp. 92 –97.

Peale, Norman Vincent. *The Power of Positive Thinking.* New York: Fawcett Crest Books, 1956.

Schwitzgebel, Ralph K., and Kolb, David A., *Changing Human Behavior.* New York: McGraw-Hill Book Company, 1974.

Sperry, Len, Mickelson, Douglas J., and Hunsaker, Phillip L., *You Can Make It Happen.* Reading, MA: Addison-Wesley Publishing Co., 1977.

PART THREE
Supervising Groups

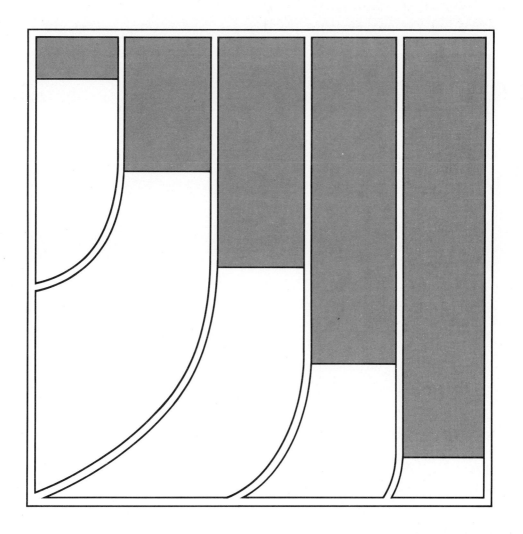

8

Understanding
Group Behavior

A house divided against itself cannot stand.
Abraham Lincoln

OBJECTIVES

This chapter provides you with the information necessary to:

1. Explain why an understanding of group behavior is important to supervisors
2. Define what a group is and what the different types of groups are
3. Explain the Homans model of group dynamics
4. Discuss the six major components of group dynamics and what is included in each component
5. Evaluate the states of development of a group and the group's overall health
6. Explain what happens within and between groups involved in intergroup conflict
7. Discuss the Blake and Mouton models of intergroup competition and problem solving

---

THE IMPORTANCE OF UNDERSTANDING GROUP BEHAVIOR

Although understanding individual behavior is an essential part of a supervisor's education, it must be complemented by an understanding of group behavior since people in organizations usually function in groups, and the dynamics of a group can

159

significantly influence or change an individual's behavior. Anyone who doubts the strong effect of groups on individual behavior need only look at current events to discover the powerful effect of groups. During strikes, we sometimes read of loyal, law-abiding citizens destroying property, threatening and sometimes taking lives, and refusing to do their jobs even when lives are at stake. We find serious students who suddenly turn to violence in a rally that gets out of hand. At work, employees can develop informal standards of behavior that support minimal performance. On the other hand, a group can motivate people to increase their productivity and inspire them to new levels of personal growth. The potential for a significant positive or negative effect on individual behavior and performance makes it very important for supervisors to understand groups and how to develop healthy and effective groups.

Some of the reasons supervisors need to understand group behavior are:

1. An understanding of what makes a group healthy and effective can be helpful in developing by design healthy group norms (behaviors that are accepted and adhered to by most of the group members) that lead to high performance and satisfaction and better end results.
2. An understanding of group behavior makes it possible to observe constructive and unconstructive behaviors in groups and make any necessary adjustments.
3. It can be used to recognize and resolve conflicts and other dysfunctional activities within and between groups.
4. It can be used to understand the dynamics of teamwork and to develop an improved team effort.
5. It can be used by leaders and individual team members to evaluate periodically group processes (decision- and problem-solving styles, how members interact and exert influence, etc.).
6. It can be used by leaders and individual team members to increase their individual acceptance and effectiveness as group members.

GROUP BEHAVIOR DEFINITIONS AND TERMS

A *group* may be defined as two or more persons joined together for a common purpose. Thus, a group could consist of the members of a particular department, committee, meeting, or even a social occasion if they are joined together for a common purpose. *Group dynamics* may be defined as the *events, activities,* and *processes* that affect the behavior of a group. Events could be past, present, or pending. Activities describe such things as the tasks and actions of group members. Processes describe the ways in which group members relate, interact, solve problems, resolve conflicts, make decisions, and exert influence.

TYPES OF GROUPS

Groups may be divided into *informal* and *formal* groups. A formal group is a group with a specific task and at least loosely defined member roles and activities. Formal groups can consist of *command* or *project* groups. A command group includes a leader and his or her followers and is part of the organization hierarchy. Project groups are formed by an organization to accomplish a specific task. They do not usually fit into the normal hierarchy of the organization and are often temporary in nature. An informal group is a group that evolves to satisfy the common needs and interests of its members but not to accomplish a specific task. Sayles also describes two types of informal groups, *interest* and *friendship* groups.[1] Interest groups form around common bonds shared by members. The common bond could be a professional, recreational, ideological, or other interest shared by the members. A friendship group forms because of the positive sentiments of members toward each other. Informal groups have the potential to exert considerable influence over the behavior of their members. In fact, informal groups often exert more influence than formal groups.

GROUP BEHAVIOR THEORY

The study of group behavior began to receive attention in the 1920s when Elton Mayo, an industrial psychologist from Harvard, and several of his Harvard colleagues began the famed Hawthorne studies at a Western Electric plant near Chicago. While the Hawthorne studies are credited by most experts with launching the human relations movement, they also created an interest in group behavior since the studies showed that the social dynamics of a group had considerable influence on the behavior of group members. One of the members of Elton Mayo's team, George Homans, later became a leader in the study of group behavior.

In the 1930s, Kurt Lewin became the acknowledged leader of the group dynamics movement. Lewin was a professor of social psychology at the University of Iowa and also taught at Stanford and Cornell and was the director of the Center for Group Dynamics at M.I.T. at the time of his death in 1947. He performed numerous experiments involving group behavior and began to develop theories explaining group dynamics. Since Lewin's death, the University of Michigan Center for Group Dynamics and the National Training Laboratories (now the NTL Institute for Applied Behavioral Science) have also been leaders in the study of group behavior. Although Lewin was instrumental in the formulation of NTL along with Kenneth Benne, Leland Bradford, and Ronald Lippitt, he died shortly before it was formally organized. NTL was primarily responsible for fostering the T-group (training or sensitivity-training group) approach to group learning.

GEORGE C. HOMANS'S MODEL OF WORK-GROUP BEHAVIOR

Figure 8.1 shows an adaptation of George C. Homans's theory of work-group behavior.[2] Homans's theory suggests that group behavior can be explained by evaluating the interaction between a group's *external* and *internal* systems, the resulting group productivity, satisfaction, cohesiveness, and individual development, and any changes that

[1]Leonard R. Sayles, *Research in Industrial Human Relations* (New York: Harper & Row, 1957), pp. 135–145.
[2]George C. Homans, *The Human Group* (New York: Harcourt Brace Jovanovich, 1950).

the feedback that these results have on the external and internal systems.

The external system that affects a group consists of *background factors* such as: (1) economic and social conditions, working conditions, leadership behavior, management assumptions and values, organizational technology and structure, organizational values, backgrounds of group members, organizational rewards and punishments, organizational rules and policies, and the status of the organization and a group within an organization, and (2) required group member *activities* (physical acts such as preparing a budget or managing people), *interactions* (the verbal and nonverbal behavior that occurs among people), *sentiments* (values, feelings, attitudes, or beliefs imposed by the organization), and *given sentiments* (those values, feelings, attitudes, or beliefs that group members possess when they join a group).

The internal system consists of *emergent* behaviors: how a group actually functions, which often differs from required behaviors. These behaviors include: (1) the groups' *emergent activities, interactions, and sentiments,* (2) the formation of group *norms* (standards of behavior that emerge in a group that become accepted and expected practices), and (3) an *internal social structure* that develops, which includes some combination of *group members* (members that conform to the group norms and are accepted members of the team) and *isolates* (members who will not conform to or accept group norms and are not accepted by most team members).

The interaction between the external and internal systems produces consequences in terms of group *productivity* and *satisfaction* and group and individual development. The consequences provide feedback for the external system, which may use this feedback to reward, punish, correct, or try to change group behaviors, which in turn may result in new emergent behaviors and consequences.

Figure 8.1 Work-group behavior. An adaptation of the George C. Homans model.

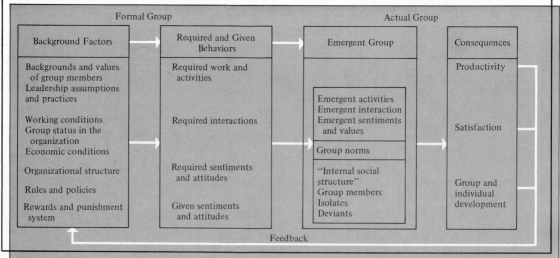

UNDERSTANDING GROUP DYNAMICS

What does a supervisor need to know in understanding group dynamics? The model in Figure 8.2 provides an overview of the basic group dynamics concepts that a supervisor should be familiar with. The model focuses on the following major concepts:

group background factors
group structure
group processes
group health
group stage of development
group results

Figure 8.2 Group dynamics model.

Background Factors	Group Structure	Group Processes	Stages of Group Development	Group Health	Results
Group leader External environment Member characteristics Group tasks Group status and influence Group history	Formal structure Group mission Group goals Required activities Required attitudes Member roles and responsibilities Policies, procedures, rules Organization Informal structure Actual structure Working conditions Work area layout Group size Space Traffic flow Pay and benefits Adequacy of supplies and equipment Noise level Lighting conditions Work area decor	Group norms Decision-making style Problem-solving style Conflict resolution style Group member roles Communication patterns Social structure Group cohesiveness Group trust Members power and influence	Stage I—Group formation Stage II—Development of task norms Stage III—Development of social norms Stage IV—Growth and maturity Stage V—Internal motivation	Healthy group Unhealthy group	Group performance Group satisfaction

GROUP BACKGROUND FACTORS

Groups, like people, may be influenced by several background factors including: (1) what the group leader is like, (2) what the external environment in which the group must operate is like, (3) the characteristics of group members, (4) what tasks the group performs, (5) the status and influence of the group, and (6) the history of the group.

Group Leader

A group's leader may have more influence on the dynamics of a group than any other factor. The group leader can motivate a group to higher levels of performance or stifle initiative. The leader sets an example for group members to follow and establishes the climate in which the members work. If the leader does not lead and fails to provide guidance and direction, an informal leader may emerge from among the group members. Understanding the group leader can be very important in understanding a group because the leader may have a major influence on:

group goals	group norms
group structure	group communication
member responsibilities	group status and influence
work climate	group socialization
group performance	group cohesiveness
group morale	group health

External Environment

The external environment in which the group operates includes many things that may influence it. Influences could range from general economic conditions to company or departmental goals, policies, leadership style, working conditions, and norms. These external influences can facilitate or inhibit the effectiveness of individual groups.

Member Characteristics

Are the group members motivated? Are they compatible? What are their social, economic, and educational backgrounds? Do they operate best with structure or freedom? Are there troublemakers in the group? Groups tend to work best when members are compatible but bring to the group new and unique experiences and ideas.

Group Tasks

The tasks performed by the group may affect both the quality and the quantity of dynamics within it. Some tasks require considerable interaction between group members, while others require little if any interaction. It is difficult for a group to develop trust and teamwork without frequent contact and interaction.

Group Status and Influence

The status and influence of a group and its leader will also affect a group. A group with low status and influence in the organization may underutilize its potential and either resign itself to second-class citizenship or fight for higher status. In either case, the group will have more than the normal internal problems.

Group History

The past can sometimes predict the future, so understanding the history of a group may be important. What style of leaders has the group had? Have they been successful? Where is the group in terms of its life cycle (growing, leveling off, declining)?

GROUP STRUCTURE

Group structure refers to the formal structure of the group, the emerging informal structure, and the physical structure. One of the keys to developing effective groups is to assure that the structure of the group is sound, given the purpose of the group, and is understood and accepted by group members.

Formal Structure

The formal structure of a group consists of the group's required activities, interactions, and attitudes; reporting and authority relationships; member responsibilities; job titles; and policies, rules, and procedures. The formal structure should be formally described in a policy manual, job descriptions, and an organization chart. Some groups never clearly define and communicate the group structure and thus keep a group confused and underutilized.

Informal Structure

The informal structure describes how the formal structure really works: who really has authority, what people in fact do, what attitudes are really like, and so forth. It consists of the emerging work activities, interactions, attitudes, group norms, social structure, and response to policies, rules, procedures, and the group leader. In healthy organizations, the formal and informal structures are very similar.

Working Conditions

Working conditions include the size of a group, office layout, and things such as office decor, noise level, lighting, space, privacy, and supplies and equipment. Interaction and cohesiveness tend to decrease as the size of the group increases. Depending on the task and the group members, it is difficult for groups of more than approximately 10 members to build quality relationships and make quality decisions. Physical layout can affect communication patterns and traffic flow. An office with an open arrangement (no private offices) increases interaction in a group but decreases member utilization because of frequent interruptions.

GROUP PROCESSES

Group processes refer to the ways in which group members relate, interact, solve problems, resolve conflicts, make decisions, and exert influence. Group processes are the most important part of group dynamics because they determine group results. Progressive supervisors periodically evaluate group processes with their group members to assure that the processes are leading to the desired end result.

Group Norms

Group norms are behaviors and procedures that are accepted and adhered to by most of the group members. They control the behavior of group members. Pressures to conform to group norms can be very strong. Group norms may form around productivity, length of breaks, attitudes toward supervision and management, vocabulary used among group members, how problems are dealt with, how decisions are made, and other activities involving the group. They have the potential to keep a group unhealthy and unproductive or assure group health and productivity. One of the best ways to build an effective group is for the leader and group members to agree on the ideal group norms that they would like to develop.

Norms develop quickly, even in a nonpermanent group that is brought together for a meeting or even a social function. Norms develop primarily around the following functions:

1. *Establishing relationships.* When groups are first forming or when new members are introduced, group members begin to feel each other out, find out how to work together, and establish initial group norms. This is usually a lighthearted and informal process. However, healthy groups do not leave relationships to chance. They strive for good relationships and take the time to mend poor ones.
2. *Establishing control and member roles.* The first process emerges into a process where members jockey for leadership, control, power, influence, and social status, test out the system, and begin to assume roles in the group. This process can be accelerated and accomplished constructively when done by design. When a group is formed or new members join, authority relationships and roles should be clearly defined and established. Also, several times a year, authority relationships and roles should be reevaluated.
3. *Task functions.* The task functions of a group refer to the work performed by the

group and to the decision-making, problem-solving, and conflict-resolution processes used by the group. Many group dynamics experts feel that the processes used to accomplish tasks are as important as the tasks themselves. For example, the processes in which decisions are made determine the quality of each decision and commitment to it. Thus, a decision that is railroaded by the boss or a powerful member may have unexpected consequences.

4. *Maintenance functions.* Maintenance functions include the efforts made to establish and maintain acceptable operating and relating procedures. These include efforts to maintain good human relations and group harmony, relieve tension, smooth out frictions, involve members in the group, and express feelings. In a healthy group, the operating and relating procedures that evolve are constructive and supportive and contribute to high group performance and satisfaction. However, in an unhealthy group, the procedures become unconstructive and unsupportive and often contribute to low group performance and satisfaction.

Problem Solving, Decision Making, and Conflict Resolution

As mentioned in the section on group norms, norms begin to emerge regarding how a group solves problems, makes decisions, and resolves conflicts. These processes are considered separately from group norms because of their importance to understanding group dynamics. A group that develops constructive and effective problem-solving, decision-making, and conflict-resolution processes will avoid many of the time-consuming problems that tend to develop in groups and that are not easily resolved because of the lack of constructive, agreed-upon processes for dealing with problems. A healthy group periodically evaluates these processes and agrees upon any needed adjustments. The problem-solving, decision-making, and conflict-resolution processes will be discussed in more depth in Chapter 9.

Group Member Roles

There are a number of roles that group members play in groups that are constructive and some that may be unconstructive. Any member of the team may display some or all of these roles. Along with identifying healthy group norms, one of the most effective ways of developing an effective group is to identify and discuss constructive and unconstructive roles and agree on how to deal with the unconstructive roles if they occur. This approach provides agreement on appropriate ways for group members to act and also provides acceptable methods for dealing with inappropriate behaviors before they have a detrimental effect on the group. Typical consequences and unconstructive roles are shown in Figure 8.3. The approach described here can be very effective in developing constructive group behaviors. Care should be taken, however, to not misuse it by calling attention to minor unconstructive behaviors that anyone could slip into and that are not harmful to the group.

Figure 8.3 Group member roles.

Constructive Roles	Unconstructive Roles
Leader Effective leaders clarify objectives and responsibilities, assure that problems are clearly defined and resolved, draw group members into the discussion, work in terms of priorities and results, and motivate group members to use their capabilities.	**Sidetracker** Sidetrackers get a group off the subject by bringing up irrelevant information, changing the subject, telling stories, pursuing hidden agendas, joking inappropriately, carrying on sideline conversations during meetings, or arriving late or leaving early.
Taskmaster Taskmasters keep the group on the task, prevent sidetracking, and assure that tasks are accomplished on time.	**Shotgunner** Shotgunners are critical, judgmental, and continuously put down ideas and people by playing the devil's advocate.
Human relations facilitator Human relations facilitators keep group harmony, relieve tension, encourage and support group members, help reconcile differences, keep communication open, show warmth and friendliness, use humor appropriately, and watch over the emotional climate of the group.	**Assumer** Assumers assume things about people and ideas without checking them out. **Isolate** Isolates withdraw from the group by being silent, showing disinterest, pouting, looking bored, or refusing to participate or cooperate with the group.
Perception checker When appropriate, perception checkers check out their understanding of what others have said, check to see if others have understood them, and occasionally summarize results and check for consensus.	**Autocrat** Autocrats dominate the group by forcing their own ideas, manipulating and intimidating group members, monopolizing group time, and making unilateral decisions.
Leveler and confronter Constructive leveling and confronting is used to get issues into the open. It is impossible to have a healthy group without leveling and confronting.	**Problem maker** Problem makers make a habit of disrupting, being poor listeners, creating and looking for problems and seldom having solutions, gossiping, ignoring the chain of command and group policies, rebelling against change or attempts to achieve change, and informally rallying group members to their causes.
Problem solver Problem solvers attack problems and not people, are good listeners, identify the key issues, explore alternatives, and motivate the group to select the best decision given the realities of a situation.	**Manipulator** Manipulators maneuver people to get their own way and send double messages by saying one thing when they mean another.
Contributor Contributing includes becoming a member of the group by accepting responsibility for one's behavior and its consequences, by getting involved, and by offering ideas and support.	

Social Structure

The social structure of a group describes how group members relate to each other and the status of each group member. Member status tends to be hierarchical but can also be influenced by knowledge, success, experience, longevity with the group, background, dress, communication skills, and leadership abilities. Imbalances in the social structure, such as a lack of socialization, too much socialization, significant differences in status, or the emergence of cliques, can make it difficult for a group to function effectively. Supervisors need to be aware of the social structure and to make possible a reasonable amount of socialization. They also need to assure that all group members, especially new members, are accepted into the social structure.

Group Cohesiveness

Group cohesiveness refers to the closeness and rapport among group members. Cohesiveness comes from interaction and personal knowledge about group members, so it is important for group members to get to know their leader and each other and to interact enough to develop trust and open communication. Group cohesiveness is important because cohesiveness usually leads to higher productivity and satisfaction.

Group Trust

Trust is essential for group members to work effectively, efficiently, and smoothly with each other. A lack of trust can quickly undermine group effectiveness. Trust is developed through straightforward, fair, and honest dealings among group members and through genuine and open communication.

Member Power and Influence

In a healthy group, power and influence are earned from constructive contributions. They are not abused or misused, and they are fairly evenly distributed among members. In unhealthy groups, power and influence are gained through manipulation and intimidation. They are often abused or misused, by the boss or a few aggressive group members.

Stages of Group Development

Groups grow and mature much like people. They move from: (1) group formation (being concerned about roles, responsibilities, policies, working procedures, rules, etc.), to (2) the development of task norms (leader's style, problem-solving, decision-making, and conflict resolution styles), to (3) the development of social norms (establishing member relationships; communication patterns, influence, and status), to (4) growth and maturity (group effectiveness, motivation, teamwork, cooperation, and learning, to (5) internal motivation (group becomes self-actualized, creative, authentic). Like people, some groups grow quickly and others never mature beyond lower stages. Until

Figure 8.4 Stages of group development.

Stage of Development	Key Processes	Key Variables
Stage 1 Group formation	**Formal and Informal Identification of:** Group membership and purpose Member roles Group policies, procedures, rules and working conditions Group activities and individual responsibilities	Leader's style and skills Legitimacy of group purpose Acceptance of group purpose by members and outsiders Working conditions Methods by which policies, procedures, rules, and wage structure are established
Stage 2 Development of group task norms	**Norms Begin to Evolve Concerning:** Leader's style Work climate Problem-solving style Decision-making style Meeting style How tasks are accomplished	Methods by which task norms are established Extent to which members are treated fairly and consistently Willingness of the group occasionally to evaluate and change problem-solving, decision-making, and meeting styles
Stage 3 Development of group social norms	**Social Structure Begins to Evolve Around:** Group and member status and influence Communication patterns Emerging member roles Group cohesiveness	Importance of interaction and cooperation in accomplishing the job Similarity of member backgrounds and attitudes Size of the group and physical proximity of group members Efforts made to orient new members to the group Level and frequency of interaction between members Willingness of group members occasionally to evaluate member roles and processes

a group reaches stage four, it is unlikely that the group will ever achieve or sustain a high level of performance and satisfaction.

Supervisors have considerable influence on what stage a group is in. They can either accelerate group development through effective supervisory practices or keep the group at a low level of development by frustrating member needs through ineffective supervision. Figure 8.4 describes the different stages of development that a group goes through. An understanding of these stages of group development is important

Figure 8.4 *(continued)*

Stage of Development	Key Processes	Key Variables
Stage 4 Growth and maturity	**Group Behavior Characterized by:** High performance Effective problem-solving, decision-making, and conflict-resolution skills Member cooperation and teamwork Open communication Willingness to learn and grow Trust	Amount and quality of training available to group members Efforts to make work challenging and interesting Opportunities for responsibility, growth, recognition, and advancement Success in confronting and resolving problems Actual productivity and satisfaction of the group Involvement and influence of the group in major decisions that affect them The type of behaviors that are rewarded
Stage 5 Internal motivation	**Group Behavior Characterized by:** High-quality work Member behavior is open, authentic, creative, and cooperative High level of honesty, trust, and ethics Members show a high degree of caring, respect, and support toward each other Creativity and innovation	Leader's style and skills Group control over its destiny Health of the group Ability of the group to continue to grow and change Organizational and group values

to understanding why a group is or is not performing. Quite often a group never realizes its potential because the early stages of development were never completed. For example, a group without clear goals and responsibilities and satisfactory leadership and working conditions is unlikely to develop its potential.

In evaluating a group's stage of development it is important to realize that although a group will have a dominant stage, it may also show some behaviors in each of the other stages.

Group Health

Group health refers to the overall effectiveness and maturity of a group. A healthy group inspires confidence, creativity, openness, trust, high productivity, and a willingness to test new capabilities. An unhealthy group creates self-doubt, stifles creativity,

Figure 8.5 Characteristics of a healthy group.

1. Productivity, work quality, and morale are high.
2. Leadership is effective.
3. Group norms are positive and constructive.
4. Commitment is high.
5. Group is task-oriented.
6. Group has clear, worthwhile, and shared goals.
7. Formal and informal structures are sound and congruent.
8. Member roles and responsibilities are clearly defined.
9. Members are compatible, valued, competent, and have high regard and respect for each other.
10. Members encourage and support each other.
11. Members have a positive attitude.
12. Members work effectively as a team, yet encourage individuality.
13. There is excellent collaboration and cooperation within and between groups.
14. Group cohesiveness and trust are high.
15. Communication is open and accurate.
16. Members are kept well informed.
17. Problems and conflicts are confronted and resolved.
18. Members are involved in major decisions that would affect them.
19. Healthy and constructive behaviors are recognized and rewarded.
20. Unhealthy and unconstructive behaviors are confronted.
21. Problem employees are helped and encouraged but not kept if they choose not to improve.
22. Group has a "big picture" focus.
23. Meetings are productive.
24. Group members unite in a crisis.
25. Group is continuously learning and growing.

and results in closed communication, distrust, minimal effort, and low productivity. The characteristics of a healthy group are listed in Figure 8.5.

END RESULT

The interaction among group background factors, structure, processes, and stage of development and health produce an end result in terms of group performance and satisfaction. The results affect the background factors, which in turn create changes in the other phases of the group dynamics model that may maintain or cause a new end result. It is a continuous, circular flow. In a healthy group, results are used to make constructive adjustments, while in an unhealthy group, the adjustments are usually unconstructive and continue to make things worse. For example, in a healthy group, low performance could result in getting the group members together and finding solutions to the problem, such as resolving some within-group conflicts or working out problems with the leader's style. In an unhealthy group, low performance would probably result in finding people to blame, tightening up controls, restricting member privileges, and consequently compounding the problem.

Performance

Performance can be defined in terms of many variables, such as productivity, profit, sales, absenteeism, and turnover.

Productivity tends to be high when: (1) there is effective leadership; (2) goals and responsibilities are meaningful, clear, and shared; (3) competent people are hired, valued, treated with respect, trained, rewarded, and kept appraised of where they stand; (4) there is a stable social structure characterized by openness, cooperation, teamwork, caring, and room for individuality; (5) group norms are positive; (6) jobs are kept challenging and interesting; (7) communication is open, genuine, and accurate; (8) responsible behavior is rewarded and irresponsible and disruptive behavior is confronted; (9) continued disruptive behavior is not tolerated; (10) problems and conflicts are dealt with openly, fairly, and constructively; (11) members' needs for growth and satisfaction are reasonably satisfied; and (12) the group is successful in accomplishing meaningful objectives.

Productivity tends to be low when: (1) there is ineffective leadership; (2) goals and responsibilities are unclear and not mutually shared; (3) anyone is hired, members are not valued, little is done to train, motivate, or appraise members of where they stand, and rewards are lacking or not connected to performance; (4) the social structure is unstable and characterized by game playing; a lack of cooperation, teamwork, and caring; and considerable pressure to conform to unhealthy group norms; (5) group norms are primarily negative; (6) jobs are boring and unchallenging; (7) communication is unconstructive and seldom accurate; (8) responsible behavior is not rewarded and irresponsible or disruptive behavior is not confronted; (9) continuously disruptive behavior is tolerated; (10) problems and conflicts are smoothed over or resolved through power and are not handled fairly; (11) members' needs for growth and satisfaction are frustrated; and (12) the group is not successful in accomplishing meaningful objectives.

Satisfaction

Satisfaction (sometimes called morale) reflects group members' feelings about themselves and the group. Satisfaction is as important as productivity in the long run because it results in either long-run productivity or problems.

Satisfaction tends to be high when: (1) group members are treated with caring, respect, and fairness; (2) group norms are positive; (3) members' needs for belonging and acceptance, growth, and recognition are reasonably well met; (4) members are involved in important decisions that affect them; (5) the social structure is stable and group members like and respect each other; and (6) collaboration and teamwork are excellent.

Satisfaction tends to be low when: (1) group members are treated unfairly and with indifference, contempt, or lack of respect; (2) group norms are negative; (3) members' needs for belonging and acceptance, growth, and recognition are frustrated; (4) decisions are dictated by management; (5) the social structure is unstable and unresolved frictions exist between group members; and (6) collaboration and teamwork are replaced by a self-serving, individualistic attitude.

INTERGROUP DYNAMICS

When groups need to relate to other groups, a new set of dynamics evolves, called intergroup dynamics, or the dynamics existing between groups. It is no small wonder that groups often have difficulties working together when you consider that they may have different goals, different time constraints, different types of personnel, different ways of solving problems, and different needs. Intergroup dynamics play a significant role in the success or failure of an organization. Intergroup problems can result in wasted time and effort, production slowdowns because of lack of coordination, considerable hostility and friction between group members, and technical and interpersonal problems between groups. Many organizations have intergroup problems. At times it appears as though an internal civil war has been declared. The marketing department is at war with the manufacturing department, the supervisors are at war with the manager, and everyone seems to be at war during the budgeting process. It is a wonder that some organizations function at all.

The group dynamics model in Figure 8.2 can also be used to understand intergroup dynamics. The background factors between the groups, structural relationships between the groups, the group processes that have evolved, and the stage of development and overall health between the groups can all be considered in understanding the dynamics among groups. However, supervisors should also be aware of two additional aspects of intergroup relations—intergroup competition and intergroup problem solving.

Intergroup Competition

A landmark study to analyze intergroup competition was undertaken by Muzafer and Carolyn Sherif at a boys' camp.[3] Their study has been replicated many times among adult groups and now serves as a reliable description of what happens when groups compete. Perhaps the most complete description of intergroup competition was developed by Edgar Schein.[4] Schein was able to identify what happens within each competing group, what happens between competing groups, and what happens to the winner and loser. An adaptation of the Sherif and Schein findings is shown in Figure 8.6, including alternatives for managing intergroup competition.

Intergroup Problem Solving

Robert Blake and Jane Mouton[5] have developed two very interesting models for understanding intergroup dynamics. The first model (see Figure 8.7) shows the assumptions made about intergroup conflict and the resulting group actions. The assumptions and their consequences are:

[3]M. Sherif and C. W. Sherif, *Groups in Harmony and Tension* (New York: Harper & Row, 1953).
[4]Edgar Schein, *Process Consultation: Its Role in Organization Development* (Reading, MA: Addison-Wesley, 1969).
[5]Robert Blake and Jane S. Mouton, "The Fifth Achievement," *Journal of Applied Behavioral Science* Vol. 6, no. 4, 1970, 413–426.

Figure 8.6 Responses to intergroup competition and conflict. Adapted from M. Sherif and C.W. Sherif, *Groups in Harmony and Tension* (New York: Harper & Row, 1953); and Edgar Schein, *Process Consultation: Its Role in Organization Development* (Reading, MA: Addison-Wesley, 1969).

	Typical Behaviors	**Possible Alternatives**
Responses Between the Groups	The goal of winning becomes the group objective and results in the groups pulling together to stop the enemy, demanding loyalty to group norms, becoming more structured, organized, and task oriented toward the goal of winning, and becoming willing to put aside internal problems and submit to whatever the leader or the group requires to accomplish the task. Considerable pressure for conformity is made on group members who do not fall into line.	Competition and conflict are viewed as challenges to be resolved. The group pulls together to identify the problem and explore alternatives in finding the best solution available. The group remains focused on resolving the real problem. Differences of opinion are allowed, but if a consensus decision is reached, group members will support the decision. Because of the high level of trust, the leader is given considerable flexibility in resolving problems. Informal leadership responsibilities may shift, depending on the expertise needed.
Responses to the Consequences	Unsympathetic or competitive groups or individuals are seen as the enemy, and trust between the groups begins to break down. Attempts are made to win over sympathetic, influential, or neutral groups or individuals to the group cause. Interaction with unsympathetic groups or individuals decreases and becomes increasingly hostile or superficially polite. Perceptions of what is happening and of conversations become distorted. Group members assume the best about their group and the worst about unsympathetic groups or individuals. As the groups become more hostile and entrenched, the actual problems that need to be solved become irrelevant, and winning becomes the real issue. Undercutting and questionable practices are justified in the pursuit of winning.	Genuine efforts are made to communicate with the other group or groups to establish a problem-solving climate to resolve the differences. Group members are careful to check out their perceptions before assuming things about their own group or another group. In attempts to resolve differences, they are well prepared, try to remain objective, and continue to focus on finding the best solution available.
Responses Within Each Group	Groups may smooth over the real issues and coexist by tolerating each other, seeking a third-party solution, seeking a compromise, continuing in a win-lose mode, or seeking to resolve the real problems constructively. If it becomes apparent that there is a winner and a loser, the loser will tend to explain away losses and look for scapegoats and then will either learn from the loss and pull together as a team or fall apart through internal conflicts, low morale, and an every-person-for-himself attitude. The winner will become more confident, more cohesive, and more cooperative—especially if the group develops new constructive goals so that it can continue to grow. Without new goals, the group is likely to become complacent and even lethargic if it does not find new goals.	Every effort is made to resolve differences constructively and to establish healthy norms between the groups regarding how to solve problems. Win, lose, or draw, the group tries to learn from the experience. Positive efforts during the problem-solving process are recognized. New, constructive goals are established to keep the group motivated.

Figure 8.7 Blake-Mouton model of intergroup conflict. Adapted from Robert Blake and Jane S. Mouton, "The Fifth Achievement," *Journal of Applied Behavioral Science,* Vol. 6, no. 4, 1970, pp. 413–426. Used by permission from the *Journal of Applied Behavioral Science.*

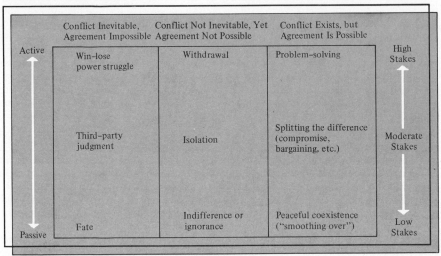

1. Disagreement is inevitable and agreement impossible. When A and B disagree, the assumption is that the disagreement must be resolved either in favor of A or B. No other solution is possible. One of three mechanisms may be used for resolution:
   A. win-lose power struggle
   B. third-party arbitration
   C. fate
2. Disagreement is not inevitable, but agreement is not possible. This situation occurs when interdependence between the groups is unnecessary. Conflict can be resolved by:
   a. One group withdrawing
   b. Maintaining indifference when there is a conflict of interest
   c. Isolating the parties from each other
3. Agreement is possible, and a means of resolving the conflict be found. Resolution is possible through:
   a. Peaceful coexistence
   b. Compromise or bargaining
   c. Problem solving

The second model, shown in Figure 8.8, illustrates how groups actually solve problems.[6] The model shows that the best way to resolve intergroup problems is through objective problem solving, the goal of which is to find the best solution to the

[6]Robert Blake, Herbert A. Shepard, and Jane S. Mouton, *Managing Intergroup Conflict in Industry* (Houston: Gulf Publishing Co., 1964), p. 195.

Figure 8.8 How groups solve problems. Adapted from Robert Blake, Herbert A. Shepard, and Jane S. Mouton, *Managing Intergroup Conflict in Industry* (Houston: Gulf Publishing Co., 1964), p. 195. Used with permission of Gulf Publishing Company.

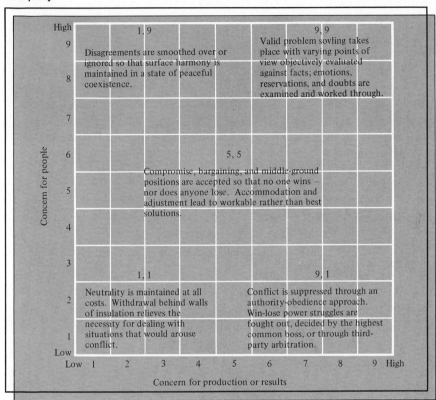

problem by objectively evaluating different opinions and facts, by working through differences, and by working toward a consensus of the best solution.

SUMMARY

An understanding of group behavior is an essential part of a supervisor's knowledge. Understanding individual behavior is not enough, since people in organizations spend much of their time in groups, and the dynamics of a group may heavily influence individual behavior. A supervisor who understands group behavior is in a position to develop healthy group norms by design, help group members become effective team members, recognize and resolve conflicts within and between groups, and evaluate the group processes and make any necessary adjustments.

   There are a number of models available for understanding group dynamics, such as the Homans model. The group dynamics model presented in this chapter contains six components: (1) group background factors, (2) group structure, (3) group processes, (4) group stages of development, (5) group health, and (6) group results. Each component has several elements that are important to an understanding of group dynamics.

Understanding intergroup dynamics is very similar to understanding group dynamics. The same concepts apply; in addition, there are special dynamics involved in intergroup competition and problem solving.

IMPORTANT TERMS

group	informal group structure
group dynamics	norms
formal groups	group members
informal groups	isolates
command groups	group cohesiveness
project groups	stages of group development
interest groups	group health
friendship groups	group results
formal group structure	intergroup behavior

REVIEW QUESTIONS

1. What is a group? What are the different types of groups?
2. How could a supervisor use the Homans model to understand group behavior?
3. What group background factors affect group behavior?
4. What group structure factors affect group behavior? What can a supervisor do to structure a group for effectiveness?
5. What group processes should a supervisor be aware of?
6. What are the five major stages of group development? How could a supervisor use his or her awareness of stages of group development to improve group performance and satisfaction?
7. What are the characteristics of a healthy group?
8. What should a supervisor look for to evaluate the overall effectiveness of a group?
9. What intergroup dynamics should a supervisor be aware of?
10. How could a supervisor use the Blake and Mouton conflict and problem-solving models?

EXERCISES

8.1 Group Dynamics Internalization

The purpose of this exercise is to help class members internalize the most important aspects of group dynamics. Meet in small groups to accomplish the following task:

1. Divide a sheet of chart paper into two equal parts. List what a supervisor most needs to know about:

    a. Understanding group dynamics
    b. Understanding intergroup dynamics

2. In developing the two lists, the group may draw from the text, other material that they are familiar with, and their own ideas and experience. Be prepared to defend your lists by explaining your choices and why you selected them.

Allow about 20 minutes for the task. Then meet in the classroom to have each group share its list (allow about 15 minutes).

8.2 Understanding Group Roles

This exercise is designed to demonstrate how to identify the constructive and unconstructive roles that people play in groups. Eight volunteers will conduct a meeting in front of the class. The volunteers should each reach into a box that has four pieces of paper that say "constructive" and four that say "unconstructive" and take one of the pieces of paper. They are not to show their paper to anyone else. Those who drew "constructive" pieces are to play constructive roles in the meeting, and those who drew "unconstructive" pieces are to play unconstructive roles.

The meeting is to last 20 minutes, and the task is to *rank* the 10 major advantages and disadvantages of the women's movement.

The class members should be asked to refer to Figure 8.3, which describes constructive and unconstructive roles, and use the model to make notes on the roles they observe during the meeting. If the equipment is available, this is an excellent exercise to videotape. It may be helpful to have the volunteers wear name cards.

After the exercise, the following questions should be discussed:

1. What constructive roles did you observe?
2. What unconstructive roles did you observe?
3. What effects did the unconstructive roles have on the group?

8.3 Dealing Constructively with Unconstructive Roles

This is a good follow-up exercise to Exercise 8.2. The class should meet in small groups and list on chart paper constructive ways to deal *in general* with unconstructive roles and *specifically* with each of the unconstructive behaviors listed in Figure 8.3. Allow about 30 minutes for the task.

Meet in the classroom to have each group share its lists.

8.4 Observing Group Dynamics: A Live Case

The purpose of this exercise is to provide a "live case" so that class members can observe the dynamics of a group. A mixed group of six volunteers will participate in a meeting to be observed by the class. Ideally the class members should observe from a room with one-way glass so that they will not disrupt the meeting. Observations should be based on the model in Figure 8.2.

The Situation (to be read by the class and all volunteers)

Five of the volunteers are to hold a meeting with the following trade. The president of their rapidly growing company has just attended an executive seminar at Harvard and feels very strongly that the company needs to establish a human resource development department. The president has hand-picked the five persons to organize and run the new department. The president is convinced that the department will become one of the most important departments in the company and that the future success of the company may depend upon the success and innovativeness of the new department. The instructions from the president are for the five to decide which position each of them should have in the new department. They have total freedom in deciding who should occupy each position. All that the president wants to know is their rationale for deciding on each position. Each of the persons selected has worked for the company for five years and is making $25,000 per year. The positions that the president wants established in the new department and the salaries that each position will carry are listed below. While some salaries represent a drop from present salaries, hopefully the opportunities will compensate for the loss in income.

> Director of human resource development—$40,000
> Head of organization development and training—$30,000
> Head of labor relations—$25,000
> Supervisor of hiring and recruiting—$23,000
> Supervisor of wages, salaries, and benefits—$20,000

The group has 40 minutes to decide who should be in each position. The president wants the task to be completed in the allotted time and will accept no excuses for not following his instructions!

Role for Sixth Volunteer (to be read only by the volunteer)

You are to play the role of an ambitious recent graduate of Harvard with an M.B.A. in human resource development who has just been hired to join the new human resource development department. You have had two years prior experience before your M.B.A. working as an administrative assistant to the personnel director of your father's company. You and your father are personal friends of the president, and your father's company is the president's biggest customer. The president has just sent you in to join the HRD meeting to become part of the team. Enter *20 minutes* after the meeting has started but do not observe the meeting prior to joining the team. You are to enter by giving them the following note from the president (have a copy made before class).

Memorandum

From: Company President
To: Human Resource Development Team
Subject: Introduction of (Write your name here)

I am sending in a new person to join your team that I just hired. I know that you will find my friend a great asset to the team. This person just graduated from Harvard with an M.B.A. in Human Resources Development. Your new colleague has two years' experience as an administrative assistant in personnel in the company that is our biggest customer which happens to be owned by your new colleague's father. I know that you will be very happy to have such an outstanding talent on the team and will find my friend a challenging position. To make room for six employees instead of five, I am taking Benefits out of Wage and Salary and creating a new position called Benefits Administration, carrying a salary of $18,000. I will check back with you in *20 minutes* at which time I want your decisions on staffing your new department.

Debriefing

At the conclusion of the exercise, everyone returns to the classroom. The volunteers meet in front of the class to discuss briefly:

1. What dynamics were you aware of in your group?
2. What were your feelings when a new member was introduced?
3. How did each of you feel about the outcome of the meeting in terms of the position you ended up with?

The volunteers then return to their seats and the class discusses the following questions:

1. What group dynamics did you observe?
2. How did the group respond to the new member?
3. How did the group solve problems and make decisions?
4. What could the group have done, if anything, to be more effective?

SUGGESTED ADDITIONAL READINGS

Bales, Robert F. *Interaction Process Analysis.* Cambridge, MA: Addison-Wesley, 1950.

Bradford, Leland D., ed. *Group Development.* 2d ed. San Diego: University Associates, 1978.

Cartwright, Dorwin, and Zander, Alvin. *Group Dynamics: Research and Theory.* New York: Harper & Row, 1968.

Hinton, Bernard L., and Reitz, Joseph H. *Groups and Organizations.* Belmont, CA: Wadsworth Publishing Co., Inc., 1971.

Lorsch, Jay W., and Lawrence, Paul R. *Managing Group and Intergroup Relations.* Homewood, Ill.: Richard D. Irwin Inc. and the Dorsey Press, 1972.

Moreno, J. L. "Contributions of Sociometry to Research Methodology in Sociology." *American Sociological Review* (June, 1947), pp. 287–292.

Shaw, Marvin E. *Group Dynamics: The Psychology of Small Group Behavior.* New York: McGraw-Hill Book Co., 1981.

Zander, Alvin. *Making Groups Effective.* San Francisco: Josey-Bass Publishers, 1982.

9

Developing
Effective Groups

A prudent man foresees the difficulties ahead and prepares
for them. The simpleton goes blindly on and suffers the
consequences.

Proverbs 14:8

OBJECTIVES

This chapter provides you with the information necessary to:

1. Conduct an effective meeting
2. Conduct a team-building session with groups
3. Understand the seven basic steps to group problem solving
4. Identify the advantages of group decision making
5. Know the six decision-making styles that groups use
6. Become familiar with group decision-making techniques
7. Indentify eight approaches to group conflict resolution and when each is appropriate

---

GROUP MEETINGS

This chapter begins with the study of group meetings because meetings provide the forum in which problem solving, decision making, and conflict resolution take place.

182

Understanding a few basics of effective meetings can enhance the likelihood of successful problem solving, decision making, and conflict resolution. Then problem solving will be considered, since effective problem solving precedes effective decision making. Next, a number of approaches to decision making will be evaluated, followed by a consideration of options for resolving conflicts in groups. Figure 9.1 provides an overview of the concepts that will be considered in this chapter.

As people advance in an organization, they spend an increasing amount of time in meetings. Meetings can be very productive and satisfying. However, considerable time, energy, and effort can be wasted in ineffective meetings.

Why Meetings Fail

People spend an increasing amount of time in meetings as they move up. Yet many meetings are ineffective. The cost of ineffective meetings becomes significant as it becomes apparent that key people may be wasting considerable time. Why are some meetings ineffective? Some of the major reasons are:

1. Meetings are often poorly planned, with no advance notices or agendas.
2. The wrong people are invited.
3. Leadership is lacking or is of a style that stifles creativity and open communication.
4. The physical setting is not conducive to the needs of the group.
5. Interruptions, disruptions, and conflicts go unresolved.
6. The meetings last too long and cause participants to lose interest.
7. The meetings take people away from work.
8. Participants sometimes use the meetings to pursue their own hidden agendas.
9. Participants don't know how to work effectively together.
10. Meeting time is used for tasks that could have been accomplished outside the meeting.
11. A lack of follow-up on decisions made in meetings.

Why Meetings Succeed

While poorly run meetings can be costly, well-run meetings have many benefits. Some of the major benefits are:

1. They are an efficient way to share information and ideas and make decisions that require input from several sources.
2. They can result in higher-quality decisions than would be made by any individual operating independently.
3. They can result in high commitment to decisions by involving group members in the decision-making process.
4. They can serve developmental purposes by helping people learn how to work together and by helping them learn problem-solving, decision-making, and conflict-resolution skills.

Figure 9.1 Approaches to group meetings, problem solving, decision making, and conflict resolution.

Group Meetings	Group Problem Solving	Group Decision Making	Group Conflict Resolution
Type of meetings Information-giving Information-seeking Problem-solving Decision-making Conflict-resolution Process-evaluation Team-building Combination **Meeting guidelines** Don't hold meetings unless they are definitely needed. Send out an agenda ahead of time with purpose, time, place, and approximate length. Select a pleasant meeting place that is physically arranged to accomplish the desired meeting dynamics and that will be free from interruptions. Make sure that all necessary administrative details are taken care of before the meeting. Invite the right people. Start on time unless there is a valid reason for not doing so. Use the appropriate leadership style and skills for the goals of the meeting. Stick to the agenda unless there are strong reasons for deviating. Monitor the process aspects of the meeting; encourage constructive behaviors and confront or ignore unconstructive behaviors. Provide closure by summarizing any decisions, agreeing on any actions to be taken, and assuring that follow-up responsibilities are understood.	Climate building and goal setting Problem definition and data gathering Exploring and evaluating alternatives and their potential consequences Process evaluation Decision making Closure Follow-up	**Decision-making methods** Delphi technique Quantitative methods Brainstorming Nominal group technique Programmed decisions Consensus testing **Decision-making processes** Decision by default Decision by powerful member Decision by minority Decision by majority Decision by compromise Decision by consensus	Fate Smoothing over Situational changes Compromise Superordinate goals and policies Superordinate authority Power struggle Third-party intervention Collaboration

5. They help satisfy socialization needs of the participants and also improve teamwork and group cohesiveness.
6. They may help identify people with leadership potential.

DIFFERENT TYPES OF MEETINGS

A supervisor can choose from a wide variety of meeting formats designed for different purposes, ranging from social meetings to meetings with a specific task to accomplish. While there are several types of meetings that will be discussed, it should be kept in mind that meetings may have more than one purpose and thus may include a combination of the types of meetings mentioned below.

Information-Giving Meetings. Informational meetings are used to provide information to the participants and occasionally to answer questions from them. Since there is a limit to how much information participants can absorb, these meetings should be fairly brief.

Information-Seeking Meetings. A meeting is called to gather information from the participants to help identify problems or make decisions.

Problem-Solving Meetings. In a problem-solving meeting within or between groups, problems are identified and resolved and follow-up responsibilities are assigned. "Gripe sessions," during which people complain without being asked to offer constructive and practical solutions, are not included in this category because they are often counterproductive and undermine morale. The problem-solving emphasis focuses on identifying and solving problems and not on dwelling on problems. It is often helpful to begin problem-solving meetings by focusing on strengths or things that are going well. This will establish a constructive and positive climate for working on problems.

Decision-Making Meetings. As the name indicates, decision-making meetings are held for the purpose of arriving at decisions. In most cases they are combined with the problem solving that precedes actual decision making. However, when decision making is the only purpose, any preliminary work on problem solving should be done before the decision-making meeting. The decision-making process used should be tailored to the desired end result of the decisions. For example, if strong commitment is needed or the decision may have a major impact on those present, a consensus approach may be appropriate; when commitment isn't crucial, a decision by majority or compromise may suffice.

Conflict-Resolution Meetings. Conflict-resolution meetings are held for the express purpose of resolving conflicts within or between groups. These meetings require some expertise in conflict resolution and must be carefully planned to achieve resolution without compounding the conflict. It is sometimes helpful to have a trained internal or external person who is not affiliated with the group or groups involved to conduct conflict-resolution meetings.

Process-Evaluation Meetings. A group meets to evaluate: (1) the effectiveness of the group; (2) the leadership, problem-solving, decision-making, conflict-resolution, interaction, and social processes of the group; and (3) improvements that could be made in how the group works together. A healthy group will usually have several of these meetings a year. It is sometimes helpful to bring in a trained person from outside a group to gather data from group members and conduct the process-evaluation meeting as long as the person has a positive, constructive, problem-solving focus.

Team-Building Meetings. Teams seldom function effectively by chance. Team-building meetings are designed to help build groups into effective teams. Most healthy teams have one or more team-building sessions a year. Such sessions are best held away from the organization and could last from half a day to several days. A typical agenda could include:

1. *Climate building.* Meeting purpose and objectives are discussed. Structured exercises or ways to get better acquainted are used to build a climate of trust, support, and genuine openness. Training may be given in problem-solving and decision-making skills, in group and meeting dynamics, and in constructive-confrontation and leveling skills.
2. *Process evaluation.* The group evaluates its leadership, problem-solving, decision-making, interaction, and social processes and decides on improvements. This may include focusing on individual as well as group behaviors.
3. *Problem solving.* The group identifies and resolves within-group, between-group, and technical problems.
4. *Goal setting and planning.* Goals are established and plans developed for a given period of time.
5. *Training.* Team-building sessions often include some training in supervision and management or technical skills.
6. *Closure.* Closure consists of summarizing what was accomplished and assigning follow-up responsibilities. This is also a good time to create a positive experience by having a strength-building session (break into smaller groups and identify the strengths of each member) or social gathering such as a dinner.

All meetings are different, so there are no hard and fast ground rules for running effective meetings. However, some typical characteristics of effective and ineffective meetings are shown in Figure 9.2.

GROUP PROBLEM SOLVING

Group problem solving is probably more of an attitude than it is a set of prescribed procedures. If those who are involved in the problem have a sincere desire to solve the problem, one way or another, a solution will probably be found. Thus, the primary key to successful problem solving is a problem-solving attitude that communicates a genuine desire to be a problem solver, to refrain from being a problem maker, and to be willing to seek the most appropriate solution to the problem. A secondary key to problem solving is developing effective problem-solving procedures. The procedures

Figure 9.2 Characteristics of effective and ineffective meetings.

Effective Meetings	Ineffective Meetings
Agenda is sent out ahead of time.	No advance notice is given.
Leader and group members are prepared.	Neither the leader nor the members are prepared.
The objectives and procedures of the meeting are clear and agreed upon.	The objectives and meeting procedures are not clear.
A time target is set for completing the meeting.	The meeting is too short or too long.
The meeting is reasonably well organized.	Organization is resisted because members are too "mature" to need it.
Group members listen, level, confront, support each other, and check out perceptions.	Group members play games, interrupt, misquote each other, do not check out assumptions and perceptions, and compete for time in the limelight.
Sidetracking, shotgunning, and hidden agendas are confronted and curtailed.	Group members often become sidetrackers or shotgunners.
Participants are enthusiastic and positive problem solvers.	Participants are negative and become problem makers.
Communication is open, on the subject, and constructive.	Communication is closed and unconstructive.
All members are involved and treated with respect.	Cliques develop.
The ideas and feelings of participants are considered.	The meeting is mechanical, and ideas and feelings are not considered.
Problems are clearly defined and prioritized.	Problems identified are often trivial, irrelevant, and unsolvable.
Several alternatives are considered along with their practicality and short- and long-range consequences.	Decisions are forced or made by default, and consequences are not considered.
The group enjoys working together.	Group members do not get along.
Group members are committed to seeking the best solution to the problem under the circumstances.	Members push for their own ideas without considering what is best for the group.
Responsibility for keeping the meeting effective is shared by all members.	The leader is held responsible and blamed for what happens in the meeting.
Quality decisions are made, and follow-up responsibilities defined.	Low-quality decisions are made, and follow-up responsibilities are taken for granted.
Group productivity is high.	Group productivity is low.
Meeting time is used only for relevant issues.	Meeting time is used for things that could have been resolved outside the meeting or that are not relevant.
Meeting time is not used for tasks, decisions, or subcommittee efforts that can be accomplished before the meeting.	Participants ask questions and answer them themselves to appear smart.
There is no need for members to compete, play games, or try to look smart.	The meeting location is poorly chosen.
The meeting location is carefully chosen.	Members show up late, come and go, take phone messages, and carry on side conversations.
Members show up on time and give their full attention to the meeting.	No record is kept of what went on.
Appropriate records are kept of the meeting.	Members provoke each other or play the devil's advocate to make things more interesting.
Members are supportive of each other and do not say things they don't mean.	

that are suggested here may provide guidance in helping a supervisor develop his or her own guidelines for solving problems.

Climate Building and Goal Setting

The purpose of this step is to build a problem-solving climate and gain commitment to a goal of finding the most appropriate solution to the problem. Where a willingness to solve the problem already exists, this step may not be necessary. Otherwise, several procedures may be useful:

1. Express a sincere desire to resolve any problems.
2. State the purpose and objectives of the meeting.
3. If necessary, seek agreement on the agenda and on any procedures needed to discuss the issues, constructively air differences, and make decisions.
4. It may be appropriate to consider any possible barriers to arriving at the most appropriate decision and to agree on how to overcome the barriers.
5. Seek agreement on the goal of genuinely endeavoring to find the most appropriate solution to the problem.

It may be helpful to do some climate building before a formal meeting by informally meeting with key people who could affect the problem-solving process.

Problem Definition and Data Gathering

The purpose of this step is to define or identify the problem or problems. In most cases a literal definition is not necessary as long as there is agreement on what has been identified as the problem or problems. What is important is that the real issues, rather than symptoms, be identified. It should be agreed upon during this step that relevant data that will help identify, illuminate, or resolve the key problems will be sought and discussed but that dwelling on problems is not appropriate to the problem-solving process. This important agreement may be necessary to prevent the focus from shifting from problem solving to general griping.

There are many ways to accomplish this step. For example, approaches may range from reviewing and modifying a previously prepared list of the problems, generating a list from the participants, meeting in small groups to identify the key issues, or using an expert from outside the group to employ more sophisticated techniques. Data gathering can be accomplished by the participants at the meeting or may be done outside the meeting if the available information is insufficient for a group to proceed. It is sometimes helpful to prioritize the final list of major problems.

Exploring and Evaluating Alternatives and Their Merits and Potential Consequences

The purpose of this step is to explore and evaluate alternative solutions. The exploration and evaluation phases are separated as much as possible to avoid stifling free and creative thinking. First, alternatives are uncritically explored or brainstormed; thereafter, the feasible alternatives are evaluated in terms of their merits and potential consequences. This task can be accomplished by the total group, by assigning smaller groups specific problems to work on, or by designating the task or parts of it to be accomplished outside of the formal meeting.

Process Evaluation

This step is an ongoing activity that could occur at any time during a problem-solving meeting. The purpose is to observe the interpersonal and problem-solving dynamics, check out perceptions of what is taking place and being said, summarize progress on key issues or decisions, and assure that the meeting dynamics are kept constructive. The process evaluation may be essential to the success of the meeting. It may uncover hidden agendas, important misperceptions, feelings, disagreements, and dysfunctional behaviors or procedures; it can also point up positive attitudes, behaviors, and feelings. It is equally important to recognize when this step is *not* needed and to make sure that it is not overdone. Some groups get so carried away with processing what is going on that they lose sight of their purpose. The processing becomes the purpose and the stated purpose becomes secondary or nonexistent.

Decision Making

The decision-making process is one of the most important processes in determining the success of a group or organization. How decisions are made determines the quality of the decisions, commitment to the decisions, and the consequences of the decisions. Many options are available for making decisions, ranging from sophisticated computer-based models to decisions by authority or decisions by consensus. Decision quality, commitment, and consequences should all be considered in selecting the most appropriate decision-making style. Once decisions are made, they should be summarized and checked against the desired end results. Decision-making alternatives are discussed in more detail in the pages that follow.

Closure

A consultant once told the executive committee of a bank after observing one of their problem-solving meetings, "You were outstanding in building a positive climate, defining the problem, exploring alternatives, communicating openly with each other, and making high-quality decisions. However, you left out one of the most important steps of all—providing closure. You completed an otherwise sterling performance by making assumptions about who would follow up on your decisions and how they would be implemented. There is a good possibility that your excellent decisions will never be carried out in the way that you assumed, or may not be carried out at all, because no one was assigned the responsibility of follow-up."

This scene is repeated all too often in problem-solving meetings. Group members are so relieved to have arrived at a decision and so eager to adjourn that nothing is done to assure that the decision is implemented. At least four things should be considered in providing closure:

1. Check for agreement and last-minute details. This is a risky but important procedure. It is risky in the sense that it may uncover issues that could undercut what has been accomplished. However, it is best to find out about such issues while something can be done about them. This procedure is not always appropriate, but it should at least be considered.
2. Accomplish any necessary action planning. Making a decision is sometimes much easier than deciding how to implement it. It may be necessary to develop action plans for carrying out decisions.
3. Assign follow-up responsibilities. Make sure that individuals or groups are assigned to follow up on any action items or decisions generated by the problem-solving group. Also assure that follow-up responsibilities are clear, when they should be accomplished, and who they should be reported to.
4. Agree on any further actions required of the group. Check with the group to see if further meetings or actions are required of the group.

Follow-up

Well-intended and high-quality decisions and action plans are sometimes never accomplished because of a lack of follow-up. Ideally, a supervisor, other central person, or committee should assume the responsibility of following up on any decisions, action plans, and agreed-upon responsibilities designated during the closure phase of the meeting.

GROUP DECISION MAKING

The advantages and disadvantages of group decision making is an often-discussed topic among supervisors, managers, and management experts. Ross Webber lists some of the advantages as the existence of a greater body of knowledge and information, greater creativity in developing alternatives, increased acceptance of decisions, and a greater understanding of the decision rationale.[1] There are other advantages, such as the possibility of higher-quality decisions, increased feelings of belonging and commitment to the decision-making team and the organization, and the personal and group development that can be gained from learning how to interact and solve problems in groups. David Hampton, Charles Summer, and Ross Webber also point out some of the disadvantages of group decision making.[2] They quote the old adage, "A camel is a racehorse designed by a committee." Then they discuss research that shows some

[1]Ross Webber, *Management: Basic Elements of Managing Organizations* (Homewood, IL: Richard D. Irwin, 1979), p. 215.
[2]David R. Hampton, Charles E. Summer, and Ross Webber, *Organizational Behavior and the Practice of Management,* 4th ed. (Glenview, IL: Scott, Foresman, 1982), p. 253.

individuals may be more effective in terms of accuracy, speed, and efficiency than groups; that the average individual is faster and more efficient than groups even though he or she makes more errors, and that while groups are more accurate than individuals, they are also much slower. Other disadvantages are that group pressures may stifle creativity and lead to conformity; dominant individuals or cliques may cancel the advantages of group decision making; member disagreements or hidden agendas may result in stalemates, hard feelings, or conflicts; and some group members may prefer to work independently and leave decision making to higher management.

The Importance of a Variety of Decision-making Processes

The advantages and disadvantages of group decision making are neither an endorsement or indictment of group decision making. They merely represent practical realities that suggest that a variety of decision-making processes need to be considered in making decisions, ranging from individual decision making to a wide spectrum of group decision-making processes. Once this is understood, decision making can be considered from a broader viewpoint. In choosing a decision-making process, such issues as the desired end result, the needs for involvement and commitment, the needs for creativity and quality, the risks involved, and time constraints can all be considered in choosing the most appropriate decision-making approach to take. One group that was very interested in being progressive and up to date in their understanding of group dynamics and group health was very relieved to learn that consensus decision making was not the only way for a healthy group to make decisions. They labored through long, needless hours in arriving at a consensus on many decisions that could have been more effectively made by the group leader, other members of the group who possessed relevant knowledge, or subcommittees.

Decision-making Techniques

The realities of decision-making techniques used in organizations have been discussed in the classic book by Herbert Simon[3] and in later works by James March and Herbert Simon[4] and Richard Cyert and James March.[5] For example, Herbert Simon points out that real-life managers usually "satisfice" in both information gathering and decision making. This means that they seek "just enough" information and choose "good enough" decisions rather than consider all possible alternatives before selecting the best choice. March and Simon suggest that actual decisions are made under conditions of "bonded rationality" since the ability of humans to make purely rational decisions is limited. Cyert and March discuss how managers will often choose the most readily available decision rather than seek optimum decisions, even though they have the capabilities for determining optimum choices. Today, supervisors have access to many

[3]Herbert Simon, *Administrative Behavior* (New York: Macmillan, 1957), pp. 40–41.
[4]James March and Herbert Simon, *Organizations* (New York: Wiley, 1958).
[5]Richard Cyert and James March, *A Behavioral Theory of the Firm* (Englewood Cliffs, NJ: Prentice-Hall, 1963).

sophisticated approaches to decision making that could increase accuracy in finding optimal decisions. However, in reality they tend to rely more on subjective approaches to decision making that result in decisions that may do the job but may not be optimal. Choosing good-enough decisions is probably satisfactory in most cases, but supervisors need to avail themselves of modern decision-making technology where accuracy and optimizing are of high importance.

In general, decision-making techniques can be described as *prescriptive, descriptive,* or *predictive.* A prescriptive approach describes the way decisions should be made in an ideal and rational sense. The *scientific method* is a good example of the prescriptive approach. The scientific method usually includes the following activities: (1) define the problem; (2) state the objective; (3) develop a hypothesis; (4) collect data; (5) classify, analyze, and interpret the data; and (6) draw conclusions. A descriptive approach describes what actually occurs such as in the Simon, March, and Cyert descriptions of decision making. The predictive approach considers information, probabilities, and other factors to predict probable outcomes of different choices. Some of the specific techniques that could be considered in making decisions are:

1. *Delphi technique.* To overcome the need for so many meetings, the Rand Corporation developed the Delphi technique.[6] Rather than meet in groups, managers fill out a questionnaire that solicits opinions on key issues. A coordinator prepares a composite of their views, sends the composite back to the managers, and asks them to respond again. After several rounds of responses, a consensus may develop without ever having to get the managers together in a face-to-face meeting. The disadvantage of this approach is that it can be very time-consuming, and face-to-face contact may in fact enable a group to reach decisions faster. An alternative that some managers use is to start out with the Delphi technique and then meet to make a final decision.

2. *Quantitative methods.* Numerous quantitative methods are available to decision making. Most are available in packaged programs. Some of the better-known methods are break-even analysis, cost-benefit analysis, operations research, computing expected values of various alternatives, using decision models that apply probability analysis, developing decision trees, PERT charts, linear and dynamic programming, and modeling and simulation. It is not our intent to describe each of these methods, since they are generally covered in statistics and management science courses. However, supervisors should be aware that sophisticated decision-making techniques are available.

3. *Brainstorming.* The brainstorming technique is a simple and efficient method for generating ideas without stifling creative thinking. Group members are asked to call off any solution or idea that comes to their mind regarding the stated problem while a recorder writes down their ideas where everyone can see them. No criticism or evaluation of the ideas is allowed until the list is complete. The ideas are then discussed and evaluated for practicality and merit (this step is often preceded

[6]A. R. Fusfeld and R. N. Foster, "The Delphi Technique: Survey and Comment," *Business Horizons,* June, 1971, pp. 63–74.

Figure 9.3 Consensus testing.

Alternatives	Choice Ranking by Members*						Total	Rank
	Member Number							
	1	2	3	4	5	6		
1. Build new building on property 1	2	1	2	2	3	3	13	2
2. Build new building on property 2	1	2	1	1	1	2	8	1
3. Do nothing	5	5	5	5	5	5	30	5
4. Remodel old building	4	4	3	4	4	4	23	4
5. Expand old building	3	3	4	3	2	1	16	3

by prioritizing the ideas). The discussion and evaluation may generate more ideas that can be added. Finally, the group narrows the list down to the best alternatives.

4. *Nominal group technique.*[7] This technique is similar to brainstorming. Group members silently list on paper every possible solution or relevant factor regarding the stated problem. A member of the group then consolidates the lists into one list for everyone to see. There is no discussion at this point other than asking clarifying questions. Once the list is completed, the alternatives are discussed by first prioritizing the items and then elaborating on them, beginning at the top.

5. *Programmed decisions.* Programmed decisions are decisions that can be based on policies, procedures, rules, standards, or past precedences. A well-thought-out and up-to-date policy manual can simplify the decision-making process, especially with regard to time-consuming routine decisions.

6. *Consensus testing.* There are many methods that can be used to test out where people stand. Voting is the most common method. Voting can be accomplished by a show of hands or having people vote on a piece of paper, if there is reason to believe that anonymity would increase the reliability of the voting. Another approach is to list the alternatives vertically on a large piece of paper and then have each member rank the alternatives, as shown in Figure 9.3. If this ranking does not provide a clear choice, the ratings for each alternative can be added together to provide totals that can be ranked. The lowest total score ranks highest. This process is also useful for prioritizing problems.

DECISION-MAKING PROCESSES

When groups make decisions, they do so according to one of many decision-making processes. The process is very influential in determining a decision and the commitment to the decision. It is important to recognize that a variety of processes are needed in group decision making. The particular process chosen may depend on:

1. The importance of the decision
2. The potential short- and long-range consequences of the decision

[7]Andre L. Delberg et al., *Group Techniques for Program Planning* (Glenview, IL: Scott, Foresman, 1975), pp. 17–39.

3. Who the decision will affect
4. The needs for quality and creativity
5. The needs for consensus and commitment
6. The time available to make the decision

The processes described here are patterned after ideas by Robert Blake, Jane Mouton, and Edgar Schein. Figure 9.4 summarizes the processes and also evaluates their potential consequences and appropriateness.

Decisions by Default

A decision is made by default when a group chooses the first reasonable decision that comes along without evaluating the merits of the decision or considering other alterna-

Figure 9.4 Decision-making processes.

Decision Process	Possible Consequences	When Appropriate
Decision by default: Any decision is accepted just to be able to say a decision has been made.	No commitment to the decision.	When quick decisions of little consequence need to be made
Decision by a powerful member: A strong and forceful member, usually the group leader, controls group decisions.	Decisions may lack quality, agreement, and commitment. Creativity, openness, and leveling may be stifled.	When decisions need to be made and there is no group agreement When decisions need to be made and group involvement isn't necessary or warranted
Decision by a powerful minority: A strong minority of the group members control group decisions.	Cliques may develop. The majority may not be committed to the decision. Conflicts may develop between group members.	When the minority has special knowledge or influence and has the commitment of the majority
Decision by majority or voting: A strong majority of the group members control group decisions.	Cliques may develop. The minority may not be committed to the decision. Conflicts may develop between group members.	When the majority has special knowledge or influence and has the commitment of the minority
Decision by compromise: A compromise of different alternatives is made in order to make a decision.	Decisions may be inappropriate and low in quality. Commitment may be low. Differences may linger.	When compromise is necessary to make a decision When time is short
Decision by consensus: Issues are openly discussed, disagreements explored, and alternatives considered until the group agrees on the best solution.	Consensus may not be possible. Reaching decisions may take too much time.	When decisions need to be high-quality and need to have high commitment

tives. This approach may result in inferior decisions and low commitment to them. However, for routine decisions of little consequence, it can be an appropriate way to make decisions.

Decision by a Powerful Member

A decision by a powerful member occurs when a strong and forceful member of the group controls the decision-making process. The powerful member is usually the boss but could also be a domineering group member. This approach has the possible disadvantages of stifling creativity, commitment, and decision quality, as well as destroying group morale and motivation. The advantages are that it takes less time to make decisions, the powerful member may be the appropriate choice to make the decision due to position or expertise, and the decision may not require group involvement.

Decision by a Powerful Minority

Decision by a powerful minority occurs when a minority of the group members control the decision-making process. This often occurs when a small but vocal and influential clique develops within a group. The danger of this approach is that it may be assumed that the powerful minority is speaking for the whole group when in fact the other members are too intimidated to voice their real opinions and feelings. If allowed to continue, it may also divide a group and have a negative effect on performance and morale. It may be a useful process, however, when a minority of the members have specialized knowledge or information or when the group designates a subgroup to make certain decisions.

Decision by a Powerful Majority

This approach occurs when a majority of the members control the decision-making process. The most common example is when a vote is taken or members are polled and the majority opinion decides. While this may seem like a reasonable way to make decisions, it also suffers from the same consequences as decision by a powerful minority, except that the numbers have shifted in terms of who is having the most influence on group decisions.

Decision by Compromise

A decision is made by compromise when concessions are made between the proposed alternatives until agreement is reached on an acceptable choice. The problem with this approach is that you may end up with a low-quality decision that no one is committed to, a win-lose situation wherein some members have more to gain than others from the choice, and bad feelings among the members. The advantage is that it is sometimes the only possible way of reaching a decision.

Decision by Consensus

A decision by consensus is made when the issues are openly discussed, alternatives are freely voiced and evaluated, disagreements are aired, and the group eventually agrees on the best choice. This is the ideal way to make decisions when decision quality and commitment are important. It does not require that everyone be in total agreement as long as the group is committed to the decision. Edgar Schein identifies an ideal form of this approach as decision by unanimous consent.[8]

GROUP CONFLICT RESOLUTION

A conflict is a struggle between opposing forces. Conflicts can occur between individuals or within or between groups and can range from minor difficulties to unresolvable stalemates. As the Blake, Shepard, and Mouton model in Chapter 8 indicated, the approaches used to resolve conflicts are based on the assumptions made about conflicts.[9] Some supervisors assume that conflict is bad and is to be avoided at all costs. Such assumptions lead them to smooth over conflicts or let them die a natural death. Other supervisors assume that conflicts are struggles that must be won at all costs to preserve authority and power. These assumptions lead to win-lose power struggles and irresponsible actions justified by the need to win or be right. Fortunately, there are also supervisors who assume that conflict is not to be feared and should be dealt with openly and constructively. These supervisors take a problem-solving or conflict-resolution approach to conflicts. In organizations where these assumptions are typical, conflicts that need to be dealt with are brought out into the open and resolved without the usual negative residual effects that accompany the first two assumptions.

Another way to view group responses to conflict is to consider the responses of healthy and unhealthy groups. Most groups probably fit in between, using some of both responses. One of the true tests of a group's stage of development is how it responds to conflict.

Healthy Group Response to Conflict

Even healthy groups are rarely free of conflicts within the group or with other groups. Healthy groups may temporarily overreact to conflicts, but their typical response includes: (1) openly and constructively facing and confronting conflicts; (2) having as a goal finding the most satisfactory solution for all parties involved; (3) attacking problems, not people; (4) focusing on the real issues; (5) using constructive, straightforward methods to arrive at a fair resolution; (6) uniting as a team to find responsible solutions; (7) learning from conflicts and not repeating mistakes; and (8) leaving residual negative effects of conflicts behind.

[8]Edgar Schein, *Process Consultation* (Reading, MA: Addison-Wesley, 1969), p. 57.
[9]Robert R. Blake, Herbert A. Shepard, and Jane S. Mouton, *Managing Intergroup Conflict in Industry* (Houston: Gulf Publishing Co., 1964), p. 195.

Unhealthy Group Response to Conflict

Unhealthy groups experience frequent open or undercover conflicts within the group and with other groups. They tend to overreact to conflicts and rarely achieve lasting and constructive resolutions. Typical responses of unhealthy groups to conflict include: (1) facing conflicts by smoothing them over, using power, or dealing with them indirectly; (2) having as a goal winning, or at least minimizing losses; (3) attacking people rather than problems and looking for scapegoats; (4) losing sight of the real issues; (5) using unconstructive, manipulative methods without regard for fairness; (6) banding together to support unconstructive causes or splintering as a group in pursuit of individual self-interest; (7) blaming circumstances for mistakes and then repeating the mistakes; and (8) internalizing any negative residual effects of conflicts.

HOW GROUPS RESOLVE CONFLICTS

A wide variety of methods is used by groups to resolve conflicts within or between groups. Quite often, the methods used are inappropriate to the situation and result in an unsatisfactory resolution for one or more of the parties involved. If inappropriate methods continue to be used, the negative consequences result in increased dysfunctional behavior. Supervisors need to be familiar with different alternatives for managing group conflicts and their advantages and disadvantages so that they can improve their ability to select appropriate methods and increase the likelihood of achieving satisfactory resolution. In his excellent article in the *California Management Review,* Stephen Robbins calls this approach to conflict a contingency model for managing conflict.[10] Robbins goes on to present an excellent discussion of many of the resolution techniques used, including a brief definition and the strengths and weaknesses of each technique. Some of the ideas that follow in discussing approaches to conflict resolution were adapted from the Robbins model.

Resolution by Fate

Conflicts are resolved by fate when nothing is done to achieve resolution in the hope that the conflict will resolve itself. There are some obvious problems with this approach to conflict resolution. When resolution is left to chance, the outcome may be unsatisfactory or the conflict may continue without resolution. As unsatisfactory solutions or unresolved conflicts accumulate within and between groups, dysfunctional behavior increases and performance suffers. Also, group members may begin to lose respect for the organization and its leaders. There are situations, however, in which resolution by fate may be appropriate. When conflicts are minor or potential negative consequences are low, this approach may be reasonable. Some conflicts do dissolve with time. It may also be the only option. Conflicts sometimes arise where there is no apparent solution or where the possibility of seeking a solution does not exist. The first possibility may

[10]Stephen Robbins, "Conflict Management and Conflict Resolution Are Not Synonymous Terms," *California Management Review* 21, no. 2 (Winter, 1978): 67–75.

occur when a solution cannot be found or when several solutions are equally attractive or even equally unattractive if an undesirable choice must be made. The second possibility usually occurs when one or more parties involved in the conflict blocks any attempt at resolution.

Resolution by Smoothing Over

Smoothing over is an important and necessary skill for anyone involved in a conflict and can be a valuable approach as long as it is not misused. It occurs when attempts are made to minimize the conflict and emphasize the need for cooperation and agreement. It is misused when it smooths over important issues, results in temporary solutions that are not likely to last, or intensifies conflict because one or more of the involved parties views it as a cover-up or avoidance procedure. It can be used appropriately when time is limited, the need for cooperation is high, and the issues are minor enough that smoothing may resolve the conflicts. Smoothing is particularly useful when the conflict is due to a misunderstanding and the parties involved are willing to discuss the issues openly and constructively.

Resolution by Situational Changes

This approach occurs when human, material, capital, or structural changes are made to achieve resolution. It may result, for example, in employees' being transferred to different positions, being involved in educational or training programs, or even being fired as a last resort. It could involve restructuring an organization or group, reallocating resources, or making facility or working-environment changes. The drawbacks are that it may not be a viable choice; it may simply postpone future problems, it could cause additional conflicts, and the costs in time, effort, and resources may be greater than any benefits. If this approach does not solve the root problem, it may simply shift the problem elsewhere. The worst misuse of this approach occurs when changes are made that reward inappropriate behaviors. For example, troublemakers may be given a new office or may even be promoted to get them out of the way. Not only will this not resolve the root problem, but it will anger the remaining members. Situational changes may be appropriate when there are no other alternatives; for example, when they eliminate the source of the conflict, when they result in a win-win solution for all parties involved, or when the benefits simply exceed the costs.

Resolution by Compromise

Compromises occur when important concessions are made to reach agreement. This definition does not recognize insignificant concessions as compromise, nor does it recognize the more traditional view that concessions have to be made to both parties. Often one of the parties will make concessions to accomplish resolution. The problems with compromising to reach resolution are that low-quality decisions are often the result, one or more of the parties involved may not be committed to the decision, and lingering bad feelings sometimes affect future relations. It could also result in one or both of the parties losing, depending on the nature of the compromises. Compromising, however, is a necessary part of conflict resolution. It may be the only way to reach a decision. It is also possible that the resulting compromise may be an improvement over other alternatives. Compromises may also be necessary to avoid having a clear winner and loser and allowing the involved parties to save face. Compromising may also be useful when expediency is important and there is little risk of a negative aftermath.

Resolution by Adhering to Superordinate Goals or Policies

Resolution can sometimes be achieved by adhering to superordinate goals or policies. This approach is very effective when existing goals or policies can be used to resolve conflicts. It is more difficult when new goals or policies must be developed and agreed to by the conflicting parties. The approach breaks down when the goals or policies used to achieve resolution are questionable. For example, a conflict may be resolved between two departments competing for limited resources by referring to company goals for the year, which require expanding one of the departments and contracting the other. However, the goal itself may have been established for political reasons and may not be based on sound judgment. Policies that are inflexible or rarely updated can also result in resolutions that are not based on sound judgment and may consequently generate negative repercussions from the conflicting parties involved. Other problems are that the approach may not deal with the root causes of the conflict, and it may also be difficult to reach agreement on superordinate goals or policies that the parties involved are willing to become mutually committed to. On the other hand, it is an excellent method if sound goals and policies exist that would resolve conflicts, and it is important to focus on commonalities rather than differences to achieve resolution. One of the best ways to prevent unnecessary conflict is to have clear goals and an up-to-date and fair policy manual.

Resolution by Adhering to Superordinate Authority

While this approach is often overused by traditional autocratic supervisors, it is sometimes underused by modern supervisors. It describes situations in which a superordinate authority is used to achieve resolution. In most cases, the superordinate authority is the boss of those involved in the conflict. However, it could also include management, a grievance committee, or perhaps designated persons in the personnel department. The approach tends to fail when the parties involved do not respect the opinions of the superordinate authority or when the superordinate authority is not impartial. Like many of the other approaches to conflict resolution, it also may not resolve the underlying problems causing the conflict. The advantages are that it is a quick and efficient way to reach resolution if the parties involved recognize and respect the superordinate authority. It is also useful for emergency situations when the stakes are too high to rely on the conflicting parties to resolve their differences or as a last resort when other alternatives have been unsuccessful.

Resolution by Power Struggle

Seeking resolution through win-lose power struggles is an option usually associated with countries that are unable to resolve major conflicts. However, such power struggles also exist in organizations when individuals or groups try to resolve conflicts with power and are unwilling to participate in rational problem solving. It is the most potentially destructive of the conflict-resolution approaches. The possible adverse consequences can be substantial, and it makes future problem solving difficult, if not impossible. It also undermines trust and cooperation and may in fact result in a lose-lose situation over the long run. In rare situations, resolution through power struggles may be appropriate. For example, it may be appropriate if it is the only available alternative or if it is a matter of survival. It may also be a necessity that is worth the struggle if there is a reasonable chance of winning.

Resolution Through Third-Party Intervention

This approach occurs when a third party is used to reach resolution through collaboration or mediation. The third party could be, for example, management, a boss, a peer, an internal or external consultant, a professional mediator, union officials, or a grievance committee. While this approach can be an excellent method for resolving conflicts, it does have some disadvantages. For instance, it may be difficult to find a capable third party who is able to facilitate resolution without bias or ulterior motives. Also, a third party could possibly intensify the conflict. This is particularly true if the third party takes an adversary position. This sometimes happens when an inexperienced internal or external consultant becomes involved and in attempting to get the problems out in the open actually worsens the situation. Another problem is that the parties involved may not have as much involvement in any solutions reached as the third party. However, if an objective and skilled third party can be obtained, this can be an excellent method for achieving resolution. A third party may have the expertise and reputation necessary to motivate the parties involved to collaborate in reaching resolution or, if collaboration is not possible, at least to acquiesce to a satisfactory solution.

Resolution by Collaboration

Resolution by collaboration is achieved by using problem-solving, decision-making, and conflict-resolution skills. It is the most effective way to resolve a conflict because the parties involved work together to find a satisfactory solution. The approach draws heavily on the problem-solving and decision-making processes mentioned previously in this chapter. Third-party resources are often used to achieve a collaborative approach to conflict resolution. The most obvious disadvantage is that the parties involved may not have the willingness or skills to achieve a "collaborative" effort. Another disadvantage is that it may be too time-consuming or costly to pursue. In addition, it may not be as well-suited to the unique characteristics of a particular conflict as other methods. It can be a very useful method, however, when mutual commitment to any resolution is of high importance, when a long-term healthy relationship between the parties involved is important, and when excellent third-party resources are available to help achieve collaboration.

WHEN YOU CAN'T WORK WITH GROUPS

Although the information in this chapter can help a supervisor develop almost any group into an effective team, there are situations that may prevent a group from becoming effective:

1. When the boss's boss is unsupportive and dictatorial and violates the chain of command by telling your people what to do.
2. When the group members are unmotivated and not committed to group objectives.
3. When the organization in which the group resides is so unhealthy that it is impossible for a healthy group to survive.
4. When funding is too limited to hire, keep, and train competent and constructive people.
5. When members who are destructive or incompetent are kept.
6. When someone who is supported by higher management decides to undermine the group.

In such situations, bringing in a third party may lead to a resolution of these problems. However, it is also possible that until the people involved in the problems are willing to seek constructive solutions, the problems may be temporarily unsolvable.

EVALUATING GROUP MEETINGS AND PROCESSES

Groups should evaluate their effectiveness periodically. A group that has a history of successful performance should evaluate itself once or twice a year. Groups that are experiencing difficulties should evaluate themselves more frequently. Evaluations can be made by considering available performance information (productivity, quality of work, absenteeism, turnover, etc.) and by interviewing group members individually or in a group meeting, as well as by having members complete questionnaires that evaluate meetings, relationships, and the problem-solving, decision-making, and conflict-resolution processes.

SUMMARY

In addition to understanding group dynamics, supervisors also need to understand the dynamics of meetings, as well as the dynamics of group problem solving, decision making, and conflict resolution. Organization members, particularly supervisors, spend considerable time in meetings. Well-planned meetings that take into account the type of meeting needed (information-giving, information-seeking, problem-solving, decision-making, conflict-resolution, process-evaluation, team-building, or a combination of several types) can be a valuable asset to a supervisor. However, poorly planned meetings can result in wasted time, money, and efforts, as well as low-quality decisions with far-reaching consequences.

Supervisors need especially to be familiar with problem-solving, decision-making, and conflict-resolution meetings. Group problem solving begins with climate building and goal setting and also includes defining problems, gathering data, exploring and evaluating alternatives and their potential consequences, evaluating processes, making decisions, providing closure, and following up on action items. Decisions can be made by default, by a powerful member, by a powerful minority or majority, by compromise, or by consensus. There are advantages and disadvantages to each decision-making process, and supervisors need to be familiar with the appropriateness of each. They also need to be familiar with different conflict-resolution processes and when each is appropriate. Some alternative approaches are resolution by fate, smoothing over, situational changes, or compromise; by adhering to superordinate goals, policies, or authority; or through power struggles, third-party interventions, or collaboration.

Finally, a supervisor needs to know when group skills are not likely to work. There are some situations in which a group has little chance of becoming effective.

IMPORTANT TERMS

information-giving meetings
information-seeking meetings
problem-solving meetings
decision-making meetings
conflict-resolution meetings
process-evaluation meetings
team-building meetings
Delphi technique
quantitative decision making
nominal group technique
conflict resolution by
   situational changes
conflict resolution by
   compromise
conflict resolution by
   power struggle
conflict resolution by
   collaboration

programmed decisions
consensus testing
decisions by default
decisions by a powerful member
decisions by a minority
decisions by a majority
decisions by compromise
decisions by consensus
conflict resolution by fate
conflict resolution by
   smoothing over
conflict resolution through superordinate goals or policies
conflict resolution through superordinate authority
conflict resolution through third-
   party intervention

REVIEW QUESTIONS

1. What are some of the major reasons that meetings are often unproductive?
2. What are some of the advantages of meetings?
3. Describe the different types of meetings and their purposes.
4. What are the typical components of a team-building meeting?
5. Discuss each step of the group problem-solving process.

6. Discuss why it is important to take a contingency (situational) approach to decision making rather than to rely on one decision-making process.
7. Describe some of the decision-making techniques being used today.
8. Discuss the six decision-making processes described in this chapter, their possible consequences, and when they may be appropriate.
9. How do healthy and unhealthy groups typically respond to conflict?
10. Discuss the nine conflict-resolution processes described in this chapter, their possible consequences, and when they may be appropriate.
11. Discuss some of the reasons it may not be possible to work with a group.

EXERCISES

9.1   Group Processes Integration

Meet in small groups to develop answers to one or more of the review questions at the end of the chapter. Each group could answer all questions or selected questions, or the questions could be divided equally among the groups. Meet as a whole group then and have each group report on its answers. This is a good exercise for integrating what has been learned from the chapter.

9.2   Evaluation of Group Meetings

Meet in small groups to develop a list of the major characteristics of effective meetings and of ineffective meetings. Use brainstorming to develop the lists, and then rank the top 15 items. It may help to put the final lists on chart paper so that they can be shared when the class meets as a group.

9.3   Intergroup Problem Solving and Conflict Resolution

The purpose of this exercise is to evaluate intergroup dynamics and problem-solving and conflict-resolution processes. The exercise works best with groups that have met together previously, although new groups can be used.

Phase I—Group Meetings

1. The class should break up into smaller groups of about five to ten people.
2. Each team should have chart paper and a box of crayons.
3. Each team is to draw a picture of itself using the following criteria:
   a. The drawing must portray the personality of the *team as a whole* and of *each team member.*
   b. Any approach can be taken—scenic, symbolic, etc.—as long as the portrayals are reasonably self-evident and no words are used.
   c. The drawing should be creative.
   d. The drawing should integrate individual efforts into a team project.
   e. A team name consistent with the drawing should be selected and placed at the top of the drawing.
4. Before returning to the main classroom, each team should select two representa-

tives (could be one or three, depending on how many groups there are) to represent the team in an intergroup meeting to select the best picture. The members of the winning team should be given an award such as an additional half grade added to their next test (B becomes B+, etc.), or each team could contribute $2 before the exercise begins to be given to the winning team.

5. Prior to returning to the classroom, each team should give its representatives instructions on what they are expected to do.
6. The teams have one hour to complete Phase I.
7. The drawings should be taped side by side to the classroom wall with masking tape.

Phase II—Intergroup Meeting of Representatives

The representatives sit in a circle at the front of the classroom. The remaining team members sit in the classroom with their team. The representatives will have *one hour* to select the best picture. They are to follow this procedure:

1. There must be a *consensus* on which picture is best.
2. Representatives should make *every* possible effort to reach a decision without stalling to avoid a decision.
3. The exercise will end promptly at the conclusion of one hour. A *timekeeper* should be appointed.
4. The meeting must take the following format:
   a. Representatives meet for 15 minutes.
   b. Teams meet with their representatives for 5 minutes.
   c. Representatives meet for 15 more minutes.
   d. Teams meet with their representatives for 5 minutes. They can also meet informally with other teams at this point.
   e. The remaining time (about 20 minutes) is to be used by the representatives in a final meeting.

Phase III—Debriefing

As a class, discuss the following questions:

1. Using the intergroup dynamics model in Figure 8.6 in Chapter 8, what intergroup dynamics did you observe?
2. What were the major strengths and weaknesses of the meeting procedures used by the representatives?
3. What steps of the problem-solving process did they follow?
4. What decision-making approaches did they use?
5. Did the group representatives use any conflict-resolution approaches? If yes, what did they do?
6. What were your major insights about intergroup dynamics, meetings, problem solving, decision making, and conflict resolution?
7. What improvements could have been made to make the representative group more effective?

Phase IV—Summary

It may be useful to point out that this exercise simulates very closely what actually happens in many organizations. Also, by using the basic procedures outlined in this chapter for effective meetings as well as for solving problems, making decisions, and resolving conflicts, most intergroup meetings can be handled successfully.

SUGGESTED ADDITIONAL READINGS

Davis, J. H. *Group Performance.* Reading, MA: Addison-Wesley, 1969.

Janis, I. L. *Victims of Groupthink.* Boston, MA: Houghton Mifflin, 1972.

Jewell, L., and Reitz, H. J. *Group Effectiveness in Organizations.* Glenview, IL: Scott, Foresman, 1981.

Katz, D., and Kahn, R. L. *The Social Psychology of Organizations.* New York: John Wiley and Co., 1978.

PART FOUR

Supervisory Management Practices

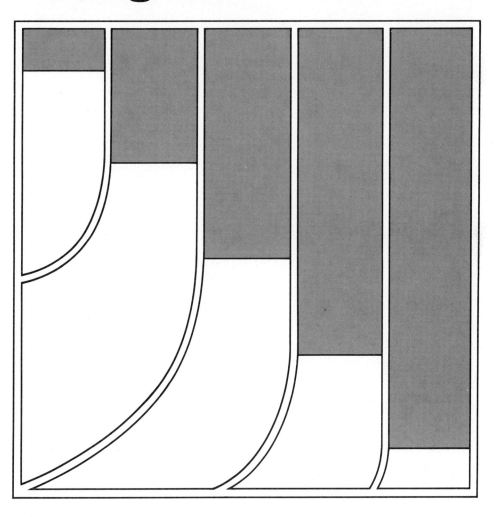

10

Leading[1]

When we think we lead we most are led.

Byron

If the blind lead the blind, both shall fall into the ditch.

Matthew 15:14

Reason and judgment are the qualities of a leader.

Tacitus

So long as I am acting from duty and conviction I am indifferent to taunts and jeers, I think. They will probably do me more good than harm.

Winston Churchill

OBJECTIVES

This chapter provides you with the information necessary to:

1. Understand the difference between leadership and supervision.
2. Explain why both leadership and supervision are important.
3. Explain the three major theories of leadership—the traits, styles, and contingency theories—and describe some of the leading models of the styles and contingency theories.

[1]Parts of this chapter were reprinted with permission from D. D. Warrick, "Leadership Styles and Their Consequences," *Journal of Experiential Learning and Simulation,* Vol. 3–4: pp. 155–172, 1982.

4. Integrate the styles and contingency theories.
5. Understand the concept of the adaptable leader-manager, recognize the adaptability clues that can be used to size up situations, and know when to emphasize different skills.
6. Describe the democratic adaptable leader concept.
7. Resolve some of the current leadership theory dilemmas.

THE IMPORTANCE OF LEADERSHIP

Of all the considerations that determine the success or failure of organizations, leadership is one of the most critical. Neither money nor machines can substitute for leadership in rallying human resources to accomplish organizational objectives in an increasingly complex and rapidly changing technological and psychological climate. Successful supervisors and managers need to be effective leaders since they must influence people to achieve objectives.

LEADERS VERSUS MANAGERS AND SUPERVISORS

While leaders, supervisors, and managers have much in common, there are important differences. *Leadership* can be defined as the ability to influence and inspire people to action. A leader could range from a political leader who rallies people to a cause, to a military leader who inspires troops to victory, to a department head who commands great employee loyalty, to a worker who emerges as an informal leader and influences group attitudes and actions.

While a leader focuses primarily on influencing and inspiring people, a supervisor or manager works with *both human and material resources* using a variety of skills, one of which is leadership, to achieve goals effectively and efficiently. Some leaders are very good at influencing and inspiring people but very inept at managing human and material resources. There are many examples in history as well as industry where the very person who inspired great accomplishments was also the primary cause of their demise through poor management. For example, in a very successful high-technology company, the leader who built the company and inspired employees to great effort and loyalty finally had to be let go by the board of directors because his lack of management skills led to financial and administrative chaos once the company grew too large to survive on charismatic leadership alone.

There are also supervisors and managers who lack leadership skills. They are very good at planning and organizing as well as other management skills, but they lack the ability to influence and inspire people to perform at maximum. This phenomenon is often found in companies with highly trained managers and supervisors who just cannot seem to spark the enthusiasm necessary for success.

The ideal, of course, is to be a leader with excellent management skills. Such a leader not only inspires and motivates people to achieve goals but also accomplishes goals effectively and efficiently.

THREE MAJOR LEADERSHIP THEORIES

Most authorities on leadership agree that the major theories of leadership are the traits, leadership styles, and contingency (sometimes called situational) theories. The leadership styles and contingency theories now dominate the current literature on leadership. It is our goal in this chapter to evaluate the three major theories, with an emphasis on the styles and contingency theories, and to provide practical guidelines on how to become an effective leader and supervisor.

THE TRAITS APPROACH

Perhaps the oldest and weakest leadership theory is the traits theory. It was thought that an effective leader must possess certain traits to be successful. Even today, much psychological testing used to select leaders is theoretically based in traits theory. The problem with the traits approach is that there is little agreement on what traits are necessary for success, and there is little evidence to substantiate a link between leadership traits and leadership success. The traits theory has generally been dismissed because of theoretical, methodological, and practical problems involved in trying to identify and support a consistent list of traits.

THE LEADERSHIP STYLES APPROACH

The leadership styles approach emerged from Ohio State University leadership studies that began in 1945.[2] The Ohio State study was responsible for many significant findings on leadership, but the most important contribution was the discovery that there are two independent leadership variables, consideration (people-oriented behaviors) and initiating structure (performance-oriented behaviors), and that when considered together, these variables describe four basic leadership styles (see Figure 10.1).

Initiating structure may be defined as behaviors by means of which the leader defines or facilitates group interactions toward goal attainment. The leader does this by planning, scheduling, criticizing, initiating ideas, organizing the work, defining member roles, assigning tasks, and pushing for production.

Consideration may be defined as behaviors by means of which the leader establishes rapport with employees, two-way communication, mutual respect, and understanding. It includes behavior indicating trust and warmth between the supervisor and his or her group and emphasizes concern for group members' needs.

Follow-up studies and theories such as those contributed by the University of Michigan,[3] Douglas McGregor,[4] Robert Blake and Jane S. Mouton,[5] Keith Davis,[6] and

[2]R. M. Stogdill and A. E. Coons, eds., *Leader Behavior: Its Description and Measurement* (Columbus, OH: Bureau of Business Research, Ohio State University, 1957).

[3]Robert L. Kahn, "Productivity and Job Satisfaction," in *Management and the Behavioral Sciences: Text and Readings,* ed. Maneck S. Wadia (Boston: Allyn and Bacon, 1968), pp. 134–143.

[4]Douglas McGregor, *The Human Side of Enterprise* (New York: McGraw-Hill, 1960).

[5]Robert Blake and Jane S. Mouton, *The Managerial Grid* (Houston: Gulf Publishing Co., 1964) and Robert Blake and Jane S. Mouton, *The New Managerial Grid* (Houston: Gulf Publishing Co., 1978).

[6]Keith Davis, "Evolving Models of Organizational Behavior," *Academy of Management Journal* (March, 1968), pp. 27–38.

Figure 10.1 Ohio State leadership study conclusions.

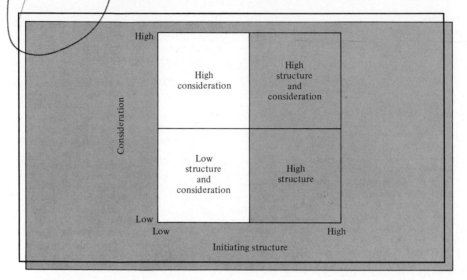

Rensis Likert[7] reinforced the leadership styles approach. Although there were some minor differences in the theories, the basic concepts were similar.

"THE MANAGEMENT GRID"

The best known of the leadership styles theories is the management grid developed by Robert Blake and Jane S. Mouton (see Figure 10.2).

Blake and Mouton described the two basic dimensions of leadership as concern for production and concern for people. The term *concern for,* as used in the grid, is a theoretical variable reflecting basic attitudes or styles of control. It does not reflect actual production or effectiveness. The horizontal axis of the management grid represents concern for mature and healthy relations among those engaged in production. Each axis is on a 1-to-9-point scale, with 1 representing a minimum interest or concern and 9 a maximum concern.

The management grid results in five basic styles of leadership: authority-obedience (9,1), impoverished management (1,1), organization man (5,5), country club (1,9), and team management (9,9).[8]

Authority-Obedience (9,1)

The 9,1 manager has a high concern for production and a low concern for people. He believes that efficiency in operations results from arranging conditions of work in such a way that human elements interfere to a minimum degree. People are viewed solely

---

[7]Rensis Likert, *The Human Organization: Its Management and Value* (New York: McGraw-Hill, 1967).
[8]Blake and Mouton, *New Managerial Grid,* p. 11.

Figure 10.2 Blake-Mouton management grid. Adapted from Robert Blake and Jane S. Mouton, *The New Managerial Grid* (Houston: Gulf Publishing Co., 1978), p. 11. Used by permission of Gulf Publishing Company.

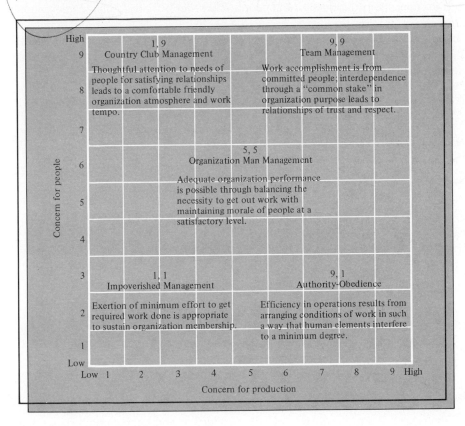

goals 9.9.

in terms of their contribution to production and, like machines, they are seen as production tools and are obligated to comply with orders given by managers whose central responsibility is to plan and control their subordinates' efforts to achieve production objectives. Thoughts, attitudes, and feelings are given little or no attention, and when conflict arises, it is suppressed through disciplinary actions.

Impoverished Management (1,1)

The 1,1 manager has a low concern for both production and people and believes that the exertion of minimum effort to get the required work done is appropriate to sustain organization membership. In other words, the manager does just enough to get by. This style usually describes a manager who has been passed by repeatedly but can still survive because of unwritten company policies that no one gets fired. Impoverished management occurs sometimes as a reaction to autocratic top management.

Organization Man (5,5)

In the center of the managerial grid is the 5,5 middle-of-the-road manager who has an average concern for production and people and believes that adequate organization performance is possible through balancing the necessity to get out work and maintaining morale of people at a satisfactory level. Thus, the theme of this theory is to push enough to get acceptable production but yield to the degree necessary to develop morale. By clever manipulation this manager believes he can prevent either of the two concerns from blocking the complete attainment of the other. A paternalistic executive of this style retains tight control in work matters but is benevolent in a personal way.

Country Club (1,9)

A 1,9 manager has a low concern for production and a high concern for people and believes that thoughtful attention to the needs of people for satisfying relationships leads to a comfortable and friendly organization atmosphere and work tempo. This management style is the reverse of task management. Production is seen as incidental to employee satisfaction through social relationships, good fellowship, and fraternity. The goal of this style is to strive for harmony, since it is assumed that contented people will produce more. It flourishes in organizations that are near-monopolies and also in bureaucratic organizations.

   The anticipated increase in production from creating a country club atmosphere is seldom realized. People in the system sense the phony quality in good human relations that are not related to achieving meaningful objectives. In addition, the "be nice" approach leads to few genuine relationships because conflict is denied and smothered in the attempt to achieve harmony.

Team Management (9,9)

A 9,9 manager has a high concern for both production and people and believes that work accomplishment comes from committed people and that interdependence through a "common stake" in the organization's purpose leads to relationships of trust and respect. The key to 9,9 management is the involvement and participation of those responsible in planning and executing work. The goal of 9,9 management is to promote conditions that integrate creativity, high productivity, and high morale through concerted team action. Some of the key elements of 9,9 management are:

1. Clear, forthright, and unobstructed communication in a climate that encourages trust, leveling, and full disclosure
2. Participative planning, organizing, directing, and controlling
3. Self-direction and control through a clear understanding of realistic goals and objectives, and commitment to those objectives because of participation in setting them
4. Flexible decision making—depending on the circumstances, the boss makes some decisions alone, some on a one-to-one basis, and some on a group basis

5. Accepting conflict as inevitable but resolvable by confronting conflict openly
6. Emphasis on innovative solutions to problems
7. Teamwork
8. Candid feedback on performance
9. A problem-solving approach

In the management grid approach, the 9,9 style is promoted as the best style. In a 1978 article in *Training,* Blake and Mouton reconfirmed their belief that the 9,9 style is the best way to manage and add that with this style, contingency theories are not needed. Their reasoning is that their two leadership dimensions are interdependent rather than independent. Next, their dimensions describe basic attitudes rather than specific behaviors. This important difference makes it possible for a leader to exhibit a variety of behaviors while using the same style. Thus, a 9,9 manager may in fact use considerable flexibility in applying his or her style. Finally, Blake and Mouton point out that one of the reasons research into leadership styles has been so inconsistent is the inconsistency in conceptualizing the different styles. They claim that when the management grid model is used, behavioral science research consistently supports the 9,9 style as the one best style.[9]

INTEGRATING THE LEADERSHIP STYLES THEORIES

In the leadership styles theories, the predominant styles are *autocratic, laissez faire, human relations,* and *democratic* leaders. They can be identified by their emphasis on performance and people (see Figure 10.3). Also implicit within each style is a leadership philosophy and a set of management skills. In understanding the leadership styles approach, it is helpful for a supervisor to understand style characteristics, the philosophy behind each style, the management skills that are typical of each style, and the likely consequences of each style.

1. *Leadership style characteristics.* Style characteristics describe the emphasis a leader places on performance and people.
2. *Leadership philosophy.* A leader's style is influenced by an implicit leadership philosophy based primarily on his or her assumptions about people and the role of a leader. A leader needs to be aware of these assumptions because they tend to be self-fulfilling prophecies.
3. *Management skills.* Each leadership style includes management skills characteristic of the style. It is important to be aware of these skills because any of them could be appropriate for a given situation.
4. *Style consequences.* Considerable research on the leadership styles theories makes it possible to predict the typical consequences of each style with reasonable accuracy (see Figure 10.4).

[9]Robert R. Blake and Jane S. Mouton, "Should You Teach There's Only One Best Way to Manage?" *Training* (April, 1978), pp. 24–29.

Figure 10.3 Four basic leadership styles.

High	**Human Relations Leader** Low emphasis on performance and high emphasis on people. Assumes that all people are honest, trustworthy, self-motivated, and want to be involved and that a participative, permissive, and supportive work environment will lead to happy workers that are productive workers. Relies on teamwork, human relations, participative decision making, and good harmony and fellowship to get the job done.	**Democratic Leader** High emphasis on performance and people. Assumes that most people are honest, trustworthy, and will work hard to accomplish meaningful goals and challenging work. Strives for a well-organized and challenging work environment with clear objectives and responsibilities and gets the job done by motivating and managing individuals and groups to use their full potential in reaching organizational as well as their own personal objectives.
Emphasis on people	**Laissez Faire Leader** Low emphasis on performance and people. Assumes that people are unpredictable and uncontrollable and that a leader's job is to do enough to get by, keep a low profile, stay out of trouble, and leave people alone as much as possible. Relies on abdicating to whomever will rise to the occasion to get the job done.	**Autocratic Leader** High emphasis on performance and low emphasis on people. Assumes that people are lazy, irresponsible, and untrustworthy and that planning, organizing, controlling, and decision making should be accomplished by the leader with minimal employee involvement. Relies on authority, control, power, manipulation, and hard work to get the job done.
Low	**Low**	Emphasis on performance **High**

Figure 10.4 Typical consequences resulting from each leadership style.

Laissez Faire Leader	Autocratic Leader	Human Relations Leader	Democratic Leader
Employees become apathetic, disinterested, and resentful of the organization and their leader. The laissez faire approach results in the lowest employee productivity and satisfaction of all the leadership styles.	Although the emphasis is on high productivity, it often breeds counterforces of antagonism and restriction of output. Frequently results in hostile attitudes, a suppression of conflict, distorted and guarded communication, high turnover and absenteeism, low productivity and work quality, and a preoccupation with rules, procedures, red tape, working conditions, status symbols, and trying to cater to the whims of the boss. Tends to develop dependent and uncreative employees who are afraid to seek responsibility.	While this style may keep employees happy, there is little evidence to support the notion that keeping employees happy and treating them well results in high productivity. The preoccupation with keeping people happy and involved often interferes with high achievement, causes employees to lose respect for their leader, results in the emergence of informal leaders, and causes problems to be smoothed over. Such an atmosphere can be frustrating to goal-oriented people.	This style leads to high employee productivity, satisfaction, cooperation, and commitment. Reduces the need for controls and formal rules and procedures. Results in low employee absenteeism and turnover. Develops competent people who are willing to give their best, think for themselves, communicate openly, and seek responsibility.

EVALUATION OF THE LEADERSHIP STYLES APPROACH

The leadership styles theories tend to portray an autocratic leader as a villain, a human relations leader as a country club director, a laissez faire leader as a nonleader, and a democratic leader as a hero or heroine. In addition, even though most leadership positions require a variety of responses to changing situations, the leadership styles theories either advocate one best style (the democratic style), one best style with a back-up style, or, in recent more advanced theories, a democratic style for some situations, an autocratic style for other situations, and in-between styles for still other situations. However, few leaders can afford the luxury of using one approach to leadership—hopefully the correct one—for all situations. Nor do they have the psychological makeup to switch from one style to another without confusing their followers or themselves. A summary of the leadership styles approach is presented in Figures 10.5 and 10.6.

THE CONTINGENCY APPROACH

The contingency or situational approach to leadership suggests that different situations require different approaches to leadership. Although the contingency approach has only recently begun to evolve as a well-developed leadership theory, Chester Barnard attempted to classify the variables found in management situations as early as 1938 in his classic book, *The Functions of the Executive.*[10] The early leaders in researching and conceptualizing situational leadership have been Robert Tannenbaum and Warren Schmidt[11] ("Choosing a Leadership Pattern"), Chris Argyris[12] ("Different Ways of Leading and Organizing"), William Reddin[13] ("3-D Management Style"), Fred Fiedler[14] ("Leadership Contingency"), Paul Hersey and Kenneth Blanchard[15] ("Life Cycle Theory of Leadership"), Robert House[16] ("Path-Goal Theory of Leader Effectiveness"), and Vroom and Yetton[17] ("Problem-Centered Approach to Leadership").

---

[10]Chester F. Barnard, *The Functions of the Executive* (Cambridge, MA: Harvard University Press, 1938), pp. 128–129.

[11]Robert Tannenbaum and Warren H. Schmidt, "How to Choose a Leadership Pattern," *Harvard Business Review,* March–April, 1958, pp. 95–101. (Reprinted in *Harvard Business Review,* May–June, 1973, pp. 162–180.)

[12]Chris Argyris, *Integrating the Individual and the Organization* (New York: Wiley, 1964).

[13]William J. Reddin, "What's Your Style?" *Management: Official Journal of the New Zealand Institute of Management,* March, 1966.

[14]Fred E. Fiedler, *A Theory of Leadership Effectiveness* (New York: McGraw-Hill, 1967).

[15]Paul Hersey and Kenneth H. Blanchard, "Life Cycle Theory of Leadership," *Training and Development Journal,* May, 1969, pp. 26–34. Also, Paul Hersey and Kenneth H. Blanchard, *Management by Organizational Behavior: Utilizing Human Resources* (Englewood Cliffs, NJ: Prentice-Hall, 1977).

[16]Robert R. House and T. R. Mitchell, "Path-Goal Theory of Leadership," *Journal of Contemporary Business* 3, no. 4 (1974): 81–97.

[17]Victor H. Vroom and Philip W. Yetton, *Leadership and Decision Making* (Pittsburgh: University of Pittsburgh Press, 1973).

Figure 10.5 Descriptions of autocratic and laissez faire leaders.

Leadership Style	Autocratic Leader	Laissez Faire Leader
Leadership Style Characteristics Emphasis on performance Emphasis on people	High emphasis on performance Low emphasis on people	Low emphasis on performance Low emphasis on people
Leadership Philosophy Assumptions about people	People tend to be lazy, undependable, dislike work, resist responsibility, work primarily for money, and prefer to be led.	People are unpredictable, and trying to understand them is a waste of time.
Assumptions about the role of a leader	Run a tight ship by planning, organizing, directing, and controlling the efforts of others.	Keep a low profile, be obedient, and don't make waves.
Management Skills Planning and setting objectives	It is the leader's job to plan and establish objectives.	Plans and establishes objectives only if required to do so.
Organizing	A formal, centralized structure is used with carefully defined rules and procedures.	Lives with whatever structure he or she is given.
Controlling	Tight controls are established to assure that employees do their jobs.	Abdicates control to employees.
Decision making	All but minor decisions must be made or approved by the leader.	Avoids making decisions as much as possible.
Motivating	Uses close supervision and tight controls, simplifies and standardizes work, and offers economic incentives and fringe benefits to motivate people.	Leaves people alone. Nothing seems to work anyway.
Communicating	Communication is primarily one-way, downward, formal, impersonal, and in a parent-to-child manner.	Communication is noncommittal, superficial, and avoided.
Developing	Development comes from hard work and experience, although some professional development may be considered if it will result in greater efficiency and productivity.	Leaves development up to employees. If people want to develop themselves, that is their business.
Use of rewards and punishment	People are rewarded for being obedient and punished for making mistakes. Punishment may take the form of withholding attention or good assignments or making people feel guilty.	Avoids rewarding or punishing people.

Figure 10.5 *(continued)*

Leadership Style	Autocratic Leader	Laissez Faire Leader
Management Skills (con't)		
Approach to handling conflicts	Conflicts are either suppressed because they interfere with work or resolved in favor of the leader.	Ignores conflicts and hopes they will disappear.
Approach to handling problems and mistakes	Attacks people and not the problem and looks for a scapegoat or someone to blame when mistakes are made.	Ignores problems and mistakes unless forced to deal with them.
Interpersonal relationship with employees	Keeps relationships formal and impersonal so that he or she can remain "objective."	Avoids close relationships and lets employees do pretty much as they please.
Use of power and authority	The use of power and authority is essential to maintaining order and high productivity.	Power and authority are abdicated to whomever wants to assume them.
Delegation practices	Fully delegates only low-risk jobs.	Responsibilities are assumed by default rather than through delegation.
Performance appraisals	Uses performance appraisal to let employees know what they are doing wrong.	Either avoids performance appraisals or gives minimum compliance to required appraisal procedures.

Figure 10.6 Descriptions of human relations and democratic leaders.

Leadership Style	Human Relations Leader	Democratic Leader
Leadership Style Characteristics		
Emphasis on performance	Low emphasis on performance	High emphasis on performance
Emphasis on people	High emphasis on people	High emphasis on people
Leadership Philosophy		
Assumptions about people	All people are honest, trustworthy, self-motivated, want to be involved in all decisions, and will give their best if kept happy.	Most people are honest, trustworthy, self-motivated, and like responsibility and challenging work.
Assumptions about the role of a leader	Minister to the needs of employees and keep them happy, because happy people are productive people.	Arrange organizational conditions to promote teamwork and high job performance and satisfaction.
Management Skills		
Planning and setting objectives	Uses group planning and objectives setting almost exclusively.	Planning ahead and establishing clear objectives are essential to effective performance and are best accomplished with heavy employee involvement.

Figure 10.6 *(continued)*

Leadership Style	Human Relations Leader	Democratic Leader
Management Skills (con't)		
Organizing	A decentralized, informal, and loosely controlled structure is used.	A decentralized and flexible structure is used, with clearly defined responsibilities and an open and participative work environment.
Controlling	Relies almost entirely on employees' controlling themselves.	Control is distributed between the leader and the employees.
Decision making	Uses a participative approach for most decisions and primarily serves as a discussion leader in helping his group arrive at decisions.	The leader is a decisive decision maker who emphasizes team decision making but also makes some decisions alone.
Motivating	Involves employees, gives continuous positive reinforcement, and provides for good working conditions, social relations, and fellowship.	Provides good working conditions and assures that jobs are challenging and offer opportunities for growth, responsibility, achievement, recognition, and advancement.
Communicating	Communication is open and two-way but is often ungenuine when conflict is involved because of the emphasis on maintaining harmony and good relations.	Communication is open, two-way, and genuine. Leveling and honesty are encouraged.
Developing	Any development activities even remotely related to the job are encouraged.	Emphasizes personal, employee, and team development.
Use of rewards and punishment	Rewards and recognition are used at every opportunity, but punishment is rarely ever used since "everyone makes mistakes."	Good work is recognized and rewarded, and punishment is used only as a last resort.
Approach to handling conflicts	Conflict is smoothed over or avoided if it might threaten good relations. Conflicts with the leader are usually resolved in favor of employees.	Conflicts are openly confronted.
Approach to handling problems and mistakes	Mistakes are ignored and problems are given to employees to resolve.	Attacks problems and not people and emphasizes finding solutions.
Interpersonal relationship with employees	Many internal and external activities are planned to promote close interpersonal relations and group harmony.	Maintains a close but objective relationship with employees.

Figure 10.6 *(continued)*

Leadership Style	Human Relations Leader	Democratic Leader
Management Skills (con't) Use of power and authority	Power and authority are abdicated to employees.	Believes that power and authority are earned, not legislated.
Delegation practices	Delegates considerable responsibility but does not hold employees accountable for results.	Delegates considerable responsibility and holds employees accountable for results.
Performance appraisals	Uses performance appraisal to let employees know what they are doing right.	Uses performance appraisal to let employees know what they are doing right and wrong.

"CHOOSING A LEADERSHIP PATTERN"

Robert Tannenbaum and Warren Schmidt[18] have consistently been progressive thinkers on leadership. They were some of the first leadership authorities to verbalize the need for flexible leadership and to develop guidelines to assist leaders in knowing when to emphasize a particular leadership style. Figure 10.7 presents the range of possible behaviors available to a leader. Each leadership approach in the Tannenbaum and Schmidt continuum is related to the degree of authority used by the boss and the amount of freedom available to the boss's subordinates in reaching decisions. The actions on the extreme left characterize the manager who maintains a high degree of control, while those on the extreme right characterize the manager who gives subordinates a high degree of freedom. The range of possible choices would be:

1. *The manager makes the decision and announces it.* This style is used for decisions made by the boss without subordinate involvement. He or she simply makes a decision and reports it to subordinates.
2. *The manager "sells" the decision.* In this case, the boss makes a decision and then tries to sell employees on it rather than announce the decision to them. The boss feels that he or she can reduce resistance to the decision by taking this approach.
3. *The manager presents ideas and invites questions.* This manager makes a decision and then allows subordinates to ask questions about it. By doing this the boss gets the subordinates involved in the decision and also gives them an opportunity to explore more fully the implications of the decision.
4. *The manager presents a tentative decision subject to change.* A manager using this approach makes a decision but allows subordinates to influence the decision before he or she finalizes it. The boss makes the final decision but strongly considers the comments of subordinates.
5. *The manager presents the problem, gets suggestions, and then makes the decision.* With this style the boss identifies the problem and the subordinates try to develop solutions. The boss considers their alternatives and then makes a final decision.

[18]Tannenbaum and Schmidt, "How to Choose a Leadership Pattern."

Figure 10.7 Continuum of leadership behavior. Adapted from Robert Tannenbaum and Warren H. Schmidt, "How to Choose a Leadership Pattern," *Harvard Business Review,* March–April, 1958, pp. 95–101. Used by permission of *Harvard Business Review.*

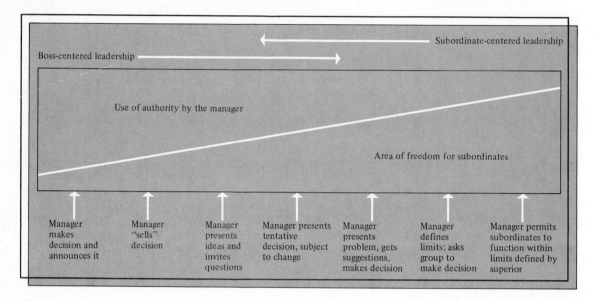

6. *The manager defines the limits and asks the group to make the decision.* A manager using this style would define the problem and the boundaries within which the decision must be made and then would allow the group to make the decision.
7. *The manager permits the group to make decisions.* When using this style, a manager gives almost total freedom to a group to make decisions. The manager may define the types of decisions the group may make but then gives the group complete freedom to make decisions.

Deciding Which Style to Use

Tannenbaum and Schmidt also give some guidelines on the factors or forces a leader should consider in deciding which leadership style to use. The primary forces to consider are: (1) forces in the manager, (2) forces in the subordinates, and (3) forces in the situation. Figure 10.8 shows how these forces might influence a leader's style in a decision-making situation.

The Tannenbaum-Schmidt leadership theory focuses on two main themes. The first is that a successful leader must be aware of the forces that are most relevant to his or her behavior at any given time. To have such an awareness a leader must understand himself or herself, the people in the group he or she is working with, and the company and broader social environment. The second theme is that a leader must be able to behave appropriately in light of his or her performance.

Figure 10.8 Leadership forces.

Forces in the Manager	Forces in the Subordinates	Forces in the Situation
The internal forces affecting the manager are: His or her value system His or her confidence in subordinates His or her leadership inclinations His or her feelings of security in an uncertain situation	The manager can permit subordinates greater freedom when they: Have relatively high needs for independence Have a readiness to assume responsibility for decision making Have a relatively high tolerance for ambiguity Are interested in the problem and feel that it is important Understand and identify with the goals of the organization Have the knowledge and experience to deal with the problem Expect to share in decision making	Situational factors that should be considered are: Organizational values, traditions, size, and geographical location Group effectiveness, teamwork, and productivity The nature of the problem Time pressures

"Life Cycle Theory of Leadership"

Paul Hersey and Kenneth Blanchard made an important contribution to leadership theory by recognizing the need for a leadership style capable of changing appropriately to changing situations:

> An effective leader must be able to diagnose the demands of the environment and then either adapt his leader style to fit these demands, or develop the means to change some or all of the other variables.[19]

The variables the leader must take into account are (1) the environment, (2) the organization, (3) the superiors, (4) the associates, and (5) the job demands.

Hersey and Blanchard did not develop these statements about leadership other than to acknowledge them. They have, however, developed an interesting theory which they call the life cycle theory of leadership. This theory is based on a curvilinear relationship between "task" and "relationships" rather than on the usual linear relationship and is an attempt to provide the leader with some understanding of the relationship between an effective style of leadership and the level of maturity of the leader's followers.

A model of this theory is shown in Figure 10.9.

According to the life cycle theory, as the level of maturity of one's followers continues to increase, appropriate leader behavior requires not only less and less structure (task) but also less and less socioemotional support (relationships). Maturity is defined by relative independence, ability to take responsibility, and achievement motivation. Beginning with highly structured task behavior for working with immature people, the theory suggests that as the follower becomes increasingly more mature, the leader's behavior should move from (1) high-task–low-relationship behavior to (2)

[19]Hersey and Blanchard, "Life Cycle Theory of Leadership."

Figure 10.9 Hersey and Blanchard's life cycle theory of leadership. Adapted from Paul Hersey and Kenneth H. Blanchard, "Life Cycle Theory of Leadership," *Training and Development Journal,* May 1969, pp. 26–34. Used by permission of *Training and Development Journal.*

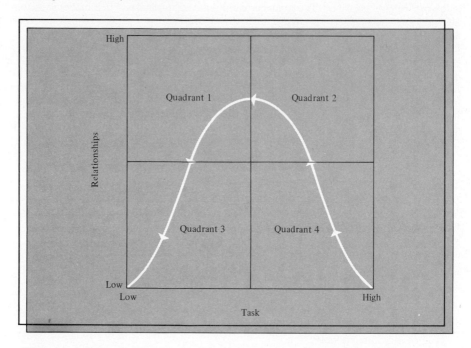

high-task–high-relationship behavior to (3) low-task–high-relationship behavior to (4) low-task–low-relationship behavior. Thus, the leader may use a high degree of structure for an immature employee, giving him detailed direction. However, as the employee matures, the leader begins to increase his or her relationships behavior by showing more trust and respect for the "child" until the "child" is mature enough to operate independently, with little structure or relationship activity.

"3-D Management Style"

Although his theory has not been widely published, William J. Reddin[20] has offered what can be considered up to this time one of the most comprehensive contingency models. He established an eight-style typology of management behavior that represents eight possible combinations of task orientation, relationships orientation, and effectiveness (see Figure 10.10).

Task orientation is the extent to which a manager directs his or her own and subordinates' efforts toward goal attainment. It is characterized by planning, organizing, and controlling.

[20]Reddin, "What's Your Style?"

Figure 10.10 Reddin's leadership model. Adapted from William J. Reddin, *Managerial Effectiveness* (New York: McGraw-Hill, 1970). Used by permission of McGraw-Hill.

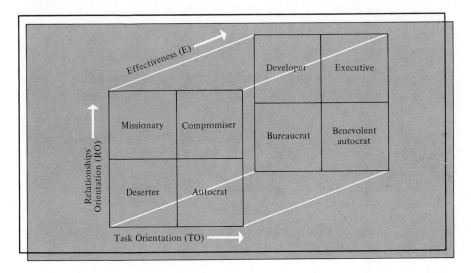

Relationships orientation is the extent to which a manager has personal job relationships. It is characterized by mutual trust, respect for subordinates' ideas, and consideration of their feelings.

Effectiveness is the extent to which a manager achieves the output requirements of his or her position. When the style of a leader is appropriate to a given situation, it is termed effective.

The eight styles, four of which are effective and four of which are ineffective, are:

Effective

1. *Executive*—a manager who is using a high task orientation and a high relationships orientation in a situation where such behavior is appropriate. He or she is seen as a good motivator who sets high standards, who treats everyone somewhat differently, and who prefers team management.
2. *Benevolent autocrat*—a manager who is using a high task orientation and a low relationships orientation in a situation where such behavior is appropriate. He or she is seen as knowing what he or she wants and knowing how to get it without creating disharmony.
3. *Developer*—a manager who is using a high relationships orientation and a low task orientation in a situation where such behavior is appropriate. He or she is seen as having implicit trust in people and as being primarily concerned with developing them as individuals.
4. *Bureaucrat*—a manager who is using a low task orientation and a low relationships orientation in a situation where such behavior is appropriate. He or she is seen as

being primarily interested in rules and procedures and as wanting to maintain control of the situation by their use.

Ineffective

1. *Compromiser*—a manager who is using a high task orientation and a high relationships orientation in a situation that requires a high orientation to only one or the other. He or she is seen as making compromises when compromising is inappropriate.
2. *Autocrat*—a manager who is using a high task orientation and a low relationships orientation in a situation where such behavior is inappropriate. He or she is seen as having no confidence in others, as being unpleasant, and as being interested only in the immediate job.
3. Missionary—a manager who is using a high relationships orientation and a low task orientation in a situation where such behavior is inappropriate. He or she is seen as being primarily interested in harmony.
4. *Deserter*—a manager who is using a low task orientation and a low relationships orientation in a situation where such behavior is inappropriate. He or she is seen as uninvolved and passive.

Reddin has made a number of important contributions with his theory. His addition of effectiveness to the task and relationship orientation usually attributed to leadership is a significant breakthrough. By adding an effectiveness dimension, he begins to integrate the concepts of leadership style with the situational demands of a specific environment. Thus, any of his basic styles may be effective or ineffective depending on the situation. The model is unlike the typologies of McGregor, Blake, Likert, and others because it does not prescribe a single "ideal leader" style. The essential qualities of effective managers in the model are diagnostic skill to evaluate the the situation and style flexibility to match the style to the situation. Reddin lists five elements which compose any managerial situation: (1) job demands, (2) corporate management philosophy, (3) superiors' styles and expectations, (4) subordinates' styles and expectations, and (5) coworkers' styles and expectations.

INTEGRATING THE CONTINGENCY APPROACH: THE ADAPTABLE LEADER-MANAGER

An adaptable leader-manager is a supervisor or manager who is an effective leader and supervisor and is able to adapt successfully to changing situations by using adaptability clues to adjust his or her supervisory skills and leadership style while maintaining overall leadership-style consistency. The word *adaptable* was chosen because it implies making appropriate choices as opposed to *flexible,* which may or may not result in good choices. The term *leader-manager* recognizes the need for both leadership and management skills.

How an Adaptable Leader-Manager Adjusts to Changing Situations

The adaptable leader-manager, either intuitively or by design, tends to incorporate the following guidelines into the process of leading and managing:

1. He or she understands the consequences of different leadership styles and recognizes the need for using a *consistent* leadership style that *facilitates* rather than limits one's ability to adapt to changing situations. Ideally, the leader uses a democratic style which tells people that high performance is expected but that they will be treated fairly and with respect. However, even if another leadership style is used, if it is consistent, genuine, and acceptable or tolerable to those affected by it, the leader will be more effective than leaders who continuously change styles and keep people confused and unsettled.
2. Management *skills* are adapted to changing situations by *sizing up the situation* and deciding on the most constructive and appropriate skills needed to achieve the desired end results. An adaptable leader-manager may, for example, use autocratic skills with an employee or group that prefers to be led and responds best to structure; laissez faire skills with an employee or group that needs little direction and works best with minimal structure; human relations skills with an employee or group that needs lots of attention and responds best to involvement; and democratic skills with an employee or group that responds best to a balance of guidance, attention, and structure. This is done, however, without changing leadership *style*.

Sizing Up Adaptability Clues

In deciding what skill adjustments are needed, if any, an adaptable leader-manager sizes up *adaptability clues* in seeking to make wise decisions. Some of the adaptability clues that may be helpful in making sound judgments are:

1. *Characteristics of the leader.* Awareness of one's leadership style, management skills, ability to adapt, and strengths and limitations can be used in evaluating options. Such an awareness can be useful in making career choices where one's approach to leadership and supervision is likely to be successful in making on-the-job decisions and in overcoming or making allowances for weaknesses.
2. *Characteristics of subordinates.* The approaches a leader uses with employees should vary with the motivation, knowledge, competence, maturity, and past habit patterns of the employees.
3. *Characteristics of the leader's boss.* The style and skills of a leader's boss may determine the boundaries within which a leader may express his or her leadership style and management skills. For example, an autocratic boss may impose conditions that make it impossible to use a democratic style or democratic skills.
4. *Organizational climate.* An organization's history, top-level leadership, objectives, policies, patterns of rewards and punishments (both formal and informal), economic status, and external environment all interact to produce an organizational

climate that, if understood, offers excellent clues for predicting which leadership styles and management skills will be successful.

5. *Characteristics of the task.* Different tasks require different skills. For example, simple, routine, highly structured tasks with narrow error margins tend to require more autocratic skills.

6. *Level of the leader in the organization.* As an individual advances in an organization, skill requirements vary from a greater emphasis on technical skills at lower levels to a greater emphasis on human relations and conceptual skills at higher levels.

7. *Scheduling and time constraints.* The need for greater leadership control and direction increases as scheduling and time constraints tighten.

8. *Importance of teamwork, interaction, and cooperation.* Another important variable is the amount of participation (human relations skills), teamwork (democratic skills), independence (laissez faire skills), and direction (autocratic skills) required to do the job.

9. *Manpower and physical constraints.* Depending on the nature of the task and the characteristics of the employees, laissez faire or autocratic skills are likely to become increasingly appropriate as the number of employees to be supervised increases and the physical setting becomes less conducive to frequent interaction.

When to Emphasize Different Leader-Manager Skills

By using adaptibility clues and research on when different skills are appropriate, an adaptable leader-manager can significantly improve his or her leadership expertise. Typical situations in which difficult skills are appropriate are shown in Figure 10.11.

Conclusions about Contingency Theories and the Adaptable Leader-Manager Concept

Learning and applying contingency theories and the adaptable leader-manager concept can significantly increase a leader's effectiveness by: (1) developing an understanding of one's leadership style and ability to adapt to changing situations; (2) using this understanding to emphasize one's leadership strengths and allow for limitations through staffing, assignment selections, or training; and (3) seeking positions and organizations where one's leadership is likely to be successful. Organizations can use an understanding of leadership style and adaptability for planning purposes by diagnosing the types of leaders needed for different jobs, placing in these jobs leaders whose style and adaptability are likely to match the job requirements, and providing leadership-style and adaptability training to prepare leaders for new assignments.

RESOLVING SOME OF THE DILEMMAS IN LEADERSHIP THEORY

The most consistent finding in the theories and studies on leadership is that there is a marked relationship between the kind of leadership an employee receives and the

Figure 10.11 The adaptable leader-manager.

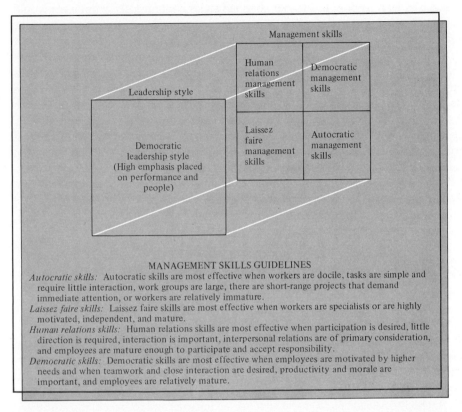

employee's job satisfaction and productivity. Beyond this point of agreement, there appear to be conflicting findings and many questions left unanswered. However, a closer examination of leadership theory reveals that many of the apparent contradictions are, in fact, not contradictions and that some of the leadership dilemmas can be explained.

Conflicting Evidence

One of the reasons that there is conflicting evidence regarding which approach is most effective is that any of the leadership styles could be successful if used under conditions favorable to the style. Another is that not all organizations reward effective leadership.

Distinguishing between Style and Skills

Some of the contingency theorists have mistakenly assumed that situational leadership means changing leadership styles with changing situations. *Style* refers to the emphasis a person places on performance and people and the characteristics, attitudes, mannerisms, and personality of the leader. In other words, style refers to the way someone comes across as a person. If a leader changed styles continuously, employees would be constantly confused in their attempts to predict and adjust to their leader's erratic behavior. *Skills* refers to the specific techniques a person uses to accomplish goals, such as staffing, planning, organizing, controlling, communicating, evaluating performance, handling problems and conflicts, and managing time. Each style of leader tends to apply these skills in a unique way because of his or her style and to emphasize some skills more than others. For example, an autocratic leader tends to emphasize centralized planning, organizing, and controlling and to apply these skills in an authoritative, impersonal way. Once one understands the difference between style and skills, it becomes apparent that what an effective contingency leader changes is not style but rather the selection of skills and the way they are applied in any given situation. Thus, an effective leader may change skills according to the requirements of the situation and still maintain a consistent leadership style. A democratic leader, for example, does not have suddenly to turn into an autocratic person to use skills such as close supervision and tight controls if they are appropriate to the situation.

The Need for a Leadership Style That Facilitates Skill Changes

An awareness of leadership styles and their consequences is very important for successful contingency leadership because a leader's style may either facilitate or inhibit skill changes. For example, a style that gains the trust and respect of those affected by the style (employees, boss, management, other departments, etc.) gives a leader considerable flexibility in changing skills with changing situations, whereas the same changes would be viewed with suspicion and resistance if a leader's style is disliked and distrusted.

Any style could facilitate change if it gained the trust and respect of those affected by it. However, in most cases an autocratic style tends to create distrust, a laissez faire style lack of credibility, and a human relations style lack of respect, thus limiting the flexibility of leaders who use these styles. The style that most consistently results in trust and respect and therefore increases the likelihood of a positive response to contingency management is the democratic style.

What the democratic style really describes is simply a reasonably healthy person who treats others with respect and places a high emphasis on both performance and people. It is the most appropriate style for contingency management and should be effective except in cases where those affected by the style resist healthy behavior, are unwilling to treat others with respect, or do not respond to a high emphasis on both performance and people.

Understanding the Importance of Style Consistency

An inconsistent leadership style causes those affected by the style to waste considerable time in trying to figure out how best to work with the leader, predict how the leader will behave in different situations, and understand what the leader really means, wants, or expects. It also slows down the decision-making and problem-solving processes and increases the stress of those affected by the leader. Even if a person has a style that is not well received, style consistency makes it possible for those affected by the style to learn to work around it. Ideally, a leader should have a style that is well received as well as consistent.

One last thing should be noted about a consistent leadership style. Consistency does not imply rigid, robotlike behavior. A style projects a particular emphasis on performance and people and can be expressed in a wide variety of ways by different people or even the same person in different situations.

The Need for Combining Leadership and Management Theories

If a leader is going to become proficient at influencing and inspiring people to action, managing human and material resources effectively and efficiently, and learning successfully to adapt to changing situations, it becomes obvious that leadership and management are both required. Remember, we are talking about a leader-manager, not one or the other. Most leaders have a predominant leadership style and one or more backup styles that they use; most managers have a predominant set of skills that they use, as well as a variety of additional skills that they use with changing situations. Effectiveness in any given situation is a result of having the right combination of leadership style and management skills.

Few One-Style Leaders

Although most leaders have a dominant leadership style, it is unlikely that they are totally autocratic, laissez faire, human relations, or democratic leaders. Thus, for example, an autocratic leader may be fairly successful and reasonably well liked because he or she occasionally switches to a human relations style or perhaps is in fact an adaptable leader who uses appropriate skills with changing situations.

Short-Range Effects

The short-range effects of leadership may not reveal the whole story. A skilled autocratic leader may take charge of an operation and cut costs, push hard for high production, weed out weak employees, quickly drive up profits, and look enough like a hero or heroine to get promoted before the long-run effects catch up. More likely than not, the long-run effects will take their toll just as a new leader takes over, and management will observe, "Sure wish we had Sally back in charge of the operation. Everything has fallen apart since the new manager took over!"

Some Professional Training May Lead to Failure

The preoccupation with the styles approach to leadership has resulted in most academic and professional management development programs' being designed to train democratic leaders. Training in democratic leadership can undoubtedly improve the effectiveness of most leaders. However, it can also train leaders to fail without understanding why, if they find themselves in situations where democratic "skills" are inappropriate or where a traditional organization does not reward progressive management.

Is It Necessary to Be an Adaptable Leader-Manager to Be Successful?

Even though a leader may not be very adaptable, the leader can still be successful as long as positions are sought where his or her approach to leadership is effective. However, the lack of adaptability does make it more difficult to advance because of the need for a greater range of leadership and management skills as one progresses upward in an organization.

SUMMARY

Many leaders limit their effectiveness because they are not good managers, and managers often limit their effectiveness because of their lack of leadership skills. Leadership and management are different skills, and both are needed to inspire and motivate people to achieve goals in an effective and efficient manner.

The three most important leadership theories are the traits, styles, and contingency theories. Little attention is devoted to the traits theories because of the lack of agreement on which traits are most appropriate. The styles theories are still popular. Four major leadership styles are usually considered: autocratic, laissez faire, human relations, and democratic. These styles are defined in terms of the emphasis a leader places on performance and people. They can be integrated by considering the style, philosophy, and typical management skills associated with each of the major styles. Contingency or situational leadership theories suggest that different situations require different approaches to leadership. The adaptable leader-manager concept offers a model for integrating and applying the contingency theories.

Some of the differences between the theories can be resolved by understanding the difference between leadership style and management skills, by recognizing the need for using a consistent style such as the democratic style that increases the likelihood of a positive response to contingency leadership (a contingency leader should change skills, not styles, with changing situations), by recognizing the need for combining leadership and management skills, and by developing practical guidelines for applying contingency theories to actual situations.

IMPORTANT TERMS

leadership	laissez faire
initiating structure	human relations
consideration	democratic
management grid	contingency
autocratic	adaptable leader-manager

REVIEW QUESTIONS

1. Define *leadership* and *supervisors* and discuss how some people can be leaders but not supervisors and others are supervisors but not leaders.
2. Discuss the three major leadership theories and what you consider to be their major strengths and weaknesses.
3. Who are some of the major contributors to the leadership styles theories? Select two and describe their theories.
4. Discuss the four major styles of leadership in terms of style, philosophy, skills, and typical consequences.
5. What are some problems with the leadership-styles approach?
6. Who are some of the major contributors to the contingency-leadership theories? Select two and describe their theories.
7. What are five important issues that can help integrate the leadership-styles and contingency theories?
8. What is an adaptable leader-manager?
9. What adaptability clues should be used in sizing up situations?
10. Describe typical situations when autocratic, laissez faire, human relations, and democratic skills should be used.
11. Discuss the democratic adaptable leader-manager in terms of style, philosophy, and skills.
12. Does a leader need to be a democratic adaptable leader-manager to be successful? Explain.

EXERCISES

10.1   Determining Your Leadership Style

Meet in small groups. Each group member should evaluate his or her predominant (primary) and backup (secondary) styles of leadership based on the autocratic, laissez faire, human relations, and democratic styles described in Figure 10.3. Then each team member should discuss the reasons for the style he or she chose.

10.2   Demonstrating Leadership Styles

The objective of the exercise is to demonstrate the effect of a leader's style on the productivity and satisfaction of employees.

Procedures

Volunteers are requested for the roles listed below. Preferably the volunteers should be selected with ample time prior to the exercise to prepare their roles (a day or more would be best, although several hours will also work).

4	leaders
2	customers
4–8	observers (optional)
4	scorers (optional)

Role instructions for each role player are contained in Exhibit 10.1. The instructor should meet with the role players to explain their role and how the exercise works. Explanations should be given to the customers and observers first so that they can be dismissed while explanations are given to the leaders. This is done to prevent bias on the part of the customers and observers. The leaders must be urged to stick to their roles so that the exercise will work.

Have the remaining people count off by four, each person being on the team with their number (all the ones are together, etc.). Each team will perform the same task over a 30-minute period, the only difference being that each team will have a different style of leader (democratic, autocratic, human relations, or laissez faire). The task is to build trademarks with Tinkertoys for a common list of 20 companies given to each leader. A trademark could include letters (for example, GM for General Motors), symbols (for example, a car for General Motors), or anything else that would serve as a suitable trademark. The exercise is ideally conducted in an area where the observers can watch from behind one-way glass.

Each leader takes a large box of Tinkertoys (each box should have identical contents) and meets with his or her group to provide instructions and begin building trademarks. The leaders must lead from the leadership style that they have accepted and not revert to other styles. One or more observers can be assigned to each group. Observers should use the observation sheet in Exhibit 10.4.

The customers should rotate continuously from group to group and rate each finished trademark on a scale from 1 (poor) to 10 (excellent). Ratings are based on: (1) how well the trademark represents a company or organization and (2) the creativity of the trademark. Once a trademark is rated, it can be torn down so that the parts can be used again. Customers must agree on the ratings before entering scores on their scoring sheet. Customers are allowed to divulge scores if asked. Exhibit 10.2 contains the customer rating sheet.

At the conclusion of the 30 minutes allowed for the exercise, the instructor tells all the groups to stop and then gives the following instructions:

1. All work must stop, but rating by the customers may continue.
2. Once all items have been rated, put the Tinkertoys back in the box.
3. The members (but not the leader) of each group complete a satisfaction survey (see Exhibit 10.3). The questionnaires are then collected by the scorers, who tabulate the scores for *each* team to determine: (1) the *average satisfaction score,* rounded to the nearest whole number (1 to 10) on *each* of the ten items in the survey, and (2) the *total satisfaction score* (the total of the ten average satisfaction scores) for each team. The scores are then posted on a chalkboard using the format of the exercise analysis sheet (Exhibit 10.5). These numbers will provide a satisfaction score for each team. Team members can be given a 15-minute break while the scores are being tabulated.
4. The customers meet to determine the total productivity (total points accumulated, divided by 2) for each team. The average score for each product can also be computed to determine the overall quality of each product. The total productivity score for each team should be posted beside the total satisfaction score.

5. The observers are asked to summarize their results and prepare a *two-minute presentation* each, explaining what they observed. Each observer should follow the format of the observation sheet in Exhibit 10.4.

6. The leaders are asked to prepare a *two-minute presentation* on what they observed as a leader regarding the effect of the leader's style on the productivity and satisfaction of their group members.

7. The instructor tabulates the total score for each team by adding together the satisfaction and production scores. The exercise analysis sheet in Exhibit 10.5 can be used to record all the scores.

Debriefing

As a suggested approach to debriefing the exercise, the following procedures are recommended:

1. The instructor reviews the results in terms of the satisfaction score, productivity score, average score for each product, and total points.

2. The instructor conducts an analysis of *each team* as follows:
   a. Team members are interviewed by asking them what leadership styles they thought their leader used, how the style affected them, and what they learned about the style of leadership that they were exposed to (4 minutes).
   b. The team observers are asked to give their report (2 minutes).
   c. The team leader is asked to give his or her observations (2 minutes).
   d. The instructor summarizes what should have been learned (2 minutes).

If the role leaders play their roles well, the total scores will generally show the following ranking in terms of overall results:

1. democratic leader
2. human relations leader
3. autocratic leader
4. laissez faire leader

Variations, particularly of the top ranking, should be explored and explanations sought. For example, a human relations leader who in fact acts from a democratic style may affect the results, or a laissez faire leader who ends up with highly self-motivated and independent people may win.

EXHIBITS

10.1   Leader Instructions and Descriptions

(one copy for each leader)

Your task is to lead your group in making trademarks for the companies listed below. *In leading your group, it is extremely important that you do a good job of leading from the leadership style that you have been assigned.* The exercise will last *30 minutes,* and you may make the trademarks in any order that you choose. After completing a trademark, you should call in the customer raters, who will evaluate the trademark on a 10-point scale depending on how well it represents the company it is for and how creative it is. After a trademark is rated, you can tear it down and reuse the parts.

Scale

Poor												Outstanding
	1	2	3	4	5	6	7	8	9	10		

COMPANIES TO BUILD TRADEMARKS FOR

ABC	Jeep
Adidas	Kentucky Fried Chicken
Arrow Shirts	Kodak
AT&T	Las Vegas Sands Hotel
Continental Airlines	McDonald's
Disneyland	NASA
Dr. Pepper	20th Century-Fox
General Motors	Rolls-Royce
Hawaii Hilton Hotel	Schwinn Bicycles
IBM	Tony Lama Boots

Role Description—Laissez Faire Leader

A laissez faire leader *places a low emphasis on people and performance.* You do just enough to get by by being vague about the task and ground rules and by offering information primarily as a result of being asked. Provide little if any direction, and let your employees do whatever they want. Take occasional breaks and, upon your return, check with the employees to find out what is going on. Try to be as noncommittal as possible and show little concern for your people or their performance. Your main purpose as a leader is to let the organization take care of itself.

Role Description—Autocratic Leader

An autocratic leader *places a low emphasis on people and a high emphasis on performance.* It should be well understood that you are the boss and make the decisions, that your only purpose is to make as many trademarks as possible as fast as possible, and that you will not tolerate disobedience. In the leadership exercise, you should begin by making these ground rules clear and by telling people exactly what you want each of them to do. You should supervise and control each employee closely, push them to work harder, and make them redo anything that you don't like. Show little interest in your employees or their feelings, and don't hesitate to reprimand anyone who challenges your authority or makes a mistake. Recognition should be minimal and should focus primarily on obedience. Your main purpose as a leader is to push for performance and maintain your authority.

Role Description—Human Relations Leader

A human relations leader *places a high emphasis on people and a low emphasis on performance.* You feel that happy people are productive people and that a leader's job is to promote good relations, seek quality rather than quantity, involve people at every opportunity, and allow people as much individual freedom as possible. In the leadership exercise, you should begin by saying that you really care about your people, that you intend to involve them as much as possible so that it will be *their* team, and that you will do everything you can to make their work enjoyable. Then explain the ground rules (task, number of trademarks, time) and explain that your goal is to produce only high-quality and creative trademarks. Push for everyone working together on each trademark or for a few small teams, but ask the group members what they think is best. Stop the group occasionally for a group meeting to make sure everyone is satisfied and likes what he or she is doing. Compliment people continuously, never chastise or push them, and avoid confrontations or conflicts at all costs. Your main purpose as a leader is to keep people happy and to use a participative style that encourages involvement.

Role Description—Democratic Leader

A democratic leader *places a high emphasis on both people and performance.* You are genuinely interested in your people, but you also expect a high level of performance in terms of both quality and quantity. You approach management as a professional and take the time to establish clear objectives, define responsibilities, and provide the necessary leadership, planning, organizing, controlling, communicating, motivating, and developing to reach a high level of both productivity and satisfaction. In the leadership exercise, begin by describing the task (produce trademarks for 20 companies during a period of 30 minutes, each trademark being rated by customers on a 10-point scale based on how well it represents the company and how creative it is). Then share your objective, which is to try to produce all 20 items and yet aim for high quality and creativity on each one. Ask for questions and make sure that the group is willing to shoot for the objective. Then suggest that, given the limited time period, the team needs to get organized and that you would suggest that they work in pairs, each pair selecting the projects they want to work on. If there is a person without a partner or who prefers to work alone, that person could work on his or her own projects or assist the pairs when they need help. Once the group is organized, the boss's job is to keep members informed about how much time is left, offer encouragement and assistance, find the customers, give feedback on their scores and give recognition when they do a good job, and help resolve any problems that arise. Your main purpose as a leader is to achieve both high productivity and morale.

10.2 Customer Instructions and Scoring Sheet

(one copy to be shared by the two persons acting as the customers)

Two persons should work together as the customers to increase the accuracy of the ratings. Rotate from group to group, and each time one of the teams completes a trademark, rate the trademark on a 10-point scale based on:

1. How well the trademark represents the company or organization it was designed to represent.
2. How creative the trademark is.

Each time you rate a trademark, enter your score on the form below. At the conclusion of the exercise, continue to rate any trademarks completed before time was called and then post the results including the *total productivity* (total points divided by 2) and *average productivity* (total productivity divided by the number of trademarks produced) scores for each team on the chalkboard or a tabulation sheet provided by the instructor.

You may be asked to make observations on the different leaders and the effect of their styles on their employees. If you are asked to share the score given to a trademark, you may do so. *The trademarks do not have to be built in the order listed below.*

Scale

| Poor | 1 2 3 4 5 6 7 8 9 10 | | | Outstanding |

Trademark	Team 1	Team 2	Team 3	Team 4
1. ABC				
2. Adidas				
3. Arrow Shirts				
4. AT&T				
5. Continental Airlines				
6. Disneyland				
7. Dr. Pepper				
8. General Motors				
9. Hawaii Hilton Hotel				
10. IBM				
11. International Jeep				
12. Kentucky Fried Chicken				
13. Kodak				
14. Las Vegas Sands Hotel				
15. McDonald's				
16. NASA				
17. 20th Century-Fox				
18. Rolls-Royce				
19. Schwinn Bicycles				
20. Tony Lama Boots				
Total Productivity $\frac{\text{(total points)}}{2}$				
Average Productivity $\frac{\text{(total productivity)}}{\text{(total trademarks made)}}$				

10.3 Satisfaction Survey

(one copy for each employee at the conclusion of the exercise)
Total Number _____

Answer the questions below based on your experience in your team by *circling* the numbers that best represent your honest feelings. After all members of the team have completed their ratings, give the ratings to a scorer.

1. I disliked my boss's leadership style.   1 2 3 4 5 6 7 8 9 10   I liked my boss's leadership style.

2. My boss was a very ineffective leader.   1 2 3 4 5 6 7 8 9 10   My boss was a very effective leader.

3. The team's objectives were not made very clear.   1 2 3 4 5 6 7 8 9 10   The team's objectives were made very clear.

4. The team was not organized to do the best possible job.   1 2 3 4 5 6 7 8 9 10   The team was organized to do the best possible job.

5. Team members were poorly utilized.   1 2 3 4 5 6 7 8 9 10   Team members were well utilized.

6. Communication with the boss was poor.   1 2 3 4 5 6 7 8 9 10   Communication with the boss was excellent.

7. Communication among employees was poor.   1 2 3 4 5 6 7 8 9 10   Communication among employees was excellent.

8. Employee commitment was very low.   1 2 3 4 5 6 7 8 9 10   Employee commitment was very high.

9. Team productivity was very low.   1 2 3 4 5 6 7 8 9 10   Team productivity was very high.

10. Team morale was very low.   1 2 3 4 5 6 7 8 9 10   Team morale was very high.

Team Averages (for scorers only)

Compute a group average score for each question, rounded to the nearest whole number, and a total score for the team.

Question Number	Group Average Score
1.	_____
2.	_____
3.	_____
4.	_____
5.	_____
6.	_____
7.	_____
8.	_____
9.	_____
10.	_____
Team Satisfaction Score	_____

10.4 Observation Sheet

(one copy for each observer—one or two per team)

If possible, observe the team to which you are assigned from an observation room with one-way glass. Otherwise, observe as quietly as possible without disrupting the team. Take notes below on the following questions, and be prepared to spend about two to three minutes sharing your observations with the class at the conclusion of the exercise.

1. What was the leader's leadership style? (Answer this after observing the group enough to determine a specific style.)

2. What were your clues to the leader's style in terms of (1) the way the leader started the exercise, (2) the way the task was explained, and (3) how objectives and responsibilities were established?

3. During the exercise, how did the leader (1) communicate with employees, (2) motivate employees, and (3) make decisions?

4. How did the employees react to the leader's style (productivity, morale, group dynamics, commitment, etc.)?

10.5 Exercise Analysis Sheet

Team Number	Leader's Style	Satisfaction Questionnaire										(A) Total Satisfaction	(B) Total Productivity	Total Points (A + B)	Average Productivity
		1	2	3	4	5	6	7	8	9	10				
1															
2															
3															
4															

SUGGESTED ADDITIONAL READINGS

Blanchard, Kenneth, and Johnson, Spencer, *The One Minute Manager,* New York: William Morrow and Company, Inc., 1982.

Boyatzis, Richard E., *The Competent Manager: A Model For Effective Performance,* New York: John Wiley and Sons, 1982.

Fiedler, Fred E., and Chemers, Martin. *Leadership and Effective Management.* Glenview, IL: Scott, Foresman, 1974.

Hersey, P.; Blanchard, K. H.; and Natemeyer, W. E. "Situational Leadership, Perception, and the Impact of Power." *Group and Organizational Studies,* December, 1979, pp. 418–428.

Hollander, E. P. *Leadership Dynamics: A Practical Guide to Effective Relationships.* New York: Free Press, 1978.

Ouchi, William, *Theory Z: How American Business Can Meet the Japanese Challenge,* Reading, Mass.: Addison-Wesley Publishing Co., 1981.

Pascule, Richard Tanner, and Athos, Anthony G., *The Art of Japanese Management: Applications for American Executives,* New York: Warner Communications Co., 1981.

Peters, Thomas J., and Waterman, Robert H., Jr., *In Search of Excellence: Lessons From America's Best-Run Companies,* 1982.

Sayles, Leonard R., *Leadership.* New York: McGraw-Hill, 1979.

11

Staffing

There is no excuse for superior authority not choosing the most suitable agents for particular duties, and not removing unsuitable agents from particular duties.

Winston Churchill

When you are aspiring to the highest place, it is honorable to reach the second or even the third rank.

Cicero

OBJECTIVES

This chapter provides you with the information necessary to:

1. Have an understanding of the overall selection process in organizations
2. Understand the role of the supervisor in the staffing process
3. Gain an awareness of the application blank and its contents
4. Describe the patterned interview as a selection tool
5. Get a grasp of the physical examination and applicant testing
6. Describe ways to improve the indoctrination and training part of the selection process

---

THE STAFFING ROLE

By design, each job in an organization fulfills a specific role in helping to achieve the objectives of the firm. The staffing process includes the necessary sequence of events to ensure that the right person is placed into a job. Whether the personnel action is initiated to fill an existing vacancy or to staff a newly authorized position within the company, the supervisor has certain responsibilities that must be fulfilled.

People are the most important asset in any organization. The staffing process supports the need of both supervisors and managers to choose the best talent available. It can serve the organization better when management personnel understand the process and use a few simple guidelines. Figure 11.1 diagrams the flow of the process for selecting individuals to join the organizational team.

All the steps in Figure 11.1 make up the staffing process. However, additional dynamics take place at the same time. From the time a prospective employee first hears about a job until a final employment decision is made, the candidate is conducting his or her own evaluation of the organization and its management team. Consequently, the organization's supervisors must work extra hard at creating a favorable impression with all job candidates. For example, assume that a supervisor interviews five candidates for one job opening. The four unsuccessful candidates will have received an impression of the organization that may or may not be positive. Interviewing candidates with the objective of creating organizational goodwill in the community—the long-range reputation of your organization—is critical.

THE STAFFING PROCESS

The company personnel department should act as a staff agency to support organizational needs. There are occasions when the personnel department performs all the functions of acquiring new individuals for the firm without adequate interaction with the line agency. We feel that the most effective techniques for using the staffing process demand considerable interaction by the managers and supervisors. Although the amount of activity by management individuals varies with organizational design and the step of the staffing process being performed, it is felt that the interaction between line and staff agencies is vital in the selection process.

Figure 11.1 The staffing process.

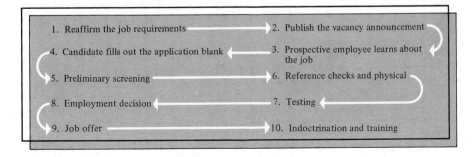

REAFFIRMING THE JOB REQUIREMENTS

The needs of the organization are typically in a constant state of upgrade and change. Too often job descriptions and job specifications accurately reflect neither the current duties of the position nor the most desirable individual characteristics needed to perform the job effectively. The supervisor should revalidate job information for the personnel department whenever vacancies occur.

Supervisors should also be involved in setting the task areas and level of performance required in the classification of new positions. Since the personnel department acquires the human resources for the organization, it is the responsibility of the line areas of the organization to reaffirm the requirements of the job to support the activity of establishing candidate qualifications.

THE VACANCY ANNOUNCEMENT

The personnel department establishes the format of position vacancy announcements using company policies consistent with the Equal Employment Opportunity Act guidelines and affirmative-action goals. The supervisor's role is again one of providing information necessary to develop an effective vacancy announcement. The first type of input usually sought from line management includes:

Levels of minimum proficiency
Amount of experience required
Preferred capabilities of applicants
Recommended scope of area for announcements

THE PROSPECTIVE EMPLOYEE

In addition to evaluating their personal competencies in comparison with the job requirements, candidates for a job bring with them many expectations, attitudes, values, and beliefs. Organizations and supervisors also have expectations, values, attitudes, and beliefs. The objective of the staffing process is to get a good *match-up* between the expectations of the candidate and the organization. There is a higher probability of a good match-up when candidates are permitted to learn as much as they can about the organization. A very common mistake made by supervisors is attempting to hide unfavorable situations and policies from candidates. If supervisors hide unfavorable things in organizations, they can set unrealistic expectations on the part of the candidate that may not be met at a later date. This will be discussed in detail later; the byword is basically, Tell it like it is!

THE APPLICATION BLANK

The first step a prospective employee ordinarily takes is completing an application (see sample in Figure 11.2). The application form is one of the most ubiquitous selection devices used by organizations. Most organizations provide a pleasant room where job

Figure 11.2 Application for employment. From Looart Press, Inc. Used with permission.

APPLICATION FOR EMPLOYMENT
LOOART PRESS, INC.
An Equal Opportunity Employer M/F

PLEASE PRINT

DATE	DATE OF AVAILABILITY	POSITION DESIRED:
SALARY REQUIREMENTS $ PER		HOW WAS YOUR CONTACT WITH LOOART INITIATED?

IDENTIFICATION

NAME FIRST MIDDLE LAST	SOCIAL SECURITY NO.
PRESENT ADDRESS	ZIP CODE PHONE
PREVIOUS ADDRESS IF LESS THAN 12 MONTHS AT PRESENT ADDRESS	ZIP CODE

DO YOU HAVE RELATIVES CURRENTLY WORKING AT LOOART? ☐ YES ☐ NO	IF YES, GIVE NAME AND DEPARTMENT
ARE YOU OVER THE AGE OF 21? ☐ YES ☐ NO	IF NO, YOU ARE SUBJECT TO PROOF OF MINIMUM LEGAL AGE UNDER STATE LAW
DO YOU HAVE ANY PHYSICAL CONDITIONS WHICH PRECLUDE YOU FROM PERFORMING CERTAIN KINDS OF WORK? ☐ YES ☐ NO	IF YES—EXPLAIN
HAVE YOU HAD ANY SERIOUS ILLNESS IN THE LAST FIVE YEARS? ☐ YES ☐ NO	IF YES—EXPLAIN
HAVE YOU EVER RECEIVED COMPENSATION FOR INJURIES? ☐ YES ☐ NO	IF YES—EXPLAIN
HAVE YOU EVER BEEN CONVICTED OF A CRIME EXCLUDING MINOR TRAFFIC VIOLATIONS? ☐ YES ☐ NO	IF YES—EXPLAIN
ARE YOU IN THIS COUNTRY ON A TEMPORARY VISA? ☐ YES ☐ NO	
WERE YOU EVER EMPLOYED BY THIS COMPANY UNDER ANOTHER NAME? ☐ YES ☐ NO	IF YES—EXPLAIN AND GIVE OTHER NAME
NAME OF PERSON TO CONTACT IN CASE OF EMERGENCY	ADDRESS PHONE

(U.S. ARMED FORCES ONLY)	BRANCH	DATE OF ENTRY	HIGHEST RANK

DESCRIBE MILITARY OCCUPATION AND ANY SPECIAL TRAINING RECEIVED

PERSONAL INTERESTS AND HOBBIES

EDUCATION

YEARS ATTENDED	NAME AND LOCATION OF INSTITUTION	COURSE TAKEN OR MAJOR	GRADUATION DATE	DEGREE
HIGH SCHOOL 19 TO 19				
COLLEGE 19 TO 19				
OTHER COURSES 19 TO 19				

DID YOU USE ANY OTHER NAME WHILE ATTENDING SCHOOL?
☐ YES   ☐ NO   IF YES, GIVE NAME

SPECIAL SKILLS

OFFICE	SHOP	OTHER
TYPING? _____ SPEED _____ SHORTHAND? _____ SPEED _____ PBX SWITCHBOARD? _____ OFFICE MACHINES? _____ _____	LIST TOOLS AND MACHINES WHICH YOU FEEL QUALIFIED TO USE WITHOUT FURTHER TRAINING— _____ _____ _____	WHAT SPECIAL SKILLS OR ABILITIES DO YOU HAVE? _____ _____ _____

applicants can complete the form. Even if no jobs are available, the receptionist should inform the applicant of that fact and then, if the applicant insists, have him or her complete an application form. The receptionist must be frank with the candidate, yet pleasant, because for some job seekers this is their only interaction with the firm.

The application form has three basic purposes: (1) It is a record of the candidate's desire for employment with the organization, (2) it becomes a reference sheet for the interview, and (3) it serves as the basic document for constructing a personnel record if the applicant becomes a permanent employee.

The application form has been legally defined as a "test" and must conform to EEOC guidelines. Supervisors should seek the assistance of their personnel department EEOC specialists before making a decision about selecting a form. Basically, any data requested from the applicant must be validated as a predictor of job-related behavior unless it qualifies as a bona fide occupational qualification. Again, this is a very technical area—consult your personnel department. If your organization does not have a personnel department, contact a regional EEOC office.

PRELIMINARY SCREENING

In most organizations, preliminary screening is done by people in the personnel department. In small businesses, supervisors may be involved in this step of the staffing process.

The purpose of the interview is to determine if the applicant is a good candidate for further interviews and/or training. Information items that should be obtained during the screening are:

Ability and aptitude to do the job
Applicant's interest in the organization
Salary expectations
Availability for work
Location desired
Past job experience

In addition to seeking this information, the interviewer should attempt to answer all the candidate's questions and set realistic expectations. If there are no vacancies or very few, tell it like it is. In the long run, the candidate will appreciate the interviewer's candor.

It is a good idea to have an "information kit" or company brochure available for all applicants. The brochure will have the answers to many routine questions and can generate goodwill for the organization. Finally, we recommend a structured format for the preliminary screening interview. Supplying the interviewer with a list of critical questions will help to ensure that all applicants are asked the same basic questions.

LENGTHY INTERVIEWS

The personal interview is used in almost all organizations in the joining-up process. The purpose of the interview is to gather more in-depth information than appears on the application. A recent study indicated that 64 percent of 2500 firms surveyed reported that the personal interview is the most important factor in the selection decision. Although many managers consider it as such, it is also probably the most unreliable. This unreliability is caused by the fact that many supervisors do not prepare for an in-depth interview. They believe they can "wing it" and play the interview "by ear," instead of planning properly. Some other erroneous attitudes are

Many supervisors believe they have an innate talent for selecting good people through the interview process. Being able to talk a good game does not necessarily ensure success with an interview.

Many supervisors are not good listeners. They should spend at least half the interview time listening to the candidate.

Supervisors have their own built-in biases and basically look for a person who reflects their value system and beliefs.

Supervisors are human and subject to the halo effect. The halo effect is when some predominant personal characteristic is evaluated in a manner that places undue importance upon it.

If the in-depth interview is unreliable, why do supervisors and managers use it so often? The answer is that most supervisors simply want to see what the applicants look like, how they present themselves, and what kind of an impression they make. Therefore, supervisors must recognize the shortcomings of the interview process and attempt to collect information from as many different sources as possible on an applicant before making an employment decision.

THE PATTERNED INTERVIEW: THE BEST APPROACH[1]

Have a comfortable physical setup.

Greet the candidate in a friendly manner and establish rapport. Remember, the candidate will probably be tense, and it is the interviewer's task to lower the threat level.

Be aware of your facial expressions. Talk in a friendly, relaxed manner and change your facial expressions. Attempt to smile more often and raise your eyebrows. If the candidate is tense, you may have to consider small talk to relax the person.

Start with a broad general question that will permit the candidate to relax and have sufficient freedom to respond: for example, "Please tell me why you are interested in working at XYZ Corporation."

Assume consent of the applicant. Word your questions in such a manner that the applicant has no choice but to answer: "Suppose you tell me about . . ."

Give positive strokes to the candidate when there is an opportunity: "You have excellent work experience for this job." This will help the candidate to relax.

[1]The authors wish to express their appreciation to Lawrence O. Short and Lynville E. Tabor for their helpful comments on this section of the book.

Use the calculated pause to your advantage. Pauses can force the candidate to talk more or add to statements. This is an excellent technique for gathering information.

Keep the interview moving in the direction you want it to go by using follow-up questions: "Tell me a little more about your previous work experience" or "That was very interesting; please tell me more about your goals."

Use your communication skills and keep your questions open-ended. Never permit the candidate to answer "yes" or "no." "Are you interested in production work?" is a poor question. A better question is "Why are you interested in production work?"

Talk the candidate's language. The more you can put yourself in the applicant's frame of reference, the more effective you will be as an interviewer.

In order to let the candidate do over half of the talking, talk only when you have information to present. Consider all aspects of the candidate—the whole person is very important: attitudes, aptitudes, motivation, and drive.

Bring the interview to a neat close. Observe time limits and gently remind the candidate when you are out of time. Close by establishing a proper verbal contract of what the candidate expects from the organization and what the organization expects from the candidate. Further, explain to the candidate who will make the next contact and when he or she will be contacted about the employment decision.

Record the interview. Immediately after the candidate leaves, record your impressions and recommendations in a short note. This information may be very important later on in the selection process.

USEFUL OPEN-ENDED QUESTIONS

The types of open-ended questions most profitable for the supervisor include those which allow the candidate to discuss issues that would be relevant to the job. Questions should also be designed to allow the candidate to reflect levels of interest in the career area, expectations from the company, and personal levels of maturity and realism regarding the job's potential. Some useful questions are:

1. How did you find out about this job vacancy?
2. What do you enjoy most about this type of job?
3. How would you describe yourself?
4. Why do you think you would be satisfied working for our organization?
5. What would you rate most important in a job?
6. If you were hiring someone for this job, what qualities would you look for?
7. What do you expect from organizational leaders?
8. How does this job fit in with your career plans?
9. Would you consider yourself a follower or a leader? Why?
10. How would you describe a perfect working group?

REFERENCE CHECKS AND PHYSICAL EXAMINATION

Normally a candidate is asked to list two or three references on the application blank. Reference checks normally consist of checking with previous employers by telephone, less frequently by letter, and sometimes in person. Recent studies indicate that over 50 percent of organizations surveyed do check with an applicant's previous employer; however, organizations are becoming more cautious because of civil rights legislation and EEOC guidelines. This check is normally done by the personnel department. However, in certain circumstances the supervisor may want to talk to previous supervisors.

Checking by letter is being done less and less because previous employers are hesitant to say too much in a letter because of the possibility of legal action and state freedom of information laws. When previous employers furnish a letter of recommendation, they tend to give the employee the benefit of the doubt and usually provide favorable recommendations. Communicating with previous employers by telephone usually increases the validity of references. Previous employers are generally more willing to discuss employees' shortcomings and weaknesses over the telephone, and this information, when added to all the other information gathered in the staffing process, can give the new organization a good overview of the whole person.

Once the applicant meets all the hiring requirements, he or she is scheduled for a physical examination, which is usually paid for by the future employer. The purpose of the medical examination is to:

Provide a medical history of the applicant. This may protect the employer from invalid future workers' compensation claims.

Protect future employees with health problems from being placed in a job that may be detrimental to themselves or other workers.

Screen out applicants who may become excessive financial burdens to the organization.

TESTING

The purpose of testing applicants is to predict performance on the job. The predictor is the test; behavior on the job (performance) is the variable. A test is a valid predictor if it has a good positive correlation with job success. If a charge of discrimination is brought against an organization, the firm must be able to prove that its tests are valid. This is a very technical area that should be handled by the organization's director of personnel in collaboration with a management consultant. However, supervisors must be aware of the legal requirement for test validation.

Tests may be divided into three major categories: (1) aptitude, (2) achievement (knowledge), and (3) general psychological. Aptitude tests are designed to measure the potential abilities of an applicant. Achievement tests measure specific skills such as verbal, typing, and shorthand. General psychological tests consist of intelligence tests, motivation instruments, and personality measures.

Aptitude and achievement tests are the easiest tests to validate; psychological tests are increasingly being subjected to questioning by the courts. Tests can be a strong plus in the staffing process when selected and administered properly. However, because of increasing EEOC pressure, many firms are reducing their testing programs. Overall, the more easily validated aptitude and achievement tests are also of the greatest value to an organization.

EMPLOYMENT DECISION AND JOB OFFER

After all candidates have been screened and interviewed, decisions must be made regarding who will be offered employment. We recommend that the employment decision be a joint decision between the supervisor and the personnel department. Although the job offer may come from the future supervisor, personnel must be involved because of equity concerns. Personnel must approve the pay grade to maintain internal organizational consistency of the wage and salary structure.

Some guidelines to remember during the employment decision are:

The supply of labor on the market will have an impact on the offer.

Define your labor market. Is it your city, county, the state, or the nation?

Don't forget the candidates who were not hired. They may be a valuable source of future labor. Give them timely feedback.

Once the offer has been made and has been accepted by the candidate, the joining-up process does not stop. It is only the beginning of the process of helping the new employee become a valuable member of the work team.

EMPLOYEE INDOCTRINATION AND TRAINING

Prior to the new employee's arrival at the organization, the supervisor should review the firm's formal on-the-job training program and directives. Next, the supervisor should consider asking a fellow employee to be a "sponsor" to help the new employee find housing, if necessary, and settle into the firm. After arrival, the supervisor must welcome the new employee and explain the organization's policies, rules, and benefits. A tour of the plant or office is a good idea early in the indoctrination process to show new employees how their tasks fit into and contribute toward the total goals and productivity of the company.

The supervisor must be aware of how the joining-up process affects the new employee's self-concept. When the new employee reports for work, basically three different types of behavior can be expected: (1) self-oriented behavior, (2) task behavior, and (3) relationship behavior.

Self-oriented behavior consists of the employee's asking himself or herself Who are the friendly people in this shop? Who are the cold and impersonal people? Who are the warm and helpful people? How much should I talk and interact with others? These are normal concerns of new employees, and the supervisor should be aware of these concerns and help the new employee through this self-oriented behavior. The sooner a new employee feels comfortable, the sooner he or she can begin task and relationship behavior, which should contribute to the overall productivity of the firm.

SUMMARY

People are the most important asset in any organization, and supervisors can improve the selection process by applying a few selective guidelines. The selection process consists of an applicant pool, good job documentation, completion of application blanks, preliminary screening, interviews, reference checks, physicals, testing, employment decisions, job offers, indoctrination, and training.

Supervisors must work very hard at creating or maintaining a good impression of the organization with all candidates. In many instances, more candidates are unsuccessful than are successful. Everyone interviewed leaves with an impression of the organization. Therefore, supervisors must strive toward creating a very favorable impression with all candidates with which they have contact.

IMPORTANT TERMS

staffing process   reference checks
application blank   testing
EEOC   employment decision
patterned interview   employment indoctrination

REVIEW QUESTIONS

1. Discuss the following statement: "People are the most important asset in any organization."
2. Discuss the steps in the selection process.
3. What are the three basic purposes of the application blank?
4. List the guidelines for the patterned interview.
5. What are the three major types of tests?
6. Explain self-oriented behavior and why it happens. Use the model of the self-concept (introduced in chapter 4) to explain self-oriented behavior.

CASES

11.1 The Joining Up of Janet Miller*

Janet Miller is 47 years old, married and the mother of two children in their twenties. Recently, Janet was hired to work in the market evaluation division of a large New York industrial firm. The market evaluation division has two sections: research and testing. Each section has approximately five women employees and a male supervisor.

*Used with permission from Wendell L. French, John E. Dittrich, and Robert A. Zawacki, *The Personnel Management Process: Cases on Human Resources Administration* (Boston: Houghton Mifflin, 1982).

The research section consists of a homogeneous group of women who have worked together for over 15 years. They range in age from 45 to 54, all have children, and some have grandchildren. They eat lunch together and use their coffee breaks to discuss, among other things, their children and grandchildren. Through the years, the group has become very close, and they often have family members visit the office.

When a vacancy occurred in research, Mike A. Taylor, the section's supervisor, asked personnel for the folders of qualified personnel seeking employment with the firm. He received five folders and asked the four female employees of research to review them and select the top three applicants. After reviewing the five folders, the four employees ranked the top three and presented their decision to Mike. Mike agreed to interview the three candidates and asked Betty Grace, who had the longest tenure in research, also to interview them. After the interviews, Mike and Betty both decided that Janet Miller was the most fully qualified and asked personnel to process the necessary paperwork to effect her immediate employment.

When Janet started working, Mike explained to her that, although he was her supervisor, Betty would conduct her training program. He further explained that all five employees of the research section must function as a team and that there was a general lack of structure and supervision because of the unique demands placed on the section by various research project officers.

Almost from Janet's first day of employment, her peers began to complain to Mike that Janet was slow, had a high error rate when computing statistics, and would sleep on the job for short periods of time. As the weeks passed and the complaints continued, Mike counseled Janet on her substandard performance. Janet denied that her work did not meet the minimum standards expected by her peers; however, she did admit that she occasionally "nodded" on the job because of the routine task.

Mike shared this personnel problem with his superior, the director of the market evaluation division, and both managers agreed to observe Janet's performance and make "memos for the record" if they observed an unacceptable attitude or behavior. Although the complaints continued, the two supervisors did not directly observe any unsatisfactory behavior by Janet during a two-month period. They did observe that Janet no longer went to lunch with the other group members and that she began to seek interpersonal relationships with people outside the research section. As communication between Janet and her peers decreased, conflict continued to increase in the section, and Mike began to receive reports from other department managers that the effectiveness of research was decreasing. Betty was observed discussing Janet's poor performance with the other team members; it was also rumored that she was discussing Janet's behavior with the testing section. The situation finally deteriorated to the point where Mike decided that he had to terminate Janet's employment for the good of the research section.

The morning after Janet's firing, George L. Kent, the supervisor of testing, stuck his head in Mike's office and asked, "Who are the women going to pick on next, now that Janet is gone?"

Questions

1. There was a rather serious conflict between Janet and her peers. What caused this conflict? Was it a personality conflict?
2. Analyze Mike Taylor's behavior. Was he an effective supervisor and counselor?
3. Discuss the overall joining-up process of the market evaluation division, and give your recommendations for increasing the reliability and validity of the process.
4. What is the predictive validity of the personal interview as a selection technique?
5. Was Janet Miller railroaded because she was new to the group? Could anyone be accepted by that group? If so, what type of person could be?

11.2 Improving Hiring Practices

A–Z Electronics manufactures small electrical components for major computer corporations. There is heavy demand for their product, and the firm is growing about 15 percent annually. To meet this demand, the organization must hire 30 new people each year. Furthermore, the job is very repetitive and boring and approximately 50 percent of the employees quit each year. Therefore, interviewing new employees is a major time-consuming task at A–Z Electronics. At present, each supervisor "wings it" during the interview.

Question

Break into groups of six to ten and brainstorm ways to improve the selection process at A–Z Electronics. Any idea is a valid idea when brainstorming. Try to be positive and don't constantly explain why an idea will not work.

SUGGESTED ADDITIONAL READINGS

ASPA. "Test Justification and Title VII." *The Personnel Administrator* (January, 1976), pp. 46–51.

Golembiewski, Robert T. "Testing Some Stereotypes About the Sexes in Organizations: Differential Centrality of Work?" *Human Resources Management* (Winter, 1977), pp. 21–24.

Gunn, Bruce. "The Polygraph and Personnel." *Personnel Administration* (May-June, 1970), pp. 32–36.

Jablin, Frederick. "The Selection Interview: Contingency Theory and Beyond." *Human Resources Management* (Spring, 1975), pp. 2–9.

Jauch, Lawrence. "Systematizing the Selection Decision." *Personnel Journal* (November, 1976), pp. 564–566.

Kessler, Clemm C., III, and Gibbs, Georgia J. "Getting the Most from Application Blanks and References." *Personnel* (January–February, 1975), pp. 53–62.

Lattrell, Jeffrey D. "Planning for the Selection Interview." *Personnel Journal* (July, 1979), pp. 466–467ff.

Leach, John. "Career Management: Focusing on Human Resources." *The Personnel Administrator* (November, 1977), pp. 59–66.

Levine, Edward. "Legal Aspects of Reference Checking for Personnel Selection." *The Personnel Administrator* (November, 1977), pp. 14–17.

Lipsett, Laurence. "Selecting Personnel Without Tests." *Personnel Journal* (September, 1972), pp. 648–654.

Maynard, Cathleen E., and Zawacki, Robert A. "Mobility and the Dual-Career Couple." *Personnel Journal* (July, 1979), pp. 468–472.

Nadler, Leonard. "Recognition of Non-Collegiate Learning Experiences." *Training and Development Journal* (July, 1975), pp. 8–11.

Nash, Allan N., and Carroll, Stephen J., Jr. "A Hard Look at the Reference Check." *Business Horizons* (October, 1970), pp. 43–49.

Schneider, Benjamin. *Staffing Organizations.* Pacific Palisades, CA: Goodyear Publishing Co., 1976.

Sibson, Robert. "The High Cost of Hiring." *Nation's Business,* February, 1975, pp. 85–88.

12

Planning and Setting Objectives[1]

No one with a day's experience in government fails to realize that in all bureaucracies there are three implacable spirits—self-perpetuation, expansion, and incessant demand for more power.

Herbert Hoover

When many are got together, you can be guided by him whose counsel is wisest—if a man is alone he is less full of resource, and his wit is weaker.

Homer

OBJECTIVES

This chapter provides you with the information necessary to:

1. Have an understanding of the overall planning process in organizations
2. List and discuss the planning guidelines
3. Have a basic familiarity with the planning chart
4. Define management by objectives

---

[1]Parts of this chapter have been adapted from J. Daniel Couger and Robert A. Zawacki, *Motivating and Managing Computer Personnel* (New York: Wiley Interscience, 1980), used with permission; and from the concepts and models of D. D. Warrick.

5. Explain why management by objectives is more than a process—it is a management philosophy
6. Have a grasp of the advantages and disadvantages of management by objectives
7. Present an overview of objectives-writing guidelines

THE PRIMARY FUNCTION OF SUPERVISORS

To accomplish work, there must be an understanding of what is to be done. Planning what is to be done is the primary function of supervisors. However, before we discuss planning, some basic definitions are in order.

Planning is the process whereby we anticipate the future and determine what steps are necessary to achieve the organization's desired results. Thus, planning involves two basic dimensions: (1) assessing the future and (2) providing the people and monies to achieve the desired outcome.

Objectives are the results that a supervisor desires to achieve. An example of an objective is, "To increase the output of assembly line C by 10 percent this calendar year."

Policies are broad, general statements of a company's objectives. For example, a common policy in an organization may be, "Each employee is permitted to take 21 days of paid vacation each year."

Rules are very specific statements indicating how supervisors implement policies and objectives. An example of a rule is, "Employees must apply for annual paid vacation at least 30 days prior to the effective date of the vacation."

You probably have assumed correctly by now that planning must come before all other supervisory functions. Further, it can be either personal or organizational. It can be short-range, intermediate-range, or long-range. And it can be formal or informal.

The breakout of the planning process in Figure 12.1 can be helpful to supervisors for several reasons. First, when supervisors fail, one of the primary reasons is that they *plan to fail.* By this we mean that they usually do not plan for the future. Usually, they do not plan for the future because they believe that they do not have ample time

Figure 12.1 Planning chart.

	Time		
Type	**Short-Range (1 year)**	**Intermediate (2–5 years)**	**Long-Range (5 years +)**
Personal			
Group			
Organization			

available to plan. Most supervisors are so busy putting out brush fires that they firmly believe that planning is a luxury. We call the above situation "getting seduced by the daily task at the expense of planning." While supervisors cannot ignore the immediate daily problems, they must recognize that proper planning is the key to effective supervision, and they must reserve some time during the week for planning. The American Management Association recommends that supervisors divide their time according to the following guidelines (recognize that these are only guidelines and that deviations are necessary and expected):

38 percent on daily problems (crisis supervision and routine decisions)
40 percent on problems and deadlines within one week
15 percent on problems and deadlines within one month
5 percent on problems and deadlines within three to six months
2 percent on problems and deadlines over one year or more away

Notice that the largest percentage of a supervisor's time should be used for daily and weekly problems and deadlines. Intermediate- and long-range planning should consume a very small percentage of a supervisor's time; however, the long-range implications of planning should not be ignored.

After recognizing the importance of planning, new supervisors usually get mentally "overloaded" because they fail to distinguish personal objectives from group and organizational objectives. For example, it may be helpful to ask new supervisors to design a personal plan of what they want to accomplish during the next year and by the end of five years. Then ask them to identify how they can accomplish some of their personal objectives by participating in the work group's and organization's objectives. This exercise forces supervisors to plan for the future in both personal and organizational terms. The linkage between personal and organizational objectives is a healthy process—and a process that is missing in some organizations.

THE PLANNING PROCESS

As previously stated, the planning process can be either formal or informal. The degree to which a supervisor formalizes a plan depends upon the importance of the plan and the amount of time and effort the supervisor wants to invest. Deciding whether and to what degree to formalize a plan is a very subjective process. However, if a supervisor is going to err, erring on the side of a formal plan is preferable.

Dr. Preston P. LeBreton, past president of the Academy of Management and professor of business administration at the University of Washington, has developed a formal planning process.[2] Professor LeBreton had a major influence on one of the authors of this book and therefore on the following guidelines. Please note that the guidelines refer only to *what* must be done. *How* to accomplish the tasks is discussed in the following section on management by objectives.

[2]Many of these planning ideas came from informal class notes taken from lectures by Professor LeBreton. His excellent ideas also appear in Preston B. LeBreton, *General Administration: Planning and Implementation* (New York: Holt, Rinehart and Winston, 1965).

1. Become aware of the need to plan:
   Are there multiple sources of input—internal or external?
   Financial, people, or information ideas?
2. Form an exact statement of the objective of the proposal:
   Formal or informal?
   Who will write the statement?
   What is the nature of the objective?
3. Prepare a general outline of the proposal:
   What is the nature of the plan?
   What resources are needed?
   What supporting evidence is there?
   What is the time schedule?
   Who is responsible for its implementation?
4. Obtain approval of the proposal:
   Who will make the presentation?
   To whom and in what format?
   Where and when?
5. Organize planning functions and assign responsibility:
   What people will be involved?
   Does plan cross departments or divisions?
   Who will notify people about the need to plan this action?
6. Contact cooperating departments and divisions:
   Who will make the contact?
   Whom will they contact?
   Formal or informal notification?
   When will they be contacted?
7. Obtain and evaluate inputs:
   What inputs do we need?
   How will they be obtained?
   Who has the information?
   What format shall we use?
   How are the data evaluated?
8. Form tentative conclusions and prepare a tentative plan:
   Compare with original objective.
   What is the probability that the planned-for events will happen?
   Is the final solution practicable?
   Have we considered all the alternatives?
9. Test the tentative plan:
   Formal or informal testing?
   What parts are to be tested?
   By whom?
   What type of tests?
10. Prepare the final plan:
    Time schedule?
    Who?

Resources needed?
Budget needed?
Is the supporting evidence included?
11. Obtain approval of the final plan:
Who makes the presentation?
Who approves the plan?
Who communicates the final plan?
To whom is the final plan communicated?
Who follows up on the implementation (action) phases?
When will progress reports be due?

A planning chart is shown in Figure 12.2.

MANAGEMENT BY OBJECTIVES (MBO)

The wise supervisor will use the preceding checklist during the planning process in real life situations. However, remember that it is only a guide to action and that the format may be shortened or even rearranged to suit the situation. The real issues in the planning process are how the objectives and plans are established and how they will be implemented. Plans and objectives can be determined automatically or in a collaborative manner. One collaborative process of establishing objectives is commonly known as *management by objectives (MBO).*

A recent study by Zawacki and Taylor of the top industrial organizations in the United States indicated that approximately 55 percent of U.S. firms are using a form of MBO.[3] Another recent study supports this, indicating that 122 out of 147 firms

Figure 12.2 Formal planning chart.

	Project	Project Leader	Team Members	Date Started	Draft of Plan Due	Budget	Completion Date
1.							
2.							
3.							
4.							
5.							
6.							
7.							
8.							
9.							
10.							
11.							
12.							
13.							
14.							
15.							

[3]Robert A. Zawacki and Robert L. Taylor, "A View of Performance Appraisal from Organizations Using It," *Personnel Journal,* June, 1976, pp. 290–299.

surveyed have a form of MBO.[4] Further, only 15 percent of the 122 companies stated that they were dissatisfied with their MBO programs.

An MBO program is based on two concepts: (1) managing a successful organization or being a successful person in one's job does not have to be a matter of luck or of letting events shape one's life or organization, and (2) an organization or person with objectives has a greater chance of making things happen and guiding a success pattern than those who simply watch things happen, criticize what happened, wonder what happened, or wait for fate to mold their organization or their lives.

The MBO Process

Management by objectives is a management method and process by means of which objectives, or goals, are established for: (1) the organization, (2) each department, (3) each work unit within each department, and (4) each employee who works in an area where the establishment of objectives would be practical and valuable (see Figure 12.3). Establishing objectives usually consists of having the key people affected by the objectives meet to: (1) agree on the major objectives for a given time period such as one year, (2) develop plans for how and when the objectives will be accomplished, and (3)

Figure 12.3 The MBO process.

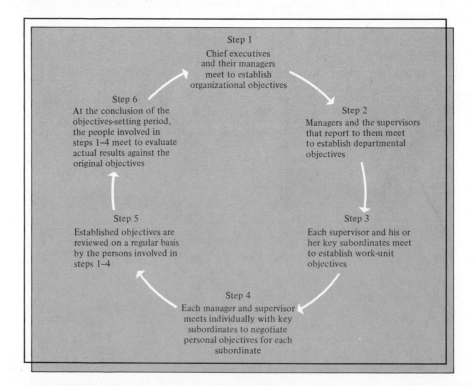

Step 1
Chief executives and their managers meet to establish organizational objectives

Step 2
Managers and the supervisors that report to them meet to establish departmental objectives

Step 3
Each supervisor and his or her key subordinates meet to establish work-unit objectives

Step 4
Each manager and supervisor meets individually with key subordinates to negotiate personal objectives for each subordinate

Step 5
Established objectives are reviewed on a regular basis by the persons involved in steps 1–4

Step 6
At the conclusion of the objectives-setting period, the people involved in steps 1–4 meet to evaluate actual results against the original objectives

[4]*Administrative Management,* June, 1973, pp. 26–29ff.

decide on the criteria for determining if the objectives have been met. Once objectives have been established, progress reviews are made regularly until the period for which the objectives were established is over. At that time the people who established the objectives at each level in the organization meet to evaluate actual results against the established objectives and then agree on the objectives for the next period.

Objectives serve the supervisor well. Properly prepared, they define targets, set expected outcomes, establish ways to measure results, and provide means of evaluating effort. The supervisor must continually balance the effects of quality, quantity, time, and cost of the operation. A good series of objectives integrates these management elements into an operating format with which the supervisor can work toward outcomes, not merely observe them.

MBO is a Management Philosophy

MBO is not simply a management technique. It is a management philosophy. It assumes that: (1) people are willing to commit themselves to objectives they participated in setting; (2) people will perform better if they can measure their progress; (3) people are objectives-oriented and desire to make a significant contribution to the organization if they are given the opportunity to do so; (4) delegation and mutual agreement on what is to be delegated are to be emphasized; (5) results rather than means are to be emphasized; and (6) people perform better when they have some control over their destiny.

Advantages and Disadvantages of MBO

MBO is not a panacea and, like most worthwhile programs, it is not without its problems. However, some of the benefits that can accrue from objectives setting are that it:

1. Forces planning ahead—looking into the future and not the past
2. Improves communication
3. Gives people a clearer understanding of what is expected of them and how well they are doing
4. Results in greater employee commitment, direction, and teamwork
5. Makes boss-subordinate relationships more of a helping relationship
6. Reduces duplication of effort
7. Reduces needless conflict resulting from unclear goals
8. Reduces busy work that does not lead to organizational objectives
9. Provides a more objective way to evaluate employees and reward effective employees
10. Forces problems in accomplishing objectives to the surface so that they can be confronted objectively
11. Shows those who wish to participate in the program that they can have a greater influence in running their organization and shaping their own careers than they had previously allowed for
12. Solves many problems before they result in crises, thus reducing fire fighting

Some of the problems with MBO are that it:

1. Requires time and commitment by the supervisor and subordinates
2. Requires hard work
3. Can become a personnel department program without any involvement of the employees in the various departments
4. Can become overstructured
5. May not permit the supervisor to link rewards with objectives accomplishment
6. May fail without top-management support
7. Requires practice and learning by the participants

Key MBO Terms

As previously stated, the words *goals* and *objectives* are used to mean the same thing in this book. Some key terms used in the MBO process are:

1. *Objectives:* major results that can realistically be accomplished during a given period of time
2. *Objectives purpose:* a simple statement of the reasons for having a particular objective
3. *Objectives plan:* a general description of what must be done to accomplish objectives
4. *Objectives measurement:* a pessimistic, realistic, and optimistic view of what constitutes accomplishing the objectives
5. *Organizational* or *strategic objectives:* a few *major* objectives that are organization-wide
6. *Departmental objectives:* a few *major* objectives to be accomplished by a department during a given time period that are consistent with organizationwide objectives
7. *Individual objectives:* a few *major* objectives to be accomplished by an individual during a given time period consistent with the individual's department objectives

Types of Objectives

There are five major types of objectives:

1. *Routine objectives:* objectives pertaining to regular duties and responsibilities that are part of a job
2. *Problem-solving objectives:* objectives related to solving specific problems
3. *Innovative objectives:* objectives pertaining to new ideas, services, or ways of doing things
4. *Personal-development objectives:* objectives related to an individual's personal and professional development and growth
5. *Organizational-development objectives:* objectives involving the development of the entire organization or a department

Identifying Objectives

A systematic procedure should be used to identify desired objectives. Figure 12.4 presents some general categories for identifying objectives. The general categories are not adequate to satisfy the specific needs of the supervisor. These must be developed.

The Objectives-Setting Process

The objectives-setting process proceeds as follows:

1. *The establishment of organizational objectives.* The procedures for establishing organizational objectives are
   a. Each supervisor of an organizational unit (department, work unit, etc.) asks for information from members of the organizational unit regarding objectives they would like to see their units accomplish. This information is passed upward to the executive team or whomever is responsible for establishing organizational objectives.
   b. Those responsible for establishing organizational objectives meet as a team to establish organizational objectives based on the information that has been passed upward. The head of the organization must assume ultimate responsibility for approving the final list of objectives. Objectives should be listed according to priority.

Figure 12.4 Organizational objectives system.

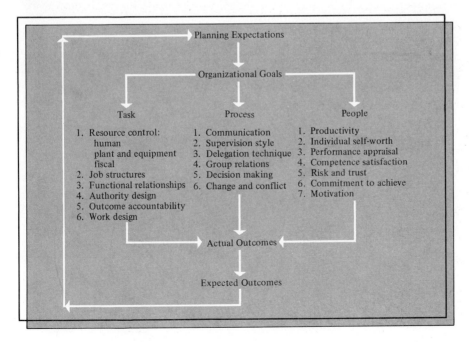

c. Major organizational objectives should be communicated throughout the organization.

2. *The establishment of departmental objectives.* Each department (personnel, computers, products, etc.) selects a few major objectives for the objectives-setting period. Peter F. Drucker, an international consultant and speaker, has specified eight areas where organizational and departmental objectives must be set: market standing; productivity; resources—human and financial; innovation and creativity; profitability; employees' development and performance; employees' attitudes; and public responsibility. The procedures for establishing departmental objectives are:

   a. Each department head meets with the supervisors who report to him or her to agree on departmental objectives.
   b. The department heads meet to share their departmental objectives and eliminate any overlaps, establish priorities, and agree on ways the departments can work together to help each accomplish its objectives.
   c. Copies of departmental objectives are given to the head of the organization and to each department head and communicated to the members of the department whenever possible.

3. *The establishment of work-unit objectives.* Each work unit (any work group or project team within a department) selects a few major objectives for the objectives-setting period. These objectives should be consistent with the objectives of the department. The procedures for establishing work unit objectives are

   a. Each work-unit supervisor should meet with his or her employees to agree on work-unit objectives
   b. Work-unit supervisors in the same department meet to discuss their objectives with each other to eliminate overlap, etc.
   c. Copies of work-unit objectives are given to the work-unit supervisors, immediate supervisor, and department head of the work unit involved and communicated to the members of the work unit.

4. *The establishment of personal objectives.* Employees who are participating in the objectives-setting program meet with their supervisors to negotiate their personal objectives for the objectives-setting period. The procedures for doing this are:

   a. Prior to the objectives-setting meeting between employee and boss, both make notes on what the employee's objectives could be
   b. Employee makes an appointment to see the boss. It is helpful for the employee to submit a copy of his or her personal objectives before the objectives-setting meeting
   c. Employee and boss meet and discuss the objectives until both agree. If it is impossible to reach an agreement on a particular objective, the boss's recommendation should be followed.
   d. Employee and boss agree on plans for reaching the agreed-upon objectives and on how objective attainment will be determined.

[5]Peter F. Drucker, *The Practice of Management* (New York: Harper & Row, 1964), p. 63.

     e. Agreed-upon objectives, objectives plans, and measurement criteria are written out and duplicated; boss keeps one copy and employee keeps the other.

        The boss's role in the objectives-setting meeting is to:

     a. Establish an informal and supportive atmosphere in which the intent is very clearly to be helpful.

     b. Help subordinates set realistic objectives and objectives plans in terms of the subordinate's capabilities and aspirations.

     c. Assure that communication in the meeting is open and two-way—the purpose of such meetings is not for bosses to hear themselves talk.

     d. Assure that definite decisions are made regarding objectives and objectives plans.

     e. Make suggestions, offer help, and propose alternatives when appropriate without imposing his or her will or forcing ideas on the subordinate.

     f. Arrange for definite dates for reviewing the subordinate's progress toward his or her objectives.

5. *Reviewing progress toward objectives.* Specific dates are set for reviewing progress toward the objectives. At these follow-up meetings, in addition to reviewing progress towards the objectives, any changes that would result in a modification of the objectives and objectives plans should be considered.

6. *Reviewing the results.* The persons involved in establishing objectives meet to evaluate actual performance against the agreed-upon objectives. The person ultimately responsible for accomplishing the objectives should prepare a brief statement regarding his or her perception of how well he or she performed on each objective.

7. *The establishment of new objectives.* The objectives-setting process begins again with step 1.

Guidelines for Writing Objectives

After you have written an objective statement, check it against the criteria shown below. If your objective seems to be poorly written, you should devote more time to improving the way you have stated it.

Well-Written Objectives Are:	Poorly Written Objectives Are:
1. Stated in terms of end results	1. Stated in terms of processes or activities
2. Achievable in definite time period	2. Never fully achievable; no specific target date
3. Definite as to what is expected	3. Ambiguous as to what is expected
4. Practical and feasible	4. Theoretical or idealistic
5. Important to job success	5. Of no real consequence

6. Precisely stated in terms of quantities, where possible
7. Limited to one important objective statement
8. Those which require stretching to improve results or personal effectiveness

6. Too brief and indefinite, or too long and complex
7. Written with two or more objectives per statement
8. Those which lack requirement for improvement or follow established routines and procedures

Guidelines for Applying MBO

Limit objectives to *major* objectives that should be accomplished during a given time period.

People should be accountable for their objectives, but there should also be enough flexibility to allow for changes in circumstances or for legitimate reasons for changing objectives or for not accomplishing them.

Objectives setting must be kept simple and flexible. Too many forms, rigid requirements, or too much time spent establishing and documenting objectives will limit the potential and possibly destroy an objectives-setting program. It is far more important to concentrate on whether a person has realistic objectives than on whether he or she followed objectives-setting procedures to the letter or completed the forms correctly.

People are unique and make different contributions to an organization. Therefore, you should tailor each person's objectives to his or her specific contribution rather than impose the same level of objectives on all your people.

You must provide guidance in helping each employee select realistic objectives. Each employee may respond differently to MBO. Employees generally fall into one of three broad groups:

1. *Underachievers.* They tend to set lower objectives than they can attain. By never committing themselves to an objective that is hard to attain, they protect themselves from risk and anxiety. They have an unfavorable self-image.
2. *Overachievers.* They announce objectives beyond their attainment. They are uncertain of what they can expect of themselves but cannot admit inadequacy. They lack self-confidence and reduce their anxiety by aiming beyond what they can achieve.
3. *Realistic achievers.* They tend to have a positive self-image, are usually successful in their endeavors, and can set challenging but reachable objectives.

Objectives cannot be set in a vacuum. Persons involved in the objectives-setting program must consider their career objectives in the context of other important areas of their lives.

Objectives plans should be stated simply, include target dates, be definite as to what is expected and when it is expected, be practical, be important to job success, and, where possible, be precisely stated in terms of quantities. An objectives-setting form is shown in Figure 12.5.

Figure 12.5 Objectives-setting form.

Objectives Level (check the appropriate one)		Period	Objectives Type (check the appropriate one)	
1. Organization (companywide)	_____	_____	1. Routine responsibilities	_____
2. Department (products, etc.)	_____		2. Problem solving	_____
3. Work Unit (project team, key punching, etc.)	_____ _____		3. Innovative	_____
			4. Organizational development	_____
4. Personal	_____		5. Personal development	_____
			6. Other	_____

Objectives (What do I want to accomplish?)	Objectives Plan (What must be done to accomplish the objective?)	Objectives Completion Target Date (When should the objective be completed?)	Objectives Attainment Measurement (How will I know when the objective is accomplished?)

SUMMARY

Planning is a primary function of supervisors. It is a process whereby supervisors anticipate the future and determine the necessary steps to achieve the desired organizational results. Plans are of three types: personal, group, and organizational. Further, there are short-range, intermediate, and long-range plans.

The planning process can be either formal or informal. The degree to which supervisors formalize a plan depends on the importance of the plan to the organization. Plans refer to what must be done. How to accomplish the plan is part of management by objectives (MBO).

MBO is a process whereby objectives are established for: (1) the organization, (2) each department, (3) each work unit within each department, and (4) every employee. Usually the key personnel in the organization meet to: (1) agree on the major organizational objectives for the next year, (2) develop plans for how the objectives will be reached, and (3) decide on the criteria for determining if the objectives have been met. Once this process is complete, regular progress reviews are necessary to keep the organization on a course that leads toward objectives accomplishment.

IMPORTANT TERMS

planning	rules
objectives	management by objectives (MBO)
policies	MBO process

REVIEW QUESTIONS

1. Discuss the steps in the planning process.
2. Is a planning chart necessary in an organization? Discuss.
3. Define MBO and list its advantages and disadvantages.
4. What is the meaning of the statement, "MBO is a management philosophy"?
5. Discuss objectives-writing guidelines and write five objectives for a real or imaginary organization.

EXERCISE

12.1 Career Planning

1. Sit where you will not be interrupted and list the five people, events, and things that have had the greatest influence on your life. You may use words, phrases, or complete sentences.
2. Rank the five entries on your list from most important to least important.
3. Describe in a short paragraph what you want to accomplish during the next year. (You should mention both personal and organizational objectives.)
4. Describe in a second paragraph what you want to accomplish during the next five years.
5. Describe how you will accomplish steps 3 and 4.

CASE

12.1 Health Care Administration

Carol A. Cretien is the director of training for Community Health Hospital. Community Health is a new city hospital that opened about two years ago and now employs about 150 persons. The managers came to Carol and informed her that they felt their hospital represented an outstanding opportunity to build an effective management team and to accomplish some unique things in health care delivery, because the hospital was not heavy in tradition or long-established rules. They then asked Carol to design and implement an effective training program for managers at all levels.

Questions

1. Using the guidelines for planning suggested by Professor LeBreton, discuss the plan that you recommend.
2. What additional information do you need to complete a detailed plan?
3. How would you measure the effectiveness of a management-development program?

SUGGESTED ADDITIONAL READINGS

Carter, Deborah Ann. "The Light at the End of the Productivity Tunnel." *Supervisory Management* (June, 1979), pp. 29–34.

French, W. L., and Hollmann, R. W. "Management by Objectives: The Team Approach." *California Management Review* 17 (Spring, 1975): 13–22.

Fulmer, Robert M. *The New Management.* New York: Macmillan, 1983, pp. 89–112.

Hollmann, Robert W. "Applying MBO Research to Practice." *Human Resources Management* 15 (Winter, 1976): 28–36.

LeBreton, Preston B. *General Administration: Planning and Implementation.* New York: Holt, Rinehart and Winston, 1965.

McFarland, Dalton E. "Planning and Control." In *Supervisory Management: Tools and Techniques,* edited by M. Gene Newport, pp. 57–69. St. Paul, MN: West Publishing Co., 1976.

Pounds, William F. "The Process of Problem Finding." *Industrial Management Review* (Fall, 1969), pp. 1–19.

Walton, Richard E. "Contrasting Designs for Participative Systems." In *Organization Development: Managing Change in the Public Sector,* edited by Robert A. Zawacki and D. D. Warrick, pp. 75–81. Chicago: IPMA, 1976.

Zawacki, Robert A., and LaSota, P. E. "Successful Staff Meetings." *Personnel Journal* (January, 1975), pp. 27–28, 63–64.

13

Organizing and Controlling

We judge ourselves by what we feel capable of doing, while others judge us by what we have already done.

Henry Wadsworth Longfellow

OBJECTIVES

This chapter provides you with the information necessary to:

1. List some guidelines for organizing
2. Have an overall understanding of when to delegate to subordinates
3. Describe the reasons why supervisors fail to delegate work to subordinates
4. Discuss the techniques of job rotation, job enlargement, and job enrichment
5. Define and discuss flexible working hours
6. Describe some control techniques and why control is necessary in organizations
7. Define and describe zero-base budgeting as a control tool

ORGANIZING

One of the secrets to the success of our free market system in the United States has been specialization. Specialization (division of work) promotes efficiency and economy because it permits an employee to work in a limited area, reducing the scope of the job. This division of work permits tasks to be performed more effectively with greater knowledge and skill because the tasks are more familiar. However, with the introduction of specialization appears the need in the firm for coordination of the tasks by supervisors. Thus, there are dual forces at work, specialization and coordination. Coming to grips with these forces is what we call the process of *organizing*. Thus, supervisors are supplied with human and financial resources; they must specify a division of labor; and then they must integrate the activities and tasks into a system of departments that maximizes outputs (see Figure 13.1).

Guidelines for Organizing

Determine Line and Staff Departments.   Line departments contribute directly toward accomplishing the objectives of the organization, while staff departments service the line organization and other staff organizations. The usual line departments in a manufacturing organization are production, marketing, and finance. Personnel is an example of a staff agency (see Figure 13.2).

Develop a Chain of Command and Establish Unity of Command.   The chain of command must extend from the top to the bottom of the organization. Each person in the organization should take orders from only one supervisor. Early management writers believed that unity of command is very critical, that without it authority is undermined, discipline is in jeopardy, and stability is threatened. However, current indications are that as technologies become more complex and the workers more knowledgeable, there is more of a need for communication between departments without going through the established chain of command. Thus, while we recommend establishing the organizational structure, we also recognize the need for flexibility in daily work relationships.

Assign Authority and Responsibility.   Authority and responsibility go together. The right and power to give orders is balanced by the responsibility for performing necessary functions. But remember, the positions in the organization, not the people, have the authority and responsibility. Harry Truman warned us that people hold power only temporarily in an organization, and when they begin to believe that they are the source of power, that will be their ruination!

Figure 13.1 The process of organizing.

Division of labor (specialization)	Combination of labor	Coordination (integration)

DIV OF LAB / COMBO OF LAB / COORDINATION

Figure 13.2 Sample organization chart.

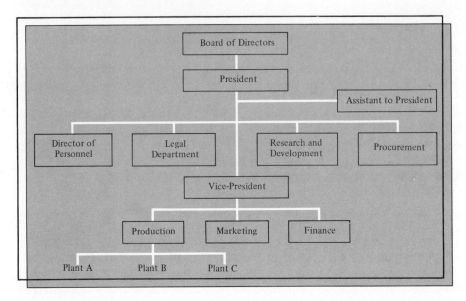

Determine the Span of Control for Supervisors.   Span of control is the number of subordinates that one supervisor can manage effectively. An advantage of a small span of control (one to three subordinates) is that it permits better coordination of the activities and tasks of the subordinates. A drawback is that a small span of control can result in oversupervision and "red tape." Oversupervision reduces the initiative and creativity of subordinates. Techniques have been developed that work toward increasing the span of control. These techniques will be discussed at the end of this chapter. Some variables to consider when determining the span of control are

a. Degree of complexity of the technology
b. Physical distance between activities
c. Need to permit subordinates to develop
d. Skills of supervisors and subordinates
e. Training needs of subordinates

Delegate to Subordinates.   This sounds logical and easy to do. Actually, when we study supervisors in organizations, we find that supervisors do not always delegate to the degree possible. One conceivable reason is that supervisors have more confidence in themselves and firmly believe that if they want it done correctly and on time, they must do it themselves. This viewpoint will soon get a supervisor in trouble. Subordinates will sense that their contributions are not needed and soon will do the bare minimum to get by in the organization without drawing attention to themselves. Decisions should be pushed as far down in the organization as possible, because the people doing the tasks are usually the people with the knowledge to make correct decisions. Two famous management writers[1] listed the following characteristics of supervisors who delegate effectively:

a. They are open to suggestions and ideas from subordinates.
b. They welcome feedback from employees.
c. They trust subordinates and are willing to give them the power to make decisions.
d. They expect subordinates to make mistakes and let them learn from their mistakes.
e. They keep communication lines open but give subordinates broad guidelines and controls.
f. They are available when subordinates need help, but they do not constantly look over the subordinates' shoulders.

Reasons Supervisors Fail to Delegate Work

There are many reasons why new (and even seasoned) supervisors fail to delegate effectively. Some possible reasons are:

1. Supervisors believe subordinates lack experience to do the job. If supervisors don't delegate to subordinates, how are they ever going to get experience?
2. Some supervisors believe that it takes more time to explain a job than to do it themselves. Supervisors must remember that they are paid to plan, organize, and direct the activities of others, not to do the work themselves.
3. Some supervisors use the excuse that a mistake by a subordinate will be too costly to the department. Supervisors must learn to develop people and know that mistakes will happen in the learning process. A department without mistakes is very probably a department without learning.
4. Some supervisors like doing the detail work and shy away from administrative duties. Remember—as supervisors assume more authority and responsibility in organizations, they must be prepared to shift from technical work to human relations and administrative work.

Techniques for Organizing and Integrating

The process of organizing is necessary and good; however, overorganizing can be a problem in organizations. One of the major criticisms of the guidelines given earlier is that they tend to encourage specialization to such a fine degree that people and their needs become lost in the process. For example, people have social needs, and many of the specialization techniques completely eliminate social interaction. To counter this dehumanization in organizing, many *human* organization techniques are being experimented with in organizations. Some of the newer techniques are described below.

1. *Job rotation.* This is the process of rotating people between jobs. For example, a new person on the automobile assembly line may put on wheels for 60 days, then

[1]Harold Koontz and Cyril O'Donnell, *Principles of Management,* S & H ed. (New York: McGraw-Hill, 1972), pp. 350–353.

assemble doors for 60 days, and so on. The goal is to reduce boredom and increase the skills of the workers. The drawbacks are increased training costs and the upsetting of informal relationships that develop on the job. Benefits from lack of boredom may be more than offset by the disruption of the informal organization.

2. *Job enlargement.* In a job enlargement program, the worker is given a greater variety of work without increasing the need for a higher level of knowledge or skills. Job enlargement does not increase the autonomy or responsibility dimensions of the job; it focuses on increasing the horizontal aspects of the job (see Figure 13.3). For example, if automobile assembly line workers are putting on wheels, we enlarge their jobs by having them put on wheels, bumpers, and trim. Although this strategy may work in the short run, workers in the long run will become bored because they are not involved in planning and organization.

3. *Job enrichment.* Job enrichment is a planned strategy to change the job content to provide the employees with a greater variety of work that requires higher skills and responsibility. They become involved in the layout of work, scheduling, and even improving the product. Basically, the strategy is to get them involved in some of the functions normally performed by the supervisor. The supervisor must be willing to delegate. This delegation provides the employees with an opportunity for personal growth and development and has a positive impact on individual motivation. Some elements to include in a job-enrichment strategy appear in Figure 13.4.

4. *Flexible working hours.* Known by many names, flexible working hours is a system whereby individual workers can come and go at their pleasure, within certain limits, as long as they work a prescribed number of hours each week. In most instances, there are certain fixed hours as well during which everyone is required to be at work.

As the examples in Figure 13.5 show, under the fixed-hour system, the normal working hours in an organization are from 7:30 A.M. to 4:00 P.M., with a 30-minute

Figure 13.3 Job enlargement.

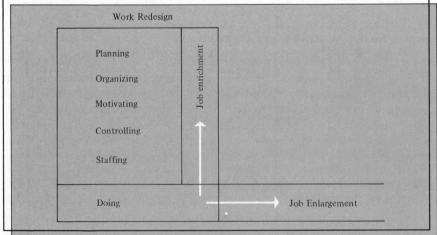

Figure 13.4 Ways to enrich jobs and increase motivation.

Environmental (Things That Enrich Work)	Job-related (Things That Enrich Jobs)
Supportive climate: Show trust Show you care	Remove controls and obstacles that cause resentment and may interfere with creativity and performance
Open communication: Listen with understanding Level with people—use sensitivity Keep informed	Give complete tasks to do, not just pieces Emphasize participation in decision making when decisions directly involve employee
Problem-solving approach: Focus on problems, not personalities Preserve mutual self-respect	Give new and more challenging tasks where possible—think possibilities through before rejecting them
Supply necessary tools for job (desks, paper, phones, etc.) to the extent possible	Recognize good performance Build on strengths—don't ignore weaknesses, but place the main emphasis on developing strengths
Emphasize results; not the way someone does something	Match appropriate leadership style with job and person

lunch break at 11:30 A.M. Under a flexible-hour system, the employees may arrive between 6:30 and 8:30 in the morning and leave between 3:00 and 5:00 in the afternoon. The traditional half-hour lunch is expanded into two alternative half-hour lunch breaks.

Although there are about as many variations on the basic work schedule as there are companies participating, in general the employee can make the decision as to what hours he or she works on any particular day.

In Europe, the span of one month is used as the period during which hours on the job must balance out to a normal workweek. The standard workweek of Sandoz Ltd, for example, is 37½ hours, but the employees may work either fewer or more hours (up to a maximum of 40 hours due to overtime restrictions) and carry

Figure 13.5 Flexible working hours.

Fixed-Hour System

A.M.   P.M.

Fixed	Lunch	Fixed

7:30   11:30   12:00   4:00

Flexible-Hour System

A.M.   P.M.

Flexible	Fixed	Flexible	Fixed	Flexible

6:30   8:30   11:15   12:15   3:00   5:00

the difference over to the following week. A maximum of 10 hours may be accumulated; these hours cannot be used to take a half or full day off.

Under current working-hour legislation and union contracts in the United States, this amount of flexibility is precluded. The rigidities we have built into our working environment to reduce uncertainty and unilateral action may have placed us in a position where we cannot realize the full potential of the flexible-hour system.

5. *Job sharing.* This technique, although used in only a few firms, has tremendous potential. It involves two people sharing one job and dividing the salary. For example, two working women with young children may share a job where one works from 8:00 A.M. to 12:00 noon and the second employee works from 1:00 P.M. to 5:00 P.M. The advantages are that both people may be classified as part-time employees, thereby reducing the cost of fringe benefits to the company. Further, where job sharing is used, the experience is that the employees tend to work more than their assigned hours. Employees want to do well and will usually work late to complete a project. This represents a salary savings for the firm.

Disadvantages of the strategy are lack of proper coordination and the fact that some jobs simply require one person doing the tasks throughout the day. As the supply of labor becomes scarcer for some jobs, we believe that supervisors and managers will view job sharing as an attractive alternative.

6. *Four-ten plan.* This is a technique that permits employees to work ten hours each day for four days, thus permitting everyone to enjoy a three-day weekend. Early returns from the recently adopted technique indicate that younger workers enjoy the extra-long weekend and are supportive of the four-ten plan. However, older workers may simply not be able to adjust to this change in structure, and many of them have little or no reason for a longer weekend. They meet their social needs on the job and prefer shorter hours and more workdays. Fatigue is an obvious factor for older people.

GUIDELINES FOR CONTROLLING

Organizations are really miniature societies that require control, just as individuals are to some degree controlled in our larger society. Examples of daily controls that our society places upon you are (1) stop signs, (2) speed limits, (3) clocks, (4) leash laws, and (5) building codes. Examples of daily controls that organizations place upon employees are: (1) time clocks, (2) working hours, (3) work schedules, (4) audits, and (5) productivity quotas.

Supervisors in organizations are subject to controls from above and must establish some controls for their subordinates. Employees must know what is expected of them and how they are being evaluated. Controls are defined as a process for regulating organizational tasks or projects to determine if the task or project contributes to organizational efficiency and effectiveness. Thus control begins with a set of objectives (discussed in Chapter 12), which must then be defined in terms of standards of performance, and finally a feedback and evaluation system must be established to measure and report progress toward objectives.

Standards can be defined in organizations in many different ways. Quality and quantity of work are very useful standards in most public or private organizations. Examples of quantity are the number of cars produced in one week at an automobile assembly plant or the number of microwafers produced at a microcomputer assembly plant each day. Quality is usually a function of the quality-control section and normally involves a sampling of products for defects and overall appearance.

General satisfaction of employees in an organization is an important measure of morale. Levels of satisfaction can be determined through a proper diagnosis of the organization using interviews and questionnaires. Other standards are employee absenteeism, product costs, share of market, and overhead costs by department.

Feedback and Evaluation Systems

Control and evaluation systems come in many forms. Some common forms are discussed here.

Budgets. Budgets and financial statements are minimum control tools for the supervisor. Budgets provide the raw data for analyzing progress toward department or organizational objectives. A very special type of budget is *zero-base budgeting.* Most of today's supervisors will be exposed to zero-base budgeting in one way or another. Although there is really nothing new conceptually in zero-base budgeting, there are specific techniques that have become formalized and certain buzzwords that should be understood. The original concept of zero-base budgeting was that each activity in an organization be able to justify its budget request in toto and that no level of expenditure be taken for granted. As former President Carter, then governor of Georgia, explained zero-base budgeting in his budget address on January 13, 1972, "Zero-base budgeting requires every agency in the state government to identify each function it performs and the personnel and cost to the taxpayers for performing that function."[2]

There are three key steps in the zero-base budgeting process:

The development of decision packages
The ranking and prioritizing of these decision packages
The allocation of resources based on the prioritizing of the decision packages

Each of these steps puts pressures at different levels in the organization. The involvement in the design of the decision packages forces the first-level operating supervisors to define their objectives and responsibilities and ways to meet them at various levels of effectiveness. The ranking and prioritizing of the decision packages forces the first and succeeding levels of management to evaluate their subordinates' rankings in terms of the overall company objectives. Clearly, not all desirable decision packages can be ranked number one. Yet the priority list is subjective at best, and various organizational behavioral pressures must be present. If top management intends to use zero-base budgeting as it was designed, the priority listing will determine the rise and fall of certain activities and the resulting influence of individual supervisors.

[2]Quoted by George S. Minmier and R. H. Hermanson in "A Look at Zero-Base Budgeting—The Georgia Experience," *Atlanta Economic Review,* July-August, 1976, p. 5.

Contoling

Cost Accounting. Each expenditure is coded and assigned against a product, ideally giving supervisors a better feel for the cost of each product. By studying cost accounting reports, supervisors can plot the cost of each product and begin the questioning process when costs appear to be out of line with expectations.

Performance Appraisal. Evaluating and giving employees feedback on their performance is a key element in the control process. Because of its importance in the organization, performance appraisal and employee development are discussed in greater detail in Chapter 16.

Contioing

Management Information Systems (MIS). Management information systems (MIS) are computerized information printouts that provide supervisors with control information on employees and projects. While not all organizations have their entire MIS on the computer, most progressive organizations are moving toward that objective. A typical personnel system computer printout may contain such items as: (1) employee's name and personal data, (2) employment history, (3) attendance record, (4) accrued vacation, (5) sick leave, and (6) projected retirement date. Other MIS printouts are helpful to supervisors—inventory levels, sales information, and cost control data, for example.

Supervisors should first determine what type of information will help them make better decisions and then investigate to determine if that information is stored in the organization's computer. If that information is available in the computer, supervisors should check with the chief of data processing and ask for a timely printout of the desired information. Most data processing supervisors are happy to help line managers. If the information is not available from the computer, supervisors may want to establish a manual MIS to aid in the control process.

SUMMARY

After planning, organizing is the key to effective supervision. Supervisors must be aware of the need for division of labor (specialization), the need to combine labor (structure), and the need to coordinate the efforts of the workers (integration). Some supervisors may not agree with or see a need for all of the guidelines and techniques discussed in this chapter. It is not necessary that you subscribe to all of the techniques; rather, it is essential that supervisors acquire a working knowledge of each technique and, given a certain situation, be able to decide if a particular technique is appropriate. Thus, each technique becomes an arrow in the supervisor's quiver, and the more arrows a supervisor has, the more options and alternatives he or she has to respond to a problem.

Controls are an important and necessary part of organizations because they help supervisors establish accountability. Controls are defined as a process for regulating organizational tasks or projects to determine the degree to which the task or project contributes to organizational effectiveness. Controls consist of objectives, standards of performance, and evaluation of objectives accomplishment. Examples of control tools are budgets, cost accounting, performance appraisal, and management information systems.

IMPORTANT TERMS

organizing
division of labor
combination of labor
coordination
chain of command
unity of command
span of control
job rotation
job enlargement

job enrichment
flexible working hours
job sharing
four-ten plan
controlling
budgets
cost accounting
performance appraisal
MIS

REVIEW QUESTIONS

1. Explain why specialization in organizations introduces the need for supervisors to be coordinators.
2. Explain why the concept of job enrichment runs counter to the ideas of specialization and division of labor in organizations.
3. Why do supervisors fail to delegate work to subordinates?
4. What are the differences between job rotation, job enlargement, and job enrichment?
5. Why is control necessary in organizations?
6. What is zero-base budgeting?

EXERCISES

13.1 Division of Labor

Break into groups of five members, and take 20 minutes to discuss the meaning of this statement: "Division of labor (specialization) automatically introduces the need for supervisors to be integrators and coordinators in an organization."

13.2 Authority versus Responsibility

Be prepared to give your opinion on the following statement before the class: "A supervisor should make decisions on all matters that come to his or her attention except those for which he or she does not have sufficient authority. Matters for which the supervisor does not have sufficient authority are decided upon by committees or higher management."

CASE

13.1 The Open Budget

Command Press, Inc., manufactures and sells a complete line of greeting cards, invitations, and party favors. In 1980, total sales exceeded $100 million and the company employed 360 people. The corporation's structure is as indicated in the chart.

Organization chart.

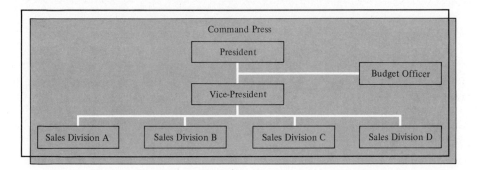

Preparation of the annual budget is the combined responsibility of the budget officer and the vice-president. The budgeting process revolves around a fiscal year from July 1 through June 30 of the following year. Around April 1 of each year, each sales division manager is requested to submit his budget proposal for the next fiscal year. After each division manager submits his manpower and financial needs, the budget officer and vice-president meet, analyze the requests, draft a narrative, and propose an overall budget for the organization. After the budget is prepared, the president then briefs the board of directors, and if they approve the budget, that approved document becomes the new budget for the fiscal year beginning July 1.

Martha Segmiller, manager of sales division A, prepared her budget proposal April 6 and submitted it to the vice-president. In her budget proposal, she requested one new salesperson because the sales of division A had increased 7.5 percent during the past year. The unwritten guideline in the company was that a division received an additional manpower authorization for every 7.5 percent increase in sales. She also requested a proportional increase in supplies, travel expenses, and telephone expenses for sales division A. She knew that her division had by far the largest sales increase for the year, and she felt confident that her requests would be honored.

After preparing and sending her budget proposal to the vice-president, Martha received the third-quarter sales figures and observed the following sales increases for each division:

A	+30%	C	+4.8%
B	+6.3%	D	+8.8%

After seeing these figures, she called a staff meeting on May 1, and her section managers indicated that they believed the increase in sales would continue for division A through the next fiscal year. Martha did not inform the vice-president of this new projection.

At a staff meeting on June 1, the vice-president told the division sales managers that the president had approved the new budget and it would be distributed within the week. The manager of sales division C asked a question about new manpower because of increased sales. The vice-president responded that sales division A would receive

1 additional salesperson, division B would receive 2.5, division C would receive 7, and division D would receive 1. Martha was shocked by the response and immediately requested a reevaluation of the budget because her division had the largest increase in sales and she was allocated the smallest increase in new people.

After leaving the meeting, Martha telephoned the budget officer and asked him if he could explain to her the logic for the allocation of new personnel. He replied that she had requested one new position and she received one new position. She countered by informing him of the third-quarter sales figures and that she now needed three new people to meet anticipated sales. She also asked, "How come division C received seven new authorizations with only a 4.8 percent increase in sales?" The budget officer responded that he didn't exactly know the reasoning behind the allocation of new personnel; however, he did know that division A received 100 percent of its requested budget, while the other divisions received less than they requested.

After the telephone conversation, Martha felt disgusted because she had been honest during the budgeting process and only requested increases that could be documented by increases in productivity, whereas it appeared that the other departments had padded their budget requests.

Questions

1. Who should Martha talk to about her problem?
2. Should she put her concerns in writing? If so, to whom?
3. What advice can you give to Martha about being candid in the budgeting process? Is padding a common practice in the public or private sectors of our economy?

SUGGESTED ADDITIONAL READINGS

Buisman, Ben A. "Four-Day, 40-Hour Workweek: Its Effect on Management and Labor." *Personnel Journal* 54 (November, 1975): 565–567.

French, Wendell L.; Dittrich, John E.; and Zawacki, Robert A. *The Personnel Management Process: Cases on Human Resources Administration.* Boston: Houghton Mifflin, 1982, pp. 121–146.

Hackman, Richard J. "Is Job Enrichment Just a Fad?" *Harvard Business Review* 53 (September-October, 1975): 129–138.

Johnson, J., and Zawacki, Robert A. "Flexible Working Hours: Pros and Cons." *Colorado Business Review* 49 (March, 1976): 1–4.

Rosenbach, William E.; Zawacki, Robert A.; and Morgan, Cyril P. "Research Roundup." *The Personnel Administrator* 22 (October, 1977): 51–61.

Suver, James D., and Brown, Ray L. "Where Does Zero-Base Budgeting Work?" *Harvard Business Review* 5 (November-December, 1977): 76–84.

Zawacki, Robert A., and Johnson, J. "Alternative Workweek Schedules: One Company's Experience with Flextime." *Supervisory Management* 21 (June, 1976): 15–19.

14

Communicating

How Communication Changes Through the Chain of Command[1]

THE COLONEL TO THE MAJOR
At nine o'clock tomorrow there will be an eclipse of the sun,
something which does not occur every day. Get the men to
fall out in the company street in their fatigues so that they
will see this rare phenomenon, and I will explain it to them.
In case of rain, we will not be able to see anything, so take
the men to the gym.

THE MAJOR TO THE CAPTAIN
By order of the Colonel, tomorrow at nine o'clock, there will
be an eclipse of the sun; if it rains you will not be able to
see it from the company street so then, in fatigues, the
eclipse of the sun will take place in the gym, something that
does not occur every day.

THE CAPTAIN TO THE LIEUTENANT
By order of the Colonel in fatigues tomorrow at nine o'clock
in the morning the inauguration of the eclipse of the sun will
take place in the gym. The Colonel will give the order if it
should rain, something which occurs every day.

THE LIEUTENANT TO THE SERGEANT
Tomorrow at nine the Colonel in fatigues will eclipse the sun
in the gym, as it occurs every day if it is a nice day; if it
rains, then in the company.

---

[1]Adapted from *DS Letter* 1, no. 3 (1971), from a speech by Dan Belles, published by Didactic Systems, Inc., Box 457, Cranford, NJ 07016.

THE SERGEANT TO THE CORPORAL
Tomorrow at nine the eclipse of the Colonel in fatigues will
take place by cause of the sun. If it rains in the gym,
something which does not take place every day, you will fall
out in the company street.

COMMENTS AMONG THE PRIVATES
Tomorrow if it rains, it looks as if the sun will eclipse the
Colonel in the gym. It is a shame that this does not occur
every day.

OBJECTIVES

This chapter provides you with the information necessary to:

1. Know why supervisors need to understand the importance of organizational communication
2. Describe the components of an organizational communication system
3. Know how to design an organizational communication system

WHAT IS ORGANIZATIONAL COMMUNICATION?

Supervisors need to be concerned about two kinds of communication—interpersonal communication and organizational communication. Interpersonal communication has already been discussed in Chapter 6. Organizational communication includes all of the formal ways an organization, department, or supervisor communicates with employees. Examples would be communicating through goals, policies, procedures, rules, the chain of command, meetings, memos, and bulletin boards.

THE COSTS OF POOR ORGANIZATIONAL COMMUNICATION

Few organizations or supervisors realized the importance of developing an effective organizational communication system, nor do they understand the consequences of allowing organizational communication to evolve by default rather than by design.

    An international study by Robert Blake and Jane Mouton showed that communication was the number one problem in organizations.[2] And it can be a very costly problem. Misunderstood policies, objectives, and instructions; communication break-

[2]Robert R. Blake and Jane S. Mouton. *Corporate Excellence Through Grid Organization Development* (Houston: Gulf Publishing Co., 1968), p. 4.

downs; too little or too much information for employees to accomplish their jobs efficiently; and delays, mistakes, and misunderstandings that can be attributed to poor communication all have a price tag.

EARLY THOUGHTS ON ORGANIZATIONAL COMMUNICATION

Henri Fayol was one of the first management pioneers to write about the communication processes in organizations.[3] Fayol recognized the need to send most communications through the chain of command but also recognized the need for exceptions. Fayol proposed a shortcut method that he called the gangplank or bridge method. The method suggests that when the chain of command would cause undue delays, involve masses of paper, or inconvenience people, direct contact is permissible even when it violates the chain of command.

Another leading management pioneer, Chester Barnard, also emphasized the importance of organizational communication.[4] He felt that effective communication was essential to organizational success and to establishing the authority structure of an organization. It was his theory that a communication is accepted only if an individual: (1) understands the communication, (2) believes it to be consistent with the purpose of the organization, (3) believes it to be compatible with his or her personal interest, and (4) is physically and mentally able to comply with the communication.

MODERN THINKING ON ORGANIZATIONAL COMMUNICATION

Today, organizational communication is beginning to come of age. Being able to rely on a few simple ground rules about communicating through the chain of command is a thing of the past. Today's organizational communication system may include new organizational structures, such as a matrix structure that render chain-of-command principles inoperable. It may also include sophisticated new communications, data processing, and word processing ideas, equipment, and systems and may even have legal ramifications in terms of what you can and cannot say to employees.

A SYSTEMS APPROACH TO ORGANIZATIONAL COMMUNICATION

One of the major reasons that communication is the number one problem in organizations is that organizations or supervisors rarely take a planned, systematic approach to communication. Various means of communication begin to appear, with no apparent design or coordination. Some information is desseminated in meetings. Other information appears on bulletin boards, in policy manuals, or in the company newsletter. What is needed is a systems approach to organizational and supervisory communication whereby formal communication is accomplished in a logical and planned way.

[3]Henri Fayol, *General and Industrial Management* (London: Sir Isaac Pitman and Sons, 1949), p. 35.
[4]Chester I. Barnard, *The Functions of the Executive* (Cambridge, MA: Harvard University Press, 1938).

Figure 14.1 A systems view of organizational communication.

Organizational Climate	Structural Communi- cation	Meetings	Information Processing, Disseminating, and Storage	Supplemental Communica- tion Systems	System Evaluation
Management philosophy	Mission statement Objectives Policies Procedures Organization chart	Orientation Staff	Word processing Data processing	Newsletter	Observation
Management style	Job descriptions and clarification of individual responsibil- ities Physical plant Reward system	Informational Goal-setting	Management information system (MIS) Records management	Suggestion box	Surveys
Organizational health	Review system Training Internal communica- tion systems (phones, intercom terminals, bulletin boards, letters, memos, reports, etc.) Grievance procedures	Team-building Problem-solving Special	Forms management Reports management Reprographics	Public relations External communica- tion with clients	Interviews Outside evaluations

It is not our purpose here to provide a detailed discussion of all aspects of a communication system. An excellent resource for such a discussion is the book *Administrative Office Management,* by Marj Leaming and Robert Motley.[5] Our purpose is to provide an overview of organizational communication so that supervisors can apply the principles to designing a communication system for the group they supervise.

We have included six important components of a communication system that supervisors should be aware of, as shown in Figure 14.1.

Organizational Climate

The climate of the organization has a major effect on organizational communication. In a healthy and well-managed organization, communication tends to be open, accu-

[5]Marj P. Leaming and Robert J. Motley, *Administrative Office Management: A Practical Approach* (Dubuque, IA: Brown, 1979).

rate, and efficient. However, in an unhealthy and poorly managed organization, communication is usually closed, inaccurate, and inefficient.

The major characteristics of the organizational climate that affect communication are management philosophy and style and the health and openness of the organization. Whether an organization's management philosophy occurs by default or design, it has far-reaching consequences. It determines how people are treated, how problems are solved and conflicts resolved, the organizational norms, and the kinds of behavior that are reinforced. The management style of an organization also affects the climate in which the people communicate. An autocratic style, for example, tends to promote one-way communication that is often distorted because of the risks and possible retribution associated with openness. On the other hand, an overly participative style may overload the organization with communications, resulting in inefficiencies and inability to act. The health of an organization determines its character and maturity and affects the level of trust and openness that exists in organizational communication as well as how straightforward and supportive it is.

Organizational climate can help or limit a supervisor. It can encourage accurate and open communication and assure that downward, upward, and lateral communication keeps supervisors well informed. On the other hand, a negative climate results in continual communication breakdowns and uninformed supervisors. Supervisors should also be aware that they create a work climate in the groups they supervise that facilitates or limits communication.

Structural Communications

Much of what is needed to have effective organizational communication can be structured into the system. For a supervisor, such a system should begin with clear goals for the group he or she supervises. These goals should be clearly communicated to group members. This should be followed by clear policies and procedures that organization members are also familiar with. A well-planned policy and procedures manual can provide most of this information. Changes should be added and communicated promptly.

An up-to-date organization chart is also useful in identifying the chain of command and how information should flow upward, downward, and laterally. Clearly defined job descriptions and responsibilities will significantly increase the efficiency of communication and will minimize confusion over what is expected. Even the physical plant should be considered in the communication process. Geographical location and office decor and layout can encourage or discourage communication.

The reward and review systems are also part of the communication process. They let people know where they stand and communicate the kinds of behavior that are rewarded by the organization.

Another important structural aspect of organizational communication is the internal communications system, including phone systems, intercom systems, on-line terminals, bulletin boards, and written communications such as memos, letters, announcements, and reports. It is important to establish an effective and efficient internal system and to develop guidelines for using each of the internal methods.

Finally, structured communication should include grievance procedures. Grievance procedures should be used when the other channels of communication fail.

Meetings

Much of organizational communication occurs in meetings—sometimes too much! Meetings can become time-wasting activity traps or efficient means of communication if carefully designed. A wise supervisor can often reduce the number of meetings required and yet improve communication by planning: (1) the types of meetings that are needed, (2) the frequency with which they are held, and (3) the meeting content.

Supervisors may use a variety of meetings to communicate with employees. Examples could be:

1. *Orientation meetings.* Orientation meetings are held for new employees to inform them of company philosophies, objectives, policies, benefits, and so on, or when something new occurs, such as the addition of a new function, product, or members. Some companies set aside a day each year when organization members and their families can tour the facilities and have someone at each key function or location available to explain that particular job.
2. *Staff meetings.* Staff meetings can be used to exchange information, solve problems, and make decisions. They can also serve to build trust and rapport between supervisor and employees and help fulfill the social needs of group members.
3. *Informational meetings.* Informational meetings can be held when important information needs to be communicated and can also be used on a planned basis to keep people generally informed about what is happening. For example, some supervisors hold quarterly meetings with all employees to inform them of sales, profits, policy changes, personnel changes, and other news and to open the meeting for questions. Such meetings keep employees informed and build trust in the organization and its leaders.
4. *Goal-setting meetings.* Many communication problems can be prevented by beginning each year with a goal-setting meeting at which supervisor and employees are involved in establishing group goals for the coming year. Some supervisors plan a retreat each year for this purpose. The goal-setting meetings are then followed up by periodic meetings to review progress.
5. *Team-building meetings.* Team-building meetings should be held periodically to evaluate team performance, team processes (how well members relate, how problems are solved and decisions made, etc.), and team strengths and weaknesses. Some organizations include this process in their annual goal-setting meeting.
6. *Problem-solving meetings.* Problem-solving meetings are used to deal with specific problems or generally to consider any problems that are interfering with group effectiveness. General problem-solving sessions are usually held once or twice a year and should include identifying strengths as well as weaknesses and should emphasize problem solving rather than the problems themselves. Problem solving is also often included in the annual goal-setting meeting. Gripe sessions are not useful and in fact can destroy morale. It is not helpful simply to hear people gripe.

7. *Special meetings.* Specialized meetings may also be used to resolve conflicts, celebrate achievements, deal with a crisis, or otherwise deal with events on an ad hoc basis.

Information Processing, Dissemination, and Storage

The technological explosion in communications technology has made information processing, disseminating, and storage an important part of organizational communication. George Grove, in an article in *Management Review,* stated:

> The electronic office of the future will be realized by integrating three major components: data processing, word processing, and telecommunications. In the text or word processing area, there have been significant developments in automatic text editing devices, dictating systems, micrographics, and reprographics. In the automated data processing area, integrated circuit technology advances have brought on the minicomputer, the microprocessor, and distributed processing. In the telecommunications area, there has been a rapid transition to the use of computer-based switching systems, digital transmission systems, software controlled systems, and satellite communications.[6]

It is not uncommon today for the computer to be a major contributor to the communication process.

Some of the areas that should be considered in planning communication connected to information processing, disseminating, and storage are:

1. *Word processing.* Many organizations today are developing word processing centers that centralize all the equipment and services necessary to transcribe written, verbal, or recorded information to typewritten or printed form. The word processing approach takes advantage of the specialization and training required to operate today's sophisticated equipment and to achieve efficient and high-quality results. It combines the tasks of dictating, typing, editing, and revising into an integrated and controlled system.
2. *Data processing.* Data processing involves the classifying, sorting, merging, matching, and recording of data. The computer has made data processing a standard part of a manager's activities. The computer can be used for reports, processing information, and decision making and has become an important communication tool.
3. *Management information systems (MIS).* MIS can provide an organization with a totally integrated computer system. It combines information processing with management systems to provide management with the information necessary for planning, decision making, problem solving, and controlling.
4. *Records management.* The information that is generated in organizations with modern technology has made records management an important function. Providing for information classification, filing, storage, security, retrieval, and disposition can be an important and difficult function. Modern technology using micrographics to store information on microfiche, aperture cards, and roll film have significantly improved the ability to store large amounts of information without incurring prohibitive costs.

[6]George Grove, "Information Management in the Office of the Future," *Management Review* (December, 1979), pp. 47–48.

5. *Forms management.* Forms in organizations seem to multiply at about the same rate as rabbits during breeding season! Forms management is an approach used to centralize and manage the forms used in an organization.
6. *Reports management.* Reports management is similar to forms management. The purpose is periodically to review required reports in terms of need and form. Through reports management, some reports are eliminated, modified, produced in a different form, or replaced.
7. *Reprographics.* Reprographics includes all reproduction services. Substantial unnecessary costs can be incurred by an organization without effective reprographics management. Reprographics is usually included as part of word processing.

Supplemental Communication Systems

Included in planning a communication system should be supplemental systems. Obvious examples would be newsletters and suggestion boxes.

System Evaluation

Designing an effective communication system should significantly improve organizational communication. However, it is also important to determine ways to evaluate the system to see if it is working effectively. The system may be providing too much or too little information, or the system's design may need modification. Some ways of evaluating the communication system are

1. *Observation.* An observant supervisor can pick up many clues that help evaluate the effectiveness of communications. Productivity, morale, communication breakdowns, misunderstandings, and having to repeat information all provide valuable information.
2. *Surveys.* Surveys can range from comprehensive surveys covering most aspects of group effectiveness to specialized questionnaires on a particular area such as communication. The advantage of surveys is that they make it possible to quantify important data so that the extent of strengths or weaknesses can be determined.
3. *Interviews.* Periodic interviews are also useful in evaluating the effectiveness of communications. The interviews can be conducted by the supervisor in an open organization where trust is high or by someone trained in interviewing, such as a person from personnel. The purpose of interviews may be for the supervisor to keep informed or to develop an agenda for problem solving.
4. *Outside evaluation.* Unless an organization has the internal expertise, it may be useful occasionally to bring in outside professionals to evaluate a group. They may use similar techniques to the ones mentioned above, but they may be able to obtain a more objective and more accurate picture of the organization.

THE SUPERVISOR'S ROLE IN ORGANIZATIONAL COMMUNICATION

Communication takes four basic forms for the supervisor: (1) from management to supervisor, (2) from supervisor to subordinates, (3) from subordinates to supervisor, and (4) between peer groups or people at the same level. These forms are usually referred to as downward, upward, and lateral communication.

Downward Communication

Downward communication may come to the supervisor from a higher source or may go from the supervisor to subordinates. The supervisor uses downward communication to inform, to instruct, to assign or explain work, to interact with subordinates to create productive output, and to support positive attitudes and behaviors towards the company.

The form of downward communication that a supervisor uses most frequently is giving job assignments. In giving assignments, a supervisor should communicate:

1. *Who* is to perform the task
2. *What* is to be done
3. *Where* performance must be accomplished
4. *How* to obtain support needed and what technical procedures to use
5. *When* it must be completed with further data to show how it ties in with other needed tasks
6. *Why* it is being performed, especially if it is a nonroutine task

Upward Communication

Upward communication for the supervisor includes keeping one's boss informed about one's activities and the activities of one's group and providing for upward subordinate communication. What the supervisor should look for in every message sent upward includes:

1. Indications of morale and level of satisfaction with the job
2. Employee response to management policies
3. The true intent of employee ideas or suggestions for improvement
4. An analysis of potential problem areas in the productivity cycle
5. Whether or not employees are merely relieving themselves of built-up stress or whether true signs of a problem exist

To provide for subordinate communication, supervisors should select the meeting formats most suited to their team and should also provide opportunities for communicating with individual employees.

Lateral Communication

Lateral communication involves sharing information on the operational aspects of the organization with supervisors of other departments. Lateral communication is required because of the interdependence of work groups needed to accomplish organizational goals.

Lateral communication supports relationships between both line and staff operating elements. If it is used correctly, it supports the coordination function by letting the other supervisors know about plans, procedures, or changes that may affect them. A good lateral communication system will foster both understanding and cooperation between groups.

DESIGNING A COMMUNICATION SYSTEM

After acquiring an understanding of the concept of organizational communication, a supervisor should be ready to design a communication system for his or her group. The design will require the involvement of the supervisor's boss, subordinates, and any lateral groups affected by the supervisor's team. A communication system can be designed by addressing the following questions:

1. What do our people need to know to do their jobs effectively? The answers to this question would obviously depend on the target group, but typical responses might be:
   Facts about the company
   Group objectives
   Personal responsibilities
   An understanding of the organization chart and lines of authority
   Company policies
   Rules and procedures pertaining to the group
   Performance-evaluation procedures
   Job-related information
2. What upward or lateral communication should be provided? The first question pertains to communication a group needs to receive and the second to communication they need to give. For example, they may want to consider:
   The information that subordinates need to provide to their supervisor
   The information that the supervisor needs to provide to his or her boss
   The information that should be funished to other groups or persons
3. What are the best ways to meet the communication needs identified on questions 1 and 2? At this point, all of the available communication methods need to be evaluated to determine the best match between communication needs and communication methods. Some typical methods would be:
   Orientation meetings
   Staff meetings
   Problem-solving meetings
   Goal-setting meetings
   Team-building meetings
   Intergroup meetings
   Informational meetings
   Bulletin boards
   Developing a policy manual
   Memos

Suggestion boxes
Developing a performance-review system
Company newsletter
Explaining the organization chart and giving each employee a copy
Explaining report requirements
Training

4. How can we find out if our communication system is working? Some possible methods have already been mentioned.

SUMMARY

Communication is the number one problem in organizations. Organizations need to be concerned about two kinds of communication—interpersonal communication and organizational communication. Organizational communication includes all of the formal ways an organization, department, or supervisor communicates with employees. While organizational communication used to be limited to a few guidelines on communicating through the chain of command, it has now evolved into a very sophisticated process involving space-age technology, legal ramifications, and new demands for dealing with the public, special-interest groups, and the media in addition to organization members.

A systems approach to organizational communication includes designing a communication system that considers: (1) the organizational climate; (2) structural considerations such as objectives and policies; (3) meetings; (4) information processing, dissemination, and storage; (5) supplemental systems; and (6) methods for evaluating the effectiveness of the communication system.

IMPORTANT TERMS

organizational communication	data processing
organizational climate	MIS
structural communication	records management
orientation meetings	forms management
staff meetings	reports management
informational meetings	reprographics
goal-setting meetings	supplemental communication systems
team-building meetings	system evaluation
problem-solving meetings	upward communication
special meetings	downward communication
word processing	lateral communication

REVIEW QUESTIONS

1. What is organizational communication?
2. Why do supervisors need to understand organizational communication?
3. Describe each of the major components of an organizational communication system and discuss why each is important to the communication process.

4. What is the supervisor's role in organizational communication?
5. How can a supervisor design a communication system?

EXERCISE

14.1 Communication in the Office

Meet in a small group and list on chart paper your answers to the following questions:

1. What basic information do most employees need to know to perform their jobs effectively?
2. If you were a supervisor with a secretary and eight subordinates reporting to you, what are some things you would include in your communication system?

Reconvene in the classroom. Each group should take a turn sharing its answers.

CASE

14.1 Organizational Growth Concerns for Communication

Over a 20-year period, a town in the Far West grew from a sleepy tourist town of 50,000 people to a sprawling modern city of over 200,000. During this period, all department areas of the city experienced tremendous increases in demand for general services. The fire department was no exception.

Originally organized with 7 station houses, the new configuration boasted over 16 locations. With the expansion also came organizational redesign. The 16 station houses were broken down into 3 divisions as shown in the diagram.

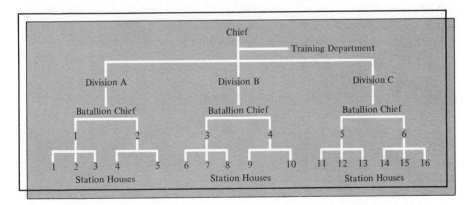

"It doesn't make any sense," Lt. Darrigan related to his unit captain. "It seems that when we compare instructions for the operating shift with other station houses, we can never agree on what we are supposed to be concerned with or how the priorities are set. Everybody seems to get different information. Our training schedules are confusing, too. I wish we could get a straight story for a change. The men seem to be losing sight of the real mission around here."

The captain was puzzled too. He knew all of the battallion and division chiefs. Most of them had been his superiors when he was a driver-engineer. It seems the procedure used for organizational communication included an informal structure. The chief was a friendly guy, too. Old Charlie felt that the more informality with the men, the closer the group would be working in harmony.

The procedure for passing information on daily routine and other informative data, such as training schedules, promotion testing, and new operating directives, took this form:

Chief briefed the division chiefs and the director of training daily. It was an informal but closed-door meeting, mostly oral.

The division chiefs were charged with disseminating the data to their two batallion chiefs. Sometimes copies of procedures and schedules were produced. On other occasions, the briefing was informal and oral.

The batallion chiefs would visit the line station houses daily and inform the unit captains of the new instructions that they felt were important.

Every working day they followed the same procedure. There seemed to be no change in results.

Questions

1. What organizational communication techniques do you see violated by the fire department?
2. How would you design a communication system for the department?
3. Do you really think that in some cases the communication received by each unit captain was totally different? Why?
4. Describe some of the significant communication barriers created by the existing systems.

SUGGESTED ADDITIONAL READINGS

Goldhaber, Gerald M. *Organizational Communications.* 2d ed. Dubuque, IA: Brown, 1979.

Ruben, Brent D., and Kim, John Y. *General Systems Theory and Human Communications.* Rochelle Park, NJ: Hayden, 1975.

Sereno, Kenneth, and Mortensen, David C. *Foundations of Communications Theory.* Reading, MA: Addison-Wesley, 1977.

Wofford, Jerry; Gerloff, Edwin A.; and Cummins, Robert C. *Organizational Communication.* New York: McGraw-Hill, 1977.

15

Supervisory Helping Skills

No man is good enough to govern another man without that other's consent.

Abraham Lincoln

Charlie Brown: *What if everyone was like you? What if we all ran away from our problems? Huh? What then? What if everyone in the whole world suddenly decided to run away from his problems?*

Linus: *Well at least we'd all be running in the same direction.*

Charles Schulz
"Peanuts"

OBJECTIVES

This chapter provides you with the information necessary to:

1. Know why supervisors need helping skills and when they can be used.
2. Understand the concept of responsibility-based helping skills (RBHS) and the helping skills principles supervisors should be familiar with
3. Understand the helping process and how to coach people to commit themselves to change.

4. Know how to give and receive feedback effectively
5. Understand what to expect from applying helping skills to the change process

WHY SUPERVISORS NEED HELPING SKILLS

It is often said that people problems take up most of a supervisor's time. Disagreements, personal problems, confrontations, lack of motivation, misunderstandings, excuses, and conflicts are all too familiar to the practicing supervisor. These problems all have one thing in common. They require supervisory helping skills to resolve. Helping skills are the interpersonal skills needed by supervisors to resolve people problems.

There are many important reasons why supervisors need good helping skills:

1. Much of a supervisor's role requires basic helping skills:
    a. Orienting employees to their jobs
    b. Giving instructions and correcting mistakes
    c. Explaining or negotiating job responsibilities and goals
    d. Evaluating job performance and goal achievement
    e. Helping and motivating employees
    f. Resolving conflicts
    g. Disciplining people in a constructive way
    h. Understanding and changing human behavior.
2. Most problems at work are people problems, and people problems lead to organizational problems, such as low productivity, morale, and creativity and high absenteeism and turnover.
3. Increasingly enlightened and aware employees expect to be valued, understood, and involved. These expectations place greater demands on a supervisor's helping skills.
4. Our changing environment, with its increased stresses, complexities, and uncertainties, is likely to result in increasing people problems in both a person's personal and organizational life.

THE MOST EFFECTIVE WAY TO HANDLE PEOPLE PROBLEMS

There are some basic helping skills that can be used in the work setting that do not require a person to be a professionally trained psychologist or counselor. These skills, which are covered in this chapter, should equip supervisors to deal effectively with most of the people problems they face. However, in learning these skills, supervisors should keep in mind that the most effective way to minimize unnecessary people problems is to create a work climate where: (1) goals, responsibilities, expectations, and policies are clear and fair; (2) communication is open and genuine; (3) responsible and positive behavior is encouraged, supported, and rewarded; and (4) irresponsible and negative behavior is confronted, discouraged, not supported, and not rewarded.

work climate

WHEN HELPING SKILLS ARE NEEDED

Supervisors use helping skills almost every day in working with employees, bosses, and others in their organizations. An employee seems to be going through a slump and can't seem to get motivated. A peer is under a lot of stress and needs someone to talk to. An employee has a negative attitude and is affecting morale or perhaps has a low self-image that results in performance far below what he or she is capable of. A peer is having a conflict with another supervisor and isn't sure what to do. It is time to meet with employees to discuss their annual performance reviews. These types of problems require primarily listening and coaching skills.

Other problems may require problem-solving skills. An employee frequently arrives late for work. An employee is a troublemaker who continually stirs up other employees. You are having a conflict with another peer or need to resolve a difference. Strife exists within your group or between your group and another group. An employee continues to perform below job requirements.

Still other situations may involve conflict-resolution skills. You have tried to help an employee with an attitude or performance problem and have even agreed on what should be done, but progress has been temporary, unsatisfactory, or nonexistent. You have reached an impasse in trying to work out a problem with another supervisor. You and your boss have a difference that you have not been able to resolve. Two employees have a conflict that you have attempted to resolve without success. You have noticed a pattern developing with another person: No matter what you try to do to solve the problem, the other person makes sure that your efforts won't work.

All of these examples are situations in which supervisors use helping skills. They listen, coach, solve problems, and resolve conflicts. When properly handled, most of these situations can have successful and satisfying endings for supervisors. However, when a supervisor does not have good helping skills, these situations often end in frustration, conflict, and communication breakdowns.

Developing helping skills is not a cure-all for people problems. Some problems may not be solvable, and supervisors are sure to make some bad calls, no matter how proficient they are in helping skills. However, by developing helping skills, a supervisor can significantly improve his or her chances of working successfully with people.

PHILOSOPHICAL BASIS FOR HELPING SKILLS

The helping skills presented in this chapter are philosophically founded on a responsibility-based approach to helping. The term *responsibility* was often used by William Glasser in his classic book, *Reality Therapy,*[1] and most recently in his book with Chester Karrass titled *RPM Both-Win Management.*[2] Many of the ideas used in this chapter were inspired by Glasser's pioneering work in simplifying the helping process to focus on the conscious mind and what people can do in the present rather than focus on the subconscious mind and trying to analyze why people do what they do. In

[1]William Glasser, *Reality Therapy* (New York: Harper & Row, 1965).
[2]Chester L. Karrass and William Glasser, *RPM Both-Win Management* (New York: Harper & Row, 1980).

Glasser's opinion, people do not act irresponsibly because they are ill; they are ill because they act irresponsibly. Therefore, the goal in working with people should be to help them deal with reality by making rational, mature, and responsible choices in the present rather than by exploring a person's past to discover the roots of problems, trying to understand why a person does what he or she does, and then working through each problem.

This approach is very useful in the work setting because supervisors usually do not have the professional training or the time to deal with people problems using more traditional helping methods. It is not necessary for supervisors to have professional training to be effective helpers. Most work-related problems do not require professional counseling skills. When someone needs professional help, they should be referred to a professional.

HELPING SKILLS: BASIC PRINCIPLES

The responsibility-based approach to helping skills is founded on the following basic helping principles:

1. The emphasis in helping should be on: (1) accepting responsibility for one's past, present, and future *choices,* regardless of who or what is at fault, and on (2) making constructive choices (choices that are responsible, mature, and self-developing). This approach recognizes that while present problems may have been caused by others, circumstances, or oneself in the past or present, solutions lie in accepting the realities of the present situation and accepting responsibility for finding present solutions, regardless of who or what caused the problem. Making others or circumstances responsible for present behaviors may or may not be justified, but nothing will change unless a person decides to take responsibility for his or her present behaviors, regardless of how they evolved.
2. Rather than focusing on past data or excuses or why a person does things, the emphasis should be on: (1) accepting present behavior without being judgmental, (2) agreeing on desired behaviors given the reality of a situation, and (3) planning how to achieve the desired results. Past information is relevant only if it contributes toward understanding and solving present problems. Dwelling on the past and on analyzing behavior is counterproductive, since solutions lie in present choices. No matter how well a person understands a situation, no change will take place until the person takes responsibility for making new choices. In fact, dwelling on the past may generate new, unnecessary additional problems, provide excuses for present inappropriate choices, or incapacitate a person to make new choices.
3. The basic ingredients for change are
   a. Awareness—change begins with an awareness that change is needed.
   b. Caring—genuinely caring for, valuing, and believing in another person may provide the incentive or hope that a person needs to be willing to change.
   c. Understanding—when people feel understood, they are often freed to solve problems.
   d. Commitment—the previous ingredients provide a climate for change; however, actual change is not likely to occur without commitment.

e. Practice—new behaviors are not likely to become habits unless they are practiced.

f. Accountability—accountability increases the incentive to change and accelerates the change process.

4. Lasting change comes from practicing new ways of *thinking* (recognizing the problem, committing to change, and changing one's attitude and perceptions) and *acting* (trying specific behaviors) until they become habits. A change in thoughts without an eventual corresponding change in actions or vice versa results in inner discomfort and tension and prevents lasting change. Supervisors should not assume that lasting change *will* take place unless they see a change in attitude and actions; nor should they believe that change *has* taken place until a new pattern of behavior is evident.

5. Devaluing another person by sending "Not OK" messages, belittling, interrupting, not listening, and other such behaviors increases the probability of an inappropriate response such as defensiveness, rebellion, and refusal to cooperate and is therefore self-defeating. Increasing the value of another person by caring, listening, and saying only what is helpful increases the probability of an appropriate response.

6. Confidentiality is of considerable importance in building trust. Information leakage can cause a breach in credibility and minimize any possibility of being helpful. Information shared in confidence should be shared with others only when permission has been granted, when there would be no adverse effects, or when you would be sharing positive information that benefits the sharer.

7. Caution and sound judgment should be used in commenting on or making conclusions about anyone not involved in the interaction if the result could have an adverse effect on that person. It is irresponsible to influence a person to make negative conclusions about another person who has no input into the interaction unless you have substantial reliable evidence to justify your conclusions or advice.

8. In applying helping skills, the primary goal should always be to solve rather than create problems and to encourage constructive rather than unconstructive actions.

9. The potential for change can be increased by: (a) providing encouragement and hope, (b) rewarding constructive behaviors, and (c) ignoring, confronting, or having reasonable consequences for unconstructive behaviors. (Punitive or unreasonable consequences cause resistance to change.)

The helping skills principles are summarized in Figure 15.1.

RESPONSIBILITY-BASED HELPING SKILLS

The responsibility-based helping process includes six skills:

Skill I	Preparing
Skill II	Rapport building
Skill III	Active listening
Skill IV	Synthesizing
Skill V	Coaching
Skill VI	Providing closure

Figure 15.1 Helping skills principles.

1. The goal should be to help and train people to accept responsibility for their present choices and the consequences of their choices and for making constructive future choices regardless of past or present circumstances or who or what is at fault. A constructive choice is choice that is responsible, mature, and self-developing. An unconstructive choice is a choice that is irresponsible, immature, and self-defeating.
2. A key assumption to accomplishing change is that a person is willing to take constructive actions. Until this assumption is true, little if any lasting change will take place.
3. The key issues in change are identifying what persons are doing now, what they would be willing to do differently, and agreeing on constructive ways to get there rather than dwelling on the past, excuses, who is at fault, or the whys of behavior.
4. The emphasis should be on what can be done in the present to solve specific problems with specific solutions in a reasonable and agreed-upon time frame.
5. Lasting change comes from practicing new ways of thinking (achieved through awareness, education, training, eliminating negative thinking, building a positive self-image, changing one's attitude, etc.) and acting until the new thoughts and actions become habits.
6. Habits are strengthened through reinforcement and repetition and weakened through nonreinforcement, lack of repetition, nonjudgmental confronting, and reasonable and fair consequences.

Supervisors need to be flexible enough to adapt the process to each situation and to develop their own helping style so that the process is applied in a genuine rather than a mechanical way.

Skill I: Preparing

Examine your willingness and ability to be helpful and objective. Prepare yourself to have a genuine desire to be helpful and cooperative, a problem solver. Clear your mind of any obstructions to being helpful, such as anger, resentment, or preconceived notions. If appropriate, prepare by gathering data and planning a strategy.

Skill II: Rapport Building

Build rapport and trust by being genuine, caring, and straightforward, by valuing the other person through unconditional acceptance, by expressing your sincere desire to be as helpful and cooperative as you can, and by being sensitive to the needs, feelings, and readiness of the other person. Assume the best about a person and his or her intentions, whether the person deserves it or not, unless such assumptions would reinforce inappropriate behaviors or would be foolish. If appropriate, discuss how you can be helpful and agree on any ground rules or procedures involved. Determine what the problem is in a nonjudgmental way. Try to create a climate or realistic hope by "normalizing" the situation (treating problems as understandable and manageable rather than abnormal); by being encouraging rather than discouraging, critical, or judgmental; and by persistently believing in the solvability of problems. Labeling people and making them feel guilty, incompetent, or abnormal is counterproductive to providing help.

Skill III: Active Listening

Listen objectively to what is being said and felt, without interrupting, overreacting, explaining away, condemning, or arguing with what is being communicated. Don't attempt to read minds! Instead of making assumptions about what is really being said and felt, check out your perceptions on important issues. Try to understand the situation from the other person's point of view, taking care not to cause the person to mistake understanding for reinforcement or agreement. Explore what the real problems are by trying to identify the key issues, soliciting clarifying data or examples, and evaluating present responses and their consequences. Active listening, understanding, and exploring require a fine balance between empathy and objectivity without magnifying problems or reinforcing inappropriate behaviors. If you find yourself continuously having to repeat Skill II, it may be a signal that a person is not willing to solve a problem and is being reinforced for having problems by your willingness to listen and understand. It is also important during this phase to be willing to level and confront in a caring, nonjudgmental, sensitive, and diplomatic way. These skills make it possible to be straightforward and share valuable information without devaluing people.

Skill IV: Synthesizing

Skill IV is designed to recognize and summarize what has been communicated, agree on the key issues, and decide if more information is needed, the problem has been resolved, and the helping process has fulfilled its purpose or if you need to move back to previous skills or forward to remaining skills. It is also important at this time to decide if the real issues are understood, if a person really needs, wants, or is ready for help, and if there is commitment to accepting responsibility for seeking constructive solutions.

Skill V: Coaching

The coaching skill is an action skill in which you help a person focus on the realities of the present situation and coach the person to accept responsibility for making constructive choices to: (1) improve the situation, (2) improve his or her responses to the situation, or (3) improve behaviors that may be contributing to the situation. Recognize that until people accept responsibility for doing whatever *they* can do individually to improve a situation, little will change. This skill begins by exploring alternatives for improving the situation and evaluating their probable consequences. Select the best of the alternatives and agree on any specific actions that will be taken and when such actions will take place. Be sure that action plans are realistic, constructive, and reasonable. In most cases, it is best to limit actions to one step at a time.

Skill VI: Providing Closure

Summarize what has been accomplished and what is to be accomplished, and check for agreement. Agree on whether further help is needed, and if so, when and in what form. If appropriate, prepare people as much as possible for difficulties and failures they may experience in implementing agreed-upon action plans. Finally, provide as much realistic encouragement and hope as you can.

GIVING AND RECEIVING FEEDBACK

One of the most important skills in the helping process is that of giving and receiving feedback. Supervisors spend considerable time giving and receiving feedback. Evaluating performance, letting people know where they stand or what they are doing well or not doing well, and trying to correct problems are all forms of giving and receiving feedback. There are several guidelines that should be considered in applying this important skill.

Giving Feedback

1. Share with caring, clearly demonstrating value and respect for the person you are sharing with.
2. As much as possible, choose a private place and assure that there will be no interruptions.
3. Try to be sensitive to the needs and readiness of the person you are sharing with. Giving advice when a person needs understanding, or vice versa, may alienate a person. Poor timing or overloading a person with more information than he or she can handle can also be counterproductive.
4. Share information in a truthful, accurate, straightforward, and yet diplomatic way. It is not helpful to share unfounded or erroneous information or to report information in an exaggerated or overly animated way.
5. Try to stick to specific behaviors and their consequences without making value judgments about the person involved and his or her motives. Making sweeping generalizations, being evaluative or judgmental, or attacking people rather than problems is not helpful.
6. Acknowledge when you are sharing an opinion or hunch rather than a fact. Implying factual information when you are sharing a personal perception can be very misleading. Support your conclusions with objective information from reliable sources as much as possible.

7. Avoid withholding valuable information that could be helpful unless you are reasonably certain that the timing is wrong or that a person is not ready for the information.
8. Listen with understanding to the other person. Check out the person's perceptions and your own perceptions of what is being said, and be careful not to overreact, which tends to magnify what is being shared.
9. Giving advice, sharing personal experiences, and exploring alternatives may be helpful if it is clear that you are not imposing your solution or way of doing things. Be sure that any advice you share is responsible and constructive. If a person responds to some well-intended advice that is not well founded, the consequences could have a significant effect on them.

Receiving Feedback

1. Try to be objective and listen without interrupting, getting defensive, or explaining away what is being shared. You may also have to do some objective sorting between old data that you have received in the past, which may or may not have been accurate, and present data, which should also be checked out for accuracy and consistency.
2. Always consider the validity of information before assuming that it is true, especially when relying on a sample of one. Remember that in most cases, people are sharing personal perceptions, which may or may not be accurate. You may want to ask for specifics or more information, compare what the person is saying with other information that you have, or even check the information out with other reliable sources.
3. Consider the source of the data. Determine if the person giving feedback is a trustworthy, reliable, and unbiased source of information.
4. Look for consistent patterns from several sources in deciding which data apply.
5. Don't discount positive feedback! Especially if the positive feedback is coming from several sources, it is probably an accurate portrayal of the way others see you, whether you feel that way or not. Remember that although others don't see you in all circumstances, the positive feedback that they give is valid for what they have seen.
6. If you are receiving inconsistent feedback, it may be because some people do not see you as others do, or you may act differently with different people. This could especially be true for differences in feedback at work and at home.
7. In disagreeing with or turning down feedback, do so tactfully without getting defensive. When you disagree with feedback, you can politely express your disagreement and possibly state your reasons, or simply thank a person for the feedback without acknowledging agreement. If you are getting overloaded with information, or feel that you cannot handle the feedback, feel free to express your needs.
8. If the person giving feedback is not giving you the feedback that you need, you can structure the feedback by asking appropriate questions.

THE HELPING PROCESS

The helping process includes three stages:

Stage I—Cognitive change
Stage II—Behavioral change
Stage III—Habit change

The helping process can be used to help people change and resolve problems and conflicts, and is designed to achieve prompt and lasting results or to recognize why results are not being achieved. It takes the emphasis off judging and condemning people for having problems and focuses on helping people improve and change in a constructive way that is likely to be successful. The eight steps of the helping process are shown in Figure 15.2. On a particular problem, a supervisor may use one or more of the eight steps and the process may be spread over several sessions.

Stage I—Cognitive Change

Change begins with a change in thinking, which can be accomplished through one or more of the following five steps:

1. Care
2. Make aware
3. Understand
4. Reason
5. Develop commitment to change

Caring is the most effective facilitator of change. Caring builds trust and confidence and sometimes is the needed catalyst that makes it possible for people to change. An uncaring supervisor inhibits change or often is the stimulus for undesirable changes. However, caring is not the only ingredient needed in the helping process. While caring may make change possible, it does not always result in change. It is also important to make people aware of what needs to be changed and to be understanding.

Hoping for change based on a person's ability to read minds or pick up hints or innuendos is likely to result in misunderstandings and unmet expectations. Understanding plays a key role in the change process because when people feel understood, they are less likely to resist and more likely to be cooperative. Finally, cognitive change is accomplished through reason and development of a commitment to change. It may be important to reason with persons about why they should change, the advantages of change, or the natural or imposed consequences of choosing not to change. All of the previous steps are designed to lead to commitment to change. *Unless a person is committed to making a change, change will not occur.* Thus it is important to check out a person's commitment. For example, you may want to inquire about what a person is willing to do to rectify the problems.

Figure 15.2 The helping process.

KURT LEWIN

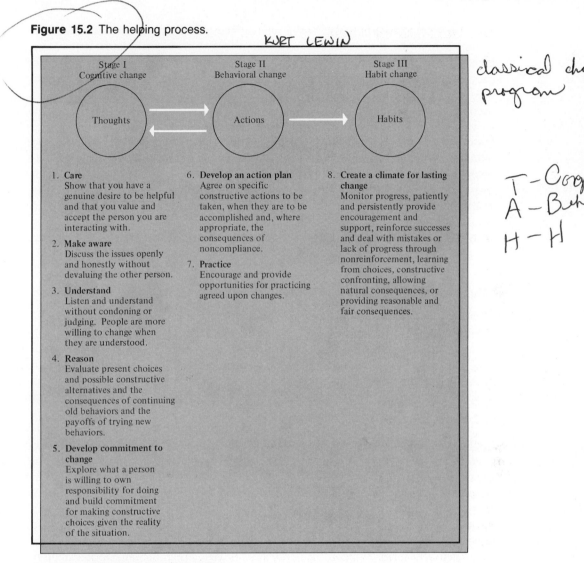

classical change program

Stage I
Cognitive change

Thoughts

Stage II
Behavioral change

Actions

Stage III
Habit change

Habits

T – Cog
A – Beh
H – H

1. **Care**
Show that you have a genuine desire to be helpful and that you value and accept the person you are interacting with.

2. **Make aware**
Discuss the issues openly and honestly without devaluing the other person.

3. **Understand**
Listen and understand without condoning or judging. People are more willing to change when they are understood.

4. **Reason**
Evaluate present choices and possible constructive alternatives and the consequences of continuing old behaviors and the payoffs of trying new behaviors.

5. **Develop commitment to change**
Explore what a person is willing to own responsibility for doing and build commitment for making constructive choices given the reality of the situation.

6. **Develop an action plan**
Agree on specific constructive actions to be taken, when they are to be accomplished and, where appropriate, the consequences of noncompliance.

7. **Practice**
Encourage and provide opportunities for practicing agreed upon changes.

8. **Create a climate for lasting change**
Monitor progress, patiently and persistently provide encouragement and support, reinforce successes and deal with mistakes or lack of progress through nonreinforcement, learning from choices, constructive confronting, allowing natural consequences, or providing reasonable and fair consequences.

Stage II—Behavioral Change

Stage II of the helping process is designed to achieve behavioral change. While cognitive change makes it possible to change behavior, it does not cause change. Change begins when new actions are practiced. Supervisors often make the mistake of assuming that talking to someone causes change. Talking may stimulate change, but actual change does not take place until an employee begins doing something different. Therefore, Stage II includes two steps designed to result in actual behavioral change:

1. Develop an action plan
2. Practice the plan

Developing an action plan begins with agreeing on the specific actions that need to be taken. In some cases where the solution is obvious or disciplinary actions are involved, a supervisor may simply specify the actions to be taken. However, in most cases it is most effective for the supervisor and employee to discuss alternatives until they both agree on the actions to be taken and how the desired actions will be accomplished. Once agreement is achieved, it may be helpful to commit the agreement to writing and provide a copy for both the supervisor and employee. If it is anticipated that the employee may perform the agreed-upon actions but does so with a bad attitude, the agreement should include provisions for a change in attitude as well as behavior. One of the problems supervisors create in achieving behavioral change is that they are unclear on specifically what they want done differently, or they do not communicate what they mean by an attitude change. The next step is to assure that the plan is practiced. Supervisors can provide opportunities for practice through assignments, training, or by having employees keep notes on their successes or failures in practicing the desired changes.

Stage III—Habit Change

Lasting change has not been achieved until a new behavior has become a habit. Persons can change the way they think or change the way they act. However, until both thoughts and actions are changed in the same direction, lasting change is unlikely. For example, making commitments that are not practiced results in short-lived change in actions. Stage III is designed to achieve habit changes and is accomplished through one step: creating a climate for lasting change. In general, creating a climate for change that is likely to result in new habits includes providing a supportive environment where successes are reinforced, mistakes are used as an opportunity for learning, and people are held accountable for their commitments. This can be accomplished by providing encouragement, praising successes, monitoring progress, creating opportunities for practice that are likely to result in success, and particularly, being patient. Mistakes or slippage need to be handled with good judgment. Some should be allowed as part of the learning process. Rescuing may even be appropriate if it does not provide an incentive for becoming irresponsible. Another option may be to allow a person to experience the natural consequences of his or her mistakes, rectify the mistakes, or evaluate the mistakes and their consequences and agree on more appropriate alternatives. Finally, it may be appropriate to confront mistakes or slippage, without being judgmental or critical, by attacking the problem and not the person and by providing reasonable and fair consequences. Consequences could include formal or informal reprimands, a loss of privileges, change in responsibilities, receiving a low performance review, personnel actions such as placing a person on probation, or, if warranted, even dismissing a person.

The positive approach to change is the preferred and most successful approach, although supervisors should not refrain from using reasonable consequences when appropriate. They should be aware, however, that if consequences are perceived as unfair or unnecessarily punitive, the result is usually temporary change, a change in behavior without a change in attitude, or retaliation.

UNDERSTANDING THE CHANGE PROCESS

When applied effectively, helping skills increase the prospects for successful problem solving and change. However, supervisors need to be realistic about what to expect from their attempts to be helpful. The following guidelines should be considered in understanding the change process and what supervisors can expect.

The Importance of Accepting Responsibility and Practicing New Behaviors

If a supervisor can coach people to accept responsibility for their behavior and commit themselves to practicing agreed-upon changes, behavior change can be accomplished in a short period of time. Most behaviors that are practiced regularly over a period of three to four weeks are likely to become habits. While such quick change is not unusual with the approach suggested in this chapter, some changes may be accomplished even more quickly, and others may take longer or may be difficult if not impossible to achieve.

Reasons Why Change May Not Occur

Most people sincerely desire to cooperate, do their best, and improve. However, hoped-for changes may not occur for one or more of the following reasons:

1. Trying to impose changes on another person will meet resistance if the person is not committed to the change. Technically, you cannot make another person change. The person must choose to change either willingly or under coercion. Coercive change rarely lasts.
2. Change often does not occur because people are unaware of what needs to be changed. Supervisors may assume that subordinates know what needs to be changed and then hold them accountable for expectations that have not been communicated. If you are going to hold a person accountable for an expectation, the expectation should be clearly communicated.
3. A person may lack the knowledge, training, or experience to make the desired changes.
4. A person may not be willing, ready, or able to make changes for legitimate reasons that may not be obvious. For example, personal problems may rob a person of the desire or energy to respond to needed changes at work.
5. The perceived rewards for change or consequences for not changing may be viewed as not worth the effort.
6. A person may also choose not to cooperate or change for inappropriate reasons, such as rebellion or a self-serving or self-centered attitude.

The Need for Patience and Understanding

Change requires patience and understanding. Rarely does change occur overnight. It takes time to develop new habits, and in the interim we often make mistakes and revert to old habits.

Focus on One Change at a Time

It is best to focus on one change at a time. Requiring a person to make numerous changes at the same time will usually prove to be overwhelming.

SUMMARY

People problems tend to dominate a supervisor's time. Conflicts, misunderstandings, personal problems, confrontations, and trying to motivate people are problems that are all too familiar to supervisors. And yet, most supervisors have not had the necessary training to handle these problems successfully. Although it isn't necessary to be a psychologist or professional counselor to handle work-related people problems, it is necessary to develop a sound philosophical basis for working with people and for using helping skills to facilitate problem solving and change. By understanding and practicing the responsibility-based helping skills presented in this chapter, a supervisor should be able to improve his or her abilities in handling people problems significantly.

The responsibility-based helping approach is based on: (1) accepting behavior without trying to place blame or judgment, (2) coaching a person to take responsibility for his or her choices given the realities of the situation and regardless of who or what is at fault, and (3) motivating a person to make constructive choices. It includes learning basic helping skills, learning to give and receive feedback, adapting the three-stage helping process to one's own unique style and to each individual situation, and being aware of what to expect in the change process.

IMPORTANT TERMS

accepting responsibility for behavior
helping skills principles
constructive choices
preparing
rapport building
active listening
synthesizing

coaching
providing closure
giving feedback
receiving feedback
cognitive change
behavioral change
habit change

REVIEW QUESTIONS

1. What are some of the most effective ways to minimize unnecessary problems at work?

2. What are some principles to consider in helping others change?
3. How can behavior be changed?
4. What are the three stages of the helping skills process?

EXERCISES

15.1   Identifying Helping Skills

Meet in small groups of about six people. Your task is to brainstorm a list of positive and negative ways to motivate people to change or improve. Check off the methods that your group considers to be the top five on each list.

Use the following format, preferably on chart paper:

Ways to Motivate Change	
Positive (Check the Top 5)	Negative (Check the Top 5)

The groups should have 20 minutes to complete the task. Another 10 minutes should be used for a class debriefing. In the debriefing, the instructor should have each group: (1) share their complete positive list, followed by an identification of the top five; and (2) do likewise with their negative list.

A good way to bring closure to this exercise is to have each participant make his own list of positive and negative ways that he or she tries to motivate change.

15.2   Practicing Helping Skills

Meet in groups of three and have each member select a role: helper, helpee, and observer. The task is for the helper to apply the three-stage helping process to guide the helpee in identifying and evaluating three possible improvements he or she would be willing to make and coach the helpee to select and develop an action plan for one of the improvements. The observer is to use: (1) the helping principles; (2) the guidelines for giving and receiving feedback to evaluate what the helper did well and what could be done to improve his or her helping skills; and (3) the three-stage helping process model.

The actual interaction between the helper and helpee should last about 15 minutes. The next 5 minutes should be used first by the observer and then the helpee to provide helpful feedback to the helper on what the helper did well and what improvement could be made. This procedure should be followed until each member of the group of three has played all three roles.

The instructor may want to debrief the exercise before the whole class by asking the following questions:

1. What helping skills did you see people use that you thought were effective?
2. What insights did you get about ways you could be more effective as a helper?

SUGGESTED ADDITIONAL READINGS

Azrin, Nathan H., and Nunn, Gregory. *Habit Control In a Day.* New York: Simon and Schuster, 1977.

Bassin, Alexander; Bratter, Thomas Edward; and Rachin, Richard, eds. *The Reality Therapy Reader.* New York: Harper & Row, 1976.

Boshear, Walton, and Albrecht, Karl G. *Understanding People: Models and Concepts.* San Diego: University Associates, 1977.

Ellis, Albert, and Harper, Robert A. *A New Guide to Rational Living.* Hollywood, CA: Wilshire Book Co., 1975.

Glasser, Naomi, ed. *What Are You Doing? How People Are Helped Through Reality Therapy.* New York: Harper & Row, 1980.

Schwitzgebel, Ralph K., and Kolls, David A. *Changing Human Behavior: Principles of Planned Intervention.* New York: McGraw-Hill, 1974.

16

Evaluating Performance

Every man is a volume, if you know how to read him.
William Ellery Channing

The conventional approach, unless handled with consummate skill and delicacy, constitutes something dangerously close to a violation of the integrity of the personality. Managers are uncomfortable when they are put in the position of "playing God."
Douglas McGregor

OBJECTIVES

This chapter provides you with the information necessary to:

1. Describe the schools of thought on performance appraisal and the basic philosophy underlying each school
2. Explain the differences between the various evaluation techniques
3. Discuss the impact of negative feedback on the worker's self-concept
4. Discuss the guidelines for performance feedback
5. Describe how to conduct a subordinate performance-appraisal interview

---

THE PERFORMANCE-APPRAISAL ROLE

The primary purpose of performance appraisal is to facilitate changes in an individual's behavior in order to stimulate achievement of both personal and organizational goals. It is one of the most important jobs a supervisor has. Since performance appraisal is essentially a personal evaluation of another, the supervising proficiency needed to conduct a successful evaluation consists of a combination of communication, technical, and human relations skills.

Performance appraisal can be formal or informal or a combination of the two. Regardless of the type of appraisal used, there are four major objectives involved in evaluating employees:

Evaluate performance considering that the outcomes of the behavior are more significant than the behavior itself

Correct shortcomings of individuals and provide information for change to more effective working habits

Aid in decisions on promotion, separation, and transfer

Evaluate future potential

The significance of these objectives explains why evaluations can materially affect the morale and motivation of the employee. To dampen any employee concern within the appraisal system it is important that the evaluation process be one of continuous communication. The dump-the-news-once-a-year approach does not contribute constructively to modification of behavior. The employees want to know how they are doing. They will tend to correct their own mistakes once they know what their mistakes are and that their supervisor's goal is to help them become more successful at what they do. Figure 16.1 illustrates the contributions that the performance-evaluation process makes to the organization's personnel system. Performance appraisal is closely related to the other personnel processes, such as rewards, fairness, leadership, and collective bargaining. Some of these other personnel processes are discussed later in this book.

TYPES OF PERFORMANCE-APPRAISAL TOOLS

Although we will briefly describe a few of the major types of performance-appraisal tools, it is our feeling that the type of appraisal tool is not as important as how the tool is applied. The tools of performance appraisal can be classified into one of two categories, conventional or emerging (see Figure 16.2).

The conventional techniques are designed to help the supervisor judge people, whereas the emerging techniques are designed to improve the working relationship between the supervisor and the subordinate. Further, the emerging school of thought is interested in what appraisal does to people and how supervisors can help subordinates grow and develop into fully functioning and contributing individuals.

A recent study indicated that 43 percent of the surveyed organizations are using

Figure 16.1 The performance-evaluation process. From Wendell L. French, John E. Dittrich, and Robert A. Zawacki, *The Personnel Management Process: Cases on Human Resources Administration.* (Boston: Houghton Mifflin, 1978), p. 192.

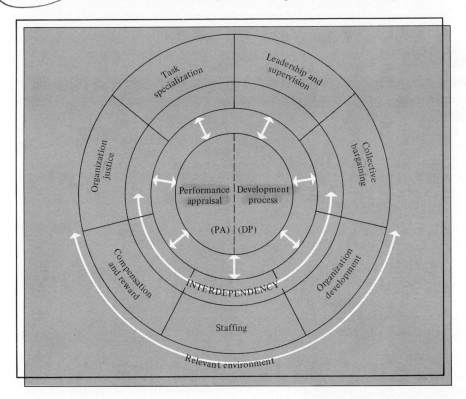

Figure 16.2 The link between performance appraisal and employee development.

started 1965

	Conventional	Emerging
Basic philosophy	Traditional (judgmental)	Collaborative (developmental)
Basic guiding question	How do we rate people?	How can we develop people and organizations?
Selected techniques	✓ most often used Graphic rating scale Forced-distribution method Peer rating	MBO BARS Organization development

PA   DP

conventional evaluation techniques and 57 percent are using collaborative tools.[1] Another study, based largely on manufacturing companies, cited that 25 percent used conventional rating systems and 75 percent used some form of MBO.[2]

The most used conventional rating systems are discussed here.

Graphic Rating Scale

The rater places a check mark on the form next to the word describing the degree of merit for each of several different traits. This is the most commonly used conventional technique (35 percent of surveyed firms), but it is also full of pitfalls for the supervisor. For example, traits are subjective and hard to measure. What does *decisiveness* or *adaptability* mean to you? These words are subject to different interpretations, and it is very difficult to communicate them to subordinates with any clarity in a way that will help them improve their performance. Another problem with this form is the halo effect. Research findings indicate that supervisors have a tendency to rate people in the same category from one rating period to another. For example, if the supervisor rates subordinate A as a 1 on the first rating, the supervisor will have a tendency to see only the good things in subordinate A and continue to rate that person as a 1 in future ratings. Another problem in organizations is scarce resources—that is, money and promotions. Therefore, supervisors tend to help their subordinates, at the expense of subordinates in other departments, by inflating individual ratings. When other supervisors hear about this inflation, they want to help their subordinates and begin to inflate their ratings. Soon a leapfrog effect takes place in the organization, and the evaluation process becomes meaningless unless organizational controls are established. One form of control is a forced-distribution method.

Forced-Distribution Method

Employees are distributed by the supervisor along one or more scales, and a fixed percentage of employees are assigned to each quarter of the scale. About 7 percent of the surveyed firms used this evaluation tool. This method corrects the inflation problem because supervisors are forced to make hard decisions about their subordinates' performances. For example, assume that a supervisor has 20 people working under his or her supervision. Using the form in Figure 16.3, the supervisor may be permitted to award only three ratings of 9 or 10, seven ratings of 5 through 8, and ten ratings of 4 or lower. Normally the personnel department is assigned the responsibility of monitoring the ratings of each supervisor and reporting any deviations to the responsible top manager.

Although this method prevents the inflation and halo problems, it introduces another problem—backstabbing. In the example above, the supervisor can award only

[1]Robert A. Zawacki and Robert L. Taylor, "A View of Performance Appraisal from Organizations Using It," *Personnel Journal* 55 (June, 1976): 290–292ff.
[2]Glen H. Varney, "Performance Appraisal—Inside and Out," *The Personnel Administrator* (November-December, 1972), p. 17.

three outstanding ratings. Therefore, if a subordinate is a 5 or 6, the only way that he or she can improve this rating is for one of the 9s or 10s to be rated lower during the next rating cycle. Lower-rated subordinates may begin to tell stories about the 9s or 10s, try to embarrass them, or even withhold critical information from them. This evaluation method discourages teamwork and collaborative relationships between people in an organization, because for someone to move up, someone else must move down.

Peer Rating

Each employee rates every other employee in his or her division at that level in the organization. This method transfers the rating function from the supervisor to the team of workers. In our example of a group of 20 subordinates, each worker would receive 19 ratings (from peers), and the 19 ratings would be averaged by the supervisor to get an overall rating for each subordinate.

The major advantage of peer rating is that it is the most valid performance-rating technique because workers generally reveal their real attitudes and behaviors when they are with their peers. Also, workers are with workers more than workers are with supervisors. Thus, the extended observation period tends to increase the accuracy of the rating. The major disadvantage of this technique is that it can introduce undesired behavior in work teams. For example, one worker may withhold information that is needed by another worker to complete a task. This may make the first worker appear more efficient in the eyes of the supervisor. This method is not recommended if the supervisor is attempting to build an effective team. It has the same shortcomings as the forced-distribution method.

Emerging Tools

While the conventional performance-appraisal tools are judgmental in nature, the emerging tools are more collaborative in nature, and the emphasis is on creating a helping relationship. The two most common collaborative tools are management by objectives (MBO—discussed in Chapter 12) and behaviorally anchored rating scales (BARS—discussed later in this chapter). The collaborative researchers are interested in what performance appraisal does to people, while the conventional researchers are interested in how we rate people.

We stated in Chapter 4 that the self-concept is a pattern of beliefs developed over a long period of time and that subordinates have a deep-seated need to preserve their self-concepts and in most cases want also to enhance or improve it. In the appraisal process, one purpose is to give employees meaningful feedback so that they can improve their performance. Research indicates that employees will normally do one of three things when receiving negative feedback (criticism): (1) act defensively, (2) leave the feedback session (either mentally or physically), or (3) change their behavior to incorporate the supervisor's recommended changes. The very objective that the supervisor is trying to accomplish (number 3) is the last thing the subordinate wants to do. The greater the threat to the self-concept, the more negative is the reaction by the subordinate to the supervisor's counseling efforts. If most people react this way when they are threatened, how can a supervisor hope to counsel subordinates without injuring their self-esteem, provoking defensive behavior, or incurring their wrath? One approach proven to be helpful is presenting the subordinates with several alternatives. The process is known as maximizing alternatives.

PRESENTING ALTERNATIVES[3]

If both people in the helping relationship agree that there is a problem and that the employee's behavior must be improved, then they have a foundation for beginning to explore alternative kinds of actions they can *both* take.

If the supervisor can get the employee to understand and explore the various courses of action available, the supervisor has taken a positive step toward solving the problem or getting the subordinate to modify his or her behavior.

The key to effective feedback is giving employees the freedom to choose the course of action that they feel is best for them under the circumstances. The employees will be much more likely to carry out a course of action that they have identified— because it is their decision and they are responsible for the outcome. This may include joint goal setting, better peer relations, increased promptness, or greater efficiency in performing a job. If the supervisor has tried to help an employee explore alternatives and arrive at a personal decision, the supervisor can be more certain that the counseling effort will achieve the desired change.

FEEDBACK GUIDELINES

Here are some guidelines to help supervisors to be more effective in the counseling relationship:

Don't Argue.   Subordinates will try to preserve their self-concepts by meeting supervisors' arguments with resistance. If supervisors increase their argumentative positions or continue to pound away at subordinates, they will provoke even more resistance and denial.

Be Prepared to Listen.   Supervisors must understand the subordinate's point of view before they can begin jointly to explore alternatives. Understanding a subordinate's point of view, however, does not necessarily mean agreeing with or supporting the subordinate's position. There's a difference between empathy and sympathy.

Let the subordinate do more than half the talking. It may be easy for supervisors, because of their experience, to get trapped in a prescribing or lecturing role. But a know-it-all position may threaten the receivers so much that they mentally leave the scene or act more defensively than if supervisors were more receptive.

[3]Freely adapted from Peter E. LaSota and Robert A. Zawacki, "The Supervisor as Counselor," *Supervisory Management,* November, 1973, pp. 16–20.

Listen actively and with understanding by genuinely trying to take an interest in, draw out, and understand the other person's point of view and feelings, even if you disagree. "I see," "I understand," "My goodness!" "Even though I don't agree with you, I can understand why you feel the way you do," "What did you do then?" are all useful expressions in such situations.

Give Frequent Feedback.   Feedback limited to a comprehensive, once-a-year performance review with subordinates will not help them develop on the job. It may even hinder their growth. Small changes effected over a long period of time will be better for the subordinate and better for the supervisor.

Look at Subordinates as Subjects—Not Objects That Make Up the Personnel Resource.   They are human beings with feelings, needs, and values of their own. Try to see the world from their point of view. Use the model of the self-concept to help you understand subordinates.

Reflect the Feelings of the Worker.   If supervisors can focus on reflecting the feelings and attitudes of the workers instead of giving advice, the workers will be better able to find their own solutions.

When a supervisor bounces back feelings that a subordinate has expressed, the worker will continue to talk about them. Frequent use of "Umm-hmm," "I see," and "Is that so?" will help bounce the conversational ball back over the net and give the subordinate a chance to elaborate.

Focus on the feelings another person transmits and restate his or her *expressed feelings* in your own words to assure that you are hearing the real (underlying) message. Used naturally, this technique is an excellent way to draw people out and find out what they are really trying to communicate: "Why do you feel that your rating is unfair?" "It seems to you that your group doesn't accept you because you have some different ideas than they do?" "You see yourself as having a lot of skills that aren't being utilized?" "You feel that I let you down?"

Perception Checking.   Check out your perceptions and others' perceptions of what has been communicated or what you or they are feeling by summarizing, repeating, or rephrasing in your own words what you have heard or are feeling: "My understanding is that . . .," "Is this what you meant when you said . . . ?" "How do the rest of you feel about what Wendy said?" "How are you feeling about the progress we have made in this meeting so far?"

Direct Comments toward Behavior That the Subordinate Can Change.   By giving people unfavorable feedback about actions over which they have little or no control, supervisors only increase subordinates' feelings of frustration and their need to defend themselves.

Give Timely Feedback.   Feedback is most helpful to a subordinate when it is given at the earliest opportunity after the relevant event or interaction. Research in this area indicates that people may have a certain tolerance level for accepting unfavorable feedback. When this level is approached or surpassed, no further learning takes place. For this reason, supervisors should give feedback often and in small quantities.

Ask Skilled Questions.   The skillful supervisor should avoid questions that can be answered with a simple *yes* or *no.* By starting questions with "How do you feel about . . . ?" or "What do you think about . . . ?" you give workers a better chance to let their feelings and attitudes emerge, along with a multitude of irrelevant facts, details, and excuses. Since the purpose of the session is to solve a problem, past facts are far less important than present feelings and attitudes.

Look for Responsibility.   Be on the lookout for signals that the subordinate is willing to make a commitment to change or accept the outcome of the helper-helpee relationship. Once a subordinate assumes responsibility for overcoming his or her own shortcomings, your task as a supervisor is easier.

BEHAVIORALLY ANCHORED RATING SCALES

As we indicated earlier, there are basically two types of collaborative methods for evaluating performance. The first method, MBO, is described in great detail in Chapter 12, and that discussion will not be duplicated in this chapter. However, we do believe that MBO has tremendous potential if it is implemented as a collaborative philosophy of management with commitment by the top executives in the organization. The study by Zawacki and Taylor in 1976 indicated that 57 percent of the organizations had MBO systems and another 15 percent planned to implement MBO systems in 1977.

The second method, behaviorally anchored rating scales (BARS), is a relatively new appraisal tool of which supervisors should have a working knowledge. BARS differs from other evaluating processes because of the focus on behavior rather than traits and because it is developed in collaboration with the employees who do each specific job. One drawback of BARS is that there must be a specific rating form for each job category in an organization. This is an expensive and time-consuming process. The steps in developing BARS are[4]

1. *Critical incidents.* Persons doing the job are asked to describe specific examples of effective and ineffective behavior on the job.
2. *Performance dimensions.* Incidents are then classified into 5 to 10 performance categories.
3. *Retranslation.* A second group of persons also familiar with the job is asked to group the critical incidents into the given dimensions.
4. *Scaling incidents.* Another group of people is asked to assign a numerical scale to each dimension. The average rating assigned to each dimension describes effective performance for that dimension.
5. *Final rating form.* The dimensions that are retained become the behavioral anchors for the number on the rating form. The final BARS instrument is a series of scales for each performance dimension.

Although BARS is expensive, there are potentially some high payoffs for supervisors. First, it defines the performance domain (scales are linked to actual job require-

[4]Donald P. Schwab and Herbert G. Heneman, III, "Research Round-up," *The Personnel Administrator* 22 (January, 1977): 54–57.

ments); second, it reduces appraisal error; and third, it is more acceptable to the Equal Employment Opportunity Commission because it comes nearer to meeting their guidelines.

PERFORMANCE-APPRAISAL INTERVIEW GUIDELINES

The performance-appraisal interview is the culmination of the appraisal process, so it is very important that it be a successful experience for both supervisor and employees. The following checklist contains some guidelines on the performance-appraisal interview process and some skills in making the interview a successful one. Some of these points were discussed in greater detail earlier.

General Guidelines

Be prepared.
Review the purpose of the appraisal interview:
    Evaluate past performance.
    Agree on ways to become more effective.
    Establish goals for the future.
Give some positive strokes—"What you stroke is what you get."
Avoid the good-news–bad-news approach.
Make it a summation of an ongoing process.
Establish a helping relationship:
    Genuinely care about helping the employee to be successful.
    Listen actively.
    Bring conflicts to the surface and deal with them.
    Understand that *your* performance may also be a point of discussion.
    Try to be sensitive to the needs and feelings of the person being appraised.

Interview Preparation

Interviewer

1. Refresh your knowledge of the employee's duties and his or her performance in accomplishing the duties.
2. Consider the type of person the employee is (sensitive, open, ambitious, etc.).
3. Plan the interview so you can highlight the employee's strengths and weaknesses in performing his or her job.
4. Consider things you can do to assist the employee in performing the job better.
5. List the objectives (personal development, professional development, and job-related items) that you would like to see the employee accomplish in the next evaluation period.
6. Select a time and place for the interview so that you will not be interrupted.

Interviewee

1. Refresh your knowledge of your job duties and performance.
2. Consider ways your boss can help you in your job.
3. List the objectives you would like to pursue in the next evaluation period.

The Interview

Try to establish an informal, supportive atmosphere and make clear that your intent is to be helpful and to confront problems constructively. Also, make sure that communication is *two-way*. It is not the purpose of the interview to listen to yourself talk.

State the purpose of the interview process if the subordinate is not familiar with it already.

Rather than start with the good news and finish with the bad news, go through the subordinate's performance item by item comparing performance to his or her duties, assignments, or objectives and soliciting comments on each item. Use specifics rather than generalities.

Discuss your overall rating of the subordinate and, if necessary, what he or she needs to do to become more successful in his or her job.

Ask the subordinate what you can do to be a more helpful supervisor.

Negotiate with the subordinate, when appropriate, objectives for the coming period, including:

Personal-development objectives

Professional-development objectives

Job-related objectives (regular duties, problems, innovations)

Set up a time for reviewing the subordinate's progress toward the agreed-upon objectives or duties.

Helping Relationships

Avoid:

Discounting

Double messages

Using loaded words

Making absolute statements

Do:

Show acceptance and a desire to help

Be specific

Admit and express your real feelings in a constructive way

Listening Skills

Avoid:

> Stereotyping
> Explaining away feelings, ideas, behaviors of others
> Indifference
> Reacting to a person's manner, appearance, delivery
> Nitpicking

Do:

> Listen actively
> Use open-ended questions
> Check out perceptions
> Reflect feelings

Skills for Handling Conflicts

Avoid:

> Judging and moralizing
> Reminiscing
> Blaming
> Communicating from your Critical Parent or Rebellious or Compliant Child
> Getting into a win-lose battle
> Interrogating

Do:

> Level
> Communicate from your Adult and Natural Child
> Attack problems—not people
> Use descriptive rather than evaluative words
> Emphasize how to solve problems rather than dwell on the whys of problems

SUMMARY

Appraising workers on their performance is a key function of supervisors. It helps the employees improve their performance by informing them of their progress toward personal and organizational goals. Also, it is a very useful mechanism to help employees grow and develop as human resources.

There are two main categories of performance appraisal tools: conventional and emerging. Conventional tools are graphic-rating scales, forced distribution, and peer ratings. Collaborative performance-appraisal tools are management by objectives (MBO) and behaviorally anchored rating scales (BARS).

The performance-appraisal interview is the most difficult aspect of evaluation because both the supervisor and the employee resist this meeting. To make the counseling session successful, the supervisor should review the employee's duties and achievements; view the employee as a caring, sensitive person; and help the employee list personal, professional, and job-related objectives. Overall, the supervisor must establish a climate of helping and caring for the employees. Employees have a unique way of sensing when supervisors are concerned about their personal and professional growth.

IMPORTANT TERMS

conventional rating tools	peer rating
graphic-rating scale	emerging rating tools
forced-distribution method	BARS
	presenting alternatives

REVIEW QUESTIONS

1. Discuss the following statement: "Most employees want feedback from supervisors yet approach the interview session with doubt and fear."
2. What are the two main schools of thought on performance appraisal?
3. Discuss the various evaluation techniques.
4. What is MBO? Identify some problems with this technique.
5. What are the main guidelines for the performance-appraisal interview?
6. What would you consider the major pitfalls of a performance-appraisal system?
7. What are the principal objectives of performance appraisal?

CASES

16.1 The Performance-Appraisal Workshop

On April 12, 1982, Dean Laura L. Beatty received a memorandum from the personnel officer at the University of Obsuk stating that a performance-appraisal workshop was scheduled for all university department heads at 9:00 A.M. on May 25, 1982. The purpose of the workshop was to bring supervisors up to date on the new state evaluation system. Administrative assistants in all departments received a telephone call on May 24, 1982, informing them of the importance of the workshop and asking if the department head planned to attend.

On May 25, at 9:15 A.M., the representative from the state personnel office entered the workshop room and started to set up his slide projector. Approximately 25 department heads had been in the room since 9:00 A.M. At 9:20 A.M., an assistant started handing out literature on performance appraisal.

After the setup time, the representative from the state personnel office presented a 10-minute slide show that illustrated a poor performance-appraisal feedback session between a supervisor and a subordinate. After the slide presentation, the participants of the workshop concluded that the supervisor in the slide presentation:

1. Was not prepared
2. Was annoyed by the session

3. Was not specific
4. Did not communicate

After this discussion, the representative then gave an overview of the new state performance-appraisal system. The appraisal steps were

1. Discuss and agree on the expected results to be achieved—a contract. Subordinates have a right to know what you expect of them.
2. Provide help with direction and training. Give subordinates a chance to show their abilities.
3. Let subordinates know how they are doing (formally and informally).
4. Compensate according to results: merit, recognition, deeds, nonmanipulation, promotion, training and development.

After presenting the steps, one department head asked, "Isn't it true that joint goal setting sets high expectations on the part of the employees, and our state merit system may not permit us to reward effort?" Another dean added, "We cannot compensate according to results because of state compensation systems." A third participant piped in, "What we are looking at is a performance-appraisal system designed around extrinsic rewards, but the only rewards available to the supervisor, in the state system, are intrinsic rewards." The state representative responded, "This is what I like—reasons why we cannot implement the system."

The remainder of the workshop had a negative tone, and many people participated reluctantly.

Questions

1. If you were the state representative, how would you answer the workshop participants' questions and comments?
2. Is a management-by-objectives program workable in a state agency?
3. What are the differences between the private and public sectors with regard to merit systems, regulations, structure, and so on?
4. Is MBO more than a performance-appraisal system? Is it a philosophy of management?
5. How often should subordinates receive feedback on their performance?
6. Are these people resisting change or are they raising legitimate questions?

16.2   The Performance-Appraisal Interview

Laura Louise has worked at Honeyriver Corporation for six months as an electronics assembler trainee. She is one of 600 employees on the night shift and performs a very routine assembly task on the line. Her supervisor, Martha Lynn, considers Laura an above-average performer who has an average absentee record. Laura is 19 years of age and is working to meet college expenses. Martha has noticed that Laura appears to become bored rather easily on the job and may have an attitude problem. However, during breaks Laura is very social and appears to have a high need to interact with her coworkers. Martha is planning the six-month performance-evaluation interview with Laura and has some apprehensions about the meeting.

Questions

1. Role-play the performance-appraisal interview between Laura and Martha.
2. Why may Martha fear the meeting?
3. Why is Laura bored with her job?
4. Do you see a future for Laura at Honeyriver? Explain your answer.

16.3 Using Performance Appraisal to Improve Performance

Review the following job-appraisal situation. Role-play for further exploration of ideas.

Supervisor:

You are about to conduct your third interview with Don Hicks. You think he is the best worker in the department and want him for a supervisor trainee. You think he is the man for the job without a doubt. To complete his requirements for the position of supervisor, however, he has to get some more education. He can be appointed a trainee without the additional education, but his chances will almost certainly be better if he is formally trained. He needs courses in management and supervision, human relations, and business communication. His production and all rating qualifications (on the board) are outstanding. You must motivate him to get the courses he needs and stay with the company.

Worker Don Hicks:

You like your job pretty well and feel you can perform among the best. You don't really care about the company. It seems to you that they don't take care of their people: no unions, pay average for the area, benefits a little below normal, too much overtime. You are a little frustrated at home, too. Your wife doesn't like overtime. She wants you to be home more. Her brother works in another department and always "puts on the dog" to show how good his department is. He thinks your department is the deadhead of the company. You are looking for another job but you don't really know if you want to leave. You just don't seem to be able to decide what to do.

Questions

1. If you sell a person on a supervisor role, will you get a good supervisor?
2. What pitfalls do you see in the supervisor's objective?
3. How would you structure the actual appraisal session?
4. Should an appraisal session be a promotion-recruiting session?

16.4   Analyzing the Performance-Appraisal Process

Review the following job-appraisal situation. Role-play for further exploration of ideas.

Manager Hillen Dale:

You are scheduled to conduct an appraisal interview. You have been in your position of manager for only six months. This is the first appraisal you have conducted. The supervisor you are evaluating is going to get a low rating. These events have occurred during your evaluation period which, to you, justify the rating:

> There is apparent unrest in his department.
> His people seem to be giving him the cold shoulder.
> You feel he is becoming too temperamental and self-centered in his job perform-ance. You know because you see him twice a week.

Supervisor Jim Paul:

You are going for your appraisal interview. You expect a good rating, as usual. Your record with the company for the past several years has been excellent, and you have come up through the ranks. These events have occurred during that period of evaluation:

> Your evaluation and recommendation for salary increases for your subordinates have been questioned, doubted, and turned down.
> Your recommendations for change in the organizational structure of your department in an effort to get better production were ignored.

> Besides this, your production rate has been on a gradual increase but you know you can make it better. You don't know if you are having a personality problem with your new boss or not. He has been there only six months, but he doesn't seem to be around much.

Questions

1. What individual dynamics are present in this appraisal situation?
2. Do you feel that a good performance appraisal could be conducted under these circumstances? Justify your answer.
3. How would you structure the actual appraisal session?
4. How would the MBO approach have aided in this appraisal?

SUGGESTED ADDITIONAL READINGS

French, Wendell L.; Dittrich, John E.; and Zawacki, Robert A. *The Personnel Management Process: Cases on Human Resources Administration.* Boston: Houghton Mifflin, 1982, pp. 181–222.

Locher, Alan H., and Teel, Kenneth S. "Performance Appraisal: A Survey of Current Practices." *Personnel Journal* 56 (May, 1977): 245–247ff.

McGregor, D. "An Uneasy Look at Performance Appraisal." *Harvard Business Review* 55 (May-June, 1975): 89–94.

Miner, J. B. "Management Appraisal: A Capsule Review and Current References." *Business Horizons* 11 (May, 1968): 83–96.

Obert, W. "Make Performance Appraisal Relevant." *Harvard Business Review* 50 (1972): 61–67.

Odiorne, G. S. "Management by Objectives: Antidote to Future Shock." *Personnel Journal* 53 (1974): 258–263.

Schwab, Donald P., and Heneman, Herbert G., III. "Research Round-up." *The Personnel Administrator* 22 (January, 1977): 54–57.

Stone, T. H. "An Examination of Six Prevalent Assumptions Concerning Performance Appraisal." *Public Personnel Management* 2 (1973): 408–414.

Taylor, R. L., and Zawacki, Robert A. "Collaborative Goal Setting in Performance Appraisal: A Field Experiment." *Public Personnel Management* (May-June, 1978), pp. 162–170.

Thompson, P. H., and Dalton, G. W. "Performance Appraisal: Manager Beware." *Harvard Business Review* 48 (January-February, 1970): 149–157.

Zawacki, Robert A., and Taylor, R. L. "A View of Performance Appraisal from Organizations Using It." *Personnel Journal* 55 (June, 1976): 290–292ff, and "Trends in Performance Appraisal: Guidelines for Managers," *The Personnel Adminstrator* (in press).

Appendix

Performance Review
Confidential

PURPOSE OF THE REVIEW

The purpose of the review is to let Employees know where they have been performing well and where they need to improve, to agree with employees on the responsibilities and goals expected of them during the coming review period, and to discuss what the reviewer can do to help the employee be successful during the next review period. The spirit in which this approach is accomplished is extremely important in making it work successfully. The approach is to be used by **both employees and their supervisors** as a vehicle for communicating openly, assuring that assignments and exceptions are understood, for solving problems, and for letting employees know where they stand and what they need to do to be successful.

PROCEDURES

1. At the end of each review period a week's notice should be given an employee regarding a performance review meeting. During this period **both** the employee and his supervisor should prepare for the meeting by evaluating past performance and considering changes in responsibilities and goals for the next period.
2. The following should be accomplished at the performance review meeting: (1) the supervisor's rating of the employee's performance should be discussed (it is possible that employee input during the discussion could result in the supervisor changing some of his ratings); (2) the employee and his supervisor should agree on responsibilities and goals for the next period; (3) both the employee and the supervisor should receive a copy of the final performance review report. The latter two steps should also be accomplished at the beginning of employment and when there are major changes in assignments.
3. A progress review of performance should be conducted at least once every six months. (Salary reviews will be made once a year.)
4. The completed performance review form should be used by both the employee and

his supervisor as a management and communications tool throughout the performance review period. Major changes in responsibilities and goals should be discussed by employees and their supervisor and should be noted on this form.

5. **All review information should be considered confidential.**

Name			Department			Job Title		
Date Joined the Firm	Last Salary Increase			Recommended New Increase				
	Date	Increase	New Salary	Date	Increase	New Salary		
Last Formal Review		Progress Reviews		Present Review				
Date	Reviewer	Dates	Reviewers	Date	Reviewer			

OBSERVATIONS

JOB RESPONSIBILITIES

A person's job responsibilities refer to the person's on-going tasks, the attitude in which the person performs the tasks, the person's use of and caring for facilities, equipment, and supplies, personal development efforts, and the person's appearance. Job responsibilities should be established in a two-way exchange between an employee and his supervisor so the responsibilities are clearly understood and agreed upon. The responsibilities should be used to give direction and purpose to a job but should not in any way be used to limit a person's willingness and cooperation in taking on responsibilities not listed below or in helping others with their responsibilities.

TASKS

ATTITUDE

With Supervisor

With Team Members

With Other Company Personnel

External (Customers, Sub-Contractors, Etc.)

FACILITIES, EQUIPMENT, AND SUPPLIES

PERSONAL DEVELOPMENT

APPEARANCE

JOB GOALS

A person's job goals include the **major accomplishments** the person has agreed to strive to achieve during a review period. Job goals could include, for example, solving a significant problem, developing a new procedure, accomplishing a job responsibility that has become very important, developing new capabilities, accomplishing agreed upon parts of a long range goal, resolving a serious problem with another department or employee, or other things that could be considered major areas of concern. It is important that goals are established in a two-way exchange between an employee and his supervisor so that the goals represent an agreement based on what a supervisor wants an employee to accomplish as well as what the employee wants to accomplish. The goal-setting approach can open up new opportunities for a person because it helps him realize that a person with goals has a far greater chance of making things happen and being successful than does a person who merely watches things happen, criticizes what happened, or waits for fate of others to shape his destiny.

Goals (what should be accomplished)	Goal Completion Target Date (estimated completion date)	How Goal Attainment Will Be Measured (how we will know when the Goal has been accomplished)

INSTRUCTIONS:

For each of the factors 1–10, place an "X" in the box which in your opinion most closely describes the progress and performance of the above employee being reviewed compared with (1) the progress and performance of others on a similar job for a similar period of time, and (2) the requirements of the position itself.

1. Quality of Work: Neatness and accuracy; frequency and degree of errors; appearance of work; also thoroughness with

Work must be consistently checked and often redone; excessive errors; leaves "loose ends" and does not follow up. Poor quality work.		Careless at times. Too many errors; quality not consistent. Work not entirely satisfactory; needs improvement.		Work satisfactory. Errors occur, but not frequently; consistently neat and orderly. Quality of work definitely acceptable.	
(1)	(2)	(3)	(4)	(5)	(6)

2. Quantity of Work: Volume of work produced or customer transactions handled; ability to meet or exceed production

Usually among the last to complete assignment. Very slow; production records poor.		Volume of work produced is not entirely satisfactory; often needs help to complete on time. Often does not meet production standards.		Satisfactory volume of work produced; maintains average production standards; completes on time; meets expectations.	
(1)	(2)	(3)	(4)	(5)	(6)

3. Knowledge of Job: Degree to which employee knows and understands the job procedures and requirements.

Knows little about the job; lacks understanding of basic principles, needs considerable further training and experience. Still a beginner.		Has fair understanding of job but needs further coaching and seasoning. Often hesitant about work and requires a more than average amount of supervision.		Employee knows the job. Meets all requirements for satisfactory job performance; requires average amount of supervision.	
(1)	(2)	(3)	(4)	(5)	(6)

4. Initiative: Extent to which employee proceeds on his own to complete assignment; degree to which he seeks to improve

Does only what is assigned or fails to follow through on assignments unless closely supervised; needs continuous prodding; wastes time. Appears to be totally indifferent.		Does little more than enough to get by; lacks enthusiasm and eagerness; needs frequent prodding and more than average supervision. Tends to be indifferent to the job.		Utilizes time to good advantage; is eager and alert; sometimes does more than assigned; seeks new challenges and responsibilities.	
(1)	(2)	(3)	(4)	(5)	(6)

5. Dependability: Degree to which employee may be depended upon to complete assignments, carry out instructions, be on

Unreliable. Assignments often left half-done. Attempts at work characterized by indifference. May be absent or late frequently.		Needs frequent follow-up to see that assignments or instructions are carried out completely and thoroughly; cannot always be relied upon; may occasionally be absent or late.		Can be depended upon to carry out assignments or instructions on his own, efficiently and on time. Seldom requires follow-up by others; seldom absent or late to work.	
(1)	(2)	(3)	(4)	(5)	(6)

6. Judgment: Employee's ability to utilize experience, job knowledge, and intelligence to identify facts, apply sound reasoning,

Employee is lost when confronted with non-routine problems or situations; impractical thinker; judgment cannot always be trusted, even on routine problems.		Has difficulty in making simple decisions without help. Definitely below average judgment and common sense.		Demonstrates good common sense. Makes sound decisions relating to normal job activities. Seldom needs to seek advice of others.	
(1)	(2)	(3)	(4)	(5)	(6)

7. Organization: Employee's ability to organize his work in such a way as to obtain maximum results in a minimum period of

Employee approaches work with obvious lack of planning and organization; work is confused and hit-or-miss; does not use time to advantage.		Has difficulty staying on top of job. Needs work on planning and organizing duties. Appears to be confused and overwhelmed much of the time.		Manages to approach work in a systematic, organized way most of the time; tries to plan duties in such a way as to use available time to advantage.	
(1)	(2)	(3)	(4)	(5)	(6)

8. Ability to Work with Others: Degree to which employee contributes to team effort, as opposed to advancement of personal

Antagonizes others; fails to gain respect and cooperation of associates; seems interested only in self; a poor group worker.		Has difficulty getting along with others and may tend to be resented by them. Lacks spirit of cooperativeness; not a good team worker.		Relationships with others satisfactory; tries to contribute to the group; does not arouse resentment or antagonism.	
(1)	(2)	(3)	(4)	(5)	(6)

9. Attitude: The employee's attitude toward his job, his associates, his supervisors, and the Company.

Highly critical and unconstructive; complains excessively. Rebellious to supervision. Dissatisfied; indifferent.		Overly critical, non-enthusiastic, or indifferent, exerts a negative and somewhat disrupting influence on others. May appear to resent supervision.		Loyal and enthusiastic. Takes constructive criticism well; responds well to supervision. Usually tries to act in best interests of the work group, the department and the company.	
(1)	(2)	(3)	(4)	(5)	(6)

10. Ability to Work under Pressure: Ease with which employee meets peak workloads and/or tight time deadlines.

Tends to "go to pieces" under pressure. Becomes highly upset and unable to perform acceptably.		Does not react well to pressure. Becomes disturbed and is unable to maintain usual performance standards.		Reacts adequately under pressure. Maintains usual performance standards and gets the job done.	
(1)	(2)	(3)	(4)	(5)	(6)

11. Attendance: Faithfulness in coming to work and conforming to work hours.

Often absent or late to work.		Lax in attendance and being at work on time.		Usually present and at work on time.	
(1)	(2)	(3)	(4)	(5)	(6)

12. Cost Performance: Use of time, company resources, labor, meeting schedules on time, etc.

Very inefficient use of time and company resources and labor can not be depended on to complete work on schedule.		Inefficient, poor use of company resources and labor, rarely completes work on schedule.		Usually efficient, fair use of company resources and labor, usually completes work on time.	
(1)	(2)	(3)	(4)	(5)	(6)

which assignments or customer transactions are conducted.

Quality definitely above average. Errors seldom made. Consistently high neatness and accuracy. Superior work.		Unusually high standards of quality. Exceptionally neat, thorough and accurate work. Errors extremely infrequent.	
(7)	(8)	(9)	(10)

standards and complete all assignments in allotted time.

Quick and steady worker; consistently high volume. Often completes work early; exceeds production standards.		Consistently tops in volume of work produced; a "pace setter" for other employees; always among the first to finish regular assignment. Exceptional producer.	
(7)	(8)	(9)	(10)

Employee knows and understands the job to the extent that he can handle difficult or unusual tasks: thoroughly experienced; needs little supervision.		Employee possesses extensive understanding and knowledge of the job: is considered an expert and provides valuable source of information about the job.	
(7)	(8)	(9)	(10)

methods or work habits, and to seek additional challenges and responsibilities.

Frequently does more than his share: seldom needs supervision; often seeks additional work and looks for new challenges and responsibilities.		Constantly accepts new duties and responsibilities: anticipates what needs to be done and does it: a self-starter all the way; always busy and productive.	
(7)	(8)	(9)	(10)

the job and fulfill responsibilities.

A very dependable and reliable worker—completely trustworthy. Never requires follow-up by others, never absent or late without good reason.		Completely reliable, dependable, and self-sufficient; always follows through accurately and completely. Never absent or late unless completely unavoidable.	
(7)	(8)	(9)	(10)

and arrive at a workable solution to a problem or assignment.

Possesses superior judgment and could handle relatively non-routine decisions with good results. A sound thinker, intelligent and practical.		Solves own problems with consistently superior results. Exceptional intelligence and reasoning ability. Could be entrusted with important decisions concerning the work.	
(7)	(8)	(9)	(10)

time, with the least possible duplication, confusion and errors.

Carefully plans work and approaches each assignment in orderly, systematic fashion; makes excellent use of available time; gets a lot done.		Is organized to the extent that work flows in and out with no time lapses, confusion, or duplication. A superior organizer and work producer.	
(7)	(8)	(9)	(10)

interests; ability to gain and give cooperation and to maintain respect and confidence.

Above-average ability to work harmoniously with others. Gives and gets cooperation and respect. An excellent team worker.		Exceptional and outstanding in ability to gain good will, inspire others, and gain their cooperation and respect. Substantial leadership potential.	
(7)	(8)	(9)	(10)

An extremely loyal and enthusiastic employee: works always to improve the company and takes a sincere interest in promoting the welfare of others and of the company.		Exerts a highly constructive influence; intensely loyal, eager, and enthusiastic: often makes constructive suggestions: always acts in company's best interest.	
(7)	(8)	(9)	(10)

Accuracy and quantity of work not adversely affected by pressure; can function well even under heavy and sustained pressure.		Reacts extremely well to pressure; can be depended upon for maximum efficiency possible in any stress or emergency situation.	
(7)	(8)	(9)	(10)

Can be depended on to be at work and report on time.		In addition to being dependable to be at work and report on time, volunteers for overtime when needed.	
(7)	(8)	(9)	(10)

Efficient good use of company resources and labor: completes work on schedule.		Very efficient excellent use of company resources and labor: completes work ahead of schedule.	
(7)	(8)	(9)	(10)

Review

☐ 6 Months Review

☐ 12 Months Review

☐ Promotion

☐ Special Review

Definition of Rating

1–2 Unsatisfactory

3–4 Meets minimum job requirements.

5–6 Performs all aspects of job in satisfactory manner

7–8 Job performance is above average.

9–10 Job performance is superior.

Supervisory Ability (Applicable to Supervisors Only)

1. Getting the Job Done and Controlling Cost.

Unreliable, has poor knowledge of job and costs.		Needs follow-up and often needs to be reminded of cost.		Adequate knowledge of job and costs, usually gets the job done.	
(1)	(2)	(3)	(4)	(5)	(6)

2. Planning, Organizing, Delegating Work and Authority.

Obvious lack of planning, cannot delegate.		Plans often inadequate, does not delegate well.		Plans, organizes, delegates work and authority adequately.	
(1)	(2)	(3)	(4)	(5)	(6)

3. Appraisal, Counseling and Development of Subordinates.

Fault finding, not fair to all.		Means well, but often needs supervision and advice, has difficulty in helping others.		Adequate in teaching, leading others. Fair in appraisals.	
(1)	(2)	(3)	(4)	(5)	(6)

4. Performance Under Pressure.

Easily excited, no help to others in stress situations.		Reacts with emotion under stress, becomes confused in procedures.		Adequate ability that is not affected under normal pressure.	
(1)	(2)	(3)	(4)	(5)	(6)

5. Take Charge Attitude.

Lacks initiative and know-how to be in control.		Irritates others, difficult to work with, over-supervises.		Accepts responsibility adequately under normal situations.	
(1)	(2)	(3)	(4)	(5)	(6)

What is your over-all evaluation of employee? (Please circle appropriate term)

| Excellent | Above Average | Average | Below Average | Very Poor |

If improvement is indicated, what are your suggestions?

_____

_____

_____

_____

_____

_____

Never wasteful, can be depended on to get a job done.		Always gets the job done easily, complete knowledge of cost and how to control.	
(7)	(8)	(9)	(10)

Gives thought to organizing, thinks through, delegates work and gives authority well.		Well organized, delegates work and authority to capable employees, maintains good control.	
(7)	(8)	(9)	(10)

Practical judgment in making appraisals. Handles grievances well, good depth in developing.		Sympathetic, cooperative, and aggressive in appraisals and counseling. Strong incentive to develop subordinates.	
(7)	(8)	(9)	(10)

Crises, distractions, interruptions have little effect in terms of upset and irritations.		Remains extremely calm under pressure, never loses control, makes employees feel secure.	
(7)	(8)	(9)	(10)

Strong and effective attitude, apparent self-assurance, dependable in most situations.		Is dominant in any situation, assumes full responsibility, making decisions presents no problem, inspires others.	
(7)	(8)	(9)	(10)

PART FIVE

Current Issues
in Supervision

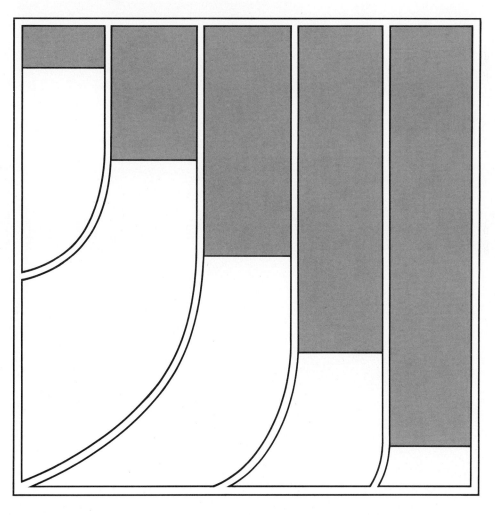

17

Supervisory Challenges: Working Effectively with Disadvantaged, Handicapped, or Alcoholic Employees

Every man is in certain respects like all other men, like some other men, like no other men.

Clyde Kluckholm and Henry A. Murray

We have not succeeded in answering all our questions; indeed, we sometimes feel we have not completely answered any of them. The answers we have found only serve to raise a whole set of questions. In some ways we feel we are as confused as ever. But we think we are confused on a higher level and about more important things.

Anonymous

OBJECTIVES

This chapter provides you with the information necessary to:

1. List and explain the major federal laws that have an impact on supervisors
2. Describe the characteristics of disadvantaged people
3. Explain some major guidelines for hiring and retaining the handicapped
4. Have an overall understanding of the Occupational Safety and Health Administration (OSHA)
5. Understand the role of the supervisor in relation to employee alcoholism

---

THE SUPERVISORY CHALLENGE

Since the early 1960s, the federal government has become increasingly involved in the management of organizations. "Three of the most significant pieces of legislation are the Civil Rights Act of 1964 (EEOC), the Occupational Safety and Health Act of 1970 (OSHA), and the Employee Retirement Income Security Act of 1974 (ERISA).[1] Our opinion is that this trend of an explosion of government regulations will continue through the 1980s and place further constraints on the options of supervisors. The purpose of this chapter is to address some of the challenges supervisors will face in the next decade.[2] Specifically, we will discuss the challenge of working with the disadvantaged, handicapped, and alcoholics.

To get a feel for the impact that federal legislation has had and will have on supervisors, please complete Exercise 17.1 at the end of this chapter.

SUPERVISOR'S COMMITMENT

Recent studies have indicated that top management professes to be more committed to hiring the disadvantaged than lower-level managers and supervisors.

One reason supervisors may be less committed to affirmative-action programs than top management in organizations is that a supervisor's effectiveness is usually measured by hard productivity indicators such as units produced, quality of outputs, and absenteeism. Therefore, supervisors attempt to hire and retain the most skilled workers possible. Many disadvantaged employees need special training that can temporarily reduce the effectiveness of a work team if top management does not give extra support for supervisors who are committed to affirmative-action programs. Top management must set an example by encouraging supervisors who take the extra steps in helping disadvantaged employees.

---

[1]Wendell L. French, John E. Dittrich, and Robert A. Zawacki, *The Personnel Management Process: Cases on Human Resources Administration* (Boston: Houghton Mifflin, 1978), p. 327.
[2]We would like to acknowledge the efforts of Bobby Jones, Diana L. Butierrez, Carmen Abeyta, Jose Guerin, Donny Rome, Dena Massie, and Mike Sanchez who gave us their time and efforts to review this chapter.

DEFINITIONS AND THE LAW

The 1964 Civil Rights Act was a national statement against discrimination in occupations, facilities, public education, and voting. Of special interest to supervisors is Title VII of the act, Equal Employment Opportunity, which is specifically about employment. It states that organizations employing more than 25 workers, employment agencies, and unions cannot discriminate against any person for any reason. It specifically states that equal treatment must be given in hiring, firing, promotion, salary increases, working conditions, and training. Further, supervisors cannot discriminate because of race, color, religion, sex, or national origin.

In 1967, the act was amended to include age. The Age Discrimination Act became effective during June, 1968, and made it illegal to discriminate against job applicants from 45 to 65 years of age.

To enforce the provision of Title VII of the 1964 Civil Rights Act, Congress created the Equal Employment Opportunity Commission (EEOC). In its first year of operation, the EEOC received approximately 9000 cases of alleged discrimination. Some 60 percent of the cases concerned racial discrimination. After a complaint is filed, the EEOC attempts to obtain compliance with the law through conferences, persuasion, and negotiation. Since its beginning, it has been swamped with discrimination cases, overburdening its relatively small staff. During President Carter's term in office, however, he placed a renewed emphasis on affirmative-action programs and doubled the EEOC budget for fiscal year 1979. Since the election of President Reagan, there have been complaints that the EEOC is not receiving adequate financial support.

CHARACTERISTICS OF DISADVANTAGED PEOPLE

Disadvantaged people in the work force have some drawbacks that set them apart from other people. Supervisors must be aware of these drawbacks and handle them. Making believe that these differences do not exist does not help the disadvantaged employees or the supervisors. Distinguishing characteristics are:

> They may have experienced numerous failures in the past and in some instances expect to fail.
> They may strike out at the very person who is trying to help them. They may distrust supervisors who attempt to help them and may be suspicious of businesses' motives.
> Many disadvantaged are typically without usable skills from the viewpoint of the organization.[3] Therefore, supervisors may have to give special attention to their training needs and the upgrading of their usable skills.

---

[3]Leonard Nadler, "Helping the Hard-Core Adjust to the World of Work," *Harvard Business Review* 48 (March-April, 1970):117.

GUIDELINES FOR HIRING AND RETAINING THE DISADVANTAGED

Supervisors must be committed to hiring, training, and retaining the disadvantaged. Subordinates are very sensitive to cues from supervisors and coworkers, and many will misinterpret negative cues about affirmative-action programs. The majority working group may interpret the negative response from the disadvantaged worker as just the excuse they need to covertly oppose an affirmative-action program.

Supervisors must function as positive role models, for all employees, through their actions and their statements.

The joining-up process is critical for disadvantaged employees. Supervisors must make an extra effort to establish two-way communication.

Supervisors should be encouraged by the organization for effectively implementing a good affirmative-action program. The encouragement may consist of favorable publicity or recognition on the annual performance report.

Special training programs for disadvantaged employees may have to be established. These programs should include such topics as: working rules, company policies, benefits, expectations, and available counseling assistance.

Jobs for the disadvantaged should not be dead-end jobs. New employees should be able to identify with other people who have moved up in the organization by starting in similar jobs.

The disadvantaged worker usually needs frequent recognition on the new job.[4] Supervisors must commend them for task accomplishment and be sensitive to their need for success.

Ideally, organizations should have a yearly affirmative-action workshop for all managers and supervisors. Topics to be discussed are: goals and timetables, progress toward goals, the law, and the need for management commitment. We recognize that this may not be financially practical in small businesses.

Supervisors must be alert for possible signs of withdrawal from the work group by disadvantaged employees.

Get unions involved in the program. Because of past discrimination, disadvantaged employees may have to be encouraged to apply for skilled jobs typically held by union members.

Supervisors must communicate, communicate, communicate. An effective affirmative-action program requires two-way communication and support from all members of the organization.

HIRING AND RETAINING THE HANDICAPPED

The 1973 Rehabilitation Act identifies the handicapped as a disadvantaged group within our society, and supervisors should be sensitive to their special needs. Generally,

[4]James D. Hodgson and Marshall H. Brenner, "Successful Experience: Training Hard-Core Unemployed," *Harvard Business Review* 46 (September-October, 1968): 148–156.

business leaders have discovered that this group can make a meaningful contribution to organizations providing some commonsense guidelines are followed.[5]

Use a "total approach" when designing an affirmative-action program.

Design a handicap-awareness program. All of the organization's personnel must be aware of the company's task in understanding the handicapped employee's needs as a proper foundation for implementing the program.

Schedule training seminars to educate all workers. One of the primary objectives of the seminar is to develop an awareness in supervisors that they must treat all handicapped workers as human beings with unique assets and problems. Don't let supervisors get trapped into stereotyping the handicapped. The two most common stereotypes are

1. *The superhuman stereotype.* This view is that the handicapped are so thankful for a job that they will put forth a superior effort, work longer hours, and have above-average productivity. The disadvantage of this sort of stereotyping is that it sets high expectations about the handicapped that may not be met. The handicapped are people who perform just like other human beings—some are above average and some are below average.
2. *The umbrella stereotype.* Many people think that all handicapped people are alike and belong to a homogeneous group. Supervisors must give attention to the uniqueness of each individual and recognize that each handicapped person has unique needs and aspirations. The handicapped should be assigned jobs according to their skills and not be grouped in one department.

Establish outreach contacts with public and private organizations that assist the handicapped. Inform these agencies of your organization's program and objectives.

Draw up a job inventory. Look at the requirements of present jobs to see if the manual requirements (dexterity, etc.) are really needed to accomplish a job. Also, look for and create new jobs that can be performed by the handicapped. The experience of firms employing the handicapped is that supervisors should attempt to give the handicapped whole jobs rather than pieces of jobs. Whole jobs can increase worker satisfaction.

Do an architectural inventory. Even the best awareness program is a failure if the disabled employee cannot get to work. Develop an accessibility plan and assign responsibility for removing any employment barriers.

Establish a follow-up and counseling program. Follow-up, especially by managers and supervisors, is the key to the success of the program. Personal follow-up by top management will demonstrate to the workers that the organization is committed to employing the handicapped in respectable and meaningful jobs.

---

[5]These guidelines are adapted from the program at C. & P. Telephone Company. For a description of their program, see Ted Bronson, "There's More to Affirmative Action Than Just Hiring 'The Handicapped'," *The Personnel Administrator* 23 (January, 1978): 18–21.

OCCUPATIONAL SAFETY AND HEALTH ADMINISTRATION

People are the most important resource in an organization; yet until 1970 there were no uniform and comprehensive policies to protect people at work from safety hazards. When Congress was considering legislation in 1970 to remedy this situation, some important statistics were:

Job-related accidents accounted for more than 14,000 worker deaths each year.
Nearly 2.5 million workers were disabled from job-related causes.
Ten times as many worker-days were lost annually from job-related disabilities as from strikes.
Estimated new cases of occupational diseases totaled 300,000 each year.[6]

Because of these problems, the Occupational Safety and Health Administration (OSHA) was established by law to:

Encourage employees to reduce hazards in the working place.
Establish a reporting and record-keeping system for work-related accidents.
Develop and enforce job safety and health standards.

The act covers all employers and their employees in the 50 states, the District of Columbia, Puerto Rico, the Canal Zone, and other federal territories. It does not cover self-employed persons or family farms. OSHA rules and standards are available free from the nearest office.

OSHA Regional Offices

REGION I (CT, ME, MA, NH, RI, VT)
18 Oliver Street
Boston, MA 02110
Telephone: (617) 223-6712

REGION II (NJ, NY, PR, VI, CZ)
Room 3445, 1 Astor Plaza
1515 Broadway
New York, NY 10036
Telephone: (212) 971-5941

REGION III (DE, DC, MD, PA, VA, WV)
15220 Gateway Center
3535 Market Street
Philadelphia, PA 19104
Telephone: (215) 596-1201

REGION IV (AL, FL, GA, KY, MS, NC, SC, TN)
1375 Peachtree Street N.E.,
Suite 587
Atlanta, GA 30309
Telephone: (404) 526-3573

REGION V (IL, IN, MI, MN, OH, WI)
230 South Dearborn Street,
32nd Floor
Chicago, IL 60604
Telephone: (312) 353-4716

REGION VI (AR, LA, NM, OK, TX)
555 Griffin Square, Room 602
Dallas, TX 75202
Telephone: (214) 749-2477

[6]U.S. Department of Labor, Occupational Safety and Health Administration, *All About OSHA* (Washington, DC: U.S. Government Printing Office, 1976), p. 1.

REGION VII (IA, KS, MO, NE)
911 Walnut Street, Room 3000
Kansas City, MO 64106
Telephone: (816) 758-5861

REGION VIII (CO, MT, ND, SD,
    UT, WY)
Federal Building, Room 15010
1961 Stout Street
Denver, CO 80202
Telephone: (303) 837-3883

REGION IX (AZ, CA, HI, NV)
Box 36017
450 Golden Gate Avenue
San Francisco, CA 04102
Telephone: (415) 556-0586

REGION X (AK, ID, OR, WA)
Federal Office Building, Room
    6048
909 First Avenue
Seattle, WA 98174
Telephone: (206) 442-5930

When OSHA was first established, there were some unfortunate cases in which OSHA officials "overenforced" the act and caused many employers to react negatively to the federal agency. However, lately it appears the agency has been enforcing the act in a more reasonable and acceptable manner. Under the act, the employer has a number of specific responsibilities and rights.[7]

Responsibilities

As an employer, you must:

Meet your general duty responsibility to provide a hazard-free work place and comply with the occupational safety and health standards, rules, and regulations issued under the act.

Be familiar with mandatory OSHA standards and make copies available to employees for review upon request.

Inform all employees about OSHA.

Examine conditions in the work place to make sure they conform to applicable safety and health standards.

Remove or guard hazards.

Make sure employees have and use safe tools and equipment (including personal protective equipment) and that such equipment is properly maintained.

Use color codes, posters, labels, or signs to warn employees of potential hazards.

Establish or update operating procedures and communicate them so that employees follow safety and health requirements for their own protection.

Provide medical examinations when required by OSHA standards.

Report to the nearest OSHA office, *within 48 hours,* the occurrence of any employment accident that is fatal to one or more employees or results in the hospitalization of five or more employees.

Keep OSHA-required records of work-related injuries and illnesses, and post the annual summary during the entire month of February each year. (This applies to employers with eight or more employees.)

[7]Ibid., pp. 28–30.

Post, at a prominent location within the work place, the OSHA poster (OSHA 2203) informing employees of their rights and responsibilities. (In states operating OSHA-approved job safety and health programs, the state's equivalent poster and/or OSHA 2203 may be required.)

Cooperate with an OSHA compliance officer by furnishing names of authorized employee representatives who may be asked to accompany the compliance officer during inspection. (If no representative has been nominated, the compliance officer will consult with a reasonable number of employees concerning safety and health in the work place.)

Not discriminate against employees who properly exercise their rights under the act.

Post OSHA citations of apparent violations of standards or of the general duty clause at or near the work site involved. Each citation, or copy thereof, shall remain posted until the violation has been abated, or for three working days, whichever is longer.

Abate cited violations within the prescribed period.

Rights

As an employer, you have the right to:

Seek advice and off-site consultation as needed by writing, calling, or visiting the nearest OSHA office. (OSHA will not inspect merely because an employer requests assistance.)

Be active in your industry association's involvement in job safety and health.

Request and receive proper identification of the OSHA compliance officer prior to inspection of the work place.

Be advised by the compliance officer of the reason for an inspection.

Have an opening and closing conference with the compliance officer.

File a notice of contest with the nearest OSHA area director within 15 working days of receipt of a notice of citation and proposed penalty.

Apply to OSHA for a temporary variance from a standard if unable to comply because of the unavailability of materials, equipment, or personnel to make necessary changes within the required time.

Apply to OSHA for a permanent variance from a standard if you can furnish proof that your facilities or method of operation provide employee protection that is at least as effective as that required by the standard.

Take an active role in developing job safety and health standards through participation in OSHA standards advisory committees, through nationally recognized standards-setting organizations, and through evidence and views presented in writing or at hearings.

Avail yourself, if you are a small business employer, of long-term loans through the Small Business Administration (SBA) to help bring your establishment into compliance, either before or after an OSHA inspection.

Be assured of the confidentiality of any trade secrets observed by an OSHA compliance officer during an inspection.

ALCOHOLISM[8]

Alcoholism is one of the leading causes of absenteeism in industry. From 5 to 7 percent of the U.S. adult population, and 7.7 percent of production and service employees in the United States, have a drinking problem. In the past it has been generally ignored by supervisors or considered a problem that the employees can correct if they want to. This approach by management assumed that alcoholism was an individual problem and not an organizational problem. Recently, the management of more progressive firms has recognized that alcoholism is a progressive illness that can be successfully treated. Normally, upon medical diagnosis of alcoholism or drug abuse, corporations provide assistance to the employee in a variety of ways—insurance coverage where possible, medical or annual leaves, and job reassignments if necessary. Continued employment usually depends upon the individual's responsible pursuit of treatment and successful rehabilitation. The organization follows the progress of the affected individual and documents this progress. Medical authorities are normally consulted on the diagnosis and progress. Figure 17.1 shows the stages of alcoholism and Figure 17.2 shows the behavior pattern of an alcoholic employee.

ROLE OF THE SUPERVISOR

The key to the successful motivation of an employee with alcoholism to accept treatment lies in the supervisor's use of the company's disciplinary procedures in a corrective manner. The social and moral stigma associated with alcoholism produces a reluctance on the part of sufferers to admit their problem. In most cases, employees with alcoholism are aware that their drinking is unlike that of most of their friends. As the disease progresses, they become increasingly aware that their drinking is becoming more uncontrollable. Such employees generally know that if they continue to drink, they will continue to have trouble with their jobs. If they could control their drinking, they would. They try and fail repeatedly. Thus, lectures or threats from anyone regarding drinking are as useless as advice to a tubercular patient to stop coughing. Logic will arrest neither of these illnesses. Yet efforts to arrest alcoholism through lectures, threats, setting of time limits of 30 to 90 days in which to "shape up," and "last chances" continue to be quite common. None of these methods works because none of them motivates the employee toward the one essential element—specialized treatment.

Experience with many cases has also demonstrated that a mere offer of treatment is as ineffectual as a lecture or repeated chances, since it does not, by itself, outweigh the intense fear of social stigma. Thus, both assurance that the acceptance of treatment

[8]The information in this section is presented with the generous permission of John Cardon, director of personnel, Hewlett-Packard Corporation, Logics Systems Division. Mary Mittman contributed many of the ideas and concepts used in Hewlett-Packard's progressive alcohol program.

Figure 17.1 Stages of Alcoholism. Adapted from "Policy and Procedures for Employees with a Drinking Problem," *Supervisor's Guide,* Hewlett-Packard Corp., undated.

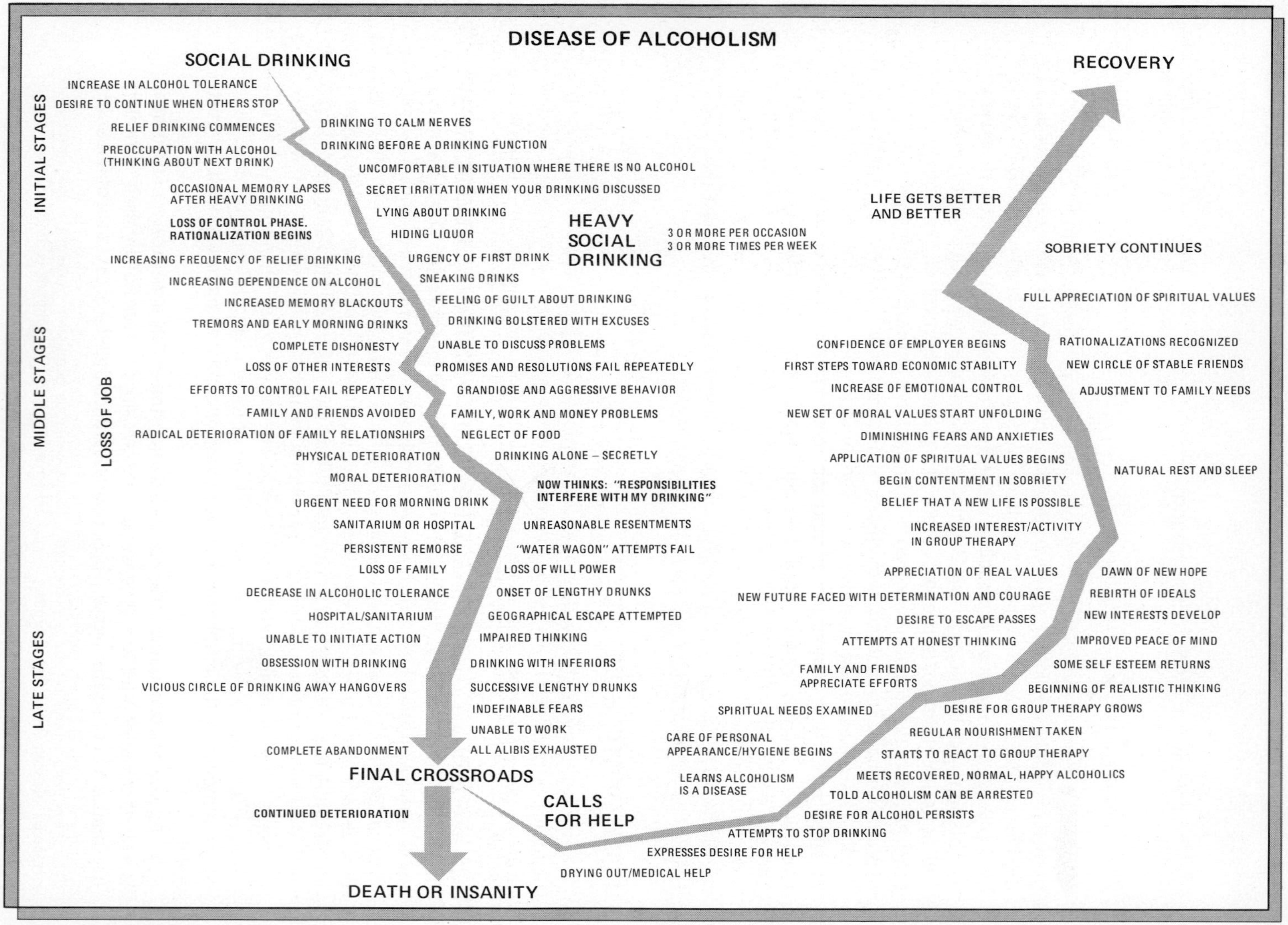

Figure 17.2 How an alcoholic employee behaves. Adapted from "Policy and Procedures for Employees with a Drinking Problem," *Supervisor's Guide,* Hewlett-Packard Corp., undated.

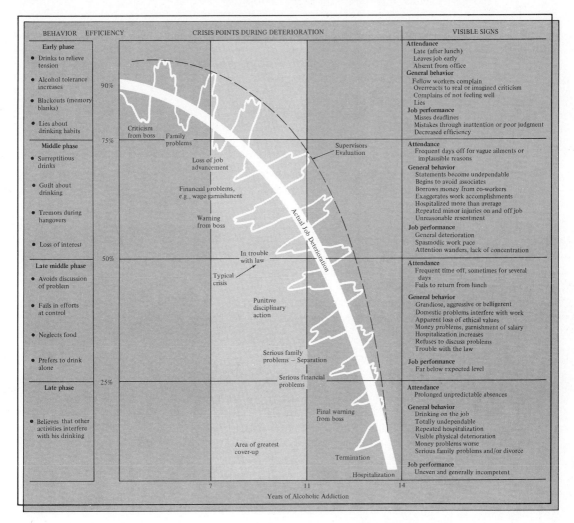

will not result in job loss and pressure to seek treatment are needed to outweigh this fear.

Industry has a legitimate tool that is currently being used with great success by a number of corporations to provide this needed pressure. It is provided through realistic and uniformly firm utilization of existing disciplinary procedures. When any illness adversely affects job performance, the company will benefit by taking corrective action, and the supervisor can take this corrective action without special knowledge of the causative illness.

In summary, the pretreatment phase of an alcoholism program can be effectively implemented by all levels of supervision through careful and thorough discharge of the responsibilities regarding employee performance.

What the Supervisor Should Look For

Patterns of excessive absenteeism, especially on Mondays, Fridays, and days before and after holidays

Unexcused absences

Frequent absences—particularly for colds, flu, bronchitis, sore throats, "peculiar" accidents on and off the job, and "family problems"

Wage attachments or other involvements with the law

Altercations with fellow employees

Deteriorating personal appearance

Odor of stale alcohol on breath in the morning, often covered by breath fresheners

"Drinking lunch" and prolonged lunch hours

Frequent disappearances at morning and afternoon coffee breaks, with obvious aftereffects

Increasingly poor judgment

Increasing spoilage

Increasing customer complaints

Tardiness and early departures

Dos and Don'ts for the Supervisor

Don't try to diagnose the problem.

Don't discuss drinking unless it occurs on the job or a person reports to work obviously drunk.

Don't moralize. Restrict criticism to job performance or attendance.

Don't be misled by sympathy-evoking tactics at which the alcoholic becomes an expert.

Don't cover up for a friend. A misguided kindness can lead to a serious delay in obtaining real help. Remember, you are not a stool pigeon if you call the fire department when you see your neighbor's house on fire!

Do remember that alcoholism is a progressive disease. It always gets worse, never better, without treatment.

Do make it clear that you are concerned with job performance. Unless job performance improves, the job is in jeopardy.

Do explain that the *employee* must decide whether or not to seek assistance.

Do emphasize that all aspects of the program are completely confidential.

Special Help for the Supervisor

Many supervisors try to go it alone with alcoholics. In most large corporations there are two additional resources that the supervisor should consult:

1. *The medical department* is available for consultation and guidance in medical problems, including alcoholism. A health counselor may be available in the medical department to assist employees with the problem in obtaining treatment and in maintaining sobriety. In small organizations, supervisors should consult with the company doctor or contact a local or state mental health agency.
2. *The personnel department* is available for consultation regarding sick leave, medical plan coverage, and severance procedures if indicated.

SUMMARY

In the next decade, supervisors will frequently face the challenge of working with the disadvantaged, the handicapped, and alcoholics.

More and more of these people have been brought into the work force since the 1964 Civil Rights Act, especially as a result of Title VII of the act, which created the Equal Employment Opportunity Commission (EEOC). Supervisors must be sensitive to the needs of disadvantaged people and give special attention to their needs during the interviewing, training, and upgrading processes.

In 1973 the Rehabilitation Act included the handicapped as a disadvantaged group within our society. Overall, managers of organizations have discovered that this group can make meaningful contributions to companies, providing some sensitive guidelines are followed.

In 1970 Congress established the Occupational Safety and Health Administration (OSHA) to encourage employers to reduce hazards in the working place, to establish a reporting and record-keeping system for work-related accidents, and to develop and enforce job safety and health standards. When OSHA was first established it may have "overenforced" the third objective. Lately, however, the agency has been enforcing the act in a more responsible manner.

Alcoholism is one of the leading causes of absenteeism in industry. In the past it has generally been ignored by supervisors and considered a problem that employees can correct if they want to. More and more organizations are now adopting a policy that alcoholism is a disease and that the supervisor and organization have an obligation to help the alcoholic employee. Sensitive but firm counseling is advisable.

IMPORTANT TERMS

OSHA	handicapped
ERISA	EEOC
1964 Civil Rights Act	1973 Rehabilitation Act
disadvantaged people	alcoholism

REVIEW QUESTIONS

1. Explain the statement, "Since the early 1960s the federal government has become increasingly involved in the management of organizations."
2. What are the characteristics of disadvantaged people?
3. Why is the joining-up process critical for disadvantaged employees?
4. What federal act identifies the handicapped as a disadvantaged group?
5. What are the responsibilities of an employer to the Occupational Safety and Health Administration (OSHA)?
6. Is alcoholism a disease? Explain your answer.
7. What should the supervisor look for to spot a possible alcoholic?

EXERCISE

Answer if each of the following practices is lawful or unlawful.

17.1 How Much Can You Legally Ask?*

1. Asking the applicant if he or she has ever worked under another name.
2. Asking the applicant to name his or her birthplace.
3. Asking for the birthplace of the applicant's parents, spouse, or other close relatives.
4. Asking the applicant to submit proof of age by supplying birth certificate or baptismal record.
5. Asking the applicant for religious affiliation, name of church, parish, or religious holidays observed.
6. Asking the applicant if he or she is a citizen of the United States.
7. Asking the applicant if he or she is a naturalized citizen.
8. Asking the applicant for the date citizenship was acquired.
9. Asking the applicant if he or she has ever been arrested for any crime and to indicate when and where.
10. Asking the applicant to indicate what foreign languages he or she can read, write, or speak fluently.
11. Asking the applicant how the ability to read, write, or speak a foreign language was acquired.
12. Asking the applicant about past work experience.
13. Requesting the applicant to provide names of three relatives other than father, husband or wife, or minor-age dependent children.
14. Asking the applicant for his wife's maiden name.
15. Asking for the maiden name of an applicant's mother.
16. Asking for the full names of the applicant's brothers and sisters.
17. Asking the applicant for a list of names of all clubs, societies, and lodges to which the applicant belongs.

*From Robert L. Menter, "Human Rights Laws and Pre-Employment Inquiries," *Personnel Journal,* June, 1972. Copyright 1972. Reprinted with permission.

Exhibit   **353**

18. Asking the applicant to include a photograph with the application for employment.
19. Asking the applicant to supply addresses of relatives, such as cousins, uncles, aunts, nephews, grandparents, who can be contacted for references.

Answers appear in Exhibit 17.1.

EXHIBIT

17.1   Answers to Exercise 17.1

Only inquiries 6, 10, and 12 are lawful.

Inquiry 1 is unlawful. There are only a few exceptions in which this inquiry would be considered lawful. The organization *can* ask for this information if the applicant had previously worked for them under a different name. If the applicant is female, the company can usually request that she indicate her maiden name.

Inquiries 2, 3, 4, and 5 are unlawful. Answers obtained could reveal the national origin, race, creed, or color of an applicant. An exception to this would be when information of this nature is required as a *bona fide occupational qualification* for reasons of national or state security.

Inquiry 6 is lawful. Organizations subject to Title VII of the Civil Rights Act of 1964 *must* ask the applicant if he or she is a citizen of the United States. Firms are also permitted to ask the applicant (1) if he or she intends to become a United States citizen and (2) if he or she has legal sanction to remain in the United States.

Inquiries 7 and 8 are unlawful. These two inquiries are incidental to an applicant's ability to perform required on-the-job duties and could easily establish race, creed, or national origin of an applicant.

Inquiry 9 is unlawful. Recent federal legislation prohibits asking applicants if they have ever been arrested. However, asking for *convictions* of crimes, date, place, and disposition of offenses is permissible.

Inquiry 10 is lawful, but *inquiry 11* is unlawful. An organization is within legal sanction to ask an applicant *what* foreign languages he or she is capable of reading, writing, or speaking (inquiry 10); these abilities can be acquired through study and do not necessarily reveal race, creed, color, or national origin. Inquiring *how* the applicant acquired these abilities is often considered an illegal preemployment practice, as this could easily determine ethnic background (inquiry 11). The *what* and *how* nature of these questions is an important element to be aware of when making preemployment inquiries that would directly or indirectly establish ethnic background characteristics of the applicant.

Inquiry 12 is lawful. This information is necessary for an organization to assess individual work experience and overall qualifications for a particular position.

Inquiries 13, 14, 15, and 16 are unlawful. Questions of this nature are usually not permissible, for they may reveal national origin, race, creed, or color of the applicant, spouse, or kin.

Inquiry 17 is unlawful. Asking the applicant to provide a specific list of names of lodges, fraternal organizations, and clubs of which he is a member could easily reveal the individual's ethnic background, religious beliefs, or color. However, the applicant *can* be asked to indicate membership in organizations that are *not* based on ethnic or religious membership practices.

Inquiry 18 is unlawful. This type of inquiry is prohibited in many states in order to protect the applicant from having recruiters make assumptions based on racial or personality stereotypes, drawn from physical characteristics in the photograph, prior to the interview.

Inquiry 19 is unlawful. Although this is considered unlawful in many states, the organization *can* ask the applicant to supply addresses of parents, spouse, or minor-age children who are living within the United States.

CASES

17.1   Alcohol on the Breath

Topics Electronics is a large manufacturing firm in the microelectronics industry. Their manufacturing facility is located in the Rocky Mountain area, and they employ approximately 650 people. Dr. Mark Thomas is chief scientist and executive vice-president for production. He is known in the business for his outstanding technical knowledge, and he recently wrote a major textbook on microelectronics. Mark's supervisor, Robert, has recently noticed that Mark has been late for some important meetings, his reports are not as timely as they once were, and he has the smell of alcohol on him when he returns from lunch. Overall, however, Mark's performance has been satisfactory.

Late one evening, Robert received a telephone call from Mark's wife stating that Mark had been placed in the hospital and diagnosed as an alcoholic. He was very ill; however, he would recover and was now very embarrassed by the unfavorable publicity he had drawn upon himself and his family.

Robert comforted Mark's wife and assured her that he would visit Mark the next day. As Robert hung up the telephone, he was shocked and wondered what he would say to Mark and his spouse the following day.

Questions

1. What advice do you have for Robert when he faces Mark?
2. Is alcoholism a disease?
3. Is the corporation responsible for helping alcoholics recover?
4. Describe the counseling relationship that you would establish with Mark.
5. How does Mark's spouse fit into this counseling program?

17.2   Drugs for Sale

Carol Anne is an employee for a fast-food chain. She is 17 years old, has worked for the company for about six months, and is considered an above-average performer by her shift supervisor and the store manager.

One night during the late shift Carol was approached by Susan Sparks, another employee, and asked if she wanted to buy some cocaine. Carol's reaction was one of shock and disbelief because Susan had a reputation for being a hard worker who was straight. Carol questioned Susan further and there was no doubt in Carol's mind that Susan was pushing drugs.

During Carol's 10-minute break that evening she approached her shift supervisor and told him about the incident. He thanked her for reporting the incident to him and told her to go back to work.

Carol's shift supervisor was a 22-year-old male named Doug Johnson. Doug had been with the company approximately two years and had worked very hard to become a shift supervisor. The practice in this company is to promote the best workers to shift supervisor. Most shift supervisors lacked practical experience and formal training in management.

About five days after reporting the incident, Carol casually asked Doug if he had reported Susan to top management. Doug responded that he had not and really did not know what to do at this time.

Questions

1. Was Carol right in reporting Susan? Evaluate the risk that she took.
2. What do you recommend Doug do at this time?

SUGGESTED ADDITIONAL READINGS

American Assembly. "Women and the American Economy." *Report of the Forty-ninth American Assembly,* October 30–November 2, 1975.

Andrewson, Dale E. "Arbitral Views of Alcoholism Cases." *Personnel Journal* (May, 1979), pp. 318–322.

Bergmann, Barbara R., and Krause, William R. "Evaluating and Forecasting Progress in Racial Integration of Employment." *Industrial and Labor Relations Review* 25 (April, 1972): 399–409.

Blitz, Rudolph C. "Women in the Professions, 1870–1970." *Monthly Labor Review* 97 (May, 1974): 34–39.

Boulding, Kenneth E. "Role Prejudice as an Economic Problem." *Monthly Labor Review* 97 (August, 1974): 40.

Bright, William E. "How One Company Manages Its Human Resources." *Harvard Business Review* 54 (January–February, 1976): 81–93.

Bronson, Ted. "There's More to Affirmative Action Than Hiring 'The Handicapped'." *The Personnel Administrator* 23 (January, 1978): 18–21.

Cruz, Daisy. "Affirmative Action at Work." *Personnel Journal* 55 (May, 1976): 226–227ff.

Domm, Donald R., and Staffor, James E. "Assimilating Blacks into the Organization." *California Management Review* 15 (Fall, 1972): 46–51.

Golembiewski, Robert T. "Testing Some Stereotypes about the Sexes in Organizations: Differential Centrality of Work?" *Human Resources Management* 16 (Winter, 1977): 21–24.

Hayghe, Howard. "Families and the Rise of Working Wives—An Overview." *Monthly Labor Review* 99 (May, 1976): 12–19.

Hedges, Janice N., and Bemis, Stephen E. "Sex Stereotyping: Its Decline in Skilled Trades." *Monthly Labor Review* 97 (May, 1974): 14–21.

Holley, William H., and Field, Hubert S. "Equal Employment Opportunity and Its Implications for Personnel Practices." *Labor Law Journal* 27 (1976): 278–286.

Kilaael, Timothy M. "A Three-Step Plan for Implementing an Affirmative Action Program." *The Personnel Administrator* 21 (July, 1976): 35–39.

Nathanson, Robert B. "The Disabled Employee: Separating Myth from Fact." *Harvard Business Review* 55 (May–June, 1977): 6–8.

"New Slant in Minority Recruitment." *Business Week,* April 8, 1977, pp. 74–78.

Pati, Gopal C. "Countdown on Hiring the Handicapped." *Personnel Journal* 57 (March, 1978): 144–153.

———, and Reilly, Charles W. "Reversing Discrimination: A Perspective." *Human Resources Management* 16 (Winter, 1977): 21–24.

Purcell, Theodore V., and Webster, Rosalind. "Window on the Hard-Core World." *Harvard Business Review* 47 (July–August, 1969): 118–129.

Schneider, B. *Staffing Organization.* Pacific Palisades, CA: Goodyear, 1976.

Sue, Stanley; Sue, Derald W.; and Sue, David W. "Asian Americans as a Minority Group." *American Psychologist* 30 (September, 1975): 906–910.

Torrey, Jane W. "The Consequences of Equal Opportunity for Women." *Journal of Contemporary Business* 5 (Winter, 1976): 13–27.

U.S. Department of Labor. "A Manpower Profile of the Spanish Speaking." *Manpower Report of the President.* Washington, DC: U.S. Government Printing Office, 1973, pp. 87–89.

18

Labor Relations

The labor of a human being is not a commodity or article of commerce.

Clayton Antitrust Act

OBJECTIVES

This chapter provides you with the information necessary to:

1. Describe the current status of the American labor movement
2. List why workers join unions
3. Describe union shops and right-to-work laws
4. Identify what supervisors can say and cannot say during the unionization process
5. Become familiar with guidelines for grievances
6. List the steps in the grievance process

LABOR RELATIONS COMPONENTS

In the United States, good labor relations is important to supervisors because they have a direct effect on worker productivity. Generally, *labor relations* consists of three main parts: the *unionization process,* the *negotiation process,* and the *grievance process.* Although the first two are important for supervisors, the grievance process is the key to good labor relations for supervisors because this is where misunderstandings and abuses of the contract are resolved. Before we discuss these processes, we will present a few facts about the American labor movement.

THE AMERICAN LABOR MOVEMENT: CURRENT STATUS AND PROBLEMS

Union membership (including associations) engaged in collective bargaining constitutes about 22 percent of the employees in nonagricultural establishments. *17 today*

In 1981 there were 22,228,000 union members.

Two of the largest unions that do not belong to the AFL-CIO are:

Teamsters — *ruled by judge*

United Auto Workers

now back in

Union membership, as a percentage of employees in nonagricultural firms, has been declining since 1953. Between 1978 and 1981 union membership dropped 652,000.

Female union membership has been increasing in recent years.

Union officials are giving more and more attention to organizing white-collar workers.

The percentage of the American labor force in professions, services, and clerical and related areas is expected to increase through the 1990s.

Workers in the public sector are joining unions and openly discussing their "right to strike."

While the American population increased at a rate of 19 percent from 1966 to 1976, the labor force increased at a rate of 26 percent.

During the same 10-year period, the male labor force increased by 16.8 percent, while the female labor force went up a dramatic 42.3 percent.

Lack of jobs for minorities is still a problem—especially at the supervisory level and in inner cities.

THE UNIONIZATION PROCESS

Workers join unions for numerous reasons. One obvious reason is to increase their pay and fringe benefits. Other reasons are: (1) to increase job security, (2) to protect themselves against arbitrary supervisors, (3) to obtain a voice in conditions of employment, (4) to meet social and fraternal needs, and (5) to satisfy mandatory requirements.

Before we discuss the unionization process, two types of laws will be defined: *union-shop agreements* and *right-to-work laws.* Union-shop agreements exist in about 30 states and basically state that a worker can be required to join a union as a condition for continued employment with the firm. Many states, especially in the South and Southwest, have also enacted right-to-work laws, which guarantee that a worker cannot be required to join a union as a condition for employment. These states have right-to-work laws (subject to changing legislation—check your state):

Alabama	Nevada
Arizona	North Carolina
Arkansas	North Dakota
Florida	South Carolina

Georgia	South Dakota
Indiana	Tennessee
Iowa	Texas
Kansas	Utah
Mississippi	Virginia
Nebraska	

The first phases of the unionization process are relatively quiet and normally involve a few employees meeting in the evening with union representatives. If the organizers believe that there is support for their union, they will begin to advertise the need for a union and attempt to sign up 30 percent of all employees. This phase of the process usually becomes more emotional, and supervisors must be very careful about the statements they make. Many supervisors and managers feel that the call for a union is a direct threat to their authority and self-esteem and become very defensive about the organization process. Good supervisors should not be threatened; they should be reviewing the guidelines on what they *may* say and *may not* say. This is no time for an emotional comment. Anything supervisors say can be—and will be—used against them.

If 30 percent of the employees request a union, the regional office of the National Labor Relations Board is petitioned to supervise the election. A majority of the votes cast by the employees in the firm is necessary for the NLRB to proclaim the union as the official bargaining agent.

What Supervisors Cannot Say or Do

Warn, or even hint, that they will take action against subordinates for choosing a union.
Make hidden threats or promises.
Avoid trying to answer union charges.
Threaten to curtail operations.
Threaten that union organizers will be worse off in the future.
Warn that unionization will result in loss of benefits.
Spy on the union.
Go to a union meeting.
Question employees about views or union activities.

What Supervisors Can Say and Do

State opposition to having a union in the firm.
Explain why the union will be bad for the firm.
Answer union charges.
Emphasize the benefits of the company.
Express views on union policies, dues, and the checkoff system.
Explain that union membership is not required for future employment.

Urge employees to vote in the NLRB election.

Advise employees that they prefer to interact directly with them on a one-on-one basis. Unions may destroy supervisors' ability to reward individual merit.

THE GRIEVANCE PROCESS

After a successful unionization drive, the *collective bargaining* process is completed with a *union-management contract* that becomes the guide for supervisors. Supervisors must study the contract. Examples of typical items in union-management contracts are:

Management options	Absenteeism
Union recognition	Contract length
Arbitration and mediation	Discharge and layoff
Discipline	Discrimination
Grievances	Seniority
Hours of work	Dues checkoff
Wages	Job posting
Vacations and holidays	Transfers
Overtime	Strikes
Renewal options	Sick leave
Rest periods	Work load
Retirement	Work clothes
Tardiness	Fringe benefits

Although good supervisors are not labor relations experts, they must know what to do when a grievance is filed and the personnel department cannot be contacted. A *grievance* is an alleged violation of the rights of the workers on the job. A list of some helpful guidelines for supervisors follows. (See also Figure 18.1.)

Grievance Guidelines

Supervisors have an obligation to protect management's rights to manage the organization. Be firm but fair and consistent.

Figure 18.1 Steps in the grievance process.

Step	Union Representative	Organization Representative
1.	Worker and union steward	Supervisor
2.	Chief steward	Supervisor's manager or plant manager
3.	Grievance committee chairperson	Personnel manager
4.	Grievance committee chairperson and national union representative	Top management
5.	Arbitration by an impartial third party	

Work with the union. The supervisor is the key link between management and the union steward.

Supervisors must be interested in any worker dissatisfaction and must be especially sensitive to a formal grievance.

Assume that the union steward and all other union leaders have the best interests of the workers in mind and are sincerely interested in improving the satisfaction and production of the work place. If they prove otherwise, then change your stand.

Approach each situation with the union in a positive, helping frame of mind.

Read and reread the contract—there is no substitute for knowledge. The union representative will respect expertise.

When a true impasse is reached between a supervisor and the union steward, forward the grievance through the procedures and channels specified in the contract.

Keep informal records and memorandums about counseling sessions and discipline problems. Good supervisors soon learn to document potential problem areas and to file those memos in a safe place. Informal files are very helpful at formal hearings or reviews.

Be alert for dissatisfaction before it becomes a formal complaint. Sometimes it may be necessary to ask for help from a third party, such as personnel, to identify potential communication and motivation problems.

If a supervisor and union steward can resolve a complaint in the early stages, the entire organization can save a lot of energy and money. Formal complaints are time-consuming and costly. Grievances should be settled as close to the problem as possible.

Supervisors are not labor relations experts. Although they should understand the contract, they should also seek advice from the labor specialists in the personnel department.

SUMMARY

Labor relations involves the unionization process, the negotiation process, and the grievance process. Some reasons workers join unions are to increase job security, to protect themselves against arbitrary supervisors, to obtain a voice in working conditions, to meet social needs, and to increase pay and fringe benefits. Supervisors must be very careful of what they say during the unionization process.

The grievance-arbitration process is very complex, and the supervisor should contact the personnel manager when a grievance is filed. However, the supervisor should also attempt to resolve the problem on an informal basis as quickly as possible. Formal complaints are time-consuming and costly. If a supervisor and worker or shop steward can resolve a problem in the early stages, the entire organization can save a lot of energy and money.

IMPORTANT TERMS

labor relations
unionization process
negotiation process
grievance process
union-shop agreements

right-to-work laws
collective bargaining
union-management contract
grievance

REVIEW QUESTIONS

1. Describe the three main parts of labor relations.
2. Describe a typical grievance process.
3. Discuss current problems in the American labor movement.
4. What is a right-to-work law?
5. Why must supervisors be careful about what statements they make during the unionization process?
6. Explain this statement: "Grievances should be settled by supervisors as close to the problem as possible."
7. Find out how one organization in your community handles grievances.

CASE

18.1 Union Problems

Carol Anne Hadley was in a tough position. She was hired two years ago by a large western insurance headquarters to be an internal change agent. When she was hired, the chief executive officer informed her that one of her measures of effectiveness would be her ability to keep the employees from voting for a union. The CEO had attended a management workshop titled "How to Keep the Union Out" and firmly believed that if managers and supervisors were doing their jobs, there would be no need for a union. He further informed Carol Anne that with her humanistic training from a good college she should be able to train supervisors to be more sensitive to the workers' needs and goals.

After two years as an internal change agent, Carol Anne felt that she had not really changed anything in the firm. Her analysis of her lack of success indicated several factors:

1. Top management was not committed to change—"We have a change agent—let her do it."
2. She lacked real power to implement change.
3. Supervisors were generally dragging their feet about making improvements.

Yesterday she saw a union handbill that indicated that a group of workers was attempting to organize for collective bargaining. Carol Anne felt an obligation to tell the CEO as soon as possible; however, she also wanted to prepare him for the potential organizing process by briefing him on what he could and could not say during the union's campaign. In addition, she feared for her job.

Questions

1. Can Carol Anne do anything to keep the union out? What would you do if you were in her position?
2. What advice should she give to the CEO?
3. Why have the supervisors been dragging their feet about making improvements?
4. Within the limits of the law, what can the CEO do to influence the employees to vote against the union?

SUGGESTED ADDITIONAL READINGS

Adams, Alan E. "No Welcome Mat for Unions in the Sunbelt." *Business Week,* May 17, 1976, pp. 108–111.

———. "Unions Step Up White-Collar Organization." *Banking* 66 (January, 1974): 12–13.

Berkwitt, George J. "Management—Sitting on a Time Bomb?" *Dun's Review,* July, 1972, pp. 28–41.

Bornstein, Leon. "Industrial Relations in 1976: Highlights of Key Settlements." *Monthly Labor Review* 100 (1977): 27–36.

Chamot, Denis. "Professional Employees Turn to Unions." *Harvard Business Review* 54 (May–June, 1976): 119–127.

Constantino, George E., Jr. "The Negotiator in Collective Bargaining." *Personnel Journal* 54 (August, 1975): 445–447.

French, Wendell L. *The Personnel Management Process,* 4th ed. Boston: Houghton Mifflin, 1978, pp. 465–535.

Jennings, Kenneth. "Arbitrators, Blacks, and Discipline." *Personnel Journal* 54 (January, 1975): 32–37ff.

Raphael, Edna E. "Working Women and Their Membership in Labor Unions." *Monthly Labor Review* 97 (May, 1974): 27–33.

Sloan, Arthur A., and Whitney, Fred. *Labor Relations,* 3d ed. Englewood Cliffs, NJ: Prentice-Hall, 1977.

19

Stress Management

Snoopy typing a story:
   And so our hero's life ended as it had begun—a disaster.
   "I never got any breaks," he had always complained. He
   wanted to be loved; he died unloved. He wanted laughter;
   he found only tears. He wanted to be rich; he died poor.
   He wanted friends; he died friendless. He wanted
   applause; he received only boos. He wanted fame; he
   found only obscurity. He wanted answers; he found only
   questions.
Snoopy considering his story:
   "I'm having a hard time ending this!"

Charles Schulz
"Peanuts"

OBJECTIVES

This chapter provides you with the information necessary to:

1. Define what stress is and understand its negative mental, emotional, physical, and behavioral consequences as well as its positive consequences when properly managed
2. Understand the ways in which people respond to stress and how you typically respond to stress
3. Identify the major causes of stress and evaluate the causes in your own life
4. Learn to prepare yourself to manage stress

---

5. Develop a short-range stress plan to manage everyday stress
6. Develop a long-range plan to minimize unnecessary stress in your life
7. Evaluate if you are a stress carrier and know what to do about it if you are

WHY STRESS MANAGEMENT IS SO IMPORTANT

Stress is becoming the number one health problem in the world today! The inability to manage stress successfully can substantially increase the likelihood of physical, psychological, and behavioral problems because of the malfunctioning it can cause in our mental, emotional, and physical systems. At work, unnecessary stress (stress that is dysfunctional) results in decreases in productivity, motivation, work quality, morale, judgment, and self-confidence, and increases in mistakes, accidents, absenteeism, turn-over, misunderstandings, conflicts, frictions within and between departments, and poor decisions. In fact, stress is estimated to cost U.S. industry over $17 billion a year.[1] Thus, stress can be very costly in our personal lives and is becoming increasingly costly to organizations as well.

Unfortunately, our lives are becoming more stressed rather than less, and this trend appears to be gaining in momentum rather than lessening. World, national, and local events; deteriorating economic conditions, led by inflation and decreasing individual productivity; environmental problems; a changing social structure; the breakdown of the family unit; the increase in divorce, alcoholism, and drug use; the liberalization of basic values; and a trend toward a society of takers and not givers—all are contributing to a stressful future.

Now the good news! Stress can have positive as well as negative consequences and does not have to be feared. For those who learn to manage stress successfully and constructively and eliminate or minimize the unnecessary stress in their lives, stress can be turned into an opportunity for increased effectiveness, growth, character development, motivation, and happiness. By learning to manage stress, you can improve your physical and psychological health, your performance, your ability to face and solve problems, and even your appearance and longevity.

THE TWOFOLD STRESS PROBLEM

Managing your own stress is only part of the problem. *Some people manage their stress by giving it away to others.* When we do this, we become "stress carriers." Stress carriers spread tension, create anxiety, and keep people on edge. In doing so, they may in fact get rid of their own stress, but they multiply their stress to others. So, managing stress is really a two-sided coin. This is especially true for supervisors, because their stress is multiplied through their employees.

---

[1]D. D. Warrick, "Managing the Stress of Organization Development," *Training and Development Journal,* April, 1981, pp. 37–41.

WHAT IS STRESS?

Stress is our *mental, emotional, physical,* and *behavioral* response to *anxiety-producing events.* It can result in serious physical, psychological, interpersonal or performance problems, or can result in increased alertness, effectiveness, and motivation. The amount of stress that we experience is based primarily on our ability to manage stress and secondarily on how much we have and how long we have it.

Our stress reaction includes four major responses:

1. Stress starts mentally when we perceive something as stressful. The way we process the event rationally or irrationally in our conscious or subconscious mind triggers harmful or adaptive emotional, physical, and behavioral responses. Negative thinking significantly increases the amount of stress that a person experiences because of the negative interpretations placed on events, regardless of whether the events themselves are positive or negative.
2. Our emotional response depends primarily on our mental response, changes in our body chemistry, and our "habitual" emotional response to different anxiety producing events. Our emotional response can increase the stress if we overreact or lose control of our feelings, or decrease the stress if we are aware of our feelings and are willing to process and express them constructively.
3. Physiologically, many things happen, including:
   a. Changes in the nervous system (voluntary activities in the central nervous system and involuntary activities in the autonomic nervous system that cause physiological changes) affecting organs, glands, muscles, and nerves.
   b. Changes in blood flow, blood pressure, and blood composition (pulse rate increases, amount of blood flow to organs and brain changes, vessels constrict and raise blood pressure, sugar and adrenaline flow into the bloodstream).
   c. Changes in glandular secretions (glands release adrenaline, cortisone, and other hormones, as well as toxins).
   d. Changes in breathing (breathing may become irregular).
4. Behaviorally we may respond by adapting with increased effectiveness and performance, or by behaving in erratic, unconstructive, self-defeating ways or, under excessive stress, by becoming immobilized.

MAJOR CAUSES OF STRESS

The causes of stress have been heavily researched in recent years. Two of the best studies were done by Beehr and Newman[2] and Schuler.[3] Figure 19.1 shows a listing of major personal and job stressors. While a list of stressors could be almost endless, there are in fact only two major causes of stress—stress-producing circumstances and our own stress-producing choices. Stress-producing circumstances include people,

[2]Terry A. Beehr and John Newman, "Job Stress, Employee Health, and Organizational Effectiveness: A Facet Analysis, Model, and Literature Review," *Personnel Psychology* 31 (1978): 665–699.
[3]Randall S. Schuler, "Definition and Conceptualization of Stress in Organizations," *Organization Behavior and Human Performance,* 24 (1982), pp. 184–215.

Figure 19.1 Personal and job stressors.

Personal Stressors	
Lack of purpose (no sense of direction, lack of worthwhile goals, lack of or confusion over religion) Attitude (negative, critical, cynical, self-centered), self-image Financial problems Death of or separation from someone close Divorce and problems associated with it Family problems with spouse, children, or relatives Change (job, residence, friends, status, living conditions, etc.) Personal problems (depression, discouragement, unresolved past events, undesirable habits, anger, bitterness, feeling unloved, loneliness, frustration, self-defeating actions, etc.) Conflict Lack of time	Lack of self-worth (feeling underutilized or undervalued, low self-image, etc.) Lack of control over circumstances Uncertainty Out-of-balance life-style (priorities out of balance, poor balance or choice of activities, too much or too little responsibility, etc.) Stressful environment (world and economic conditions, crime, lack of morality, noise, neighborhood, overcrowding, traffic, etc.) Stressful stage of life (feeling of lack of accomplishment, behind in career and life objectives, concerned about age, etc.) Fears (fear of failure, success, rejection, harm, etc.) Physical problems (poor health, pain, sleeping difficulties, poor condition, overweight, sexual problems, handicap, appearance, etc.)
Job Stressors	
Not feeling valued Tasks (overwork, underwork or boredom, uneven work load, unreasonable time constraints, lack of training, etc.) Management (ineffective, unfair, or excessive supervision) Role ambiguity (unclear responsibilities, expectations) Organization structure (unclear or unfair goals and policies, lack of organization and planning, too much red tape, lack of communication, too many or too few meetings, etc.)	Work climate (tense, unfriendly, unsupportive, unfair, untrusting, etc.) Working conditions (noise, poor pay, crowding, poor lighting, poor office layout, unpleasant decor, lack of space or privacy, frequent interruptions, inadequate supplies, poor fringe benefits, inadequate facilities, poor job security, etc.) Reward system (unfair, unclear guidelines, little opportunity for advancement, etc.) Social conditions (interpersonal conflicts, favoritism, cliques, too much or too little socialization)

events, problems, and situations that result in stress. Stress-producing choices include our own thoughts, feelings, physical conditions, and behaviors that result in stress.

Although we have a tendency to attribute most stress to circumstances, stress-producing choices are by far the bigger culprit. It isn't actual circumstances that cause us stress as much as our mental, emotional, physical, and behavioral responses to circumstances. Stress is primarily caused by our own irrational or negative thinking, our own lack of emotional self-control, our own abuse of our bodies, and our own unconstructive choices.

CONSEQUENCES OF STRESS MISMANAGEMENT

When people mismanage stress, they experience mental, emotional, physical, and behavioral consequences. Some of the potential consequences are shown in Figure 19.2. It is important to become familiar with these consequences for several reasons. First, it is important to realize the serious negative effects that stress can have if it is not properly managed. Also, if you can recognize when you are beginning to mismanage stress, you are at least in a position to take constructive actions for dealing successfully with it. Finally, you can begin to recognize stress symptoms in others, which should make you more sensitive to their needs and more understanding of their behaviors and also may enable you to offer needed assistance.

ADVANTAGES OF MANAGING STRESS

A study done by Laurence E. Hinkle, Jr., and his colleagues at Cornell University Medical College showed that rates of coronary heart disease were higher among nonmanagers than those in management. The findings were based on a five-year study in the Bell Telephone system that included 270,000 men.[4] This study and other similar studies have exploded the myth that people at executive levels experience the most stress in organizations. They may in fact have the most stress of any members of the organization, but they experience the least because of their ability to manage stress. How did these effective managers get into such key positions? The ability to manage stress is an important factor in getting promoted.

A famous study conducted by cardiologists Dr. Meyer Friedman and Dr. Ray Rosenman identified two types of behavioral patterns among executives.[5] Managers with Type A personalities live under constant stress that is primarily of their own making. They are always in a rush, are compulsive overworkers, and need to perform to prove themselves. They are impatient, nervous, restless, aggressive, ambitious, and competitive, and they play as hard as they work. They seldom have time for their families, close relationships, and leisure activities. They not only experience a great deal of stress, but they also spread it to others.

Type B personalities are good stress managers. They are easy-going, calm, and relaxed and tend to pace themselves and set realistic goals. They know their capabilities and their limitations. They can be high performers and make excellent executives, since they make carefully thought out decisions and also create a work climate conducive to sustained good performance. The study showed that high-stress Type A personalities were three times more likely to have heart attacks than Type Bs. The study suggests that good stress managers live longer, are better adjusted, and are less likely to experience serious illness.

A sociological study at Johns Hopkins University and the University of Pittsburgh showed that people who sincerely try to do their best and are considerate of others

[4]Jere E. Yates, *Managing Stress* (New York: AMACOM, 1979), p. 36.
[5]Meyer Friedman and Ray H. Rosenman, *Type A Behavior and Your Heart* (Greenwich, CT: Fawcett, 1974).

Figure 19.2 Possible consequences of stress mismanagement.

Psychological Consequences	
Mental	**Emotional**
Negative, unconstructive, and self-defeating thoughts Distorted perceptions Confusion, inability to concentrate Loss of perspective on issues and events Loss of memory Difficulty processing data rationally and thinking clearly Subconscious negative thoughts Decreased self-image and self-confidence	Feelings of inadequacy, inferiority, worry, anxiety, fear, helplessness, hopelessness, and being unloved or unliked Oversensitivity Feeling depressed, demotivated, paranoid, discouraged Feelings of anger, rage, resentment, hostility, bitterness Negative feelings from the past Feelings not connected to the actual reality of a situation
Physiological Consequences	
Typical Physiological Stress Effects	**Other Physiological Stress Effects**
Dissipates energy (wears us out) Affects blood flow, blood pressure, and blood composition Increases heartbeat Changes amount of blood flow to organs and brain Increases blood pressure May result in flushed face, headaches, heartburn, nosebleeds, high blood pressure, blood vessel constriction, heart attacks, etc. Raises flow of sugar and adrenaline into the bloodstream Affects glandular secretions Secretes toxins into the body May result in dry mouth, increased perspiration, throat irritation, nervousness Tenses muscles and results in aches, cramps, and muscle spasms Causes nervous system malfunctions May affect the respiratory system and result in breathing difficulties	Increases likelihood of illness, infections, digestive problems, etc., because of the physiological malfunctioning. This includes increasing the potential for ulcers, diabetes, kidney diseases, cancer, heart diseases, arthritis, etc. Adds wrinkles from the pull of tense muscles on the skin Wear and tear on the physiological system speeds up the aging process May cause sleeping difficulties Could result in frigidity or impotence
Behavioral Consequences	
Impaired performance Accidents and mistakes Irritability, moodiness, defensiveness, strained relationships Overly aggressive or passive behavior, or swings back and forth Unconstructive, self-defeating behaviors such as excessive eating, drinking, smoking, socializing, playing, working, etc., or becoming rebellious, domineering, or resorting to old bad habits	Withdrawal into oneself Decreased ability to give and receive love and caring Suppression of problems or blaming them on others or circumstances Self-centeredness Exaggerating weaknesses or strengths Becoming helpless or incapacitated

Figure 19.3 Advantages of learning how to manage stress.

1. Better mental, emotional, and physical health resulting in a happier and more fulfilled person.
2. Increased energy, motivation, performance, and potential.
3. Substantial reduction in downtime (time when performance is significantly lower than usual).
4. Greater feelings of self-worth from managing problems and not being a victim of circumstances.
5. Improved interpersonal relationships.
6. Improved appearance (relaxed and lively rather than tense and dreary).
7. Longer life.
8. Fewer problems and stress caused to others; may actually improve others' performance.
9. Freedom from most fears and anxieties that prevent you from doing your best.
10. Becoming a more responsible and mature person.
11. Character development that can help you learn self-control and how to turn difficulties into opportunities.

live longer, are less accident prone, and are less likely to collect guilt that is eventually expressed in inappropriate behaviors. These descriptions are very close to Type B personalities.

Another study at the National Institute of Health at Cornell University Medical Center showed that people who practice the golden rule have fewer colds, digestive upsets, and headaches and are generally less subject to all types of serious ailments and diseases. They also recover faster.

These studies and others suggest some consistent emerging characteristics of good stress managers and also portray the extensive payoffs of good stress management. The effective stress manager tends to live by the golden rule, gives his or her best while striking a balance between living and making a living, enjoys life, is considerate of others, is calm in a crisis, is relaxed, and paces himself or herself while setting realistic goals. Some of the advantages of good stress management are shown in Figure 19.3.

HOW DO PEOPLE RESPOND TO STRESS?

Our typical response to stress is a learned behavior. The reason we respond the way we do is that we have practiced our response so long that it has become a habit. For example, some people respond by being calm, some by getting upset, and others by going through a combination of both behaviors. Still others respond constantly in one way in certain situations and another in other situations. New situations may produce a new response. However, most of our responses are highly predictable because they have become habit. There are four major types of responses to stress:

1. Aggressive
2. Passive

3. Problem-solving
4. Combination

Aggressive Approach to Handling Stress

This is the "fight" approach: You deal with stress aggressively by throwing tantrums, slamming doors, taking your stress out on others, or actively expressing stress in unconstructive ways. What is deceiving about this approach is that it may work in the short run but may also have some side effects and long-run consequences. For example, aggressively blowing off steam may in fact take care of the immediate stress. However, it may have serious side effects on the people you blow off steam on and may also have long-run personal consequences in terms of your feelings about yourself. It is difficult to feel good about hurting others and handling your behavior in such immature ways.

Passive Approach to Handling Stress

This is the "flight" approach: You deal with stress passively by suppressing it, running away from problems, withdrawing, storing it up and then cashing in on someone, or indirectly expressing your stress in unconstructive ways such as subtly discounting yourself or others or developing dependencies on overeating, drinking, smoking, drug use, gossiping, or some similar activity. While the passive approach is less harmful to others than the aggressive approach, it is more harmful to yourself. Suppressing feelings and dealing with them indirectly builds up resentments, causes confusion over who you are, and causes problems in experiencing and perceiving things accurately.

Problem-Solving Approach to Handling Stress

The problem-solving approach to managing stress consists of recognizing your mental, emotional, physical, and behavioral stress symptoms and managing the stress constructively and rationally before it begins to have harmful consequences. For a person who has learned to manage stress this way, few things are experienced as stressful because they are placed in proper perspective with the belief that one way or another they can be managed successfully. Although this approach may appear simplistic, it is often very difficult to apply because it requires more self-control, responsibility for one's behavior, and maturity than the aggressive or passive approach.

Combination Approach to Handling Stress

Most people probably take a combination approach to managing stress. They may go from aggressive to passive responses or passive to aggressive or possibly aggressive to passive to problem-solving or some other combination. Whatever the combination is, it is probably a predictable response for most situations.

MANAGING STRESS

There are four basic alternatives for managing stress:

1. Give up our excuses for being stressed. Even though our excuses may be valid and justified, we are not in a position to manage stress until we give up our excuses and accept responsibility for managing our stress regardless of who or what is at fault.
2. Change our stress-producing circumstances. Once stress-producing circumstances are identified, a person is in a position to minimize, reduce, or eliminate the stress they are producing. Stress-producing circumstances could include such things as being overcommitted, working in a high-stress job, financial problems, getting involved in stress-producing activities or with stress-producing people, living in a stressful neighorhood, etc. We should evaluate our stress-producing circumstances frequently and explore constructive alternatives for managing them.
3. Change our stress-producing behaviors. Since most stress is self-inflicted, it follows that we often engage in stress-producing behaviors that could be changed. Examples of stress-producing behaviors are over- or undereating, smoking, excessive drinking, drug use and abuse, being a negative thinker or tempermental, being disorganized or constantly late, etc.
4. Change our stress response. A new, more effective stress response can be developed by: (a) practicing seeing ourselves as an effective stress manager so our self-image will allow us to manage stress; and (b) developing a stress plan and practicing it until it becomes a habit or normal way to respond under stressful conditions.

DEVELOPING A STRESS PLAN

In learning to manage stress, we first need to develop a stress plan to manage day-to-day stress. As long as your choices are constructive, the specific choices that you make to manage stress are not nearly as important as the fact that you made the choice! Your mind and body are probably not too concerned about whether you meditate to relax or just decide to relax or whether you use certified special methods of deep breathing or just breathe with the intent to manage the stress that you are feeling. In other words, the intent is much more important than the method. It is, however, helpful to develop an actual stress plan that works for you and practice it until it becomes a habit. Unfortunately, when stress strikes, it is much easier to give in to it and let it run its natural course than it is to choose to manage it. Therefore, carrying a stress plan with you on a 3- by 5-inch card or piece of paper can be very helpful because making the choice to manage stress is probably the most difficult part of stress management.

Figure 19.4 shows what a stress plan might look like. Although you might not personally have as many items on your stress plan or may have different items, including these four main steps in developing your stress plan is important:

1. Know your stress symptoms.
2. Get in balance mentally and emotionally.
3. Get in balance physically.
4. Develop an action plan.

Figure 19.4 Developing a stress plan.

"As long as your choices are constructive, the specific choices that you make in dealing with stress are not as important as the fact that you made the choice!"	

1. Know Your Stress Symptoms (Symptoms that signal that you are getting stressed)

Pulse-rate increases (about 60–80 beats per minute is OK)	Assuming the worst about others or yourself
Rapid or difficult breathing	Withdrawal
Aches and pains	Becoming fidgety, nervous, and impatient
Fatigue or hyperactivity	Denying feelings or expressing them unconstructively
Loss of perspective of reality	Lack of motivation
Becoming defensive or reverting to self-defeating thoughts and behaviors	Depending on unconstructive outlets such as temper tantrums, drinking, smoking, overeating, using drugs
Blaming others for your problems and becoming critical and judgmental	Becoming very self-centered
Irritability	Worry and anxiety

2. Get in Mental and Emotional Balance

Mental Balance	Emotional Balance
Choose to process information rationally and objectively	*Choose* to be in charge of your emotions, to deal with negative feelings in a mature way, and to exercise self-control
Place the problem in proper perspective	Clear your mind of any anger, hostility, bitterness, grudges, or negative thinking, knowing that such thinking increases stress
Gather enough data to see the issues clearly and to check out your initial perceptions	View your problems as opportunities for growth
Reflect on positive thoughts, memories, or inspirational material	Test your feelings by trying to identify what they are, where they came from, and if they are based on reliable information
Seek the advice and counsel of wise people	Learn to rely on facts and sound judgment when your thoughts and feelings are out of control or are motivating you to act irresponsibly
Pray	*Choose* to express your feelings constructively *even if you don't feel like it*

3. Get in Physical Balance

Exercise regularly and eat a nutritious diet	Listen to relaxing or motivating music
Breathe deeply	Take walks
Exercise vigorously	Read something relaxing
Use muscle-tension-releasing exercises	Slow down
Rest or catnap	Work on a hobby
Take a hot bath	Do anything constructive that relaxes you (yard work, housework, etc.)

4. Learn How to Problem Solve

Learn how to problem solve	Learn to take your eyes off yourself and to do something positive for someone else
Define and express the problem accurately	Develop a support system that you can rely on when you need it
Gather and evaluate relevant data	Accept responsibility for not spreading your stress
Explore constructive and realistic alternatives	Identify the source of the stress and determine if it would be wise to seek a resolution
Choose the best alternative given the realities of the situation	Learn to recognize when a problem is not solvable and when stress reduction must come from a change in your response
Develop a plan for implementing your solution	
Know yourself well enough to know when to postpone any actions	

The stress plan follows the stress definition. When you mismanage stress, you malfunction mentally, emotionally, physically, and behaviorally. Therefore your task in managing stress is to get each of the items in balance when you start to experience stress. Often, simply making the choice to use your stress plan will eliminate the stress. If you practice the plan enough, your mind, emotions, body, and behavior may automatically respond to your choice to manage the stress in most situations. On the other hand, in a highly stressful situation you may need to work very hard at implementing your stress plan and to keep working at it day after day until you gain control of the stress. It may also be helpful to realize in practicing your stress plan that the exact order of the four steps isn't always important.

Know Your Stress Symptoms

Your stress symptoms are the things you do that signal that you are under stress. Once you can identify these symptoms you are in a position to manage the stress. If you are not aware of your symptoms, then the stress manages you. Some typical symptoms are getting nervous, having difficulty breathing, developing aches and pains, getting touchy and irritable, denying your feelings or expressing them unconstructively, becoming worried or anxious, losing your perspective by blowing things out of proportion, overeating, smoking, and drinking.

Even if you are not aware of your stress symptoms, someone else is! We tend to go through very predictable "stress rituals" when we are feeling stress or about to blow, and those close to us learn to recognize these symptoms so that they can prepare themselves or quickly retreat when we start into our patterns. It is surprising how perceptive people are about our stress rituals. A twitchy nose or a pattern of self-depreciation may be all the signal they need to know that you are about to get in trouble and that they will probably also get in trouble if they stay around. Subordinates, for example, learn to watch for such signals in their supervisor, and when they occur, they avoid their boss like the plague! Therefore, it may be helpful to ask those close to you what your stress symptoms are.

It should be pointed out that having stress symptoms is perfectly natural and that what is important is that we learn to recognize them so that we can do something about it. In some cases it may be appropriate to alert others that we are feeling some stress, but keep a handle on it so they won't have to get nervous too.

Get in Mental and Emotional Balance

Stress often throws us off balance mentally (our conscious and subconscious thoughts) and emotionally (our feelings). A negative chain reaction starts when we start thinking negatively; this in turn creates negative feelings and makes it almost impossible to deal constructively with stress.

There are numerous alternatives for getting in mental and emotional balance. We can choose to think constructively and be in charge of our emotions or deal with our negative thoughts and feelings in a constructive and rational way. We can carry in our memory bank some especially positive experiences that we can call up. We can also carry inspirational quotes, pray, talk to positive people and avoid negative people, or even view our problems as opportunities for growth and character development. We may also try to slow everything down long enough to gain a proper perspective of the actual issues and their ramifications. When we are under stress, sometimes our mind spins so fast that we can't concentrate or get things in proper perspective as our mind races from one thought to another. When this happens, we need to calm down, recognize and work through our feelings, try to evaluate the situation and its possible consequences objectively, and realize that worry and anxiety will only compound the problem. When our thoughts and feelings lead us to unconstructive actions, that is when we need to rely on responsible choices, whether we feel like it or not.

Get in Physical Balance

Stress can stimulate our physical systems to increased effectiveness and performance, or it can throw our system out of balance and result in malfunctioning, which may give us headaches, cramps, acid stomach, heartburn, pain, a clogged or dry throat, muscle spasms, hypertension, nervous laughter, and other symptoms. If our system starts to malfunction, we need to get it back in balance to manage stress successfully without harmful consequences. Regular exercise and a nutritious diet are essential to physical balance and our ability to manage stress. It takes considerable energy to manage stress, and if we don't have the needed energy, we either succumb to stress or wear our body out from making demands on it that it is not conditioned to deliver. The latter often happens to supervisors who are out of shape but operate at a high energy level and eventually suffer the consequences of misusing their bodies.

Physical stress can also be managed through deep breathing, exercises to release muscle tension (stretching), resting or catnapping, and physical exercise such as calisthenics, jogging, swimming, or sports, as long as your intent is to rid yourself of the stress and relax. Listening to relaxing music, taking a walk, reading something relaxing, working on a hobby, taking a hot bath, or anything constructive that gets rid of the tension or is relaxing will work.

Persons who practice getting in balance physically can stay relaxed in a high state of activity and tension and can get rid of almost all aches and pains except for those that are organically based. Stress-related aches come primarily from tensing muscles or flooding an area of the body, such as the head, with too much blood. Exercises to release muscle tension, massaging areas that ache or hurt, and relaxing will eliminate most of our aches and pains.

Develop an Action Plan

The first three steps will usually get rid of any unnecessary stress except in situations where the stress is severe or prolonged. However, we may still need an action plan to deal constructively with the actual cause of the stress. The situation may dictate the actual alternatives that can be considered. However, it is helpful to experiment with a variety of actions that seem to fit your own personal way of managing stress and practice those actions until they become natural responses. Some people need to go immediately to the root of the problem and find a resolution. Others may need to postpone action, gather more data, check out their perceptions of the problem, seek the advice of wise and integrated people (don't seek advice from those who are out of balance themselves or are not known for their wisdom), or stop long enough to put the problem into proper perspective.

For difficult problems it may be necessary to develop a support group to meet with on a regular basis until the stress is under control; to seek professional help; to attend motivational or informative talks, retreats, or workshops; or to accept the fact that a problem may not be solvable at the present time.

LEADING A MINIMAL STRESS LIFE-STYLE

In addition to developing a short-range stress plan, we also need to take responsibility for leading a minimal stress life-style. A balanced life-style with a meaningful purpose reduces stress, while a chaotic life-style with no sense of direction creates stress. Happy, successful lives rarely happen by chance, nor do lives characterized by strife and stress. While some stress in our life is beyond our control, there are many things that can be done to lead a life that reduces most of our unnecessary stress so that we can lead happy and productive lives and be at the mercy of fate or circumstances.

Included in a minimal stress life-style should be:

1. Developing an attitude that problems and stress are not to be feared but are to be used as opportunities for growth and character development.
2. Frequently evaluating your goals, values, and priorities. To have an adventurous, purposeful, and rewarding life, we need meaningful goals, backed by sound values and properly ordered priorities. If you don't know what goals to pursue, don't wait for lightning to strike. Pick some, give them your best, and if they lead you in the wrong direction, pick some new ones. Your values need to be philosophically sound. Values not based in wisdom eventually result in stress. Priorities should be continuously reevaluated. Losing a sense of proper priority also results in stress.
3. Learning to manage your time and your life. Poor time and life management increases stress, while good time and life management based on worthwhile goals, values, and priorities significantly reduces stress.
4. Learning to learn from mistakes. When you blow it, don't make a big deal out of it and heap guilt and self-condemnation on yourself. Learn to learn from your mistakes, leave them behind, and move on without dragging them with you.
5. Taking one step at a time in getting your life in order. It isn't necessary to have everything in order to enjoy the benefits of a minimal stress life-style. Being willing to take the first step—and each succeeding step—brings its own satisfaction, and with it the realization that you can manage your life and your stress.
6. Take a periodic stress inventory of the sources of stress in your life and decide which ones you can or are willing to do something about.

SUMMARY

Stress is the number one health problem in the world today. Stress can cause mental, emotional, physical, and behavioral problems and can even kill. At work it can cause a loss in productivity and morale and increases in turnover, absenteeism, mistakes, accidents, conflicts, and misunderstandings. On the other hand, if stress is constructively managed, it can increase our effectiveness and be turned into an opportunity for growth, character development, success, and happiness.

Stress is our mental, emotional, physical, and behavioral response to anxiety-producing events. People respond to stress with an aggressive, passive, problem-solving, or combination approach. It is caused primarily by our own behaviors—particularly by our thoughts, actions, and habits. However, some stress can be attributed to actual circumstances, some of which we can do something about and some of which we can do nothing about.

To manage stress we need to: (1) give up our excuses for being stressed; (2) change or manage our stress-producing circumstances and behaviors; and (3) develop a stress plan and practice it until it becomes a habit. Our stress plan should include: (1) knowing your stress symptoms; (2) getting into mental and emotional balance; (3) getting into physical balance; and (4) developing an action plan. Leading a minimal stress life-style includes taking responsibility for your life-style and its consequences and getting your life, goals, values, and priorities in proper balance and order.

IMPORTANT TERMS

stress

personal stressors

stress management

stress plan

stress symptoms

stress carrier

job stressors

stress mismanagement

minimal stress life-style

REVIEW QUESTIONS

1. Why do supervisors need to know how to manage stress?
2. What is stress and what are its positive and negative consequences?
3. What are the four ways in which people respond to stress?
4. What are the major causes of stress?
5. What should a person do to prepare to manage stress?
6. Describe each of the steps of a short-range stress plan.
7. Discuss what should be included in a long-range stress plan.
8. What is a stress carrier?

EXERCISES

19.1 How Stressed Are You?

Take a survey in the class to find out how people evaluate themselves on a 10-point scale (10 is high and 1 is low) on the following questions:

1. In evaluating the stressful circumstances in your life, how much stress do you have?
2. Considering that stress is relative to how we experience it, how much stress do you *experience?*

How many people in class are predominantly Type A personalities and how many are predominantly Type B personalities?

19.2 The Major Causes of Stress

Break into small groups and brainstorm a list of the major causes of stress and then rank the top 20 items (this should take about 20 minutes). Write the top 20 items on chart paper. Meet in the classroom and have each group share its list.

19.3 Managing Stress

List on the stress analysis form (see Exhibit 19.1) the major stressors in your life. Then complete the requested information in each column. After completing this information, meet in small groups and have each person share several of their stressors and what they plan to do to manage the stress. Additional suggestions should be offered by other team members.

EXHIBIT

19.1 Stress Analysis

1. In column 1 list the major stressors in your life.
2. In column 2 try to be specific regarding what causes you stress. For example, in column 1 you may list Past events and in column 2 you might list Divorce, Getting fired, Not completing my education.
3. In column 3 try to describe what you do when you are stressed by each of the items in column 2.
4. In column 4 try to describe the consequences of your responses in column 3— . . . for example, "I relieve the stress," "I make people angry," "I get depressed."
5. In column 5 try to identify some constructive ways that you handle *each* of the items that is causing you stress. Then, on the back of the page list the constructive and unconstructive ways in which you handle stress and some new constructive ways that you would be willing to try. Also consider if you are a stress carrier and evaluate ways you could minimize or eliminate the stress that you cause others.

1 Stress Sources	2 Specific Causes of Stress	3 How I Respond to the Stress	4 Consequences of My Responses	5 Possible Constructive Alternatives

SUGGESTED ADDITIONAL READINGS

Brief, Arthur P.; Schuler, Randall S.; and Van Sell, Mary. *Managing Job Stress.* Boston: Little, Brown, 1981.

Kiev, Ari, and Kohn, Vera. *Executive Stress.* New York: AMACOM, 1979.

McLean, Alan A. *Work Stress.* Reading, MA: Addison-Wesley, 1979. (See also the series of books on stress published by Addison-Wesley.)

Pelletier, Kenneth R. *Mind as Healer, Mind as Slayer.* New York: Dell, 1977.

Selye, Hans. *The Stress of Life.* New York: McGraw-Hill, 1969.

———. *Stress Without Distress.* New York: McGraw-Hill, 1976.

Yates, Jere E. *Managing Stress.* New York: AMACOM, 1979.

20

Time Management

The best way to kill time is to work it to death.

Anonymous

*Dost thou love life? Then do not squander time; for that's
the stuff life is made of.*

Benjamin Franklin

OBJECTIVES

This chapter provides you with the information necessary to:

1. Know whether you are a time manager or a time mismanager.
2. Understand that time management is a life philosophy, not a gimmick.
3. Explain the principles of effective time management.
4. Prepare your organization to reflect proper time-management concepts.
5. Identify the time wasters in your job as well as ways you could save personal time.
6. Organize your time so that you will be in control of yourself.

THE TIME RESOURCE

Time is a precious resource that we all possess. The way we use this valuable resource affects our character, our self-image, our values, our families and relationships, our knowledge, our achievements, our careers, our health, our destiny—all aspects of our life and often the lives of others. It is not a resource to be taken lightly, yet most people have never learned to manage their time effectively. We are far more skilled at time *mis*management than we are at time management. Does your life show signs of time mismanagement? Look for these clues:

Your life lacks direction and purpose.

The days slip by and you don't know where all the time has gone.

You are behind in your work but are so disorganized that you don't know where to start.

Your time is primarily controlled by others or by circumstances.

You don't have enough time for yourself, others, or the important things in life.

You constantly reshuffle papers that never get taken care of.

Much of your time is spent in unproductive meetings, conversations, efforts, relationships, etc.

Much of your time is spent on trivial tasks.

You are so busy making a living that you don't have time to live and enjoy life.

Your dreams rarely come true.

You collect books that are never read and ideas that are never pursued.

The way supervisors and managers spend their time largely determines how effective they are. Do they waste time? Do they invest their time in low-priority activities? Have they become workaholics because of poor management? Poor time management leads to management by crisis, confusion, and inefficiency; when the person who is leading a group of people is a poor time manager, it affects the whole group by leaving little time for proper management activities.

ADVANTAGES OF EFFECTIVE TIME MANAGEMENT

People sometimes incorrectly assume that effective time management implies that a person must become highly structured and insensitive and never waste a minute. In fact, the word *effective* implies a positive and constructive outcome to the way a person spends his or her time. Effective time management should have some of the following positive outcomes:

A more satisfying and productive life

More free time to do what you want

A substantial reduction in the stress caused by lateness, procrastination, disorganization, and lack of accomplishment

More time for others.

TIME MANAGEMENT IS A LIFE PHILOSOPHY

Time management is not a technique that can magically make you successful. It is a philosophy that becomes a way of life: It begins with such philosophical issues as Why am I here? What do I hope to accomplish in life? What do I want to do with my life? How do I want to spend my time? Without an attempt to address these issues, the value of time management can rightfully be questioned. Being the most efficient at accomplishing nothing of true value hardly merits the effort and discipline involved in time management. Thus, time management begins with thinking about the meaning of life, of what is important, and of evaluating and establishing long- and short-range goals that give meaning to our use of time and provide direction as we choose among many options and pressures. This is a continuous process that must be frequently reevaluated or adjusted. A sound life philosophy integrated with a person's own unique strengths provides a solid foundation for managing time.

PRINCIPLES OF EFFECTIVE TIME MANAGEMENT

Think in Terms of Effectiveness, Not Efficiency

Good time managers have learned to distinguish between being effective and being efficient. One manager was very efficient at keeping the office neat and orderly and very ineffective at accomplishing meaningful and purposeful tasks. The word *efficient* refers to accomplishing anything, meaningful or not, with a minimum of waste. The word *effective* implies achieving meaningful results. The ideal is to be both effective and efficient.

Think in Terms of End Results, Not Activity Traps

Effective time managers think of desired end results before deciding if, when, and how to invest their time. Time mismanagers think in terms of activity traps. Activity traps are time-consuming activities that have little or no purpose or value. Faithfully working on reports that no one uses, spending several hours each day watching television, or requiring people to document how they spend each day are examples of possible activity traps.

Think in Terms of Priorities

A characteristic that good time managers have in common is that they think and plan in terms of priorities. They invest most of their time and energy in high-priority items and progressively less time and energy on medium- and low-priority items. Most effective time managers make a list each day of the things they want to accomplish and prioritize the list. Then they concentrate on the high-priority items. One highly successful executive managed his time and his life successfully by first listing his life priorities. In his case, they were God, spouse, children, work, and personal interests. In planning his personal and career goals, as well as his daily list of what he wanted to accomplish, he tried to keep his life priorities in mind.

Think in Terms of Goals

Effective time managers organize their time around goals. Although the formality and methods of goal setting will vary with the individual, it is almost impossible to use time effectively without some form of goal setting to provide purpose and direction to the many options available for investing our time. Aiming at nothing and getting something is luck! Setting realistic goals, prioritizing them, and organizing one's time to reach them teaches one the art of making things happen and not having to go through life being a victim of circumstances or relying on luck for success. Ideally, goals should:

1. Cover all aspects of one's life (career, family, finances, recreation; mental, physical, and spiritual health; etc.)
2. Be realistic, written, and prioritized
3. Include a list of long-range goals, yearly goals, and possibly monthly goals.

While the process itself may seem overly time-consuming, in actuality long-range and yearly goals can usually be established in about a half day, monthly goals in about 20 to 30 minutes, and daily goals in about 5 to 10 minutes. If you don't know where to start or what goals to pursue, start with anything that seems realistic and is appealing, and make adjustments or set new goals as doors become closed or new opportunities become available. The important thing is to get started rather than wait for a perfect plan to suddenly strike you.

Invest Most of Your Time in Building on Your Strengths

Time mismanagers spend an excess of time worrying about their weaknesses, trying to overcome them, or trying to discover the reasons for them. Effective time managers develop an awareness of their strengths and limitations, build on their strengths by investing most of their time in doing the things they do best, continuously develop new strengths, and spend a minimal amount of time on weaknesses. Spending too much time on weaknesses is a waste of time! This is not to say that effective time managers ignore their weaknesses. They do, however, realize that many of their weaknesses will be resolved as they build on their strengths and that in focusing primarily on building on their strengths, they gain the confidence to confront the weaknesses that need attention.

Know Your Cycles

A careful observation of your behavior may reveal patterns that should be kept in mind in organizing your time. When do you work best? When do you work less well? Are you a morning person? Day person? Night person? As much as possible, high-priority and difficult tasks should be scheduled during high periods and routine tasks during low periods. Adjustments can be made on days when the cycle changes. For example, on a day when you are tired, it may be best to schedule primarily routine tasks rather than waste the whole day. The ideal would be to eliminate your cycles and therefore substantially increase your high-productivity time! It is quite possible that your cycles are due to habit, eating too much at lunch, being out of shape physically and therefore not having enough energy, having a bad diet, office practices, starting the day off balance, avoidance of unpleasant tasks, a medical problem, too little or too much sleep (too much sleep will make you sluggish), or energy-draining stress.

Develop a Rhythm to Your Life

Joggers understand the concept of rhythm. Until you establish and adhere to a routine or schedule, it is very difficult to get started and maintain the discipline necessary to jog regularly. Circumstances or laziness that break up the rhythm often make it very difficult to get started again. Effective time managers seem to have a rhythm in their life that enables them to operate at a high level. They start the day right, have some order to their schedule and life (stable relationships, weekly tennis matches, weekends with the family, jogging at lunch, etc.), and discipline themselves to maintain enough order to develop a life rhythm. Time mismanagers are just the opposite. Their lives are chaotic and disorganized, they run hot and cold in terms of their productivity, and there seems to be little order or rhythm to their lives.

Organize and Reorganize

Time management is not possible without being reasonably well organized. Having goals, lists of things to do, and necessary information facilitates good time management; not being able to find these things once you have them leads to time mismanagement. People need to find organizational balance to live at their best. They also need to reevaluate frequently how well their degree of organization suits their own unique way of doing things. Some essentials to getting organized are

1. Developing a system for planning, prioritizing, and scheduling time. A simple system that can be purchased is a pocket or desk Day-Timer[1] or something similar that makes it possible to:
      List yearly, monthly, and daily goals either ranked from most important to least important or by top-, medium-, and low-priority.
      Have a yearly calendar for scheduling appointments and assignments. Such a system provides excellent records.
2. Developing an effective, labeled filing system for organizing and storing work and information.

Keep in Balance

Most systems in this world—solar, chemical, economic, engineering, etc.—work on principles of equilibrium or balance. Human beings are no exception. We need to recognize that each of us is a whole person and that we operate at our highest level when we are in relatively good balance mentally, emotionally, physically, and spiritually. Many of our problems are a result of the inner whole person's being out of balance or of a life-style out of balance. Problems take time and energy and hinder our ability to control and manage our time and life; they interfere with our ability to have a strong, healthy self-image that allows us to live at our best. Therefore, an essential part of our

[1]Available from Day-Timer, Allentown, PA 18001.

time management should include keeping balanced mentally, emotionally, physically, and spiritually. Balancing the whole person takes care of our *inner self*. However, we also need to think in terms of balancing our *outer activities*. This means that given our responsibilities, circumstances, and needs, we need continuously to seek a reasonable balance of time spent on family, work, personal development, recreation, and other aspects of living. Balancing one's inner self and outer activities is perhaps the most difficult task in time management. However, it is also the most necessary and rewarding task and gives meaning to time management as well. The goal in this endeavor is to do your best, and that is enough.

Start the Day Right

A chaotic start at the beginning of a new day makes it very difficult to regain the momentum and rhythm necessary to manage your time. Often people start the day by jumping—or falling—out of bed too late, rushing to get dressed, throwing down or skipping breakfast, and driving too fast to work to avoid being late. They arrive at work tense and disoriented, and it takes most of the morning and many cups of coffee for them to calm down enough to be moderately productive. They start the day behind the eight ball and probably end most days the same way. We would be in a far better position to manage our time if we would spend more time preparing for the day so that we can start in balance and with a plan. The difference in productivity, control, and the ability to handle stress is sometimes staggering! Depending on one's circumstances and responsibilities, most people need about one hour to prepare for the day (exercising, praying, eating, planning, etc.). Some people prefer to do their planning at the end of the previous workday.

Think Constructively

What we do with our time is significantly affected by the way we think about ourselves, others, our capabilities, and events such as good or bad breaks. Negative thinking is a waste of time for you and everyone affected by you! Negative thinking limits our potential, fosters discouragement, biases our perception of reality, dissipates energy, causes physical and emotional problems, and is perhaps the largest cause of time mismanagement. Since the way we think determines the way we act, negative thinking produces negative actions that can result in considerable time losses. Arguments, misunderstandings caused by erroneous negative assumptions about people or events, grudges, and temper tantrums all take valuable time. You are a victim of negative thinking when you dwell on the weaknesses or failures of yourself or others or when you devote your valuable time to worry, unfounded fears, resentments, jealousy, envy, anger, or the reasons why things won't work. A constructive thinker looks for and focuses on the best in self, others, and environment. He or she makes the best out of difficulties by accepting them if nothing can be done about them, by working them through, learning from them, changing them, or turning them into opportunities.

Figure 20.1 Distribution of the supervisor's time.

Activity	Approximate Percent of 8-Hour Day	Approximate Number of Minutes
1. Production supervision	25%	120 min.
2. Personnel administration and grievances	20	96
3. Concerns with machines and equipment	15	72
4. Appraising worker performance	8	38
5. Concern with materials	8	38
6. Planning and scheduling work	5	25
7. Meetings and conferences	3	15
8. Other	16	76
Total	100%	480 min.

Figure 20.2 Supervisor's time spent with others.

Contacts	Percentage of the Day Guest	Evans
1. Time spent alone	43%	33%
2. Time spent with subordinates	26	30
3. Time spent with other supervisors	7	8
4. Time spent with superiors	6	7
5. Time spent with service and maintenance personnel	8	6
6. Time spent with other persons	10	16
Total	100%	100%

SUPERVISORY TIME

Many studies have been done on how a supervisor spends his or her time. Surprisingly, they show many similarities, although they may differ widely in specific details. Figure 20.1 is a composite constructed from several studies including some by Richard Plunkett.[2] It is presented as a guide and is useful when one examines the use of time and the identified responsibilities of the supervisor as Plunkett sees them. Items 2, 3, and 4 together fill more than half the supervisor's day. Plunkett also emphasizes that all of the listed tasks involve direct contact with subordinates.

Figure 20.2 contains a comparison of two studies published approximately one year apart. These studies, one by Guest[3] and the other by Evans,[4] show remarkable similarities. Again, they are intended as a guide. However, they do substantiate the representative roles previously cited by Plunkett.

It soon becomes obvious that the basis of effective supervisory time management

[2]Richard W. Plunkett, *Supervision: The Direction of People at Work* (Dubuque, IA: Brown, 1975), p. 41.
[3]R. H. Guest, "Of Time and Foreman," *Personnel* 32 (May, 1966): 482.
[4]Chester E. Evans, *Research Report No. 30: Supervisory Responsibility and Authority* (New York: American Management Association, 1947), p. 27.

lies in the review of time not only within a personal framework but also within an organizational framework. Organizational considerations that supervisors need to take into account in managing their time are:

1. Task time
   a. Performing tasks
   b. Establishing priorities for tasks
   c. Determining agreed-upon tasks
   d. Determining required tasks
2. Meetings
   a. Attending meetings
   b. Scheduling and organizing meetings
3. Personal contact with others
   a. Contact with subordinates
   b. Contact with superiors
   c. Contact with associates
4. Conducting discussions for normal duties
5. Administering approvals and disapprovals
6. Assigning work loads
7. Giving instructions and clarifications

TIME WASTERS AND TIME SAVERS

While the essence of time management is to integrate time-management principles into a sound life philosophy and productive life-style, there are specific steps that a supervisor can take to eliminate or minimize time wasters and to save time. Figure 20.3 shows a list of typical time wasters and time savers on both a personal and work level. Supervisors can use Figure 20.3 for a personal evaluation of how they may be wasting time or could improve their time management.

APPLYING TIME MANAGEMENT

A concept called *time mapping* can be used to apply time management. Time mapping is an eight-step procedure for evaluating and changing time-management choices.

Use the following sequence of actions to analyze your use of time:

1. Performance mapping
   a. List briefly the duties and responsibilities directed by your job. Official source should be an approved job description.
   b. List other duties and responsibilities not specifically outlined in your job description. This would include all actions performed because "we've always done it this way" or "it's been like this since I got here."
2. Using the duties and responsibilities identified in step 1, map the decision patterns relating to each of the identified duties that affect job outcomes. Type of decisions and their relationship to the following patterns are important for identifying time use. Establish the types of decisions that are made:

Figure 20.3 Typical time wasters and time savers.

Time Wasters	Time Savers
Work	
Unclear goals and responsibilities	Have a life philosophy and a sense of direction
Too much time spent on low-priority items	and purpose
Poor filing system	Implement good planning
Constant interruptions	Establish clear goals and resonsibilities for
Crisis management due to lack of planning	yourself and your employees
Unnecessary paperwork	Hire and keep effective people
Ineffective and unnecessary meetings	Plan meetings
Fatigue	Eliminate unnecessary meetings, reports, policies,
Procrastination	and all forms of activity traps
Doing things others could be doing	Dictate letters and reports into a cassette
Gossip	recorder
Disorganization	Train your employees (especially secretaries) well
Going over problems, assignments, information,	and delegate as much as possible
etc., more than once	Have a secretary screen calls, visitors, and mail
Working long hours	and write routine letters
Junk mail	Develop an effective filing system
Red tape	Set deadlines
Duplication and rework	Use lunch and coffee breaks for personal
Government regulations and information	development
requirements	As much as possible, work on high-priority items
Communication breakdowns	during your peak periods and routine items
Lack of deadlines	during your low periods
Unresolved personnel problems	Do your best the first time
Oversocializing	Become a good listener and learn to check out
Lateness	your perceptions of what you heard others say
Poor training	and their perceptions of what they heard you
Misuse of coffee and lunch breaks	say
Ineffective management, employees, or secretaries	Work smarter, not harder
Lack of records or too many records	Develop some protected time that can be
Not having enough time to do things right the first	interrupted only by emergencies
time (Where does the time come from the sec-	Learn to use computers and other time-saving
ond time?)	technological advances and machines
Open-door policy	Admit mistakes and correct them
Distracting working conditions (poor pay, not	Throw away everything that you don't need
enough space, out-of-date equipment, etc.)	Take care of things when you first get them
Personal	
Negative thinking (dwelling on failures,	Do your best and be satisfied
weaknesses, worry, resentment, envy)	Think constructively
TV	Learn to concentrate
Being bothered by the actions or habits of others	Tell people how much time you have
Unselective reading	Do something constructive during lunch
Unplanned errands	Sleep less
The need for perfection	Listen to motivational or technical tapes while
Insisting on being right	driving, traveling, or getting dressed
Destructive relationships	Read selectively
Saying *yes* to more than you can do	Learn to say *no* kindly
Arguing	Learn to relax
Dishonesty	Learn to express your needs, level with people,
Poor health	and confront problems from a caring position
Imbalance as a whole person	Be honest
Being overly organized	Start the day right
Attacking people rather than problems	Achieve balance as a whole person
Excess of escapism (socializing, daydreaming)	Take speed-reading and memory courses
Detrimental habits such as smoking, overeating,	Take something to do while waiting in lines
and drinking	Allow for recreation and renewal time

a. By the boss only
b. Jointly by the boss and the supervisor
c. By the supervisor alone
d. By the supervisor and coordinated with fellow supervisors
e. By the supervisor and a designated subordinate
f. By a designated subordinate alone using delegated authority and responsibility.

    Where patterns of decision making show an overdependence upon joint decisions, ask yourself why. These time-use patterns identify such organizational ills as: (1) supervisors who refuse to use the resources under their control and want to do everything themselves, (2) managers who have not become comfortable with their organizational position and still want to get into the operating action of the first level, (3) managers and supervisors who are not delegating adequately, (4) subordinates who do not want to be held accountable for delegated responsibility, and (5) organizational procedures involving other departments that need to be placed into the form of written directives.

3. Establish the importance of the tasks being performed by:
   a. Identifying and prioritizing from the most important to the least important the 10 most significant performance requirements of your job.
   b. Complementing this, prioritize from the most important to the least important the 10 job tasks you personally find the most satisfaction in doing. The satisfaction can be either personal or professional.

4. Establish the types of tasks you actually do. On the last two full days you worked, what activities did you perform and what percent of the total time in the workday was spent in each of these activities? Analysis of a seven-day period might prove even more useful. Prepare a list with two columns such as:

                  Activity   **Percent of time**

5. Compare the activities listed in 4 to both sections of item 3. The analysis of what you actually do compared with what is most important and from which activities you derive the most satisfaction can show patterns of: (1) favoring things you like or derive satisfaction from over more important things, (2) important items being little of what you actually do, and (3) being insensitive to high-priority items of your job while performing in a more take-it-as-it-comes operating style.

6. Validate the expectations and priorities you place upon the job tasks with your manager. Ensure that your expectations and priorities are similar to those of the organization and that the priorities agree. This form of validation will create continuity between levels of management and will facilitate the next step in the analysis process.

7. Identify your major time wasters. Eliminate the low-priority time consumers. Review patterns of time consumption that do not contribute to your personal productivity and the productivity of your subordinates. As you identify areas of lower priority or possible time wasters, use the model in Figure 20.4 to make decisions regarding their disposition.

Figure 20.4 Activity rationale.

What do I do?	What would happen if I didn't do it?	Must I be the one to do it?	Is it possible to delegate this type task?

Be sure to include in your listing those items in your decision-making patterns for which decisions are made by two people.

8. If you establish items that could be delegated or reassigned, consider the following checklist to make the decision easier:
   a. What is the activity to be delegated?
   b. To whom will it be delegated?
   c. Is this person willing to do it?
   d. Is this person capable of doing it?
   e. How much control will be required to ensure satisfactory completion?
   f. Can all of the task be delegated, or only part of it?
   g. What time elements are important to the delegation?
   h. Will feedback be required if delegated?
   i. Will I allow the individual to make mistakes?
   j. How will the mistakes be handled?
   k. Will my expectations and those of my subordinate be met?

SUMMARY

Time management is often viewed as a kit of techniques that will magically make you highly productive and efficient and still leave you time on your hands. Effective time management is in fact a life-style, not a technique. The way you use your time affects all aspects of your life and often affects others as well. It reflects your life philosophy, which may be a carefully thought out philosophy or one that is implicit in the way you use your time. It also reflects your priorities, your values, and your self-image. It can contribute significantly to your personal and organizational worth. Time is one of our most valuable resources, and the way we manage or mismanage it influences whether we lead a satisfying and happy life or one of frustration and disappointment. Now is the time to take the time to start managing your time.

IMPORTANT TERMS

time management	activity traps
effectiveness	time wasters
efficiency	time savers
end results	time mapping
priorities	

REVIEW QUESTIONS

1. What are some clues that a person is mismanaging his or her time?
2. Why does a supervisor or manager need to manage his or her time effectively?
3. What are some of the advantages of effective time management?
4. Describe the major principles of effective time management.
5. Discuss as many time wasters and time savers as you can.
6. Discuss why time management is a life philosophy and not a gimmick.

EXERCISES

20.1   Time Management Inventory and Planning Questionnaire

The purpose of this exercise is to help you evaluate what is important to you in life, how you are spending your time, and how you can manage your time more effectively.

Part 1

Make a list below of everything that is important to you in life. Something is important if you *spend time on it, think about it a lot,* or *would like to spend time on it.* Disregard whether you feel good or bad about an item. Simply list everything that is important to you. Several examples are listed below. Then rank each item according to what you would *ideally* like your priorities to be and what they *actually* are, based on the quality and quantity of time you spend on each item. This part of the exercise will help you to develop a frame of reference for managing your time.

Work	Drinking	Dwelling on the past	Being jealous, envious, angry, or resentful
Spouse	Sports		
Children	Socializing	Looking good	
Self	Going to meetings	Being successful	Being rebellious
Giving love		Taking care of my body	Spreading hope
Receiving love	Helping others		Being a problem solver
Smoking	Arguing	Hobbies	
Having friends	Being right	Vacationing and relaxing	Being a problem maker
Being a loyal friend	Unproductive relationships	Entertainment	Being positive
TV	Productive relationships	Covering up mistakes	Being negative
Faith			Going to classes

What is Important to Me in Life		
	Order of Importance	
List of What is Important	Ideal Priorities	Actual Priorities

Part 2

On the form below make a list of the things you tend to do on a *typical day, monthly,* and *a few times a year.* Your typical day should include all 24 hours of the day. *List the activities in chronological order.* Some activities that you may want to consider are listed. The term *wasted time* refers to time that was obviously misused.

Personal Time	**Work Time**
Getting out of bed	Planning
Exercising	Organizing
Planning	Following up on projects
Meditating or praying	Motivating others
Dressing	Staffing
Eating breakfast	Developing others
Socializing before work	Developing myself
Driving to work	Giving instructions
Breaks	Employee evaluations
Lunch	Budgeting
Driving home from work	Reports
Dinner	Meetings
Socializing after work	Personnel problems
Watching TV	Other problems
Personal hobbies	Socializing
Dealing with problems (mine or others')	Personal business
	Unanticipated interruptions
Daily recreation	Phone
Vacations	Correspondence
Working (non-job-related work, bills, etc.)	Travel
	Keeping up to date in my field
Family time	Paperwork
Sleeping	Productive work
Wasted time	

Category	Typical Day (List Activities)	Approx. Amount of Time	Priority	Control	Monthly (List Activities)	Approx. Amount of Time	Priority	Control	Yearly (List Activities)	Approx. Amount of Time	Priority	Control
Personal Time												
Work Time												
Total Amount of Time		____				____				____		

1. Beside each item, list the approximate amount of time that you spend on the item.
2. Next, evaluate each activity according to its priority: top (T), medium (M), or low (L).
3. Finally, evaluate which activities—you have some control over—and which ones you cannot control. The purpose of this step is to help you decide which items are potentially changeable and which are a waste of time trying to change.

Part 3

1. Evaluate your activities and the quantity and quality of time you devote to each and complete the following:
   a. Are your *personal* activities consistent with your ideal priorities? Circle the number that is most representative.

Ideal Priorities

Very inconsistent   1 2 3 4 5 6 7 8 9 10   Very consistent

Your comments:

   b. Are your *work* activities consistent with your ideal priorities and work priorities?

Ideal Priorities

Very inconsistent   1 2 3 4 5 6 7 8 9 10   Very consistent

Work Priorities

Very inconsistent   1 2 3 4 5 6 7 8 9 10   Very consistent

Your comments:

2. What are you doing that to you is a waste of your time and talents?

Personal	Work
1.	1.
2.	2.
3.	3.
4.	4.
5.	5.
6.	6.
7.	7.
8.	8.
9.	9.
10.	10.

3. What could you do to eliminate, control, or delegate your controllable time wasters?

Personal	Work
1.	1.
2.	2.
3.	3.
4.	4.
5.	5.
6.	6.
7.	7.
8.	8.
9.	9.
10.	10.

4. What could you do to save time or to make better use of your time?

Personal	Work
1.	1.
2.	2.
3.	3.
4.	4.
5.	5.
6.	6.
7.	7.
8.	8.
9.	9.
10.	10.

5. Share parts 1 through 3 with several trusted and knowledgeable people and ask for feedback or suggestions on each item.

Part 4: Reorganization

1. Rank your major ideal priorities as you now see them. Refer to part 1 to see if your ideal priorities have changed. If you are uncertain, list some ways in which you can find out.

2. Rank your major work priorities top, medium, and low, as you now see them. Refer to part 2 as it pertains to your work. (Students can refer to their role as a student as work.) If you are uncertain, list some ways in which you can find out.

3. What are some of your long-range career objectives? If you are uncertain, list some ways in which you could find out.

4. Based on the information you have generated in this exercise, list some ways in which you could better manage your time and then reorganize your activities.

SUGGESTED ADDITIONAL READINGS

Dayton, Edward R. *Tools for Time Management.* Grand Rapids, MI: Zondervan Publishing House, 1978.

Douglas, Merrill E., and Douglas, Donna N. *Manage Your Time, Manage Your Work, Manage Yourself.* New York: AMACOM, 1980.

Douglas, Stephen B. *Managing Yourself.* San Bernardino, CA: Campus Crusade for Christ, 1978.

Ferner, Jack D. *Successful Time Management.* New York: Wiley, 1980.

Lakein, Alan. *How to Get Control of Your Time and Your Life.* New York: Signet, 1973.

McCoy, James T. *The Management of Time.* Engelwood Cliffs, NJ: Prentice-Hall, 1959.

Mackenzie, Alec R. *The Time Trap.* New York: McGraw-Hill, 1975.

Name Index

Subject Index

85 86 9 8 7 6 5 4 3 2